Santa Barbara

All photos licensed by Shutterstock.com.

Page 1: Mission Santa Barbara.

Page 2: (top left) Stearns Wharf at Christmastime; (top right) Fishing boat leaving Santa Barbara Harbor; (bottom) Jogging along a Santa Barbara beach at sunset.

Page 3: (top) Birds roosting on a pierced rock near Anacapa Island, Channel Islands National Park; (bottom left): Goleta Beach; (bottom right, upper) The quaint Danish village of Solvang; (bottom right, lower) One of Santa Barbara's scenic vineyards.

Page 4: (top) A secluded garden patio in Santa Barbara; (bottom) View of Santa Barbara from the pier.

INSIDERS' GUIDE® TO

SANTA BARBARA

FIFTH EDITION

LESLIE A. WESTBROOK

INSIDERS' GUIDE

GUILFORD, CONNECTICUT
AN IMPRINT OF GLOBE PEQUOT PRESS

All the information in this guidebook is subject to change. We recommend that you call ahead to obtain current information before traveling.

INSIDERS' GUIDE ®

Editor: Kevin Sirois
Project Editor: Heather Santiago
Layout: Joanna Beyer
Text Design: Sheryl Kober
Maps by XNR Productions, Inc. © Morris Book Publishing, LLC

ISSN 1536-8580
ISBN 978-0-7627-7323-7

Printed in the United States of America
10 9 8 7 6 5 4 3 2

CONTENTS

CONTENTS

Directory of Maps

ABOUT THE AUTHOR

Leslie Andrea Westbrook is a third generation Californian who has been a newspaper columnist, magazine editor, and freelance writer for most of her adult life. She has written books and articles on travel, the 100-year history of a college, design, and weird people she has known. She lives in Summerland, California, where she writes with a view to the sea. The *Insiders' Guide to Santa Barbara* is truly that: With the exception of surviving the cold winters during 2.5 years in New York City, she has resided in sunny Santa Barbara, California, for over 30 years.

Courtesy of Mark Robert Halper

ACKNOWLEDGMENTS

Rome wasn't built in a day and updating this guide took a team of hard working "Insiders" who assisted me. It may take a village to raise a child, but it takes a tribe to dig into every detail of this tiny, but culturally rich, destination.

First, I should offer thanks to my predecessor Nancy Shobe, who updated the last edition of this tome. Nancy was kind enough to pass the baton (because she was too busy running a museum, fund-raising, and, hopefully, working on her own writing). Thanks also to the original author, Karen Hastings, and to all those who came in between.

My UCSB editorial interns—Reyes Gonzalez, Kelly Delany, Jana Barrett, and Deanna Melin—aided in fact-checking copious amounts of details to ascertain that we don't send readers astray. It wasn't always easy. Dana Davis (UCSB) and Parker Babbe (Norwich College) helped pinch-hit toward the end of the project.

While learning about the town they have adopted while in college (or in Parker's case, his hometown), these future writers added a younger perspective to nightlife, shopping, cultural attractions, and recreational activities in our 'hood—and hopefully learned a lot in the process.

We did meet some resistance along the way, but overall most businesses and organizations were happy to oblige with helping us to keep our readers informed and au courant when we let our fingers do the walking.

Other Santa Barbara Insiders who offered their expertise and thoughts (and to whom I am grateful) include Kathleen Sullivan (City of SB Parks and Recreation Department); Shannon Doherty (formerly of the Santa Barbara Conference and Visitors Bureau); Jim Fiolek of the Santa Barbara County Vintners Association; Laura Kath of the Santa Ynez Valley and Solvang Visitors Associations; Yvonne Menard, Chief of Interpretation and Public Information Officer, Channel Islands National Park; and Mrs. Lemon Jelly, a foodie if ever there was one, who added some tasty tidbits over a couple of dinners out for the Restaurants chapter.

Thanks to my family, especially my mom, Marcella Meharg, and my dear friends, Janet Lees and Ewy Axelsson, among others, who were patient with me while I became crankier and crankier the closer my deadline loomed.

Thanks also to Globe Pequot editors Kevin Sirois and Heather Santiago for their thoughtful care with the manuscript and eagle eyes.

I am also grateful to my sweet friend Roberto in Santa Fe. Knowing that when I finished this humongous task I'd get to spend time travelin' with you was the proverbial carrot at the end of the stick.

To you, dear readers: Enjoy exploring my town to the fullest, while using this handy-dandy guide as you travel the not-so-dusty trails of Santa Barbara and beyond. There's a lot to be discovered and savored in my neck of the woods.

Most of all, thank you beautiful Santa Barbara. I couldn't have done this without you!

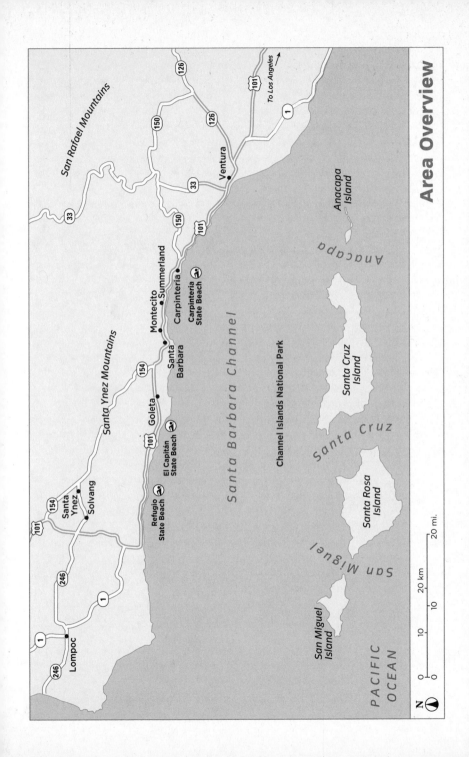

Area Overview

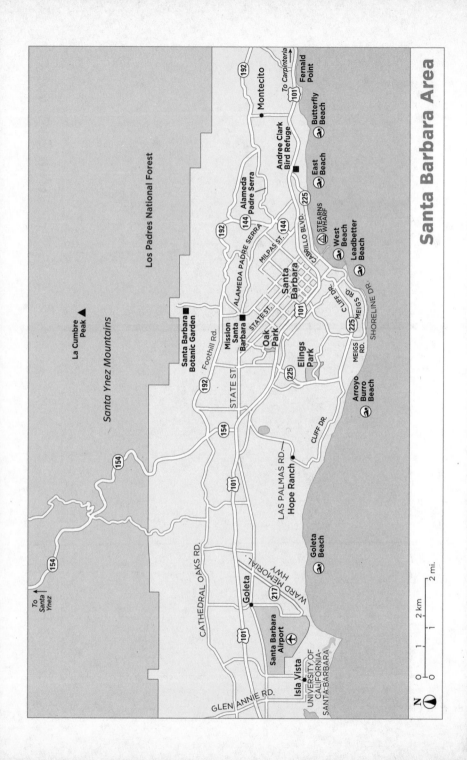

Santa Barbara Area

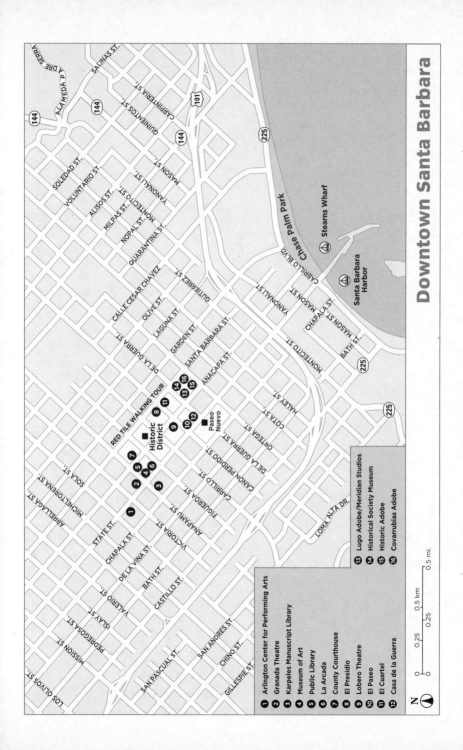

Downtown Santa Barbara

① Arlington Center for Performing Arts
② Granada Theatre
③ Karpeles Manuscript Library
④ Museum of Art
⑤ Public Library
⑥ La Arcada
⑦ County Courthouse
⑧ El Presidio
⑨ Lobero Theatre
⑩ El Paseo
⑪ El Cuartel
⑫ Casa de la Guerra
⑬ Lugo Adobe/Meridian Studios
⑭ Historical Society Museum
⑮ Historic Adobe
⑯ Covarrubias Adobe

N

0   0.25   0.5 km
0   0.25   0.5 mi.

RED TILE WALKING TOUR

Historic District

Paseo Nuevo

Stearns Wharf

Santa Barbara Harbor

Chase Palm Park

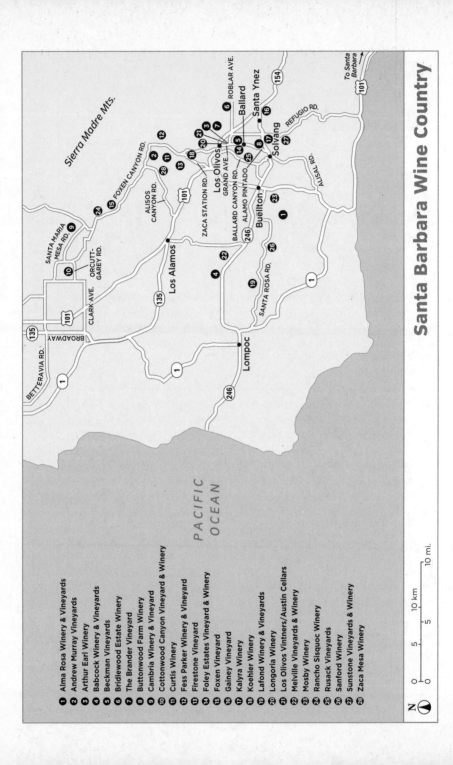

Santa Barbara Wine Country

1. Alma Rosa Winery & Vineyards
2. Andrew Murray Vineyards
3. Arthur Earl Winery
4. Babcock Winery & Vineyards
5. Beckman Vineyards
6. Bridlewood Estate Winery
7. The Brander Vineyard
8. Buttonwood Farm Winery
9. Cambria Winery & Vineyard
10. Cottonwood Canyon Vineyard & Winery
11. Curtis Winery
12. Fess Parker Winery & Vineyard
13. Firestone Vineyard
14. Foley Estates Vineyard & Winery
15. Foxen Vineyard
16. Gainey Vineyard
17. Kalyra Winery
18. Koehler Winery
19. Lafond Winery & Vineyards
20. Longoria Winery
21. Los Olivos Vintners/Austin Cellars
22. Melville Vineyards & Winery
23. Mosby Winery
24. Rancho Sisquoc Winery
25. Rusack Vineyards
26. Sanford Winery
27. Sunstone Vineyards & Winery
28. Zaca Mesa Winery

INTRODUCTION

Whether approaching Santa Barbara by land, air, or sea, visitors are visually delighted both en route and upon arrival to this jewel of a destination. From the south, especially at dusk, if you wind up the coast from Los Angeles, relaxation sets in the minute you cross the county line, with the Pacific Ocean to the west, hugged by mountains at your shoulder as you travel the coastline. From the air, a bird's-eye view reveals mega mansions, lush agricultural swaths, hillsides, and the sprawling University of California at Santa Barbara campus—at the very least. By train, from north or south, again the sparkling Pacific offers a welcoming aesthetic to this historic tourist town situated on a south-facing bay. Once you've landed in town, drive, walk, ride a bicycle, or take a trolley along Cabrillo Boulevard, the main artery that parallels the Pacific Ocean, or cruise the windy curves of the Riviera section of Santa Barbara, and you might think you are in the south of France or on the Italian Riviera. But we speak English (and a lot of Spanish) as well as surf lingo in this idyllic seaside town. Twelve hundred palm trees lining the oceanfront—all hand watered when they were first planted—are just part of the allure that converts visitors into permanent residents, if they can afford to live here.

Visit Santa Barbara, and no doubt you will see bronzed bodies spiking volleyballs and jogging along the shore, but also Spanish Revival architecture—bubbling fountains, cream-colored stucco, and red-tiled roofs—coloring the landscape. In fact, on the surface, Santa Barbara is alluringly seductive and glamorous. But read this book, get to know the town more intimately, and you will learn that Santa Barbara's beauty is more than "skin deep."

Despite all the images of glittering materialism and the high cost of living, Santa Barbara is actually quite unpretentious. Shunning the conspicuous consumption of big-city life, the town prefers instead to bask in its wealth of natural beauty. Few spots on earth are blessed with such a stunning mix of natural assets—broad, sunny beaches; rugged coastal peaks; golden valleys; and windswept islands. Cruise the sparkling waters, and you might spot seals, dolphins, and migrating whales. Hike the canyons, and you'll feel as though civilization is a million miles away.

Beneath this wildly beautiful visage, Santa Barbara's culture and history run deep. It may have the soul of a small beach town, but it exudes all the sophistication of a world-class city. Opera, theater, ballet, art galleries, museums, and gourmet restaurants abound, and Santa Barbara's renowned educational resources attract students from around the world.

As culturally diverse and pristine as Santa Barbara is, Santa Barbarans love to party. No matter what time of year you visit, you're sure to find something fun—whether it's the Old Spanish Days celebration each August ("Fiesta" to the locals), the colorful floats of the eclectic Summer Solstice Parade, or the annual Santa Barbara International Film Festival.

And then there's us—the people who live here. Many traveled here for vacation and vowed to return—permanently. Others were lucky enough to be born here. We are artists and authors, students and professors, builders and gardeners, engineers and entrepreneurs. And yes, there are even celebrities and film folk among us. Though we come from diverse backgrounds, we all choose to live in Santa Barbara for the same reason—we simply cannot find the same quality of life anywhere else on the planet.

We especially love our nearly year-round Santa Barbara sunshine which allows us to stay outdoors. As you explore our little piece of paradise, we'll be right beside you—hiking the wilderness trails, kayaking, cycling, surfing, fishing, and sailing. Don't be surprised if we strike up a conversation or wave you ahead of us in traffic. If you're visiting, use this book to find the best of Santa Barbara in the short term. If you're moving here, congratulations. To ease your transition into Santa Barbara life, we've included detailed information on education and child care, newspaper and television options, health care, and retirement opportunities. Don't let Santa Barbara's high cost of living scare you away. Bargains abound, and we'll show you where to find them.

For whatever reason you've turned to the *Insiders' Guide,* we hope this book serves as a trusty companion. Take it with you on your adventures. As you flip the pages, you'll get to know the real Santa Barbara including our quirks, fancies, pet peeves, and charms. We're much more down-to-earth than you may have imagined. So relax, "kick back," and enjoy the views!

HOW TO USE THIS BOOK

Santa Barbara, despite being welcoming and friendly, does have a caste system. If you are an eighth- or ninth-generation Santa Barbaran, you are unquestionably local. Born here? You are in. But if you have lived here for anything less than 25 or 30 years, you could be considered a newcomer.

We've tried to make this guide so informative that you will feel like an Insider.

Stash it in your beach bag, backpack, purse, or car. Mark it up, shake out the sand, and dog-ear the pages you turn to the most. Know that many Insiders have worked extremely hard to bring you the best information possible to enjoy our town. Whether you're lounging on the beach, hiking the mountains, cruising the ocean, or sightseeing in town, treat this book like a trusted companion. It's meant to help you discover the best Santa Barbara has to offer, from entertainment and recreation to attractions, lodging, and more. We've arranged the book to give you quick and easy access to specific information.

The region covered in this book stretches along US 101 from Gaviota in the west to Carpinteria in the east. (Don't be confused yet: Santa Barbara sits on a south-facing bay, so we are oriented west–east, which confuses not only first-time visitors, but longtime residents, as well). Channel Islands National Park; the wineries in the North County on the other side of the Santa Ynez Mountains; and Cachuma Lake, a recreation area about 35 miles north of Santa Barbara, are also featured in these pages.

Where appropriate, the chapters in this book are divided into geographic sections based on this west–east orientation. First, we cover Santa Barbara (the main city): Then we explore Goleta at the western end (including the beaches and rural areas between Gaviota and Goleta), followed by the towns east of Santa Barbara: Montecito, Summerland, and Carpinteria.

As you're planning your trip, you'll probably want to consult the Accommodations chapter first. If you've just arrived and want to head straight for the sand, flip to the Beaches & Watersports chapter to decide which beach you'll visit first. When you're craving some mouthwatering Santa Barbara cuisine, including freshly caught Santa Barbara spiny lobster and other delights of the sea, turn to the Restaurants chapter for an overview of your options.

The History chapter will shed light on Santa Barbara's unusual architecture and location names. The Area Overview chapter will help you understand who we are and what makes us tick.

The Getting Here, Getting Around chapter explains the layout of the city to keep visitors from getting lost, which is easy to do when you're navigating our many one-way, dead-end streets and traffic "roundabouts" for the first time. The Attractions chapter highlights favorite things to see and do.

We've spiced up every chapter with handy **Insiders' Tips** (represented by an ⓘ) and illuminating **Close-ups** on noteworthy people and places. We highly recommend that you read the Area Overview; Getting Here, Getting Around; and History chapters before embarking on your explorations.

You'll also find listings accompanied by a ✳ symbol—these are our top picks for attractions, restaurants, accommodations, and everything in between that you shouldn't miss while you're in the area. You want the best this region has to offer? Go with our **Insiders' Choice.**

Finally, if you're moving to the Santa Barbara area or already live here, be sure to check out the blue-tabbed pages at the back of the book. There you will find the **Living Here** appendix that offers sections on relocation, media, child care, education, health care, and retirement.

AREA OVERVIEW

Santa Barbara has been nicknamed the American Riviera®, the last unspoiled city in a Mediterranean climate, and even paradise, for many reasons. Cruise under mostly blue skies unhampered by any skyscrapers blocking the mountain views. Wander through the beautifully groomed parks and gardens that adorn almost every neighborhood. Skim across the ocean to the wind-whipped Channel Islands and you'll discover an untamed dimension of pure wilderness to explore. Secluded coves and sea caves lace the shores, and an amazing diversity of wildlife still thrives on these rocky isles and in their surrounding waters. Cradled between these rugged islands and towering coastal peaks, Santa Barbara has a nearly perfect climate. For most of the year, it's so bright and brilliant and sunny that even longtime residents still revel daily in the beauty of our surroundings.

Fiercely protective of our lovely home, we Santa Barbarans work hard to preserve the qualities that make our region so special, and many issues are close to our hearts. Mention development, affordable housing, or offshore oil drilling, and be prepared for a lively discussion.

NATURE IS MOSTLY KIND

Overall, Santa Barbara enjoys very pleasant weather. Temperatures are generally balmy along the coast for most of the year, with monthly averages between 65 and 75 degrees Fahrenheit (approximately 18 degrees to 24 degrees Celsius). Inland, temperatures can be quite a bit higher during the day (especially in summer) and much cooler at night. To cope with changing weather conditions, most Santa Barbarans have mastered the art of layering when dressing, wearing a sweater or jacket over a long-sleeved shirt over a still lighter shirt in case the day warms up.

About 15 inches of rainfall is normal for the year, with most of it falling between December and March. Fog is often a factor in spring and early summer, when it can hang over the coastline until late morning or early afternoon. We call it "June Gloom," but we have even experienced "May Gray" and "Fogtober" in recent years. In most cases, it's a high fog that blocks out the sun, but the thick, drippy, wet, turn-on-your-windshield-wipers kind occurs at various times of the year as well. The Mesa neighborhood, Summerland, and the Santa Barbara Airport have been known to be foggy, while downtown and the hills are bright and sunny on any given day. On the other hand, in late summer and fall, mild and sunny conditions occasionally give way to temperatures in the 90s or 100s (30s or 40s Celsius), especially if hot Santa Ana (or "sundowner") winds blow in from the north.

i Santa Barbara is sunny 85 percent of the year. No wonder everybody wishes they could live here.

Californians often joke about earthquakes and brush fires, but Insiders know that ignoring the potential for either is foolish. Santa Barbara suffered from two major earthquakes during the past 200 years and had a rash of terrible fires—the Tea and Jesusita blazes—that destroyed many homes in the past decade, as well as other blazes in the later part of the last century. Knowing what to do during an earthquake or fire, having a map in case of an evacuation, or keeping shoes and flashlight next to your bed will help you stay safe if and when a disaster strikes.

DIVERSITY IS OUR MIDDLE NAME

The population of the city of Santa Barbara is just over 90,000, roughly a quarter of the total population of greater Santa Barbara County. Several unincorporated areas lie outside the city boundaries, including parts of Goleta to the west; Montecito to the east, with about 10,000 residents; and Hope Ranch east of Goleta, a relatively small community tucked between the city of Santa Barbara and the sea.

With a large population of its own, **Goleta** debated for decades on whether to become an incorporated city or be annexed to Santa Barbara. In November 2001, voters finally approved a proposal to incorporate parts of Goleta, creating the South County's second-largest city (population 29,182) behind Santa Barbara. **Montecito** and **Hope Ranch** are the most expensive areas of Santa Barbara, with sprawling estates and

ranch homes rimmed by gates and security fences. East of Montecito is the funky hillside community of **Summerland** (famous for its antiques stores) and **Carpinteria,** a friendly, family-oriented beach community where agriculture thrives.

The large Latino population currently accounts for a sizable 43–48 percent of Santa Barbara County. (While the SB Chamber of Commerce cites the Hispanic population at 35 percent, other sources claim it to be in the 43–48 percent range.) Some Latino families trace their roots to the city's original Spanish and Mexican occupants, and a strong sense of tradition permeates Santa Barbara. Spanish dance studios are full of young women hoping to one day lead the Old Spanish Days parade as the "Spirit of Fiesta" in honor of their heritage. (See the Annual Events chapter for more information on Fiesta.) Because of this large Hispanic contingent, many government and agency officials are bilingual in English and Spanish.

Santa Barbara has a diverse mix of industries—social services, the retail trade, tourism, government, and agriculture employ the most workers locally. The University of California at Santa Barbara is a major local employer, as are several high-tech and software firms, school districts, and major health care facilities. The heart of Santa Barbara's agricultural activity is the "North County," between 45 and 100 miles up the coast from the city proper. Broccoli, wine grapes, olives, lemons, flowers, strawberries, avocados, and the famous Central Coast pinquito bean are all part of the local agricultural scene, and many of these crops are celebrated in annual festivals such as Lompoc's Flower Festival (June), Goleta's California Lemon Festival (October), and the California Avocado

Festival (October), held in the city of Carpinteria each fall. The Santa Barbara Conference & Visitors Bureau has practically claimed October as foodie month with its special culinary events (see the Annual Events chapter).

All things considered, Santa Barbara has a lot going for it, but the city has no plans to rest on its laurels (if not its grapevines). The community continually strives to preserve and enhance the qualities that make Santa Barbara such a desirable place to live and visit. Currently, the city is tackling issues ranging from the homeless, transient, and panhandling population to gang activity. Maintaining the city's natural beauty is one top priority, and you can bet Santa Barbarans are involved in every decision as they continue to fight for the environmental integrity of their beloved city.

JUST A FEW CAVEATS

Santa Barbara would indeed seem to have it all: glorious weather, friendly people, beautiful ocean vistas, a healthy lifestyle, an impressive offering of cultural arts, and a collective consciousness dedicated to preserving it all for generations to come. Despite its shiny image, however, we feel obliged to let you know that the city probably falls a few notches short (but just a few) of being paradise. So, in the interest of full disclosure, here are a few things to watch out for.

In Spanish, Montecito means "little mountain," Goleta means "schooner," and Carpinteria was named after the Spanish word for "carpenter's shop," because the Chumash Indians used to build their canoes *(tomols)* there on the beach.

In a time when travelers sometimes become victims, Santa Barbara is proud of its low crime rate. Serious crimes are rare, but the increase in gang violence has upset residents and city politicians and kept law enforcement busy. Let common sense be your guide. Despite the appeal of a late-night solitary stroll on the beach, unescorted women need to consider safety first. Also, local police recommend you lock your car and stow valuables out of sight, especially when parking at a trailhead or even in public parking structures.

It's so easy to be seduced by our gorgeous beaches. Standing at the foot of Stearns Wharf and looking back at the mountains as the sun sets provides one of the most spectacular views in California. Residents and tourists alike look to the beaches for solace and beauty, and most times the beaches deliver. However, bacteria contamination, especially after heavy rains, has become a concern. An Ocean Water Quality Hotline has been set up by Santa Barbara County Environmental Health Services (805-681-4949; www.sbcphd.org/ehs/ocean.htm), and reports are published in local newspapers or online. Although your day at the beach is not likely to be ruined by such pollution, it's wise to check the charts and watch for signs that indicate beach closure.

Tar is an all-too-familiar fact of life for Santa Barbara beachgoers. Locals often differ about whether beach tar comes from natural seepage on the ocean floor or is somehow caused by oil drilling in the Santa Barbara Channel, but the reality is that nearly every visit to the shoreline calls for tar removal. This is especially a problem at Summerland Beach.

Santa Barbara Resources

Santa Barbara Conference & Visitors Bureau and Film Commission
1601 Anacapa St., Santa Barbara
(805) 966-9222, (800) 676-1266
www.santabarbaraca.com
www.filmsantabarbara.com

Santa Barbara Region Chamber of Commerce
924 Anacapa St., Ste. 1, Santa Barbara
(805) 965-3023
www.sbchamber.org

Water, Water—Almost Everywhere

Santa Barbara doesn't really discuss its "water problem" these days because it seems as if it's been solved. The truth is, though, that rainfall varies from year to year, and long-term droughts are often followed by exceptionally rainy seasons. After a series of drought years that left local reservoirs close to empty, citizens succumbed to the temptation of buying into California's state water system. Currently, Santa Barbarans receive their water supply from Cachuma Lake and the Gibraltar Reservoir, the State Water Project, and recycled water. Droughts in Santa Barbara prompted city officials to build a $34 million seawater desalination plant in 1991–1992. Because of rainfall, the plant is not operating (something some locals find amusing), but city officials consider it money well spent if there is another severe drought or catastrophic event.

Unreal Estate

To put it succinctly, real estate in Santa Barbara is expensive, although prices have dropped somewhat since the housing bubble. A three-bedroom tract home can run around $1 million, and you can easily pay a few thousand dollars a month to rent a two-bedroom, two-bath unfurnished house, or over $1,000 for a studio apartment in some parts of the community. Although the median home price of above $1 million has dropped, locals are shaking their heads wondering where the 20 percent devaluation has hit. We haven't seen it. Sure, it's expensive to live in Santa Barbara. But would so many people be looking for homes here if they were just putting out big bucks for wood and stucco? We doubt it. Insiders know that when you buy a house here, the price includes the beach, the sunsets, the nonprofit social scene, warm winters, and many more perks and benefits.

There is a downside to this unquenchable demand. As property prices skyrocketed, the lack of affordable housing reached crisis proportions, perhaps the worst in the state if not the nation. Unforgiving mortgages and rents forced low-income workers out of the region long ago. To solve the problem, the county has several high-density housing projects on the drawing board. But, while everyone agrees that something needs to be done, most residents (NIMBYs) don't want the increased development in their own backyard.

i Conservation is a way of life in Santa Barbara. Efforts by Insiders to conserve water have reduced the per capita water demand by 25 percent since 1988.

To Grow or Not to Grow?

For years, "pro-growthers" and "slow-growthers" have been at war in Santa

Santa Barbara Vital Statistics

Santa Barbara's nickname: The American Riviera®

Population: Santa Barbara City: 90,300; Carpinteria: 14,100; City of Goleta: 44,000; Montecito: 8, 965; Summerland: 1,547

Santa Barbara County: 424,400

Average temperatures: Sunny 85 percent of the year

January high/low: 67/43 degrees Fahrenheit, 18/6 degrees Celsius

July high/low: 75/57 degrees Fahrenheit, 24/13 degrees Celsius

Average annual rainfall: 15 inches (38 cm)

Major universities and colleges: University of California at Santa Barbara, Santa Barbara City College, Antioch University, Brooks Institute of Photography, Fielding Graduate Institute, Music Academy of the West, Santa Barbara College of Law, Santa Barbara College of Oriental Medicine, Southern California Institute of Law, Westmont College

Driving laws: Passengers and drivers must wear seat belts at all times. Children must be properly secured in a child seat that meets federal safety standards until they are at least 6 years old or weigh 60 pounds. A child who weighs more than 40 pounds and is riding in a car without combination lap and shoulder belts in the back seat may wear just a lap belt.

Newspapers: *Santa Barbara News-Press* (daily); *Santa Barbara Daily Sound* (Tuesday through Saturday); *Santa Barbara Independent* (weekly); *Montecito Journal* (weekly); *Montecito Messenger* (weekly)

Online local news: www.noozhawk.com; http://edhat.com; http://craigsmithsblog.com

Sales tax: 7.75 percent

Room tax: 12 percent (10 percent county, 2 percent allocated toward Creeks Fund) plus 50 cents to $2 for TBID (Tourism Business Improvement District), depending on room rate tax

Average household income: $63,000 (median income: $47,498)

Barbara, making every local election a down-and-dirty quest for power. Nearly every campaign addresses the issues of growth versus quality of life, progress versus stagnation, and developers' rights versus preservation. Most of these political battles are the focus of races for mayoral or city council seats in Santa Barbara, and races for the Board of Supervisors, which administers the affairs of Santa Barbara County. When the balance of slow-growthers and pro-growthers in a local governing body is at stake, you're guaranteed both a heated battle and a close election, and Insiders know that every vote counts when the future of the city or county is on the line. With adamant advocates on both sides of almost any local issue, the political sparks are always flying.

Pushing the Comfort Zone

Santa Barbara is only 90 miles north of Los Angeles but a world away in attitude. Life is slower here. Development is carefully controlled, and a laid-back approach is the order of the day. But locals are very much aware that the Big City is knocking at our back door. For some residents, the ever-expanding megalopolis of L.A. is getting too close for comfort, but others enjoy the proximity for the cultural and recreational events. A trip to Disneyland, attending a big-league athletic event, or a museum opening is easily doable in a day, but after such an excursion, Santa Barbarans inevitably rush home and swear they wouldn't be caught dead suffering the indignities of L.A. gridlock on a daily basis.

The reality is, though, that you sometimes feel like you're in L.A. sitting in bottlenecks on US 101 in Santa Barbara. The freeway has been widened, but citizens are

i The shoreline juts sharply to the west just north of Ventura County, and all of southern Santa Barbara County's beaches are south-facing, hence the name "South Coast," which is often used when referring to the South County.

fed up with the ongoing construction. The thought of Santa Barbara becoming "another L.A." is unsettling, and residents cast anxious glances southward as a hazy cloud of smog continues its almost imperceptible crawl up the coast.

Despite our traffic woes, we still like to think of Santa Barbara as a pristine enclave— a sanctuary from the stress of the Big City. Of course, Santa Barbara isn't perfect. What place is? But as long as the jobs, the housing, and the water hold out and Mother Nature behaves herself, we'll continue to adore our beloved city and be forever grateful that we are perched on one of the most favored plots of land on the planet.

GETTING HERE, GETTING AROUND

Santa Barbara has all the transportation options needed to get you here from almost anywhere. You'll also be pleased to know downtown Santa Barbara is easily walkable. Most of the shops and historic attractions lie in a compact area a short stroll from each other. (See the Red Tile Walking Tour Close-up in the Attractions chapter for a self-guided tour of Santa Barbara landmarks.) Still, getting to (and parking) around Santa Barbara proper can be tricky for a number of reasons, so we've included information to help you find your way around town.

HIGHWAYS & BYWAYS

US 101 is the West Coast's major north–south freeway and the "main drag" through Santa Barbara. You can take US 101 south to the Mexican border or north to the Canadian border, and because it literally bisects Santa Barbara, it's within a few minutes' drive of anywhere in the city. You can get stuck in traffic at any time of the day in both directions—especially in the summer when hordes of holidaymakers travel along this major West Coast corridor. If you have a choice, try to travel during off-peak times of the day, and you should avoid the bottlenecks. The widening of the freeway to six lanes was met with scorn by many local residents, who preferred not to have any more pieces of paradise bulldozed to accommodate what they perceive as a glut of weekending Los Angeles drivers. Most people agreed, though, that something had to be done. CA 154 (San Marcos Pass), which connects Santa Barbara's South County with Solvang, Cachuma Lake, the wine country, and the rest of the North

County, is a mixed blessing. You can get to the same places by taking US 101, but it takes about 15 minutes longer than zipping over the pass. Unfortunately, zipping is what people have a tendency to do on this winding narrow road, which has no center divider. Combine a few impatient, speeding, or intoxicated drivers with darkness, high winds, fog, or other weather problems, and you have the potential for a serious accident. In fact, there is legislation pending that will ban large trucks from the San Marcos Pass. This was introduced after a big rig's brakes failed and it plowed into a home, killing a family of three.

i Choose your time to travel US 101 carefully. Northbound from Ventura to Santa Barbara is bumper-to-bumper from 7 to 9 a.m. Southbound from Santa Barbara to Ventura is gridlocked from 4 to 6 p.m. Vacationers know that heading south on Sunday afternoon or early evening is no picnic either.

This can be an extremely dangerous stretch of roadway, so if you take the pass, drive defensively. In inclement weather, the pass is subject to rock or mudslides, which often close the road for hours or even days and add another element of danger.

In short, if you're going to drive the pass (and yes, Santa Barbarans do it all the time), be careful.

CA 217 is a short stretch of highway that links northbound US 101 with the University of California at Santa Barbara (UCSB), the Santa Barbara Airport, and the rest of Goleta. The exit is just past the northbound Patterson Avenue off-ramp for US 101, and from CA 217 you can reach the airport and Goleta Beach Park by taking the Sandspit Road exit. Downtown Goleta is off the CA 217 Hollister exit. The highway ends at the entrance to the UCSB campus.

i Insiders know that gasoline is more expensive in Santa Barbara than just about anywhere else. When traveling to Los Angeles, they leave Santa Barbara with half a tank, then fill 'er up in Ventura, Los Angeles. However, savvy Insiders frequent Risdon's 76 in Carpinteria. It has the cheapest prices in town, and as an added bonus, friendly employees politely direct the line of cars waiting to take advantage of this station's bargain gas prices.

IN SANTA BARBARA

"Blame It All on Captain Haley," wrote Barney Brantingham, a local newspaper columnist and author, referring to Santa Barbara city streets. Indeed, it seems that Captain Haley has to shoulder most of the blame, even though he died decades ago and isn't around to hear the modern-day commentary on his 1851 survey. Salisbury Haley was a sea captain, after all, who just happened to be in port when the city was taking bids for the laying out of Santa Barbara's streets. Figuring he could make a quick $2,000 (which turned out to be the lowest bid), Haley became a landlubber just long enough to do the job, which looked good enough on paper to city planners. Problem was, Haley's survey chain had broken and been repaired with rawhide thongs that shrank and expanded, depending on the weather. So by the time he was finished, everything was off by just a little—and sometimes by a lot. Later surveys showed that none of the city blocks Haley measured were the same size, with some being as much as 14 feet over the proposed size of 450 square feet. Haley, of course, had long since gone back out to sea.

Today, the streets are still crooked, city blocks are all different sizes, and there are enough one-way streets crisscrossing downtown to practically ensure that taking the most direct route to anywhere will still require going a block or two out of your way. Add the perennial road construction, potholes, cracks, torn-up streets, wooden barriers, and detours, and you have a typical day's drive in Santa Barbara.

It won't take you long to notice (whether you read the map or not) that Santa Barbara street names are both confusing and difficult to pronounce. (See the Close-up in this chapter for an Insiders' look at the origins of the city's street names.) Then there is our unique geographical orientation. Many Insiders who have lived here for years still can't point out which way is north. As one of the few stretches of Pacific coastline between Alaska and the South Pole that

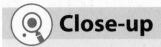

Close-up

Car-free and Carefree

Tired of parking hassles and exorbitant gas prices? Below are a few local organizations that will help you explore Santa Barbara car-free.

- For an overview of alternative travel options, check out **Santa Barbara Car Free** (www.santabarbaracarfree.org). Led by the Santa Barbara County Air Pollution Control District, this cooperative venture helps visitors and residents find ways to travel around Santa Barbara without their cars—and save 10–50 percent on hotels, dining, attractions, and transit.

- **Traffic Solutions** (805-963-SAVE; www.trafficsolutions.info), a division of the Santa Barbara County Association of Governments, publishes commuter carpool match lists and vanpool vacancies, as well as an excellent bike route map.

- **Santa Barbara Metropolitan Transit District** (MTD; www.sbmtd.gov) operates local buses and electric shuttles. To plan your trip, call (805) 963-3361 and speak to a transit adviser. Bus passes may be purchased online at www.sbmtd.gov, and schedules may be downloaded to your PDA.

- **Santa Barbara Trolley Company** (805-965-0353; www.sbtrolley.com) operates narrated trolley tours of Santa Barbara attractions, running from Stearns Wharf to the Santa Barbara Mission. Save dollars when you purchase tickets online.

has mountains running east–west, Santa Barbara also has south-facing beaches. To everyone who knows that the Pacific Ocean is always to the west in California (and almost everyone does know that, don't they?), this state of affairs causes no end of confusion. Whether Salisbury Haley gave much thought to compass directions is debatable, but he chose to lay out the city's streets running diagonally from southeast to northwest and from southwest to northeast. In the middle is State Street, the main downtown business thoroughfare; once you've found your way there, you have a good point of reference for exploring the rest of the city.

Our best advice? Study your map before you go exploring, or—if all else fails—ask someone. We Santa Barbarans are unbelievably friendly and helpful.

Parking

Compared to big cities, parking in Santa Barbara is reasonably stress-free. However, you may find it a challenge on busy summer weekends and holidays—especially during festivals and events. If you're headed downtown, you'll find 12 public parking lots near State Street between Victoria and Haley Streets with easy access from Chapala or Anacapa Streets. Both streets run parallel on either side of State Street. But beware: Anacapa Street is one-way, as is the section of Chapala Street north of Carrillo Street, so you may have to double back a few blocks to reach your destination. Public parking facilities are open 24 hours a day, 7 days a week, and parking is free for the first 75 minutes. For every hour or part of an hour thereafter, you'll pay $1.50, which accrues until you leave. To see a map of downtown parking lots, visit www.santabarbaradowntown.com.

When public lots are full, you may be forced to park on a side street, as no parking is permitted on State Street in the downtown district. This can be difficult. Nearly all downtown streets have only 75- or 15-minute parking zones (except Sunday), and vigilant parking authorities regularly patrol, writing tickets for infractions. If you do park in one of these zones, make sure you move your car before the time is up. To be on the safe side, we suggest you allow 10 minutes for parking your car and walking to your destination—perhaps a little longer during peak holiday periods. That way, if you nab a spot quickly, you can take your time and do a little window-shopping along the way.

Take the Bus

If all this talk about traffic and parking has you feeling nervous about driving downtown, you have several other options to get you there and get you around. The Santa Barbara Metropolitan Transit District (805-963-3366; www.sbmtd.gov) provides bus service throughout the greater Santa Barbara area, from Carpinteria to Ellwood. There are also electric shuttles such as the Downtown-Waterfront Shuttle (fare: 25 cents) and the Seaside Shuttle in Carpinteria (fare: 25 cents). You can pick up a schedule at the main transit center (1020 Chapala St., Santa Barbara),

on MTD buses, or at visitor centers and most waterfront hotels. For help planning your route, call (805) 963-3366 and speak to a transit adviser. If you're already out and about, look for the bus stops with the yellow-and-black MTD signs every few blocks along the route. Exact change is required for all passengers. The standard one-way fare is $1.75; seniors 62 and older and disabled persons (including blind passengers) pay 85 cents, and the Downtown-Waterfront Shuttle, which runs up and down State Street, costs just 25 cents. Children no taller than 45 inches (with shoes on) accompanied by an adult ride free. Note that 30-day discounted passes are $52 for adults, $42 for youth K–12, and $20 for seniors 62 and over, offering a great savings for frequent travelers.

Bike & Bus

If you'd like to take the bus and then bike your way around town, consider the Bike & Bus program, which allows you to stow your bike on a special rack on the bus, then disembark and ride away. Taking your bike incurs no extra charge, but Bike & Bus options are available only on certain lines. To find out which lines, call (805) 963-3356, visit MTD's website, or pick up a *Routes & Schedules Guide* available at the main transit center (1020 Chapala St., Santa Barbara), on MTD buses, or at visitor centers and most waterfront hotels.

Downtown-Waterfront Shuttle

An extremely popular way to get around is the Downtown-Waterfront Shuttle, also operated by the MTD. Making use of this service, you can shop State Street, tour the waterfront, then take the kids over to the zoo, all without the hassle of negotiating traffic jams or parking lots. The little electric shuttles with the blue-and-black sailboat symbol are a familiar sight on State Street. Just hop aboard! The Downtown Shuttle runs daily from State Street at Sola Street to Stearns Wharf and back again, with service every 10 minutes between 10:15 a.m. and 6 p.m., depending on the time of year. Fare is 25 cents one way. Children under 45 inches tall ride free. You can get on or off at any stop along the way (the shuttle stops on every block). Transfers to the Waterfront Shuttle are complimentary, but you need to ask your driver for a shuttle transfer when you first board. The Waterfront Shuttle runs daily from 10 a.m. to 5:45 p.m. along Cabrillo Boulevard from the Santa Barbara Zoo to the harbor every 30 minutes. There is nonstop service between the zoo and the Arlington Theatre every 30 minutes from 7:30 to 10 a.m. Mon to Fri, 8 to 10 a.m. Sat, and 9 to 10 a.m. Sun.

- **Downtown summer schedule:** 9 a.m. to 10 a.m. every 30 minutes; 10 a.m. to 6 p.m. every 10 minutes; Fri and Sat evenings: 6 to 10 p.m. every 15 minutes.
- **Waterfront summer schedule:** 10 a.m. to 6 p.m, every 15 minutes; Fri and Sat evenings, between the Zoo and the Wharf only, 6 to 10 p.m. every 15 minutes.
- **Downtown schedule for fall and winter:** 9 to 10 a.m. every 30 minutes; 10 a.m. to 6 p.m. every 10 minutes.
- **Waterfront schedule for fall and winter:** 10 a.m. to 6 p.m. every 30 minutes.

In Carpinteria

Climb aboard the electric Seaside Shuttle and you can cruise in ecofriendly style between Carpinteria's downtown shopping district, residential areas, and the beach. The shuttle also connects with MTD's other lines for trips to downtown Santa Barbara, but to make the transfer, you must pay the $1.75 bus fare and ask your driver for a transfer when you pay. It's 25 cents for a one-way ride; children no taller than 45 inches (with shoes) are free. The shuttle operates every 15 to 30 minutes Mon through Fri from 6 a.m. to 7 p.m. and Sat and Sun from 8:45 a.m. to 5:50 p.m. or 7 p.m., depending on the season. Call (805) 963-3366 or click on "Seaside Shuttle" on www.sbmtd.gov for more information.

i Looking for a quick trip from the waterfront to downtown? For 25 cents, you can't beat the Downtown-Waterfront Shuttle. TotalSantaBarbara .com has an excellent map of the shuttle's route at www.totalsantabarbara .com/dws.shtml.

For Disabled Passengers

The **nonprofit Easy Lift Transportation** (805-681-1181; www.easylift.org) provides curb-to-curb, wheelchair-accessible transportation for passengers with disabilities and covers southern Santa Barbara County. The service runs Mon through Fri from 5:25 a.m. to midnight, Sat from 6 a.m. to 11:20 p.m., and Sun from 6:20 a.m. to 10 p.m. The fare is $3.50 a ride. Reservations are essential and can be made up to 2 weeks in advance.

Taxis

There's a joke in Santa Barbara that all you need to do is think of a color, and you have the name of a taxi service. The cost for a trip from the airport to downtown Santa Barbara will run you around $28 to $30. Call the Rose Cab Company (805-564-2600), Gold Cab (805-685-9797), Yellow Cab Company (805-965-5111), A-1 Yellow Cab (805-964-1111), or Blue Dolphin Cab (805-966-6161). There is even a Rockstar Taxi & Limousine (805-882-9191), but Lucky Cab's ecofriendly Prius may be the ticket to ride (805-968-5020).

Limousine Service

Since there are plenty of celebrities (and plenty of celebrity wannabes) in Santa Barbara, the city has more limo companies than you might expect. Most provide everything from sedans to super-stretch limos, so if you have something special in mind, be sure to ask (being aware, of course, that the fancier you get, the more it will cost). In general, limo transportation from the airport to downtown runs around $150 to $200, including tax and gratuity. Choose a company from the following list, and ride in style.

**AMERICAN INTERNATIONAL
  TRANSPORTATION SERVICES**
(805) 643-5466, (888) 334-5466
www.aitslimo.com

EXECUTIVE LIMOUSINE SERVICE
(805) 969-5525, (800) 247-6980
www.goexeclimo.com

LIMOUSINE LINK
(805) 564-4660, (888) 399-5466
www.santabarbaralimousinelink.com

ROCKSTAR TAXI & LIMOUSINE INC.
(805) 451-9999, (877) 418-7267
www.rockstarsb.com

SPENCER'S LIMOUSINE & TOURS
(805) 884-9700
www.spencerslimo.com

ZEUS TRANSPORTATION LLC
(805) 571-1400
www.zeuslimo.com

Rental Cars

You can find most major rental car companies in the Santa Barbara area. Currently, Avis, Budget, Enterprise, Hertz, and National have counters at the airport. Thrifty has an off-site location and offers shuttle services. Courtesy phones are located in the terminal. Not all companies provide pickup service, so you may need to hoof it a short distance to get to your car or take other airport transportation to the rental office if it's downtown. Be sure to ask what the company policy is if you need pickup service either from the airport or from a downtown location.

AVIS RENT-A-CAR
(805) 965-1079, downtown
Santa Barbara
(805) 964-4848, airport
(800) 331-1212
www.avis.com

BUDGET CAR & TRUCK RENTAL
Airport only
(800) 527-0700
(805) 683-3012
www.budget.com

ENTERPRISE RENT-A-CAR
(805) 966-3097, downtown
Santa Barbara
(805) 683-0067, Goleta
(800) RENT-A-CAR (736-8222)
www.enterprise.com

HERTZ RENT-A-CAR
(805) 967-0411, airport
(805) 962-5305, downtown at
Doubletree Resort
(800) 654-3131
www.hertz.com

i Honking your horn while driving is simply not done in Santa Barbara. According to state Motor Vehicle Code, it's illegal to blast your horn out of anger.

NATIONAL CAR RENTAL
(805) 967-1202, airport
(800) CAR-RENT (227-7368)
www.nationalcar.com

THRIFTY CAR RENTAL
(805) 681-1222, airport
(800) 367-2277
www.thrifty.com

U-SAVE AUTO RENTAL
(805) 963-3499, downtown
Santa Barbara
(805) 964-5436, Goleta
www.usavesantabarbara.com

THE SANTA BARBARA AIRPORT

Quaint and *charming* would be the words we'd use to describe the Spanish-style Santa Barbara Airport (SBA) complex, which lies about 8 miles west of downtown. You, on the other hand, might think of something a bit more disparaging, especially if you're used to big-city technology and efficiency. But Santa Barbarans love their open-air airport, and most visitors think its beautiful architecture and colorful Mission gardens are fitting for the gateway to a town so steeped in Spanish history. In February 2007, the city's Architectural Board of Review and Planning Commission provided concept approval to a $60 million redesign called the Santa Barbara Airport Terminal Project. The project aims to increase the size, accessibility, and traffic at the airport while preserving

"the Santa Barbara experience." Construction of the new terminal was completed in summer 2011, with the entire project's execution, including restoration of the old terminal and a new short-term parking lot, to come sometime in 2012. The new terminal features art and tile work by Santa Barbara artists, including a historic mural by local favorite Channing Peake (1910–1989).

Like all the nation's airports, Santa Barbara Airport has tightened security since 9/11. Expect frequent baggage checks and passenger screenings, and make sure you keep your boarding passes and identification handy. The airport is often crowded, but in a friendly sort of way. There are no snug walkways out to your plane, so you have to cross the tarmac and go up the ramp. This means you'll need an umbrella if it's raining. Special assistance is available if you can't climb the steps.

Keep in mind that air service is limited and generally requires a nonstop connecting flight to Los Angeles, San Francisco, Seattle, Denver, or Phoenix (these can change) in order to board an international flight or even one that goes to the eastern half of the country. But if everything goes according to plan, you can enjoy a one-stop journey to around 200 destinations from our little airport and save the time of a 2-hour trek to Los Angeles International Airport.

Currently, the airport has nearly 60 daily commercial flights. Major airlines servicing Santa Barbara include **Alaska Air** (800-252-7522; www.alaskaair.com), **American Eagle** (800-433-7300; www.aa.com), **United Express** (800-241-6522; www.ual.com), and **US Airways** (800-428-4322; www.USAirways.com). But remember, the travel industry is volatile, and airline affiliations and services change from time to time. Santa Barbara's

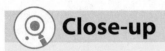

Close-up

Street Names

In addition to the tricky geographical orientation of Santa Barbara, visitors are often struck—and sometimes confused—by the city's downtown street names. Spanish military men, Chumash chiefs, and early settlers are all memorialized on signs, a fact that may leave you wondering whatever happened to Main Street, Maple Lane, and other classics. (Well, we do have State Street.)

ALAMEDA PADRE SERRA

Called simply APS by Insiders, this winding road just above Mission Santa Barbara leads to the city's Riviera. It was named in honor of Father Junipero Serra, the Franciscan friar who founded the mission.

ANACAPA STREET

Anacapa comes from the Chumash word meaning "ever-changing" or "mirage." The natives noticed that, depending on the weather conditions, Anacapa Island could appear as one large mesa or, when the island was reflected in a mirage, a body of land much bigger than its actual size. Anacapa Street points in the direction of Anacapa Island.

ARRELLAGA STREET

José Joaquin de Arillaga was governor of California from 1792 to 1794, although the street is a misspelling of the governor's name.

BRINKERHOFF AVENUE

This avenue is named for Samuel Bevier Brinkerhoff, the city's first medical doctor.

CANON PERDIDO STREET

Literally "Lost Cannon Street," this downtown thoroughfare's name marks a famous local incident in 1848. Four boys stole a cannon from the beach as a practical joke, but local military leaders were convinced that someone was trying to stock-pile weapons for a rebellion against the American occupation forces. The military governor of California, Richard Mason, decided that if the cannon wasn't promptly returned, the people of Santa Barbara would have to pay a $500 fine (a pretty hefty fee in those days). Local residents were forced to cough up the money, and the cannon was eventually found mired in Mission Creek in 1859.

CABRILLO BOULEVARD

Named for Juan Rodriguez Cabrillo, the Portuguese explorer who sailed into the Santa Barbara Channel in 1542 and the first European to see the Santa Barbara coastline.

CARRILLO STREET

The name of this street reflects the role of the Carrillo family in Santa Barbara's history. Jose Raimundo Carrillo served as captain of the Presidio, and his son, Carlos Antonio de Jesús Carrillo, was appointed governor of California in 1837.

DE LA GUERRA STREET

The name literally means "of the war," but in this case it honors the family of Jose Antonio Julian de la Guerra y Noriega (better known simply as Jose de la Guerra), who became commandant of the Presidio in 1815, serving until 1842.

FIGUEROA STREET

Jose Figueroa was a popular Mexican governor in early California.

GUTIERREZ STREET

Benigno Gutierrez was a Chilean who came to California in 1849 to make his fortune in the gold fields. After amassing a substantial sum of money, he came to Santa Barbara in 1854 and became the city's first pharmacist.

HALEY STREET

This street is named for Salisbury Haley, a steamship captain who came to Santa Barbara in 1851 and, with questionable surveying skills, laid out the streets.

INDIO MUERTO STREET

The translation is literally "dead Indian"—Captain Haley found one here as he was doing his survey.

LOS OLIVOS STREET

"The Olives" Street once bisected the Mission's olive grove.

MICHELTORENA STREET

Mexican governor Manuel Micheltorena became governor of California in 1842 after Mexico overthrew the Spaniards.

MILPAS STREET

Milpas comes from a native word meaning "ground sown to grain," and the word *milpo*, an Americanized Spanish word, means "cornfield." The street is named for the farmland overseen by the natives and padres from Mission Santa Barbara.

ORTEGA STREET

Lieutenant Jose Francisco de Ortega was chosen in 1782 to be the builder and first commandant of the Presidio.

SALSIPUEDES STREET

In Spanish, *salsipuedes* means "leave if you can," a concept that residents continue to take literally when winter rains turn the area into a swamp.

SOLA STREET

Pablo de Sola was the last Spanish governor in California.

VALERIO STREET

Valerio was an infamous Native American robber who lived in a cave in the Santa Ynez Mountains and made forays into the city to steal from local residents.

YANONALI STREET

This name is a variation on Yanonalit, who was the Chumash chief when the Spanish arrived to establish the Presidio in 1769.

runway is relatively short, so air travel in or out of the city is almost always by regional jets. Most of the local airlines are linked to major airlines, so you can easily make connections, and you can even get a boarding pass and seating assignment for a longer trip as you board in Santa Barbara, saving time later.

Information on airlines serving the Santa Barbara area, the types of planes they fly, and their worldwide connections, as well as parking instructions and rates, are available from the Airport Information Line, (805) 683-4011. Better still, visit the Santa Barbara Airport website at www.flysba.com.

Airport Parking

The good thing about the short-term parking lot at the Santa Barbara Airport is that it is adjacent to the terminal—an easy walking distance. You can whiz into the lot 5 minutes before Grandma's plane arrives and be at the gate in time to see her disembark.

This doesn't help you if you're picking up passengers, however, and you may find your best bet is a quick stop in front of the terminal. If you do choose that option, don't leave your car unattended at the curb. If you plan to park in the short-term parking lot, located to your left as you enter the airport, you'll pay $1 for up to 15 minutes, $2 for 16 to 60 minutes, and $1 for each additional hour, with a maximum $16 daily fee. Parking information is available online at www.flysba.com, or you may contact the parking office during the week at (805) 967-2745.

The entrance to the long-term parking lot is farther east than the main airport entrance, which puts you farther away from the terminal, but it's still not much of a walk for the physically fit. Senior citizens, however, may find the trek a bit of a hardship, so you may want to drop them (and any heavy

bags) off at the terminal before parking. Rates for long-term parking are $2 for the first hour, $1 for each additional hour (with a $9 daily maximum). Long Term Lot 2 is also available off Hollister Avenue near Fairview Avenue. A free airport shuttle will take you from there to the terminal, but you should arrive 2 hours before your flight to allow enough time for parking and checking in. The overflow-parking rate is $9 a day. Note that all the parking rates are raised periodically, and all airport parking lots accept cash and major credit cards.

i If you're heading northbound to Santa Barbara on US 101, read the signs carefully. Cabrillo Boulevard, Carrillo Street, and Castillo Street are all US 101 exits in close succession. Cabrillo (Cabr-EE-o) Boulevard runs along the Santa Barbara waterfront, Carrillo (pronounced Ca-REE-o) Street is one of the main downtown exits, and Castillo (Cas-TEE-o) Street will take you to Bath Street and the Santa Barbara Harbor.

Leaving the Airport

To head to downtown Santa Barbara from the airport, turn right as you exit the parking lot and follow Sandspit Road past Goleta Beach Park, merging onto CA 217. Stay in the left lanes, which merge with southbound US 101 at Patterson Avenue, and continue until you see the signs for downtown Santa Barbara. If you're staying in Goleta or headed farther north, exit the airport to your left and follow Fairview Avenue to Hollister Avenue or Calle Real, two major thoroughfares in downtown Goleta. If UCSB is your destination, it borders airport property on the west, so you're not far away. To get there, turn

GETTING HERE, GETTING AROUND

right out of the airport parking lot and take a quick left as the signs direct (if you go past Goleta Beach Park, you've gone too far). This will link you to the last stretch of CA 217 and take you to the entrance of the university.

EOS TRANSPORTATION
(805) 683-9636, (800) 977-1123
www.eostransportation.com
Eos Transportation provides on-demand, door-to-door shuttle service for $20 to $40 (depending on the location), and $5 per additional passenger. Reservations need to be made 24 hours in advance. They also do wine tours, so you could just head straight for wine country or their nightclub (Eos) downtown (see Nightlife section).

Shuttle Service to LAX
CENTRAL COAST SHUTTLE
SERVICES, INC.
Santa Maria Public Airport
3249 Terminal Dr., Ste. 102, Santa Maria
(805) 928-1977, (800) 470-8818
www.centralcoastshuttle.com
Although most of their shuttles originate in Santa Maria or Buellton, Central Coast Shuttle Services also offers Flag Stop Services from Santa Barbara Airport or Santa Barbara to Los Angeles International Airport (LAX) six times daily. Services depart from Santa Barbara Airport from 5:15 a.m. to 6:45 p.m. and return from LAX anywhere from 11:15 a.m. to 12:15 a.m. Reservations may be made online. Rates from SBA to Santa Maria $50; SBA to Buellton $45; SBA to LAX $55.

ROADRUNNER SHUTTLE AND
LIMOUSINE SERVICE
240 S. Glenn Dr., Camarillo
(800) 247-7919
www.rrshuttle.com

One of our favorite ways to hitch a ride to Los Angeles is with the courteous and reliable door-to-door service from Roadrunner. They have airport shuttles or chartered vehicles, from private cars to buses to limousines. The shuttle is an economical and environmental ride-share service to LAX, BUR (Burbank's Bob Hope Airport), and SBA.

The van transportation takes significantly longer to arrive at LAX due to its many stops, so if you can afford it, splurge on the private town-car service. Or, if price is really no object, then shoot for the stretch H2 Hummer that will have heads turning all the way to L.A. Roadrunner also has a host of other excursions that will tickle your fancy. Visit their website to check fares and reservations.

SANTA BARBARA AIRBUS
5755 Thornwood Dr., Goleta
(805) 964-7759, (800) 423-1618
www.sbairbus.com
Santa Barbara Airbus is a friendly, locally owned company that aims to save travelers the hassles of driving between Santa Barbara and LAX. It offers 16 trips daily to and from LAX in comfortable buses driven by great drivers, and there's free wireless Internet for your laptop computer. The Santa Barbara Airbus departs from the company's Goleta office and stops for pickups in Santa Barbara (at the Hyatt Santa Barbara, 1111 E. Cabrillo Blvd.) and Carpinteria (outside the International House of Pancakes at 1114 Casitas Pass Rd.). Service is very reliable, and the cost is less than connecting with LAX via a commuter flight. Fare to LAX for one person (if you make and pay for a reservation at least 24 hours ahead) is $44 one-way and $84 round-trip. You can walk on without a reservation, but the fare goes up to $48 one-way and $90 round-trip. Discounts apply

19

if two or more passengers travel together. There are no baggage fees for two bags and a small carry on. If you exceed this amount or need to transport unusual items such as bicycles, surfboards, large boxes, or trunks, an excess-baggage charge may be applicable. Wheelchair-accessible vehicles are available but require 48-hour advance notice. The Santa Barbara Airbus also offers day-trip tours to destinations throughout California.

i The first road to be closed due to inclement weather is almost always CA 154, so call CalTrans for highway conditions, (800) 427-7623, before setting out.

TRAINS

AMTRAK
209 State St., Santa Barbara
(800) USA-RAIL
www.amtrak.com
Pulling into our Spanish Mission Revival–style railway station in the heart of downtown is a great way to arrive in Santa Barbara. The Santa Barbara station is fully staffed daily with ticketing and checked baggage service, and there's an indoor waiting room with restrooms. Long-term parking is available in a lot operated by the City of Santa Barbara.

Separate, unstaffed, no-frills boarding platforms are in Carpinteria, at 475 Linden Ave., and in Goleta, at 25 S. La Patera Ln. between US 101 and Hollister Avenue, but most passengers board in downtown Santa Barbara, just 2 blocks from the beach.

Santa Barbara is served daily by two Coast Starlight trains, which run between Seattle and Los Angeles, and the Pacific Surfliner, which offers round trips daily between here and San Diego as well as north to San Luis Obispo. Amtrak also offers Thruway motor coach services to Solvang, Lompoc, Santa Maria, and Bakersfield when purchasing a through-train ticket.

LONG-DISTANCE BUS SERVICE

GREYHOUND LINES INC.
(805) 965-7551, (800) 231-2222
www.greyhound.com
Greyhound bus services will connect you to almost anywhere in the continental United States. Service is offered to Los Angeles and San Francisco. Information on all Greyhound routes and fares is available at the terminal (located adjacent to the Amtrak station), by calling the toll-free number above, or accessing their website. The local telephone line is often busy, so you might want to try the toll-free number first.

HISTORY

L et's say you've just arrived in beautiful Santa Barbara for a week's vacation. You can't wait to get to the beach, you've been looking forward to sampling some local wines, and you plan to take in a concert or check out the latest exhibit at the Santa Barbara Museum of Art. You'd just as soon skip the historical sights and get on with the good stuff.

Guess what? You don't have to go looking for history in Santa Barbara. It's there every time you turn around.

Santa Barbara's roots are deep, and their evidence is in the architecture, the street names, the celebrations, the shopping malls, the public parks and monuments—even the food. Pretty soon you'll be so intrigued by everything around you that you'll be begging to learn more. Really.

IN THE BEGINNING

Long before the celebrities and tourists hit the Santa Barbara beaches, the virgin stretches of sand and sea were home to the Chumash Indians, a gentle people who called their home "the land of the gods—the place where man was born."

Remains of Chumash villages have been found on both the mainland (the center of the Chumash capital city of Syukhtun was located on the present-day intersection of Cabrillo Boulevard and Chapala Street) and on the islands more than 20 miles offshore (now called San Miguel, Santa Rosa, Santa Cruz, Anacapa, and Santa Barbara or, collectively, the northern Channel Islands).

Ten thousand years ago, finely crafted 20-foot boats (called tomols) hand-carved from driftwood and fallen Northern Californian redwood trunks, sealed with the abundant local tar, carried the Chumash back and forth across the Santa Barbara Channel as they brought their wares to market at Syukhtun or gathered to celebrate with dance, music, storytelling, and sacred ceremonies. The Chumash lived off the land and sea and developed a complex language, economy, and system of trade and taxation. When the Portuguese explorer Juan Rodríguez Cabrillo sailed to the Channel Islands in the fall of 1542, the Chumash paddled their massive canoes out to meet his two small ships, never realizing that his visit heralded changes that would eventually decimate their lives and culture.

SANTA BARBARA, PROTECT US!

Many seafaring explorers followed Cabrillo (who is reportedly buried on San Miguel Island), including Sir Francis Drake. On December 3, 1602, the eve of the feast day of Saint Barbara, patron saint of mariners,

Sebastian Vizcaino's ship was in the channel when a violent storm erupted.

Fearing that he and his entire expedition were about to be swept to a watery grave, Vizcaino called upon the ship's friar to appeal to the saint, who was credited thereafter with sparing their lives.

In gratitude, the friar christened the channel Santa Barbara. None of the expedition disembarked, and it would be another 167 years before the land on either side of the channel was claimed for Spain.

THE ROYAL PRESIDIO

On August 14, 1769, José Francisco de Ortega, a scout for the land expedition of Captain Gaspár de Portola, became the first non-Chumash of record to set foot in this area. The expedition, under the commission of King Carlos III of Spain, was sent with Father Junípero Serra to establish a series of both military and religious strongholds along the California coast in hopes of putting the entire region under the control of the Spanish crown.

Thirteen years later, Lieutenant Ortega brought a band of settlers and soldiers back with him and selected a spot for a fort approximately 1 mile inland from the south-facing shore. The last military outpost of the Spanish Empire in the New World thus originated on what is now the corner of Canon Perdido and Santa Barbara Streets. Father Serra celebrated a mass, and the fort was christened El Presidio Real de Santa Bárbara (The Royal Fort of Saint Barbara).

MISSION SANTA BARBARA

By the late 1780s, several more structures had been added to the Presidio, including high walls with locked gates to surround it.

Security had been one of the highest priorities of the Spanish, and with the settlement now enclosed and guarded, they were ready to turn their attention to building a mission for Father Serra. Unfortunately, the good father, knowing that construction of the mission would not begin until after the Presidio was completed, had already gone north to Carmel, where he died. His successor, Padre Fermín de Lasuén, raised and blessed the cross at Mission Santa Barbara on December 4, 1786. In addition to marking the dawning of organized religious life at the Presidio, the day's ceremonies were the beginning of the end of the Chumash culture.

> **i** The original name of La Purisima Mission in Spanish was La Misión de La Purísima Concepción de la Santísima Virgen María. This mission was founded on the Feast Day of the Immaculate Conception of the Blessed Virgin on December 8, 1787.

It was the Chumash who had provided most of the labor for the building of the Presidio and the mission. The first structures were made of logs and mud, and the mission itself looked nothing like it does today. A small chapel, a kitchen, a granary, and separate quarters for the padres and the servants, arranged in a quadrangle, made up the early mission complex. Amid these humble surroundings, more than half of the Chumash population—including their chief, Yanonalit—eventually embraced Christianity, taking up residence nearby in a village that grew to include more than 250 adobe houses by the year 1800. Although the Chumash learned agriculture, animal husbandry, and other skills, the arrival of the Europeans

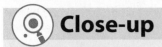
Close-up

Earthquake!

On December 12, 1812, a major earthquake wreaked havoc on the mission and surrounding areas. Following the initial shock, which caused most roofs to collapse, a series of tidal waves thundered as far inland as the Presidio, crushing and scattering what was left of the buildings. The Chumash were terrified, and many fled the area, never to return.

In the ensuing weeks, aftershocks caused even more devastation, mud bubbled up from the ground, landslides buried many foothill canyons, and it seemed as though life would never be the same at Mission Santa Barbara. As the earth began to quiet, however, the rebuilding process began. In 1815 the remaining Chumash, aided by soldiers and local artisans, started reconstructing the mission church using pink sandstone blocks and limestone mortar.

The new Mission Santa Barbara building, reportedly inspired by a drawing of a temple by Roman architect M. Vitruvius Polion from the first century BC, had a single bell tower that was hung with six bells brought from Peru. On September 10, 1820, eight years after the disastrous quake, a formal dedication followed by a 3-day fiesta celebrated its completion. A second tower was added just over 10 years later.

La Purisima Mission in Lompoc—one day's travel by horseback—was completely destroyed by this same earthquake: its mission bells ringing, as Padre Señan would write, "without benefit of a bell ringer."

Another strong temblor, occurring a little more than a century later in 1925, leveled Santa Barbara and set the stage for the rebuilding of the devastated town into a charming destination that would later become famous for it's red-tile roofs and graceful Spanish architecture.

If history repeats itself, Santa Barbara stands poised for the Big One, but hopefully the many buildings that have been retrofitted to meet strict earthquake standards will stand their ground.

took a terrible toll. Between 1787 and 1841, more than 4,000 natives died, most from European diseases. By 1812, however, the faithful Chumash had been instrumental in building two successive churches on the mission site, including one adobe structure with six side "chapels". That mission church was destroyed by the great earthquake of 1812. The long *convento* wing with its row of stone rooms survived. This made it clear to the padres that the church should be rebuilt in stone. By 1820 the new structure was completed—with 6–foot-thick stone walls and just two side-altar chapels, plus an actual crypt room under the floor. There are 18 people buried in this crypt at Mission Santa Barbara. Of the 21 Spanish California missions, only two—Carmel and Santa Barbara—are built of stone rather than adobe, and only one—Santa Barbara—has an actual burial crypt.

THE REBELLION

After the reconstruction of the mission, the Chumash began to sorely resent their role as servants and builders. No longer free to roam the land they loved, they were sick, tired, and hungry, and they were often beaten for being lazy or disobedient.

The Mexicans, who took over the local government after the success of the Mexican Revolution in 1822, were no kinder to the local tribes than the Spanish had been, and in early 1824 the Santa Barbara Chumash joined forces with Chumash at La Purisima, Ventura and Santa Inés missions to overthrow their oppressors.

After the severe beating of a young Chumash in February 1824 at Santa Inés, tribesmen seized the mission and set fire to it. Demonstrations of support were staged at the three other missions, but the rebels were ultimately forced to flee when the military was called in to stop the revolt. After seeking refuge for a time with the Tulare tribe in the interior valley, the Chumash returned to Santa Barbara when the regional governor issued a guarantee of amnesty.

THE MEXICAN PERIOD

Not long after Santa Barbara came under the political control of independent Mexico, foreign trade laws enforced under Spanish rule were abolished, and the city began to trade tallow and hides with the New England states, drawing Yankee traders such as William Goodwin Dana and his ship, *Waverly*, to the Santa Barbara area. (It was William Dana's cousin, Richard Henry Dana, who wrote *Two Years Before the Mast*, describing the latter's voyages to the area.)

The traders' visits were often filled with a whirlwind of social events arranged by hospitable Santa Barbara residents, including wealthy landowning Spanish dons and doñas whose families had stayed on after the Mexican Revolution.

On more than one occasion, dashing young sea captains fell in love with dark-eyed Santa Barbara señoritas and converted to the Catholic faith in order to marry them. William Dana fell for the charms of Josefa Carrillo, daughter of Carlos Antonio de Jesús Carrillo, whose four sisters also married Americans.

El Cuartel or "Soldiers Quarters," built in 1782 and preserved in El Presidio de Santa Barbara State Historic Park downtown, is the oldest residence in Santa Barbara and the second oldest in California. It is located next door to the US Post Office on E. Canon Perdido Street.

Soon, it seemed everyone had heard of Santa Barbara, and its economic importance began to draw the attention of the US government. During the Mexican War, in the late summer of 1846, a contingent of US marines led by Commodore Robert Field Stockton came ashore and raised the American flag over the Presidio. By Christmas Day, attempts by the Mexicans to regain control of the city had been put down by Captain John Fremont, and Santa Barbara belonged to the Americans.

The Californios (Hispanic residents who lived in Santa Barbara before it was captured by the United States) were furious about the takeover. As Americans continued to pour into Santa Barbara, Californios began to lose both their rights and their property; land was sold to the newcomers for 25 cents for an acre of farmland and $1 for a city lot.

Frustrated and angry, the Californios began to strike out at the Yankees by robbing them and plundering at every turn, but their efforts were futile. A drought in

1863–1864 was the final economic blow to most of the remaining Californios, and many were forced to move to the poorer sections of town.

Soon after, Chinese laborers displaced from the California gold country moved into the city and often into the abandoned homes of the Californios. Shops, laundries, and gambling houses sprang up along Canon Perdido Street between State and Santa Barbara Streets. In response to some of the illegal activities of the Chinese, a law was eventually passed forbidding them to own land and thus forcing most to move to the outskirts of town. The social and economic future of Santa Barbara now rested squarely on the shoulders of the Americans, who by the late 1800s wielded most of the power and controlled nearly all of the land and the money.

THE AMERICAN PERIOD

Full "Americanization," which included the adoption of English as the official language, slowly began to change Santa Barbara's character. By the later half of the 19th century, it was a growing American city with its own newspaper, boarding school, wharf, and expanding number of tourist attractions. Articles in major publications, including some New York City newspapers, praised the city's climate, hot springs, and other amenities, and before long tourists were coming in droves to stay at an increasing number of new hotels and boardinghouses. The first wharf, Chapala Street Wharf, was a failure, but after Stearns Wharf was completed in 1872 at a cost of $40,000, Santa Barbara became accessible by sea. The Lobero Theatre, also completed in 1872, offered a new venue for the cultural arts and would become the oldest continuously operating theater in the state. When the Southern Pacific Railroad connected Santa Barbara with Los Angeles in 1887 (the same year that State Street installed electric lights), the city became a full-blown tourist destination, hosting such luminaries as John D. Rockefeller Sr., Andrew Carnegie, the Vanderbilts, and the Du Ponts.

The Lighthouse Lady

California's first female lighthouse keeper, Julia Williams, "wo"-manned Santa Barbara's lighthouse for over 40 years. The "Lighthouse Lady" assumed her position in 1865 after her husband quit the job. Julia faithfully beacon-tended while also raising their six children. As if that wasn't enough, she oversaw lighthouse improvements and the sinking of a 50-foot well and copiously documented oil usage, hours burned, and weather conditions.

By the turn of the century, Santa Barbara was booming. In 1912, the city became the "Film Capital of the World" when the American Film Company opened its Flying A Studio on the northwest corner of State and Mission Streets. The rugged backdrop of San Marcos Pass was often used for filming Westerns, and local beaches served as stand-ins for exotic island shores. Movie stars often sought respite in luxurious beachside hotels or relaxed in one of several local mineral springs.

With the continued Americanization of the city, Santa Barbara's Spanish architecture began to be eclipsed by more "modern" buildings, resulting in a sort of hodgepodge look in the downtown area. Although many found this trend disturbing, no one was sure what to do about it. On June 29, 1925, a solution emerged in the form of a major earthquake that destroyed most of the downtown buildings, opening the way for reconstruction in what was to become the classic Santa Barbara style, thanks to the civic-minded Pearl Chase (known as "The First Lady of Santa Barbara" for her legendary work in historic preservation and civic planning), who had the foresight and saw to it that the town was carefully rebuilt in the Spanish Revival style. During the 1930s, Santa Barbara's population continued to grow, and it remained a popular getaway for the rich and famous. Posh hotels such as Ronald Colman's San Ysidro Ranch catered to an upscale clientele.

Times were leaner during the Great Depression, and because the city was perched on the Pacific shoreline, there were many anxious moments during the war years that followed. In February 1942 a Japanese submarine fired on a beach approximately 10 miles west of the city, marking the first enemy shelling of the American mainland since 1812. Little damage was done, but tensions grew and coastal property values fell as a result of the incident. After World War II, Santa Barbara enjoyed the economic boom experienced by the rest of the country. The University of California at Santa Barbara campus and Santa Barbara Junior College (now Santa Barbara City College) accommodated young soldiers seeking an education on the GI Bill, and local government officials scrambled to secure enough water to meet the needs of the growing population. Bradbury Dam was completed in 1953, Cachuma Lake spilled over five years later, and the city's water problems seemed to be solved.

City boundaries expanded between 1960 and 1970, and Santa Barbara's population grew from 19,000 to more than 60,000. Research and development companies employed more than 160,000 workers by 1974, as families came to Santa Barbara from all over the country, drawn by the healthy economy and alluring lifestyle. The booming tourist economy was almost dealt a deathblow in 1969 when a Union Oil platform 5 miles off the Santa Barbara coast blew out, sending thick waves of black crude oil onto local beaches. Tourism, as well as sea creatures and birds, took an extremely hard knock until the mess was cleaned up, and local environmentalists were livid, vowing to protect their beaches in the future. This event was considered the birth of the environmental movement, and GOO (Get Oil Out!) led the way. Since then, the activities of oil companies, who own drilling and tankering rights in the Santa Barbara Channel, have been under constant scrutiny.

Wildfires have also plagued Santa Barbara; the 1990 Painted Cave fire killed one person and destroyed hundreds of homes and several businesses. Started by an arsonist, the blaze roared from the top of San Marcos Pass to the outskirts of Hope Ranch, driven by hot down-canyon winds. The threat of a brush fire is ever present in Santa Barbara, especially during drought years, when the canyons are overgrown with tinder-dry brush. Fire was also the problem in November 1998 when one of the city's most popular tourist attractions—Stearns Wharf—was hit by a $12 million blaze that destroyed 20 percent of the pier. Broadcast throughout the country, scenes of the spectacular conflagration (as well as early reports that the wharf had been completely destroyed) led some to exclaim that Santa

Barbara would never be the same. "Nonsense!" exclaimed city officials, who promptly plopped down a 70-foot Christmas tree on what was left of the rubble. With the burned-out section roped off, the pier reopened to the public a few days after the fire, and repairs on the rest of the pier have restored the landmark to its former glory.

> **i** On June 29, 1925, a magnitude 6.8 earthquake destroyed many of Santa Barbara's downtown buildings. After the quake, Pearl Chase and the Plans and Planting Committee joined with the Architectural Board of Review and recommended all new buildings be constructed in the Spanish-Mediterranean style, creating Santa Barbara's famous skyline of red-tile roofs you see today.

More recently the Tea fire (2008) and Jesusita fire (2009) had the town living in a state of evacuations, flames, and ash for months on end. Over 200 homes were destroyed in the Tea fire, which consumed almost 2,000 acres. On the heels of the Tea fire—with residents proclaiming, "Oh no, not again!"—8,733 acres were burned and 80 homes destroyed in the May 2010 Jesusita fire. The scorched hills soon came back to life, after winter rains and the resilient citizens (at least those who were properly insured) rebuilt their homes in Santa Barbara and Montecito.

Given that Santa Barbara's past is fraught with political skirmishes, water woes, environmental disasters, and economic downturns, the city has done well to maintain its reputation as a modern-day paradise. No matter how turbulent, every era of history has in some way left its mark, and the Chumash, Franciscan friars, Spanish dons, Mexican landowners, and irrepressible Yankee traders have all added something to the flavor of Santa Barbara. If you've any doubt, spend a few hours enjoying the festivities at the Old Spanish Days celebration, held each August (see the Annual Events chapter). On any given evening, you can watch flamenco dancers, see a living representation of Saint Barbara (a local woman is chosen to represent the saint), and eat tacos in the plaza or enjoy a cold cerveza or salty-rimmed margarita in a historic cantina setting. In no time at all, you'll be shouting "Viva la Fiesta!" right along with the natives.

ACCOMMODATIONS

Some of the world's most exclusive hotels can be found bookending downtown Santa Barbara businesses. Beanie Babies toys mogul Ty Warner, named on the *Forbes* 400 Richest Americans list, refurbished the world-renowned San Ysidro Ranch and the Five-Diamond Four Seasons Resort The Biltmore Santa Barbara, both located in Montecito. Santa Barbara also has a myriad of very affordable accommodations—everything from cozy inns and historic hotels to family-friendly waterfront lodgings.

Staying at an intimate bed-and-breakfast gives you a great opportunity to experience Santa Barbara's rich history and character. The area's first official bed-and-breakfast, the Old Yacht Club Inn, opened in 1980. A number of regional inns have since joined the ranks. Most are beautifully restored, turn-of-the-20th-century Victorian or California Craftsman homes filled with antiques and memorabilia.

OVERVIEW

Bear in mind that you can score discounts on even the priciest accommodations during the off-season (generally November through March, although many hotels consider the Christmas holidays peak season) and there are often "Third Night Free" and other promotions. It's always best to check the Santa Barbara Conference & Visitors Bureau website (www.santabarbaraca.com) for special deals.

A 12 percent occupancy tax is added to all hotel room rates in the greater Santa Barbara area, so figure the extra into your total cost. Some hotels and bed-and-breakfasts have a 2-night minimum on weekends—especially during the high season (summer). Most hotels and motels listed here offer discounts (AAA, corporate, AARP, etc.), cable television with at least one premium channel (HBO, Showtime, etc.), and free wireless Internet service. They all accept major credit cards, but only a few accept pets. We've noted the pet-friendly spots.

i Many Santa Barbara hotels offer Internet specials on their websites. Look before you book.

Price Code

These prices are based on a 1-night, double-occupancy stay in the high season and do not include taxes and fees for added services. Bear in mind that these are averages, so some rooms may be quite a bit more expensive. And, of course, fancy suites or cottages can run you into the several hundreds or thousands at the finest resorts.

$................	$120 to $150
$$	$150 to $190
$$$	$190 to $250
$$$$	More than $250

HOTELS & MOTELS

Santa Barbara

By the Beach

BRISAS DEL MAR, INN AT THE BEACH　　$$$–$$$$
223 Castillo St., Santa Barbara
(805) 966-2219, (800) 468-1988
www.sbhotels.com

The Brisas Del Mar offers a comfortable alternative to the oceanfront Cabrillo Boulevard hotels. Although Castillo Street is busy with beach traffic during the day, it mellows at night, and rooms are set back from the street. West Beach and the harbor are just 2 blocks away, and you can walk to restaurants, downtown State Street, and Stearns Wharf.

Accommodation choices range from Mediterranean-style standard rooms with a king-size or 2 queen-size beds to penthouse suites for up to six guests with full-size kitchens, marble inlay counters, and fireplaces. Every room comes with a refrigerator, coffeemaker, hair dryer, and TV, and all are nonsmoking. Outdoors, you can splash around in the heated pool, soak in the Jacuzzi, and lounge on the scenic sundecks overlooking the dolphin fountain. Fitness buffs will appreciate the new exercise room. Rates here include a complimentary continental breakfast, evening wine and cheese, and bedtime milk and fresh-baked cookies. Parking is free, and guests can use the coin-operated laundry on-site. If you're planning on staying a while, ask about weekly and monthly rates.

CABRILLO INN AT THE BEACH　$$
931 E. Cabrillo Blvd., Santa Barbara
(805) 966-1641, (800) 648-6708
www.cabrillo-inn.com

This modest, nonsmoking, family-run motel is not exactly deluxe, but it offers a relaxed atmosphere, sparkling clean rooms, and great oceanfront location at a surprisingly affordable rate. It's just a stone's throw from East Beach and the Cabrillo Bathhouse and about a mile from Stearns Wharf and downtown's State Street. Second-floor rooms have the best views of the ocean and islands, and some rooms have private balconies. Each of the 39 rooms has a king-size or 2 queen-size beds, an in-room refrigerator, HBO, and a phone (local and credit card calls are free).

Enjoy the views from the second floor sundecks, heated pool area, or the new garden terrace.

Every morning you can head down to the ocean-view lounge for a complimentary continental breakfast. The Cabrillo Inn at the Beach also has 2 Spanish-Mediterranean-style vacation cottages adjacent to the hotel that rent weekly or monthly. Each 1,600-square-foot unit has 2 bedrooms, 2 bathrooms, a large living room with a gas fireplace and sofa bed, a large, fully equipped kitchen with a dishwasher and microwave, direct-dial telephones with a private number and answering machine, laundry facilities, a DVD player, and daily maid service. Cottage guests also have access to a lush garden area and common patio and gas barbecue, and full use of the inn's amenities. Weekly seasonal rates range from $1,950 off-season to $3,650 summer season.

CASA DEL MAR　$$
18 Bath St., Santa Barbara
(805) 963-4418, (800) 433-3097
www.casadelmar.com

For those seeking a little more serenity, come to Casa Del Mar—a charming Mediterranean-style "house by the sea." It's a cross between a bed-and-breakfast inn and a small hotel, with very friendly service and a helpful staff. Although you won't see the ocean from your room, the inn lies in a quiet neighborhood a 1-minute walk from West Beach. Some of the 21 rooms and suites have full kitchens, and 12 have mini-kitchens (a refrigerator and microwave), so this is a good choice for vacationing families, business travelers, and anyone who likes to prepare a few simple meals at "home." You can relax in the whirlpool spa or sit on the courtyard sundeck amid the colorful geranium gardens. Guests also score a discount at Spa del Mar at nearby Fess Parker's Doubletree Resort. All rooms have king- or queen-size beds and private baths, and some have a gas fireplace. Thoughtful touches include fresh flowers from the local farmers' market, hair dryers, coffeemakers, and irons in every room.

Every morning guests enjoy a generous breakfast buffet in the lounge. In the evening you can mix with other guests over wine and cheese. Business travelers appreciate the desk and telephone in every room and the fax service in the inn's office. All rooms at Casa Del Mar are nonsmoking, and golf packages are available. Dogs and cats are welcome at an extra charge of $15 per night per pet, but they must never be left unattended. Note that Casa Del Mar offers special discounts on their website at certain times of the year.

Dog Walks

Time to attend to Rover's need for a daily walk? Head over to the dog-friendly Douglas Family Preserve, Chase Palm Park, Shoreline Park, Oak Park, or the beach below Summerland's Lookout Beach Park for a trek along waterfront stretches or over untamed land. Just be sure to pick up any little messes Rover may leave behind. (Some parks provide plastic bags.) Santa Barbarans are very insistent on keeping their environs pristine.

**FESS PARKER'S DOUBLETREE
    RESORT**   **$$$$**
633 E. Cabrillo Blvd., Santa Barbara
**(805) 564-4333, (800) 879-2929 (outside
805 area code)**
www.fpdtr.com
You can't miss this sprawling white stucco and red-roofed resort as you drive along the Santa

Barbara waterfront. It's one of the city's largest and most eye-catching hotels, with 338 rooms and 22 suites, all set on 24 beautifully landscaped oceanfront acres about a 0.5 mile (1 kilometer) east of Stearns Wharf. With its expansive meeting and banquet facilities, the resort draws large numbers of conferees, but it's also popular with tourists. Even if you don't stay here, you can stroll, picnic, and people-watch in the grassy expanse that fronts the hotel (it's a city park, though you won't see too many signs announcing this fact).

"Extra oversize" is the best way to describe the guest rooms at the Doubletree—each averages 425 to 450 square feet and holds either a king-size or 2 queen-size beds with feather pillows. Decorated in casual coastal style, each room has a patio or balcony, bathroom with a double vanity, minibar, sitting area, work desk, iron and ironing board, and coffeemaker. Make sure you request a room close to reception if you have difficulty walking around.

In many ways, this resort resembles a health spa: You can play tennis on the lighted courts, swim some laps in the pool, hit a few balls on the putting green, work out in the fully equipped fitness center, or indulge in some relaxing treatments at Spa del Mar. Many guests rent bikes or in-line skates (for a fee) and cruise along the beachfront bike path across the street. You don't have to go far to replenish yourself after burning up all those calories. The restaurants on the premises—Cafe Los Arcos, Rodney's Steakhouse, and Barra Los Arcos, with ocean-view outdoor patio—serve excellent food. If you're starving at 2 a.m., you can call upon the 24-hour room service to sate your hunger pangs. Believe it or not, this is a pet-friendly resort. All you need to do is sign a Pet Policy and pay a $25 nightly pet fee.

Visiting Santa Barbara with Fido and need information on pet-friendly services? Go to www.allfor animals.com and click on the "Santa Barbara Animal Directory" link. You'll find listings for doggie day care, emergency hospitals, groomers, and specialty stores.

FRANCISCAN INN $–$$
109 Bath St., Santa Barbara
(805) 963-8845
www.franciscaninn.com

If you're looking for an affordable Spanish-Mediterranean hideaway a few blocks from the beach, we highly recommend this friendly, family-owned inn. It's in a quiet residential area, and you can easily stroll to West Beach, the Santa Barbara Harbor, Stearns Wharf, State Street, and many shops and restaurants from here. The hotel's moderate size enables the owners to maintain a tranquil, family-style atmosphere and a high level of personalized service. Many guests return year after year and rave about the Franciscan's dedicated staff, some of whom have worked here for a decade or longer.

Brightened with homey floral touches, the 53 rooms and suites were designed to meet a variety of budgets. Choices range from a cozy room with a single bed to spacious suites with a living room, wet bar, and fireplace. Many rooms feature comfortable sitting areas, and nearly all the suites provide fully stocked kitchenettes (one comes with a full kitchen). All rooms and suites include direct-dial telephones with free local calls, hair dryers, coffeemakers, big TVs, and DVD players, and guests can use the free video library and reading library. Outdoors you can swim in the spacious pool or soak in the private spa tucked away in a secluded garden setting. The Franciscan attracts many business travelers and extended-stay visitors and has free wireless Internet service. Ask about their weekly rates if you plan on staying a while. Other extras at the Franciscan include complimentary continental breakfast, an afternoon tea-and-cookie hour, self-service laundry facilities, and valet service for dry cleaning.

HARBOR VIEW INN $$$$
28 W. Cabrillo Blvd., Santa Barbara
(805) 963-0780, (800) 755-0222
www.harborviewinnsb.com

Luxurious yet casual, this Four Diamond, family-friendly Spanish-Mediterranean resort ranks among our favorite beachside hotels. It enjoys a prime waterfront location, overlooking Stearns Wharf and West Beach, just a half block west of State Street (you can't get much closer to the tourist action). Originally built in 1985, the inn has undergone extensive makeovers and now includes luxury rooms and suites (most with ocean views), a gift shop, and business center. Under the same ownership, the adjacent Eladio's Restaurant & Bar serves high-quality California cuisine with the same delicious ocean views as the hotel.

Offering ocean or mountain views, the 102 spacious, air-conditioned guest rooms and 13 luxury suites are tastefully decorated with specially designed fabrics, upholstery, tile, and artwork.

Many rooms feature oversize marble baths, sunken tubs, cathedral ceilings, wet bars, sliding louvered shutters, and garden patios or balconies. Other touches include minibars, teakettles, safes, robes, TVs, free Internet access, and an iron and ironing board in every room.

Outdoors, you can soak up the sun across the street at the beach or on the second-floor sundeck, then unwind in the recreational-size pool (young children can splash about in their own separate wading pool). Health buffs can work out in the tiny fitness center, and at day's end you can stroll in the gardens and stargaze while relaxing in the outdoor Jacuzzi. Room service runs from 6:30 a.m. to 9:30 p.m. The lobby is always open and staffed by friendly professionals who really do go the extra mile to make your stay enjoyable. The on-site Spa Meaumontia offers massages, facials, and body wraps. The entire complex is nonsmoking.

HYATT SANTA BARBARA $$$–$$$$
1111 Cabrillo Blvd., Santa Barbara
(805) 882-1234, (800) 643-1994
www.santabarbarahyatt.com
This sprawling Mediterranean-style oceanfront property is ideal for family vacations and relaxing getaways. East Beach, the Cabrillo Bathhouse, and a beachfront playground are just across the boulevard, and the zoo is a half block away. To reach Stearns Wharf and State Street (about a mile down the road), hop on the electric shuttle that stops right in front of the hotel.

The hotel takes up an entire city block, and the rooms are spread out in four buildings, so be sure to request accommodations close to the facilities if you have mobility problems. Hyatt Santa Barbara offers 171 guest rooms, most with panoramic ocean or mountain views and either a king-size or 2 queen-size beds. Built in 1931 to take advantage of the ocean views, the hotel has been remodeled to also take advantage of the Old World charm in a New World way. You and the kids can splash in the heated outdoor

pool and gaze at the ocean at the same time, or sink into the new Jacuzzi for a relaxing soak. When you feel like working out, just head for the hotel fitness center.

If you don't feel like venturing far away for meals, you can dine at the ocean-view Bistro Eleven Eleven, "where the food gets dressed up, but you don't have to." The restaurant serves breakfast, lunch, and dinner.

INN BY THE HARBOR $$–$$$$
433 W. Montecito St., Santa Barbara
(805) 963-7851, (800) 626-1986
www.sbhotels.com
Inn by the Harbor sits right next to the Brisas Del Mar, Inn at the Beach—they both belong to the same hotel family. Built in the Spanish Colonial tradition, this white adobe inn features red-tile roofs, inlaid tile staircase, and wrought iron embellishments. From here you can walk 3 blocks to West Beach and the marina, then just a few more blocks to Stearns Wharf and State Street.

The inn offers 42 rooms, all nonsmoking and decorated in Spanish-Mediterranean-style furnishings. The inn serves a continental breakfast, wine and cheese in the evening, and milk and cookies at bedtime. Room choices range from standard rooms with king- or queen-size beds to family suites with kitchens. One of the inn's best features is a peaceful, enclosed tropical courtyard pool area, where you can sit and soak up some rays.

LAVENDER INN BY THE SEA $$–$$$$
206 Castillo St., Santa Barbara
(805) 963-4317, (800) 649-2669
www.sbhotels.com
Lavender Inn by the Sea is directly across the street from the Brisas Del Mar, Inn at the Beach. The inn's 23 guest rooms feature

pillow-top beds, down duvets, lavender-scented bath amenities, and a welcoming bottle of champagne. If the beach wasn't so alluring and only 2 blocks away, you might never leave your room. Continental breakfast, afternoon wine and cheese, and evening milk accompanied by freshly baked cookies are all served in the sunroom. Have some questions about Santa Barbara? Just ask the lobby receptionist, who is a veritable warehouse of knowledge.

**WEST BEACH INN
    AT THE HARBOR $$$$**
306 W. Cabrillo Blvd., Santa Barbara
(805) 963-4277, (800) 716-6199
www.westbeachinn.com
The 3-story, Mediterranean-style West Beach Inn is fresh, cheery, and has a great location right across the street from the harbor and near West Beach. Each of the 44 sparkling rooms has a refrigerator, coffeemaker, complimentary high-speed wireless Internet access, hair dryer, iron and ironing board, bathrobes, and air-conditioning. Many rooms also have views of the yachts bobbing in the harbor. Choose a 1-bedroom suite if you'd like a kitchen. During the winter months, you might prefer a 2-bedroom suite with a fireplace. The pool and spa overlook the ocean, so you can easily check out what's happening across the way. The inn serves a complimentary continental breakfast every morning and wine and cheese every afternoon.

Long-term visitors or large families may be interested in the 2,000-square-foot suite. It sleeps up to eight and features 3 bedrooms, a kitchen and dining room, and 5 plasma TVs.

In Town
**BEST WESTERN PLUS ENCINA
    LODGE AND SUITES $$–$$$**
2220 Bath St., Santa Barbara
(805) 682-7277, (800) 526-2282
www.sbhotels.com
This well-managed hotel, which lies about 2 miles inland and 1 mile from downtown, is cheerful and well maintained. Tucked into a residential neighborhood about a half block from Santa Barbara Cottage Hospital and the renowned Sansum–Santa Barbara Medical Foundation Clinic (see the Health Care & Wellness chapter), the property caters to medical guests, many of whom are visiting local clinics or providing support to hospitalized friends or family.

The range of accommodations is exhaustive, with seven buildings housing regular guest rooms, apartments (some with 2 bedrooms and/or full-size kitchens), town houses, pool suites, and efficiency units with kitchenettes. Quilted bedding and floral accents in the rooms create the quaint country charm.

The 121 units have a hair dryer, refrigerator, iron and ironing board, and coffeemaker, wall safe, DVD player with complimentary movie rentals, and Crabtree & Evelyn bath products in every room. The staff puts hard candy, apples, oranges, and packaged cookies in each room every day, which is another of those small touches that make you feel at home.

A large pool, whirlpool, massage facility, beauty shop, and aviary are located on the grounds. The on-site restaurant, Las Aves Cafe, is open for breakfast, lunch, dinner, and happy hour.

In addition to the standard discounts, Encina Lodge offers discounts for anyone going to a Santa Barbara medical facility and will provide free transportation to doctors' appointments in the area as well as to the Santa Barbara Airport or the train station.

BEST WESTERN PLUS PEPPER
TREE INN $$–$$$
3850 State St., Santa Barbara
(805) 687-5511, (800) 338-0030
www.sbhotels.com
Dotted with palms on Santa Barbara's busy State Street, this well-maintained Spanish-Mediterranean hotel is similar in many ways to its sister, the Best Western Plus Encina Lodge. Friendly staff, comfortable rooms, attractive grounds, and reasonable rates make this a popular choice. The inn is set on 5 beautifully landscaped acres in the Upper State Street shopping district, across the street from La Cumbre Plaza Mall. You'll need a car if you want to head downtown to the heart of the tourist action. Each of the 150 individually decorated guest rooms has a private patio or balcony overlooking garden courtyards. Guest rooms feature complimentary bottled water, whole fresh fruit and Lorna Doone cookies, bathrobes, Crabtree & Evelyn bath products, refrigerators, coffeemakers, iron and ironing board, hair dryers, complimentary high-speed wireless Internet, and DVD player and complimentary DVD rentals from the hotel's media library. Extra amenities include 2 large tiled pools and whirlpools, an exercise room, a sauna, a massage room, hair salons, valet laundry service, and a gift shop. The Treehouse Restaurant and Lounge serves breakfast, lunch, and dinner in a casual atmosphere and will also deliver to your room or poolside. When you need a ride to or from the airport or train station, just make arrangements with the staff for complimentary transportation.

CANARY HOTEL $$$$
31 W. Carrillo St., Santa Barbara
(805) 884-0300, (877) 468-3515
www.canarysantabarbara.com
Want to be in the heart of the action? The 97-guest room, 5-story hotel, has 22 suites plus a Presidential Suite (with a large balcony), all handsomely decorated by noted interior designer Michael Smith. Televisions with DVDs and CD players, wireless Internet service access, minibar, coffeemaker, and robes are also part of the package. The popular Coast Restaurant & Bar off the hotel lobby is popular for happy hour. The Perch, the rooftop outdoor terrace and pool, offers amazing 360-degree views of Santa Barbara and its red-tiled roofs. Under a canopy of a brilliant nighttime sky, Perch makes for a memorable evening. Valet parking and a great staff add to the comfort of this hotel. The Canary Hotel's rooftop wine tasting every Mon night (from end of May through Sept, $20 per person, reservations recommended) at the Perch from 5 to 8 p.m. features top local wines from Santa Barbara County paired with delectable artisan cheeses. Imbibers soak up the stunning Santa Barbara views.

DAYS INN & SUITES $$
1601 State St., Santa Barbara
(805) 966-0807, (800) 669-8979
www.daysinn.com/hotel/45035
Family-owned and operated, the former El Prado Inn is not one of those splashy Santa Barbara accommodations, but rather a cozy little motor inn on busy State Street offering personalized service. The lobby is homey and welcoming to new arrivals. Guests can enjoy the daily paper while sipping a cup of tea or coffee in the lobby.

The inn has spacious rooms with queen- or king-size beds and suites with refrigerators, microwaves, sitting areas, and patios. Free continental breakfast is provided, and meeting space is available. Amenities include a heated pool and patio and complimentary wireless Internet; a coin-operated laundry and a market are right across the street, and you can walk to many of the area's restaurants and attractions in just minutes.

i During Fiesta in early August, it's nearly impossible to find lodgings in Santa Barbara. Make your reservations well ahead of time. For more affordable rates, try booking a room in Carpinteria or other areas outside the city.

HOLIDAY INN EXPRESS—HOTEL VIRGINIA $$–$$$
17 W. Haley St., Santa Barbara
(805) 963-9757, (800) 549-1700
www.hotelvirginia.com
One of downtown Santa Barbara's boutique hotels is the Holiday Inn Express—Hotel Virginia, which is currently listed on the National Registry of Historic Places. It features a mosaic fountain in the lobby and replicas of Malibu and Catalina tile work throughout. This is a great spot to stay if you're in town for business or want easy access to the shops, restaurants, and downtown businesses. You won't find a pool on-site, but the hotel is only 4 blocks from the beach. The 61 guest rooms are decorated in classic California Spanish Revival style and feature free wireless Internet, a free lobby computer and printer, luxurious bedding, hair dryers, and ironing boards with irons. Upstairs rooms are the best picks; some have views of the city. Guests also receive a complimentary hot breakfast and can park their cars in a private lot for a fee—a big bonus in the downtown area. This is a nonsmoking hotel.

HOTEL SANTA BARBARA $$–$$$
533 State St., Santa Barbara
(805) 957-9300, (800) 549-9869
www.hotelsantabarbara.com
Before the Hotel Santa Barbara opened in mid-1997 after a $4 million renovation to the 100-year-old building, there wasn't one hotel on lower State Street that we would have included on our "best and brightest" list. This hotel changed all that in a big way, providing well-appointed lodgings in the heart of downtown's social scene.

Although the hotel is on bustling State Street, the indoor corridors make it quiet and secluded. It's near downtown shops and restaurants and within 5 blocks of Stearns Wharf and the waterfront. There are 75 air-conditioned rooms and 3 junior suites appointed with queen- or king-size beds plus pullout sofas in the suites. All rooms are nonsmoking and have coffeemakers, hair dryers, and bottled water. Guests may request refrigerators. A complimentary continental breakfast, including waffle maker, is offered to guests each morning, and coffee is available in the lobby throughout the day. Two conference rooms are also available along with complimentary high-speed Internet access throughout the hotel. If the view is important to you, ask for one of only four rooms that overlook State Street and the mountains, subject to occupancy.

As we see it, the only drawback to Hotel Santa Barbara is its tricky parking situation. There is one pullout space in front of the hotel for loading or unloading, but the main parking lot is located behind the hotel with valet parking access in an extremely narrow driveway on Cota Street. Rates are slightly higher during special events dates such as Fiesta and graduation weekends.

INN OF THE SPANISH GARDEN $$$$
915 Garden St., Santa Barbara
(805) 564-4700, (866) 564-4700
www.SpanishGardenInn.com
Deep in Santa Barbara's oldest neighborhood amid a mix of low-rise businesses and residences, this intimate Spanish-Mediterranean boutique hotel has received rave reviews since it opened in 2001. Highlighted as "Inn of the Month" in *Travel + Leisure* magazine, it lies only a few blocks from downtown, so you can easily stroll to restaurants, shops, theaters, and businesses. Leisure guests and business travelers love the personalized service, plush rooms, and refined touches at this stylish inn, where modern technology mixes well with Old World charm. All of the 23 spacious guest rooms and suites are air-conditioned and come with luxuriously comfortable king- or queen-size beds with fine linens, complimentary wireless Internet access, French press coffeemakers, cozy robes, hair dryers, flat-screen TVs, DVD players, and ceiling fans. The rooms also feature Spanish-style tiling, high ceilings, fireplaces, secluded garden patios or balconies, private baths (with oversized soaking tubs in most), and deluxe toiletries. All are nonsmoking. In your free time, you can paddle in the lap pool, work out in the fitness room, or snuggle around the outdoor fire pit on cool nights. Guests love the included gourmet continental breakfast, and each evening local wines are available by the glass or bottle for purchase. The inn offers free underground parking and an intimate boardroom for business meetings.

THE PRESIDIO MOTEL $$$
1620 State St., Santa Barbara
(805) 963-1355
www.thepresidiomotel.com
The Presidio Motel is a small boutique motel located on upper State Street, not far from the Santa Barbara Mission. The motel offers 16 rooms, each being spacious, clean, simple, and airy. What makes the Presidio different is the carefully applied vinyl decals and mobiles on the walls of each room that create a youthful, fresh, and creative ambience. You might just find yourself in a room inspired by a Southern home, the Wild West, a peacock, or a garden (to see pictures, visit their website). These trendy rooms were designed by local artist Stephanie Mansolf and Kat Trajano. Morning coffee and tea are available; if you hunger for more, Cantwell's, a deli and mini grocery store across the street, offers fresh fare. Parking is free, and you can explore downtown on complimentary bikes. The wharf is just a trolley ride or 20-minute walk away.

ℹ Surprise! The fun Presidio Motel has a teensy boutique in the lobby. The Supply Room carries offbeat clothing, shoes, personal items (forget your toothbrush?), and home accessories that reflect the owners' hip style. For a sneak peek, info on trunk shows, and events showcasing local artisans, go to www.thepresidiomotel.com/blog.

THE UPHAM HOTEL $$–$$$
1404 De la Vina St., Santa Barbara
(805) 962-0058, (800) 727-0876
www.uphamhotel.com
At the stately Upham Hotel, established in 1871, guests experience a bit of Santa Barbara history. This elegant city landmark is

the oldest continuously operating hostelry in Southern California. The Victorian hotel and garden cottages occupy a corner of De la Vina and Sola Streets, just 2 blocks from State Street and within walking distance of the Arlington Theatre, the Museum of Art, restaurants, and shops.

The Upham was built by Boston banker Amasa Lincoln (a distant cousin of Abraham Lincoln) in 1871. The Lincoln House (its original name) was an elegant, New England–style boardinghouse made of redwood timbers. Since it was built before mule-powered streetcars and the railroad came to town, the first guests arrived on foot or by horse or steamship. A subsequent owner, Cyrus Upham, changed the name to Hotel Upham in 1898.

Today the Upham continues its tradition of warm hospitality. The hotel features a cozy lounge with a large fireplace and comfy sofas, and guests love the tranquil gardens. The atmosphere is very much bed-and-breakfast style—in fact, the Upham frequently appears in bed-and-breakfast listings.

Fifty guest rooms and suites are available in the original main building, three Garden Cottage buildings, the Lincoln Building, the Carriage House, and the Jacaranda and Hibiscus buildings. Each unit is individually decorated and filled with antiques and period furnishings.

Units in the Garden Cottages feature porches or secluded patios; several have gas fireplaces. For the ultimate splurge, book the master suite with a Jacuzzi tub, fireplace, wet bar, and private yard, where you can nap peacefully in the hammock.

Rates include a continental breakfast buffet and afternoon wine and cheese. Oreos and milk await you in the lounge

every evening, and coffee, tea, and fruit are always set out. The popular Louie's California Bistro adjoins the main lobby. Louie's offers innovative lunch and dinner menus featuring fresh seafood, pasta, and California cuisine crafted by a head chef who's been with Louie's for over 20 years. You can dine on the wide, wooden veranda year-round. (See the Restaurants chapter for details.)

Goleta

BACARA RESORT & SPA $$$$
8301 Hollister Ave., Goleta
(805) 968-0100, (877) 422-4245
www.bacararesort.com

Set on 78 palm-studded beachfront acres, 13 miles north of Santa Barbara, the exclusive Spanish Colonial–style Bacara (pronounced Ba-CAR-ah) Resort & Spa opened its doors in September 2000. Bacara promises "the Good Life," and with its 311 luxury guest rooms, 49 suites, 3 gourmet restaurants, sprawling pools, impressive recreational facilities, grand ballroom, and multilevel spa, it seems poised to deliver. Wander the light, airy interior and you will see handwoven rugs imported from India, rich mahogany accents, and corridors full of commissioned art. Bacara's fine dining restaurant, Miró, is one of the region's top dining establishments, albeit a very, very pricey one; with a impressive wine list to match. The Spa Cafe overlooking one of the pools serves up healthy fare, and the Bistro offers ocean views from both indoors and its alfresco seaside terrace.

The landscaping is tropical meets the Mediterranean, with plenty of palms, bougainvillea, lush courtyards, and gushing fountains. In your spare time, you can pamper yourself in the opulent spa, relax on the beach, jog along the seaside running track, go horseback riding, play tennis on the Har-Tru courts, or hit a few rounds at the celebrated Sandpiper Golf Course next door. The stylish guest rooms feature raised king-size or twin beds with Frette linens, warm-toned Spanish tiling, mahogany furnishings, video entertainment systems, high-speed Internet access, robes, and in-room ameni-ties. All have private balconies or patios with ocean, mountain, or garden views. Half are warmed by gas log fireplaces, and some of the suites boast romantic candlelit Jacuzzi tubs. Bacara strives to evoke the beauty and glamour of a bygone era, but to stay here you'll have to pay a pretty price.

BEST WESTERN PLUS SOUTH COAST INN $$
5620 Calle Real, Goleta
(805) 967-3200, (800) 350-3614
www.santa-barbara-hotel.com
This spiffy little Three Diamond inn lies only 2 miles from Santa Barbara Airport and UCSB. It's a great choice if you're visiting the univer-sity or Goleta businesses. Accommodations include 121 well-appointed guest rooms with queen- or king-size beds. Each room has air-conditioning, a fridge, a microwave, a hair dryer, a DVD player, and cable TV. Busi-ness travelers appreciate the voice mail, free local calls, and high-speed wireless Internet throughout the hotel. A complimentary hot-and-cold breakfast buffet is served daily in the lobby. A free shuttle whisks guests to UCSB, the airport, and Goleta businesses.

For recreation, guests enjoy the heated pool and whirlpool, relax on lounge chairs around the sundeck, or play a few rounds of table tennis on the patio. Topiary gardens and a soothing fountain add a touch of elegance to the grounds. Guests also have free use of a local athletic club nearby.

EXTENDED STAY AMERICA $
4870 Calle Real, Santa Barbara
(805) 692-1882, (800) EXTSTAY
www.extstay.com
Geared to the business traveler who plans to stay for a week or more, this good-value hotel lies near the western edge of Goleta just off US 101, about 10 minutes from downtown Santa Barbara. The hotel includes 104 rooms, most with queen-size beds, a kitchenette (with full-size refrigerator, elec-tric stovetop, and dishes for two), desk, dataport phones, and voice mail. There are also two suites, each with a separate sitting area and king-size bed, but they're usually booked up.

You won't find a lot of frills here—no pool, Jacuzzi, or food service (but then, you'll be cooking in your room, remember?). The hotel's rates are flexible, but two people can stay for around $650 a week during high season in Santa Barbara.

Everything's fresh and clean here. You have freeway access right out the front door, and there are enough restaurants and gro-cery stores nearby to meet your needs (and a coin laundry is on the premises). We think this is a great bet for the business traveler or for anybody relocating to the area and need-ing transitional accommodations.

i Hotels in Goleta are closer to the Santa Barbara Airport and the University of California at Santa Bar-bara than lodgings in the city of Santa Barbara.

HOLIDAY INN $$
5650 Calle Real, Goleta
(805) 964-6241, (888) HOLIDAY
www.hisantahbarbarahotel.com

The Holiday Inn in Goleta is a full-service hotel conveniently located 2 miles from the Santa Barbara Airport, the University of California at Santa Barbara, and 8 miles from downtown Santa Barbara's shops, museums, and attractions. The 160 guest rooms are generously proportioned and handsomely furnished. The grounds are nicely manicured and feature a large resort-style pool adjacent to a recently added 2,000 square foot patio terrace with alfresco bar and anchored by a raised fire pit.

The hotel's Remington's Restaurant serves breakfast, dinner, and room service. Within easy walking distance there are 23 other restaurants (including quick-serve and a 24-hour Denny's), 3 grocery stores, a bowling alley, and a 3-screen movie theater. Take advantage of a complimentary pass to the nearby Goleta Valley Athletic Club. This hotel attracts corporate travelers as well as families looking for familiar Holiday Inn quality and amenities.

PACIFICA SUITES $$$
5490 Hollister Ave., Goleta
(805) 683-6722, (800) 338-6722
www.pacificasuites.com
An all-suites hotel in the Santa Barbara area, this charming property takes the restored 1880 Joseph Sexton house as its centerpiece. To design the house, Joseph Sexton, a successful Goleta nurseryman, enlisted the services of local architect Peter J. Barber, who also designed the first Arlington Hotel and the historic Upham Hotel.

After the Sextons died, the house had a number of owners but then fell into disrepair until the Invest West Financial Corporation acquired it in 1984. Before the complex was developed into a lodging property, the original home and grounds were completely restored, and many of the large trees that had been lost over the years were replaced.

Today the towering trees and expansive lawn create a parklike setting, and the old Sexton House is available for business or social functions. The plush sitting area just off the lobby has a fireplace and bar and is used for social functions or for guests who want to sit back and relax. The design of the rest of the complex echoes that of the Sexton House, with the same elegant architectural style and soothing colors.

The hotel offers 87 suites, each with a living room featuring a pullout sofa and separate bedroom offering a king-size bed or 2 double beds, a coffeemaker, refrigerator, comfortable robes, and deluxe bath products as well as complimentary high-speed Internet access. A full, cooked-to-order complimentary breakfast is served to guests in the breakfast room or on the outside terrace. Evening receptions are held 5 to 7 p.m. Mon through Fri.

There is a pool and Jacuzzi as well as amazing flora and fauna throughout the property. Pacific Suites is adjacent to CA 217. Pets are welcome in designated rooms for an extra fee of $20.

RAMADA LIMITED $$
4770 Calle Real, Santa Barbara
(805) 964-3511, (800) 654-1965
www.sbramada.com
Known as the Cathedral Oaks Lodge until the locally owned property joined forces with Ramada, this motel has 126 rooms and three suites. The courtyard in the middle of the complex features a lovely freshwater lagoon and gardens that are home to ducks, turtles, koi, and goldfish.

The rooms face indoor corridors and open onto patios or balconies that look out on either the courtyard or the parking lot (if you'd rather see the lagoon, you'll pay more for the privilege). All are air-conditioned, and each comes with a coffeepot, free premium cable with HBO, iron and ironing board, desk, and 2 phones with voice mail. Local calls are free. Upstairs rooms have higher ceilings, and there's a modest amount of meeting space on-site. A complimentary deluxe continental breakfast with made-to-order waffles is served every morning. In your spare time, you can swim in the heated pool or relax in the hot tub.

The Ramada is near the eastern boundary of Goleta, about 10 miles from downtown Santa Barbara. You are not particularly close to any tourist attractions here, but the motel is moderately priced, and it's only a 10-minute drive to Santa Barbara's waterfront and other attractions and 5 minutes to UCSB and the Santa Barbara Airport.

Montecito

COAST VILLAGE INN $$
1188 Coast Village Rd., Montecito
(805) 969-3266, (800) 257-5131
www.coastvillageinn.com
Modest by Montecito standards, this little motel is cheerful, well kept, and near the exclusive boutiques and restaurants that line Coast Village Road (the local farmers' market is held across the street on Friday). The property was opened in the 1930s but has been upgraded on a regular basis. (You may want to avoid the back rooms, which open onto the parking lot.)

The 28 nonsmoking rooms and suites are decorated with country pine furniture. Typical features include ceiling fans, cable TVs, phones with voice mail, and wireless high-speed Internet access. You won't find many amenities at this quiet little spot, but guests can enjoy the inn's heated pool, free parking, complimentary use of bicycle cruisers, and a $5 credit toward a full breakfast at Peabody's next door.

FOUR SEASONS RESORT THE
BILTMORE SANTA BARBARA $$$$
1260 Channel Dr., Montecito
(805) 969-2261, (800) 332-3442
www.fourseasons.com
This newly minted, Five Diamond hotel and Coral Casino club just completed a 6-year, $305 million renovation funded by Ty Warner Hotels & Resorts. The 207 guest accommodations, including 12 one-story cottages, are situated on 20 acres of some of the world's most exclusive turf. Even with a train running behind the property, this is a place of elegance and romance where the well-heeled love to stay.

Originally built in 1927 and designed by renowned architect Reginald Johnson, this Spanish Colonial–style complex offers only the finest in hotel amenities. Down pillows (hypoallergenic ones are also available), plush terry robes, CDs and DVD players, refrigerated bars, and twice daily housekeeping services are just a few of the luxuries this property has to offer.

Situated directly across from Montecito's stunning Butterfly Beach, the property offers easy beach access. Fitness facilities and 10,000 square feet of spa services are on-site. Basking by the pool, playing tennis, sharpening your putting skills on the practice greens, and exploring the scenic routes on complimentary bicycles are some of the other options. Windsurfing, horseback riding, sailing, and parasailing are all within no more than 20 minutes' reach. No wonder celebrities and business moguls flock to the Biltmore (as Insiders know it).

The on-site restaurant Bella Vista is a casually elegant dining facility where the patio seating with ocean views is most popular along with special prix-fixe buffet dinner nights. It's known for Chef Alessandro Cartumimi's eclectically delicious, local, seasonal California cuisine. Or guests can dine at Tydes, the casually hip ocean-view restaurant that is part of the Coral Casino (a private club with the best swimming pool on the West Coast), set directly on the Pacific, across the street from the main hotel grounds. The Ty Lounge, with its mesmerizing ocean view and fireplace, offers a splendid location for an evening nightcap or pre-dinner cocktail.

Traveling with children can be a task, but not so at the Biltmore. If you provide the names and ages of your children when you make your reservation, your kids will each receive a welcome amenity, child-size bathrobe, and complimentary baby or child toiletries. There's a special children's menu at Bella Vista, and babysitting services can be arranged 24 hours prior to your need. The complimentary Kids for All Seasons program includes activities for the young ones.

MONTECITO INN   **$$$–$$$$**
1295 Coast Village Rd., Montecito
(805) 969-7854, (800) 843-2017
www.montecitoinn.com
The minute you drive up to the Montecito Inn, you know it's a different kind of small hotel. For one thing, you'll see Charlie Chaplin's face on the sign out front—a theme the hotel carries throughout, with statues of Chaplin in the lobby, his figure etched on the door of the meeting and banquet room, and authentic art posters hanging in the public areas.

Chaplin was one of the original investors in the hotel, which opened in 1928 and drew the rich and famous of the day, including Lon Chaney Sr., Carole Lombard, Wallace Beery, and Norma Shearer, to name a few.

Since its Hollywood heyday, the hotel has enjoyed some refreshing face-lifts. In 2003 management treated the rooms to a major Mediterranean makeover, and they now exude Old World elegance with fresh carpet, paint, fabrics, new furnishings, and historic photographic prints of Santa Barbara on the walls. Ceiling fans cool the 52 standard rooms, and all include refrigerators, hair dryers, large TVs, DVDs, high-speed Internet access, and petite bathrooms. Nine luxury rooms come with a diversity of things such as air-conditioning, separate living rooms, fireplaces, and soundproofing.

In your free time, you can tour upscale Montecito on the complimentary bikes, tone up in the workout room, or relax in the small pool, sauna, and Jacuzzi (although their proximity to the freeway makes the area a bit noisy). If you're feeling nostalgic, you can pick a flick from the complete library of Charlie Chaplin films. Each morning, the staff lays out a complimentary continental breakfast in the lobby for you to enjoy in the sunny Montecito Cafe, by the pool, or in the privacy of your room.

This charming little inn is truly unique for Santa Barbara, with a personalized, European feel. A 2-night minimum stay is required for Saturday arrivals.

✳SAN YSIDRO RANCH   **$$$$**
900 San Ysidro Ln., Montecito
(805) 565-1700, (800) 368-6788 (from
outside the 805 area code)
www.sanysidroranch.com

Set far from the touristy beachfront in the Montecito foothills, the 540-acre San Ysidro Ranch has been cloistering the rich and famous of the world for more than a century. The first cottages were built on the property in the 1890s, and guests began arriving in January 1893.

In the 1930s, actor Ronald Colman bought the property, and soon the likes of Gloria Swanson, Merle Oberon, David Niven, Fred Astaire, Groucho Marx, Lucille Ball, and other Hollywood luminaries were on the guest list. John Huston finished the script for *The African Queen* while ensconced in a ranch cottage, and Vivien Leigh and Laurence Olivier were married in the Wedding Garden at the stroke of midnight.

A $120 million renovation of the San Ysidro Ranch was completed in 2009. Forty individual cottages were designed in true bungalow style, most with king-size beds, fine linens, fireplaces, and private patios. Hot tubs sunken into outdoor decks, rain showers, radiant-floor heat, hand-cut stone decks, and a multitude of exquisite antiques accentuate the decor.

To woo a special someone, try out the Kennedy Cottage. Sleep where Jackie and John placed their honeymooning heads. This cottage continues to exude romance today with its newly refurbished twin master suites, each hosting a king bed, fireplace, private bathroom, and ocean-view deck. The Warner Cottage is a charming country European single-level home featuring 2 master bedrooms, 2.5 baths, 3 wood-burning fireplaces, a living room and dining area, and a full kitchen. A private fenced yard has a heated pool, hot tub, and gas grill. What more could a couple in love really need?

If you haven't experienced San Ysidro Ranch, there's nothing like it. You won't want to leave the property or even your room. If you do decide to venture out, there's so much to enjoy—hiking along the 17 miles of trails in the Santa Ynez Mountains, sipping robust reds in Santa Ynez's abundant wine country, biking, golfing, or indulging in a spa treatment.

Gwyneth Paltrow and Coldplay's Chris Martin hid out at the Ranch for their private wedding, and Julia Roberts and Danny Moder followed in the Kennedys' steps by making the Ranch their honeymoon choice. J-Lo and Marc Anthony paid a visit just after their wedding. It seems like romance is always abloom at this luxurious, first-class resort.

Locals have been enjoying the Stone-house, San Ysidro Ranch's exquisite restaurant, for years. Located in a 19th-century citrus packinghouse, this hideaway provides the ideal dining spot. Recommended is the outdoor terrace, but if you can't get that, then cozy up to the indoor fireplace.

This is not a hotel for the faint of heart. The average price can set you back, but if you're in the mood for the finest or just trying to avoid the paparazzi, then San Ysidro Ranch should be your choice. By the way, pets are welcome for $100 a stay.

Carpinteria

BEST WESTERN PLUS CARPINTERIA INN $$
4558 Carpinteria Ave., Carpinteria
(805) 684-0473, (800) 780-7234
www.bestwestern.com/carpinteriainn
Rimmed by colorful geraniums, this attractive Spanish-style hotel is a great choice for families, business travelers, and anyone who wants a comfortable yet affordable place to

stay in the South County. It's just 3 blocks from downtown Carpinteria's main street, and you can walk to Carpinteria Beach. When you want to visit downtown Santa Barbara, just hop in your car and drive 9 miles up the freeway.

The 144 nonsmoking air-conditioned guest rooms and suites are equipped with refrigerators, hair dryers, safes, irons and ironing boards, coffeemakers, cable TVs, and high-speed Internet access. Amid the red-tile roofs of the inn's main buildings, you'll find a lovely courtyard with a swimming pool, Jacuzzi, fountains, and a koi pond, and you can keep fit in the inn's small workout room. When you're hungry, you can feast at the hotel's Sunset Grille Restaurant and quench your thirst at the full bar.

BED-AND-BREAKFAST INNS

The majority of Santa Barbara's bed-and-breakfasts are located in historic residential areas close to mid State Street, where you can escape from city noises but easily walk to restaurants, theaters, and shops. Several offer a peaceful refuge near the beach, while a few cater to those who prefer off-the-beaten-track hideaways.

Smoking is absolutely forbidden at all the bed-and-breakfasts listed here. If you're a smoker, you can usually light up outside in the garden or patio, but only if other nonsmoking guests aren't out there sharing your smoke. Some bed-and-breakfasts even enforce stiff fines on guests caught smoking in their rooms. Sorry, pets—Santa Barbara's gracious bed-and-breakfast hospitality doesn't extend to you. None of the inns we've listed here allow animals of any kind.

Santa Barbara Beach Area

THE OLD YACHT CLUB INN $–$$$
431 Corona del Mar Dr., Santa Barbara
(805) 962-1277, (800) 549-1676 in
California, (800) 676-1676 outside
California
www.oldyachtclubinn.com

If you're longing for a convivial bed-and-breakfast experience, along with easy access to the beach, this friendly inn will fulfill your wishes. Erected as a private family home on East Beach in 1912, the Craftsman-style building served as headquarters for the Santa Barbara Yacht Club during the Roaring 20s after the first clubhouse washed out to sea in an unusual storm.

In 1928 the building was moved just a block inland to its current location tucked behind two olive trees on a peaceful residential street. The Old Yacht Club Inn was opened in 1980 as Santa Barbara's first bed-and-breakfast inn and remains the only Santa Barbara B&B with a beachside location. Eilene Bruce and Vince Pettit's trademarks are a tradition of warm hospitality and fantastic food. Breakfasts alternate between mouthwatering egg dishes, such as egg soufflé, and bread dishes, such as cinnamon swirl french toast.

The inn offers five guest rooms with private bathrooms in the main building. The adjacent Spanish-style Hitchcock House, built in 1926, has two large suites with whirlpool tubs, as well as rooms with private entrances and a long-term rental with private kitchen. A 3-bedroom, 1-bath family suite can accommodate up to six guests. Both houses are filled with classic European and Early American antiques, Oriental rugs, historic photos, and memorabilia.

Beach towels and chairs and bicycles (free of charge) are available to tool around the waterfront or hit nearby East Beach. A 2-night minimum stay is required on weekends if a Saturday is included. Special business and midweek rates are available from October to May. A 3-night stay is necessary with weekend bookings in July and August and some holidays and special events.

i Many bed-and-breakfasts offer special packages as well as reduced rates on weekdays and/or in the low season (usually November through February). Be sure to inquire about possible deals when you make reservations.

VILLA ROSA $$–$$$$
15 Chapala St., Santa Barbara
(805) 966-0851
www.villarosainnsb.com
Although this cozy residence looks and feels like a small hotel, it has many characteristics of a typical bed-and-breakfast: a historic structure (built in 1931 in Spanish Revival style), personalized service, a satisfying continental breakfast, and the *Los Angeles Times* delivered to your door every morning. But the best thing about Villa Rosa is its location: It's only 84 steps from West Beach and a hop, skip, and jump from the marina and Stearns Wharf.

The building was remodeled in the early 1980s as a Santa Fe–style bed-and-breakfast. You can choose from 18 rooms with ocean, harbor, garden, or mountain views (but only two have glimpses of the sea). Several deluxe rooms feature fireplaces and/or private gardens, and the upstairs corner rooms are among the brightest units thanks to their extra windows and elevated views. Though the rooms lack televisions, all have tiny private baths (some are especially cramped),

telephones, clock radios, bathrobes, hair dryers, and sitting areas.

Relax in the cozy lounge, take a dip in the small, solar-heated pool and Jacuzzi, or soak up some sun on the lovely outdoor garden patio. Complimentary port and sherry are available in the lounge every evening. Nightly turndown is sweetened with Belgian chocolates. Children are welcome as long as they are at least 14 years old, because the pool is unfenced. A conference room accommodates 20. The clientele is eclectic but typically includes young couples and groups of friends looking for a more affordable option to the pricier beachside hotels in this area.

Santa Barbara

THE CHESHIRE CAT INN AND
**   COTTAGES** $$–$$$$
36 W. Valerio St., Santa Barbara
(805) 569-1610
www.cheshirecat.com
An extremely popular destination for honeymoons and romantic getaways, Cheshire Cat is set amid colorful English gardens in a quiet residential area just 1 block from State Street and a 5-minute walk to restaurants, shops, and theaters. Owner Christine Dunstan, an experienced innkeeper from Cheshire, England, has done an incredible job of restoring and remodeling 2 neighboring Queen Anne Victorian homes (now more than 100 years old), a coach house, and 4 nearby cottages into a sophisticated, romantic retreat. She added modern conveniences (flat-screen TVs, free Internet, and in-house computer) and charming personal touches, such as English antiques and Laura Ashley wallpaper and draperies. As a special bonus, the inn offers an enticing array of facials, massages, and spa treatments to soothe the mind and pamper the body. Treatments can be

administered in your own room or in the on-site spa rooms.

As you might guess, the inn's theme hails from the English classic *Alice's Adventures in Wonderland*. Most of the sparkling clean 18 rooms are named for characters in the book. For the ultimate romantic retreat, stay in Tweedledum, a luxurious 2-room suite with a Jacuzzi, fireplace, sitting room with Oriental rugs, a king-size brass bed, and a wet bar/kitchen. If you don't need a kitchen, try the Queen of Hearts—an equally romantic but smaller room with a Jacuzzi.

Even if you don't have a Jacuzzi room, you can soak in the outdoor spa and enjoy the tranquil gardens. All rooms have private baths, robes, and direct-dial phones, TVs, DVD players, and beautiful potted orchids. Breakfast is served daily on Wedgwood china, either outside on the lovely brick patio or in the privacy of your room. On the weekends, you'll be treated to pecan cream cheese–stuffed french toast, poached pears or apples, or a Mexican casserole dish.

Recently, the inn opened the Woodford, Prestbury, Bramhall, and Mobberly Cottages, named after three villages in Cheshire. Each has 2 bedrooms (1 with a queen-size bed and 1 with a king-size), a private redwood deck, and a hot tub. Other features include a large living room with TV and VCR, a fireplace, a dining nook, a full bathroom, and a kitchen. The cottages may be rented by the day, week, or month. The Mobberly Cottage has a Spa Therapy Room for one or two people. Treatments are offered between 8 a.m. and 8 p.m. Mon through Fri or in your room on the weekends. Children are allowed only in the cottages, which can also be rented as 1-bedroom suites; tots younger than 5 stay free. This meticulously maintained inn oozes personality and is a top choice for those who yearn for a historic bed-and-breakfast experience with a delightful English twist and a dash of whimsy.

THE COUNTRY HOUSE $$–$$$$
1323 De la Vina St., Santa Barbara
(805) 963-2283, (800) 999-5672
www.tiffanycountryhouse.com

Honeymoon, wedding, getaway, business—whatever your reason for coming to Santa Barbara, you'll find an intimate getaway at the 100-plus-year-old Country House. In late 1999, Vintage Hotels, owners of the Upham (see p. 37), purchased this grand Victorian, stripped some of the frills and ruffles, and exposed more of the inn's dark woods, adding to its feel of formal elegance. Perhaps the best feature of this inn is its convenient location just 3 blocks from State Street and the heart of downtown, an easy walk to restaurants, shops, and museums.

The Country House's 7 rooms all have telephones, TVs, DVD player, and private baths, and all but 2 come with Jacuzzi tubs. The award for most spacious and comfortable quarters goes to the Penthouse Suite. It occupies the entire third floor and offers a sprawling bedroom with a fireplace, a private terrace, spectacular city, mountain, and ocean views, a refrigerator, a double Jacuzzi tub, and a sitting area and writing nook. The staff delivers a full gourmet breakfast directly to the Penthouse Suite every morning.

Just got hitched or want to celebrate a special anniversary? Go for the romantic Windsor Suite, which is also warmed by a wood-burning fireplace.

If you're staying in one of the less expensive rooms, you'll find your equally delicious breakfast of homemade granola, crepes, quiches, or waffles waiting in the dining room downstairs or out on the deck. Be sure to try some of the freshly baked cookies the cook sets out every evening and to stroll in the beautiful rose garden.

SECRET GARDEN INN AND
COTTAGES $-$$$
1908 Bath St., Santa Barbara
(805) 687-2300
www.secretgarden.com

The lush gardens of this secluded enclave aren't really secret, but they certainly enhance its peaceful, romantic atmosphere. In 1999 French artist Dominique Hannaux purchased the inn and added her own sense of warm hospitality and European flair. Dominique is a delightful host and loves to cultivate artistic talent. Works by local artists adorn the inn's common rooms, and every few months, Dominique hosts art openings with performances by local musicians.

Set back off the street in a quiet residential area about 6 blocks from downtown, the Secret Garden includes 11 rooms and suites dispersed among a historic main house (ca. 1905) with 9 rooms in cottages, all with private entrances. Five rooms feature private outdoor hot tubs. Many of the baths have antique claw-foot tubs. Other amenities in certain rooms include fireplaces, private decks, refrigerators, beautiful hardwood floors, Oriental rugs, and European art. One of the most popular rooms is the bright and sunny Meadow Lark in the main house, which offers great value and comes with an antique queen bed, a beautiful bay window, and a private bath with tub and shower. The Oriole and Hummingbird cottages with hot tubs are also popular, and the Nightingale offers a fireplace. The Garden has a striking French blue decor, honey-colored hardwood floors, a sky-lit queen-size bed, and a spacious bath done in white Italian tile.

Breakfast is a buffet of quiche, breads, scones, bagels, and croissants served in the kitchen. Guests can also dine in the privacy of their rooms or in the gardens, beneath the persimmon and avocado trees. None of the rooms have telephones (but there are TV/DVD players if you must "connect"). In the evening, help yourself to cookies, brownies, and hot cider. English tea ($17) is served from 1 to 2:30 p.m. by request on the weekends. Children are welcome. Special midweek winter packages are available. This secluded inn appeals to couples, families, and artistic types who prefer chic European decor to fussy frills and ruffles.

i Celebrating a birthday or anniversary? With advance notice, most bed-and-breakfasts will offer fresh flowers, champagne, or a gift basket in your room. Ask when you book.

*SIMPSON HOUSE INN $$$$
121 E. Arrellaga St., Santa Barbara
(805) 963-7067, (800) 676-1280
www.simpsonhouseinn.com

This world-class inn is not just the empress of Santa Barbara bed-and-breakfasts, it's North America's only Five Diamond bed-and-breakfast. Guests are guaranteed a one-of-a-kind experience, well worth every dollar spent.

Located just a few blocks from State Street, the Simpson House Inn has rooms, suites, and cottages interspersed among several buildings. The original house contains 6 guest rooms, a formal dining room, and a living room with a fireplace. Victorian Estate rooms in the main house have elaborate wallpaper treatments, king- or queen-size beds, and rooms with large, outdoor decks.

The restored 1878 Carriage House features king bedrooms, each with a sitting area, fireplace, TV and DVD players, stereo, and wet bar. The English Garden cottages have Jacuzzis, fireplaces, and antique queen-size canopied beds. All accommodations have private baths, telephones, CD players, TVs, and DVD players, and guests can choose films from the extensive video library. You can read and relax in the lovely gardens and stroll among mature oaks, magnolias, exotic plants, and manicured lawns, serenaded by the soothing sound of flowing water from strategically placed fountains. Sandstone walls and tall hedges promote a sense of privacy and conceal the street from the oasis within.

The full gourmet vegetarian breakfast is a real treat, with organic California juices, fruits, and house specialties. You can choose to eat in your room or on the veranda or garden patios. In the afternoon, feast on a lavish Mediterranean hors d'oeuvres buffet featuring local wines.

Pamper yourself with European spa services in the privacy of your room. Since the Simpson House is such a highly rated establishment, you might expect snootiness and snobbery to prevail among the staff and clientele. Not here—the casual atmosphere (and the super-friendly staff) will make you feel at ease as soon as you arrive.

i If you want to avoid crowds, plan your trip to Santa Barbara during the winter months. The weather's still mild, fewer people are on the beach, and the clear winter skies provide fantastic views of the mountains and Channel Islands.

Summerland

INN ON SUMMER HILL & SPA $$$–$$$$
2520 Lillie Ave., Summerland
(805) 969-9998, (800) 845-5566
www.innonsummerhill.com

The Inn on Summer Hill rests on a hillside just off the freeway near the shores of Summerland. You can easily walk or bike to Summerland Beach, while village shops, antiques stores, and restaurants are a short stroll down the road. The inn's decorated rooms evoke an English country feel, and leave no inch uncovered, with their king- or queen-size canopy beds, billowy down comforters, country pine antiques, and custom floral fabrics. All have double-paned windows and double-insulated walls to block out noise from the nearby US 101 freeway. All 15 mini-suites include imported furniture, sitting areas, TV/DVD players, stereo cassette players, hair dryers, tea- and coffee-making facilities, minifridges, phones, fireplaces, and whirlpool tubs. Whichever room you choose, you can take in glorious sunset views across the ocean from your private balcony or patio. Guests rave about the inn's hearty breakfasts served in the downstairs dining room amid a collection of antique teapots, which features such treats as Italian eggs Benedict, frittata, and omelets. Feel like lounging around? For an additional fee, you can order breakfast in bed. In addition to the delicious breakfasts, you can feast on hors d'oeuvres from 3 to 5 p.m. and end your evening with a complimentary dessert from 7:30 to 9 p.m.

The Inn on Summer Hill offers various special packages, some seasonal and a few throughout the year. Check out the Romantic Getaway package with massages for two and breakfast in bed. This inn appeals to anyone seeking the traditional flourishes of the bed-and-breakfast experience with a fresh country feel, outstanding noshing, and sparkling sea views.

VACATION RENTALS

To find a vacation home for rent in Santa Barbara, plan way ahead. The high price of real estate discourages ownership of investment property, so the demand for seasonal rentals far outpaces supply in this fair city-by-the-beach. If you're planning a summer vacation, you need to start looking (and in some cases, making reservations) at least 6 months ahead. We've listed here some of the available options, which include rental units in complexes and on hotel grounds and, for those willing to forgo staying in Santa Barbara proper, accommodations in seaside Carpinteria. Few local hotels offer "vacation rentals" as such, but they may offer weekly or monthly rates that represent a savings over the regular room rate, so ask when making reservations.

A few cautions: Always ask exactly what is included in the cost of your rental. Some places charge for the use of towels and other necessities, which will run your bill higher than just the cost of the lodging. Also ask what you're required to bring. When linens are not supplied (at a cost or otherwise), you may have to lug along towels, sheets, and other personal items. Find out what's in the kitchen and what the parking situation is. Figure security deposits (usually refundable if you leave the rental in the same condition that you found it in) and occupancy taxes into your total cost, and be sure to ask for an immediate confirmation of your reservation after you've paid.

Rental Agencies

In addition to the companies listed below, which specialize in vacation rentals, several other real estate agencies in town handle vacation rentals as part of their services. Check the Relocation chapter for a listing of local real estate firms and inquire about vacation rental opportunities.

COASTAL PROPERTIES
1086 Coast Village Rd., Montecito
(805) 969-1258
www.coastalrealty.com
Coastal Properties is the only vacation rental company in Santa Barbara that is a member of the National Vacation Rental Managers Association—and it has the largest inventory of vacation rentals in the area. It handles upscale owner-occupied Santa Barbara properties that rent for between $750 and $7,500 a week while the owner is absent. Homes come with absolutely everything (including linens), and Coastal Properties can arrange extras, such as maid service and chefs. The vast majority of the homes are nonsmoking, many do not allow pets, and all rentals require a cash payment 60 days in advance of occupancy (no credit cards are accepted except to hold a rental temporarily). Rental periods vary from a required 3-day minimum (a week on beach properties) to leases of several years, and renters often love the area so much that they end up buying a home. Most of Coastal's summer rental properties are booked 3 to 6 months in advance. Winter rental of beach properties can cost as much as 33 percent less than summer rentals.

ACCOMMODATIONS

i A 12 percent tax on short-term accommodations is automatic everywhere in the city of Santa Barbara (10 percent in Carpinteria), so be sure to figure in the extra amount when assessing your rental costs.

Rental Complexes

CARPINTERIA SHORES
4975 Sandyland Rd., Carpinteria
(805) 684-3570, (800) 964-8570
www.carpinteriashores.com
This 3-story vacation-rental condo complex is the only one directly on the oceanfront. Both oceanfront and west-facing units have great views. With a newly added elevator, access to top floor units is now more desirable. Each fully furnished 2-bedroom, 1-bath unit is individually decorated, so you may not know what's in store. Ground-floor units on the beach with patios are most popular, and winter snowbirds and desert summer birds return year after year. There are full kitchens, private gated parking, communal barbecues, private-beach access, and outdoor showers. Rates range from $1,100–$2,000 a week (low season) to $1,900–$3,000 a week (high season), depending on floor. Free wireless Internet; most units have master bedroom and 2 twins or even double twin bunks in the smallish bedrooms.

✴LINDEN HOUSE
789 Linden Ave., Carpinteria
(805) 574-0031
www.789linden.com
This charming 3-bedroom historic house set in the heart of downtown Carpinteria on Linden Avenue—the town's main drag—is just blocks from the beach. Perfect for families or wedding parties and guests, Linden House sleeps up to 6 people.

There are bicycles (and helmets), a barbecue, and other beach supplies but—be forewarned—only 1 bathroom with access off the downstairs master bedroom. There's a charming side porch that is right out of the pages of *Coastal Living*. Rates range from $350 to $250 per night (2- or 3-night minimum off season) to $3,000 a week during peak season.

SUNSET SHORES
4980 Sandyland Rd., Carpinteria
(805) 684-3682, (800) 343-1544
www.carpinteriasunsetshores.com
Sunset Shores is a 2-story condominium complex across the street from the "world's safest beach" in Carpinteria, with a year-round heated pool and spa. The units include studios that sleep up to four guests and 1- and 2-bedroom condos that range in cost from $900 a week for a studio in winter to $1,900 a week for a 2-bedroom in summer. Furnishings and utilities are included, but you must bring your own towels and sheets. A security deposit of $500 is required, plus additional cleaning. The reservation fee is $35.

i Be aware that there are no truly "beachfront" homes in Santa Barbara city proper. Some may overlook a beach from a bluff or cliff, but you may have to drive 10 or 15 minutes to dig your toes in the sand.

VILLA ELEGANTE
402 Orilla del Mar, Santa Barbara
(805) 565-4459
www.villaelegante.com
Built a block from East Beach in Santa Barbara in 1997, family-run Villa Elegante comprises 7 Mediterranean-style units with spacious 2- and 3-bedroom suites in duplexes. All

the units are nonsmoking and are rented by the week or month. Everything is provided, including linens, and each suite has air-conditioning, a gourmet kitchen, TV, VCR, DVD, stereo, washer and dryer, wood-burning fireplace, free wireless Internet, and individual parking garage. Upstairs units have balconies and ocean views. Book way ahead, as these units go quickly. Rentals are Saturday to Saturday (some exceptions may apply). Villa Elegante accepts pets in one of the units.

Prices are not for the faint of pocketbook: They start at $1,700 a week (low season Oct to June); $5,440 a month in nonpeak season (Oct through May); $1,900 a week or $6,080 a month in semi-peak season (early June, month of September); and $2,200 a week or $7,480 a month in peak season (mid-June to Labor Day). The city's 12 percent hotel tax and $2-per-night tourism assessment apply unless the stay exceeds 30 days.

RESTAURANTS

ew cities in the country boast as many restaurants per capita as Santa Barbara. In fact we beat out Los Angeles and San Francisco in percentages. There are more than 500 in the greater Santa Barbara area, and during the busy summer months and holiday seasons, nearly all are filled to capacity with diners from around the world. Our restaurants represent all colors of the culinary spectrum. The mind-boggling array of international cuisine means you can always find the type of meal you're looking for, whether you're hankering for tacos or the latest California farm cuisine.

The burgeoning local wine industry has contributed to this restaurant renaissance, and many dining establishments offer pairings of acclaimed local wines with seasonal meals. (For more information on local wines, read the Santa Barbara Wine Country chapter.)

Don't worry if you're not an epicurean—you'll find plenty of restaurants to please your palate as well as your pocketbook. Wholesome fare reigns supreme in health-conscious Santa Barbara, and most menus include vegetarian and low-fat entrees. California cuisine—which features artistic presentations of seafood, grilled meats, seasonal vegetables, and salads made with fresh, locally grown produce—dominates the current restaurant scene. Chefs create their own versions of California cuisine, often adding local avocados, citrus fruits, and salsas to their concoctions.

Pacific Rim seafood, spices, and sauces are currently in vogue. Ahi tuna, for example, appears in creative variations on many local menus. You can order it as sashimi or a sushi roll, seared, pan-broiled, grilled, or coated with peppercorns or sesame seeds. If your palate seeks adventure, take a culinary safari to our many international restaurants, from Mexican and Moroccan to Thai. Restaurants serving traditional American fare—burgers, french fries, pizza, steak, and potatoes—will never go out of style here. Several local restaurants have been serving the same hearty American meals for more than 50 years.

OVERVIEW

In this chapter we focus on the dining experience. Several restaurants offer music, dancing, and/or other entertainment in addition to meals, and we've highlighted these in the Nightlife chapter. You can also find more information on hotel restaurants in the Accommodations chapter. Nearly all the restaurants listed here accept reservations as well as credit cards. If not, we've noted it in the description. We recommend that you always call ahead to reserve a table on weekends and holidays and at any time during the busy summer months. The most popular restaurants fill up quickly, and if you don't have a reservation, you might have to wait for an hour or two before you're seated.

California law prohibits smoking in any restaurant or bar. Some restaurants have cigar terraces reserved for smokers. We've mentioned these in the individual write-ups.

Dogs are allowed on some outdoor patios, at the discretion of the restaurant or cafe owners. To help you out, we've mentioned in the individual write-up if the restaurant offers an alfresco eating area. At least that way, you can sit where you can see your little buddy.

Children's menus are available at many restaurants, and unless we've mentioned otherwise, the eateries listed here are wheelchair accessible. Casual dress is fine at most,

and we know only a few that require a coat. If you're going to an expensive restaurant for dinner, however, you probably want to change from your shorts, T-shirts, and flip-flops into somewhat dressier attire. Bon appétit!

Price Code

The price key symbol in each restaurant listing represents the average cost for a dinner for two, excluding appetizers, dessert, cocktails, beer or wine, tax, and tip.

$ .... **Less than $20**
$$ .... **$20 to $40**
$$$ .... **$40 to $60**
$$$$ .... **More than $60**

La Super-Rica Taqueria, Santa Barbara, Mexican, $, 73

Los Agaves, Santa Barbara, Mexican, $–$$, 74

Los Arroyos, Santa Barbara, Mexican, $–$$, 74

Louie's California Bistro, Santa Barbara, American & California Cuisine, $$, 60

Lucky's, Montecito, American & California Cuisine, $$$–$$$$, 60

Madam Lu, Santa Barbara, Chinese, $–$$, 67

Montecito Cafe, Montecito, American & California Cuisine, $$, 61

The Natural Cafe, Santa Barbara, Vegetarian & Vegan Fare, $, 78

Nordstrom's Cafe, Santa Barbara, American & California Cuisine, $, 61

The Nugget, Summerland, American & California Cuisine, $, 61

Olio Pizzeria, Santa Barbara, Italian, $$–$$$, 70

Olio e Limone Ristorante, Santa Barbara, Italian, $$$, 70

Opal Bar and Restaurant, Santa Barbara, American & California Cuisine, $$, 61

Pacific Crepes, Santa Barbara, French, $, 67

Padaro Beach Grill, Carpinteria, American & California Cuisine, $–$$, 62

The Palace Grill, Santa Barbara, Cajun, $$–$$$, 66

The Palms, Carpinteria, American & California Cuisine, $, 62

Pane e Vino, Montecito, Italian, $$$, 71

Paradise Cafe, Santa Barbara, American & California Cuisine, $$, 63

Pascucci, Santa Barbara, Italian, $, 71

Petit Valentien, Santa Barbara, French, $$, 67

Restaurant Mimosa, Santa Barbara, French, $$, 68

Roy, Santa Barbara, American & California Cuisine, $$, 63

Rudy's, Santa Barbara, Mexican, $, 74

Saigon, Santa Barbara, Vietnamese, $–$$, 79

Sakana, Montecito, Japanese, $$, 72

Santa Barbara Brewing Company, Santa Barbara, Brewpub, $$, 65

Seagrass, Santa Barbara, American & California Cuisine, $$$, 63

Shanghai Chinese Restaurant, Santa Barbara, Chinese, $–$$, 67

Sojourner, Santa Barbara, Vegetarian & Vegan Fare, $, 78

Spice Avenue, Santa Barbara, Indian, $, 68

Spiritland Bistro, Santa Barbara, Vegetarian & Vegan Fare, $$, 79

Stella Mare's, Montecito, American & California Cuisine, $$–$$$, 63

Stonehouse Restaurant, Montecito, American & California Cuisine, $$$$, 64

Sushi-Teri, Santa Barbara, Japanese, $–$$, 72

The Tee-off Restaurant and Lounge, Santa Barbara, American & California Cuisine, $$, 64

Tupelo Junction Cafe, Santa Barbara, American & California Cuisine, $$, 64

Via Vai Trattoria & Pizzeria, Montecito, Italian, $$, 71

Wine Cask, Santa Barbara, American & California Cuisine, $$$$, 65

Your Choice, Santa Barbara, Thai, $$, 77

Your Place, Santa Barbara, Thai, $$, 78

Zaytoon, Santa Barbara, Middle Eastern & Greek, $$, 75

Zen Yai, Santa Barbara, Thai, $$, 78

Zookers Cafe & Juice Bar, Carpinteria, American & California Cuisine, $$, 65

AMERICAN & CALIFORNIA CUISINE

ARTS & LETTERS CAFE $$
7 E. Anapamu St., Santa Barbara
(805) 730-1463
www.sullivangoss.com
Hidden in a walled garden courtyard behind Sullivan Goss Gallery (see the Arts chapter), this evocative Mediterranean-style cafe is a delightful spot for lunch. Sip a glass of wine by the bubbling fountain, and you'll feel as though you're in a romantic European gem. The menu varies with the seasons and draws from the fresh local bounty. Lunch dishes include delicious hot soups, gourmet salads, such as Riviera seafood, roast chicken, and smoked turkey; panini sandwiches; and a range of entrees, including risotto, roast chicken, and grilled salmon. The cafe has a full bar and is open for lunch 7 days a week, and their 3-course $24.99 Artists Dinner makes for a great pretheater stop before a show at the Granada or Arlington.

BELLA VISTA $$$
1260 Channel Dr., Montecito
(805) 969-2261
www.fourseasons.com/santabarbara
Bella Vista is the main dining venue at the Four Seasons Resort The Biltmore Santa Barbara. Guests are treated like royalty, and the ocean views on the patio, as well as special prix-fixe buffets dinners (Italian, seafood) with special or no corkage fees and the ever-popular Sunday brunch make Bella Vista popular with locals as well as hotel guests. Chef Alessandro Cartumimi has a special flair for interesting creations, pairing his Italian sensibilities with local seasonal ingredients to present delicious cuisine such as wild mushroom risotto, tagliatelli with braised short ribs, crispy branzino sea bass with seasonal beans and cucumber. Check out the coconut mojitos. Bella Vista is open for breakfast, lunch, and dinner daily.

i You have to be a hotel guest at the Four Seasons Resort The Biltmore Santa Barbara or a member (or guest of a member) to gain access to the exclusive Coral Casino beach club (memberships are pricey) and dine at Tydes, the ocean-view seafood restaurant and bar overlooking the Pacific Ocean. The vibe is Miami cool, and the views are to die for (as are the prices).

BLUE AGAVE $$
20 E. Cota St., Santa Barbara
(805) 899-4694
www.blueagavesb.com
This trendy, 2-story restaurant and bar opened in 1995 and quickly became a popular hangout for young professionals, Hollywood celebrities, and chic singles and couples. Blue Agave's popularity has a lot to do with its winning combination of contemporary decor, soft romantic lighting and seating, creative cuisine, a full bar stocked with dozens of different tequilas, and lively crowds.

The menu is eclectic, including tortilla soup, chicken mole, and the can't-get-enough-of Cowboy and Cowgirl Plates. Upstairs, you can order a martini, lounge on couches around the fireplace, or head out to the cigar balcony overlooking Cota Street. For parties of four, we think the best dining nooks are the cozy and very private booths on this upper level. Blue Agave is open for dinner daily. Only parties of six or more can make reservations. If your party has fewer than six people, you'll be seated on a first come, first served basis. It's best to show up before 8 p.m. if you don't want to wait for a table.

BOUCHON $$$

9 W. Victoria St., Santa Barbara
(805) 730-1160
www.bouchon.net

If you can't make it to the wine country for a meal, come to Bouchon instead. The name is French for "wine cork," and owner Mitchell Sjerven opened this very civilized eatery in the summer of 1998 with a desire to conjure a wine-country dining experience in the heart of downtown Santa Barbara. He must be doing something right. Since its launch, Bouchon has earned a place at the table with Santa Barbara's restaurant elite, receiving enthusiastic reviews from *Wine Spectator* and the local press. From the cozy exhibition kitchen, the experienced chef concocts an imaginative menu of regional wine-country cuisine using fresh local produce. Depending on the season, you can feast on such specialties as lime-seared sea scallops, Santa Barbara spiny lobster pie, braised Kurobuta pork shank, and the popular bourbon-and-maple glazed duck breast with fava bean, butternut squash, and apple wood–smoked bacon succotash. And if that's not enough of a mouthful, Bouchon's wine list will dazzle your palate. Oenophiles can choose from an impressive lineup of more than 50 Central Coast wines by the glass, as well as bottles from Northern California, the Pacific Northwest, and France. You can sit in the bright and airy dining room or alfresco on the covered garden patio fronting Victoria Street. Planning a special party? Reserve the private Cork Room, lined with—you guessed it—cork, and the chef will design a special menu just for you and your guests. Of course, all this doesn't come cheap, but this is a special spot for special occasions. It's open for dinner 7 nights a week.

DOWNEY'S $$$

1305 State St., Santa Barbara
(805) 966-5006
www.downeyssb.com

Downey's is proof that good things come in small packages. Only 15 tables are tucked into this little dining room, but Chef John Downey consistently serves up some of the finest cuisine in the city (just look at all the awards amassed on the wall, and Zagat's rates it tops for food in Santa Barbara).

The menu changes often, incorporating the freshest local and seasonal ingredients. Such specialties as Santa Barbara mussels with sweet corn and chile vinaigrette and homemade duck sausage with lentils are favorites. A few heart-smart options are sprinkled throughout the menu as well. Don't resist the traditional dessert either: The signature Raspberry Mille Fleur Cake is to die for.

In addition to the fabulous food, Downey's offers a superb wine list, spotlighting local wines, and attentive service. Reserve ahead or you may be disappointed. Downey's serves dinner only Tues through Sun.

ELADIO'S RESTAURANT & BAR $$$

1 State St., Santa Barbara
(805) 963-4466
www.harborviewinnsb.com

In a prime location directly across Cabrillo Boulevard from Stearns Wharf in the heart of the tourist district, Eladio's is under the same ownership as the adjacent Harbor View Inn and draws many guests from that hotel and others nearby. Now exuding a more formal ambience and wearing a bold sea-themed decor with a dramatic frescoed ceiling, the restaurant serves up seasonal menus of high-quality California cuisine prepared with fresh local produce. Sink into the well-cushioned banquettes and enjoy sweeping views of Stearns Wharf, the beachfront bike path, and the mountains while you dine. On warm days, you can also dine alfresco by a fountain in the courtyard. The lunch menu offers elaborate seafood, chicken, and beef dishes as well as gourmet salads and sandwiches. Dinners and desserts are just as delicious, and the menu offers a good selection of wines, ports, and single-malt whiskeys. Eladio's has a full bar and is open for breakfast and dinner daily and lunch Mon to Sat.

FRESCO CAFE $
3987-B State St., Santa Barbara
(805) 967-6037
www.frescosb.com
This small cafe has grown in size and stature since its beginnings in 1995. Mark and Jill Brouillard, proprietors, developed a popular system, with food orders placed at the front. Patrons then seat themselves, and the dishes are delivered when they are ready. There's something about this cafe that makes you just want to slide down into your seat and slip into conversation with your friends. Even though the tables are relatively close, the acoustics are so good you can't hear the conversations at neighboring tables. The all-day menu brims with salads, sandwiches, homemade soups, and desserts. Our personal favorite is the warm goat cheese salad and the turkey club triple-decker. One Insider notes that there is a high ratio of women to men here, so single fellas take note. Breakfast, lunch, and dinner are served every day except Sun.

FROG BAR & GRILL $$
405 Glen Annie Rd. (at the Glen Annie Golf Club), Goleta
(805) 968-6400
www.glenanniegolf.com

Overlooking the rolling greens of the Glen Annie Golf Club, the Frog Bar & Grill is a popular spot for lunch and special events. The dining room has a cozy feel and affords gorgeous views of the coastline. You can also pick a table on the spacious patio, which has a fireplace and heaters for chilly days. The food is upscale and well prepared, and the lunch menu offers everything from sandwiches, crepes, pizza, and salads to seared-ahi wraps, Sicilian chicken pizza, and chicken panini. You can order a cocktail from the full bar or choose a bottle from the wine list. The Frog Bar & Grill serves lunch Mon through Fri, and the patio cafe serves breakfast and lunch with counter service from dawn until dusk daily. The Glen Annie Golf Club is also a great venue for weddings, birthdays, anniversaries, meetings, or any other group-catered event. The value is extraordinary, and the setting and service are exceptional.

THE HABIT $
216 S. Milpas St., Santa Barbara
(805) 962-7472
www.habitburger.com
The Habit is true to its name for a loyal flock of locals who come here regularly to get their fix on fresh, juicy charburgers. Just head to the general vicinity of the stores, and the aroma of sizzling beef, chicken, and fish will lead you to the source. In 1976 owner Brent Reichard went from flipping burgers in a Goleta walk-up window to buying the joint with his brother Bruce. Together they introduced the famous chargrilled burger, and the rest, as they say, is history. Today that modest stand has grown to over 40 locations across Southern California (and now Arizona) with casual on-site dining. All the burgers are made to order with only the highest quality ingredients, and the buns are baked

fresh on the premises. Local addicts swear by the classic charburger and fat onion rings, but you can also order burgers bulging with charbroiled chicken, fresh albacore, pastrami, tri-tip, and even a vegetarian patty. Top off your meal with a creamy shake and a chocolate sundae, and you'll be on a high for the rest of the day. The Habit is open for lunch and dinner daily. The Hollister Avenue (5735 Hollister Ave., Goleta; 805-964-0366) and State Street (628 State St., Santa Barbara; 805-892-5400) locations have no indoor seating, but there are awnings and arbors.

Go Local

Laurence Hauben (www.market forays.com, 805-259-7229), a local slow-food guide, provides a unique culinary experience for cooks and foodies who want to learn how to prepare and then nosh on local fish and green foodstuffs. The adventure starts by shopping for ingredients at the Fisherman's Market at the Wharf, the farmers' market, C'est Cheese, Chocolate Maya, and Our Daily Bread. Then, participants learn how to prepare a locally fresh and tantalizing meal before settling down to a marvelous lunch paired with local wines.

THE HARBOR RESTAURANT $$$
210 Stearns Wharf, Santa Barbara
(805) 963-3311
www.stearnswharf.org
Halfway down Stearns Wharf, with ocean views to die for (and pay for), the Harbor Restaurant can't help but be a touristy kind

of place. It's always full of out-of-town visitors looking for fresh seafood and a seaside perch from which to enjoy the busy waterfront scene.

The restaurant's interior is upscale and nautical, but casual dress is perfectly acceptable, and the Harbor Restaurant often draws diners from the busy Stearns Wharf foot traffic. How do we say it politely to foodies? Keep it simple: oysters and a glass of chilled Pinot Grigio, soak and the views, and you won't be disappointed. In addition to seafood, the menu offers steak, prime rib, and chicken, plus pastas, salads, and sandwiches. You'll also find a full bar here and a fair wine list. The Harbor is open for lunch and dinner daily, and breakfast on the weekends.

HARRY'S PLAZA CAFE $$
3313 State St., #13, Santa Barbara
(805) 687-2800
www.harryssb.com
Opened in 1968, this lively, old-style restaurant has a 30-year tradition of serving down-home American food and very strong drinks. The atmosphere is pure old-fashioned Santa Barbara history: about the deep, red-leather booths hang photos of everything from Flying A Studios to autographed photos of many celebs who have popped in over the decades, including Robert Mitchum. An experienced Santa Barbara restaurateur bought the venue in 2001 and has managed to preserve the cafe's unpretentious personality. You'll find steak, seafood, pastas, salads, sandwiches, and daily specials. The regulars at Harry's form an eclectic group that transcends all ages: It's not unusual to see motorcycle riders, construction workers, retirees, and business professionals in suits seated side by side at the bar. We love the waitstaff: Local authors meet here monthly for lunch, and the staff provides

individual checks for the table of up to 20 chatty writers. Harry's is tucked in a corner of the Loreto Plaza shopping mall at the corner of Las Positas Road and State Street. It's open daily for lunch and dinner.

INTERMEZZO $$
813 Anacapa St., Santa Barbara
(805) 966-9463
www.winecask.com

This delightful little wine bar addition to the Wine Cask (see p. 65) offers light, bistro-style dining in a casual and intimate atmosphere. Relax on the patio or cuddle on the couch inside near the fireplace while enjoying a glass of wine from the awesome tap wine system. The menu is as casual as the surroundings, with an emphasis on salads, pastas, pizzas, and sandwiches—great for lunch, a pretheater drink, or a late-night stop after the theater. We love the flatbreads (try the duck), and you can order a glass of wine made by one of the co-owners, Doug Margerum, from his label or one of the other vintners he consults.

Popular entrees include lamb kibbe, wild mushroom napoleon, truffle fries, and the three-cheese plate. All of the desserts are homemade, and the wine list, drawn from the Wine Cask's selection, is one of the best in the city. Intermezzo also offers a martini menu and other mixed drinks from the bar and sells cigars, which you can puff on the front patio. Intermezzo is open daily for lunch and dinner.

JANE $$
1311 State St., Santa Barbara
(805) 962-1311

This sister restaurant to the very popular Montecito Cafe has garnered a whole new rash of fans thanks to a similar formula: delicious fresh food, pleasant service, and friendly prices. Menu favorites include grilled breast of duck, seared ahi and prawn salad bowl, and a natural hamburger. The setting, two doors down from the historic Arlington Theatre, in a Spanish building with a floor-to-ceiling fireplace in the 2-story-high room is welcoming, as is the family-style communal dining table, should you find yourself dining solo; or with friends who want to gab with others. Open for lunch and dinner.

JOE'S CAFE $$
536 State St., Santa Barbara
(805) 966-4638

Joe's is one of the oldest and most famous restaurants in all of Santa Barbara. Joe Ferrario opened the original restaurant at 512 State St. in 1928 during Prohibition, and according to local legend, Joe's was a popular speakeasy.

In the 1980s the restaurant moved just a few doors up from the original to larger quarters on the corner of Cota and State Streets and continued to draw huge crowds. In 2003 local restaurateur Gene Montesano (owner of Lucky's and Ca'Dario plus more) added Joe's to his burgeoning portfolio of Santa Barbara eateries. We recommend you stick to the two Bs here: breakfast and booze (but not necessarily at the same time).

The same unpretentious Italian diner ambience with red-checked tablecloths and a raucous bar serving some of the stiffest drinks in town prevails. The menu lists long-time favorites, like home-style fried chicken, French dip, pot roast, spaghetti, calamari, prime rib, club sandwiches, and charbroiled steaks using only prime-grade midwestern beef. Joe's is open daily for lunch and dinner and breakfast Sat and Sun. Note: Over the years the ambience has changed slightly. There are now bouncers on the weekends to regulate things as the nightlife scene heats up, because the crowd at the packed bar can sometimes get rowdy.

✳JULIENNE $$–$$$
138 E. Canon Perdido, Santa Barbara
(805) 845-6488
www.restaurantjulienne.com
In a small, unprepossessing storefront with glass windows and cozy tables set close together, you will discover some of the best farm-to-table cuisine in Santa Barbara. Emma and Justine West (he's the chef-owner, she's the wife and co-owner) present 100 percent local seafood and imaginative and tasty dishes sourced from the local farmers' market. From the delicious house-made charcuterie (lamb, pork, *foie gras,* and more) to pork belly or soft-shell crab, it's hard to go wrong here. We recommend the tasting menus (3, 5, or 7 courses) with wine pairings (prices range from $45 to $125 depending on number of courses and if you do the pairings or not). Global and local wine list is superb. They do charge $2 for bread. So be it.

LOUIE'S CALIFORNIA BISTRO $$
1404 De la Vina St., Santa Barbara
(805) 963-7003
www.louiessb.com
Pamper yourself at Louie's, a sweet California-style bistro in the historic Upham Hotel (see the Accommodations chapter for a detailed description of Santa Barbara's oldest hostelry). Louie's is a favorite with the local business lunch crowd, and the intimate, casually elegant atmosphere makes it a perfect place for a birthday lunch or dinner or romantic tête-à-tête. You can dine inside or on the heated wraparound veranda.

The restaurant is best known for gourmet cuisine at prices that won't make a huge dent in your budget. Dishes include Louie's famous Caesar salad with blackened chicken or shrimp, chicken in puff pastry, stuffed Anaheim chile, and quiche. Louie's serves beer and wine only. It's open for lunch Mon through Fri, 11:30 a.m. to 2 p.m., and for dinner 7 days a week.

LUCKY'S $$$–$$$$
1279 Coast Village Rd., Montecito
(805) 565-7540
www.luckys-steakhouse.com
This sleek steak house in the old Coast Village Grill location is the hip hangout in Montecito for locals, celebrities, and wannabes. Owner Gene Montesano (of Lucky jeans fame) and his partners have infused this place with some minimalist glamour. From the old black-and-white photographs of celebrities adorning the walls to the smartly clad waiters, the valet parking, and the impressive list of champagnes, Lucky's exudes a kind of nouveau nostalgia. It's famous for its juicy steaks aged well and cooked to order—the filet porterhouse and the New York strip steak among them. Side selections include golden, skinny onion rings that must be devoured quickly while they are hot (not hard to do), home fries, and creamed spinach. You'll also find a few enticing seafood options. If you're dining alone, you can perch at the bar and watch your favorite sports game or pick a people-watching spot on the street-side patio. The wine list is excellent, with many French selections and a few big-ticket bottles that are a good indication of the clientele here. Lucky's is open daily for dinner and Sat and Sun for lunch. It's not for the miserly, but the beef is worth the bucks.

MONTECITO CAFE $$
1295 Coast Village Rd., Montecito
(805) 969-3392
www.montecitoinn.com

The Montecito Inn was a famous Hollywood hangout back in the 1920s and '30s (read more in the Accommodations chapter), and some of the light, romantic history is preserved in the charming Montecito Cafe, just off the lobby. Popular with the rich Montecito crowd who like to watch their pennies, as well as regular folk, the California cuisine here is excellent, and the prices extremely reasonable for such high-quality fare. You'll find imaginative dishes, such as grilled chicken breast with roasted Anaheim chiles, a peppered New York steak, and fettuccine with a pesto cream sauce and grilled lamb sausage—all under $16. An excellent list of wines and champagne provides the perfect accompaniment. The Montecito Cafe is open daily for lunch and dinner.

NORDSTROM'S CAFE $
17 W. Canon Perdido St., Santa Barbara
(805) 564-8770

Mothers and daughters alike love capping off their morning of shopping with a delicious lunch at the third-floor Nordstrom's Cafe. Sit outside on the terrace for a bird's-eye view of the coast and Santa Ynez Mountains. Although the decor is unimpressive, this is a classic case of not judging a book by its cover. Our perennial favorites are Chinese chicken salad and lime chicken salad, as well as the soups.

THE NUGGET $
2318 Lillie Ave., Summerland
(805) 969-6135

This saloon-style restaurant with an Old West theme seems a bit out of place amid Summerland's colorful Victorian cottages, but it's been a steadfast local favorite for more than 50 years. The Nugget was reprieved from its "everything fried" menu a while back, but it still has the best french fries in town. The salmon salad, pork chops, and T-bone steaks are safe bets, but check out the reasonable bar menu for tasty pork sliders or succulent lamb chops as well. The Spicy Bloody Caesars are terrific, and Monday nights are packed with a moneyed Montecito crowd who dress down and "rough it" to drink up and gossip after a weekend of socializing The Nugget is open for lunch and dinner daily, and they also have a Goleta outpost at 5687 Calle Real; (805) 964-5200.

OPAL BAR AND RESTAURANT $$
1325 State St., Santa Barbara
(805) 966-9676
www.opalrestaurantandbar.com

The casual and cozy bistro-style dining room at Opal Bar and Restaurant is always bubbling with the chatter of happy diners, and if you like a wide selection of innovative international dishes, you'll love it here too. The menu is "California eclectic" with influences from around the world, and the daily specials add even more diversity. Favorite dishes are lemongrass-encrusted fresh salmon fillet with a Thai curry sauce and the gourmet pizzas cooked in a wood-burning oven. Be sure to leave room for one of the incredible desserts. A popular pick is the Like Water for Chocolate Surprise, a decadent mix of white and dark chocolate mousse. More than 300 bottles from around the world grace the award-winning wine list, plus you'll find a good variety of unusual beers and spirits, and you can top off your meal with a frothy cappuccino. Opal is open for lunch Mon through Sat and for dinner nightly.

PADARO BEACH GRILL $–$$
3765 Santa Claus Ln., Carpinteria
(805) 566-9800
www.padarobeachgrill.com

Packed with beachgoers in the summer, this family-friendly eatery near Padaro Lane is ideal for an alfresco meal before or after a day in the sun. The kid's sandbox and fenced lawn make this a paradise for parents with young kids in tow (see the write-up in the Kidstuff chapter), and the setting, set off from Santa Claus Lane Beach by a fence, is a hit with everyone. There are 4 types of sandwiches, burgers, and salads to choose from, in addition to sides like onion rings and sweet potato fries. There is a full menu for kids and 8 different beers on tap for parents.

After closing in December 2009, this local favorite was reopened by Habit Burger founders/brothers Brent and Bruce Reichard, who aimed at revamping the Santa Barbara staple with a more wallet-friendly menu and an exciting atmosphere. The new Beach Grill hosts live music and serves barbecue items on weekends, and has an outdoor patio with a fire pit and beautiful views of the Santa Barbara coast.

Place your order, then pick a picnic table on the lawn and relax with a glass of beer or wine while you wait for your meal. (The kitchen will buzz you on your personal pager when it's ready). Beach Grill at Padaro is open for lunch and dinner daily in the summer. In winter the restaurant serves lunch daily. A special brunch menu is also available on weekends. Live concerts and a barbecue on Sundays add to the fun.

Tip: Leashed pets are welcome on the street side of the lawn.

Food Trucks

As "mobile cuisine" gains popularity, keep an eye out for the **O Street Truck** (French-Vietnamese fusion fare including French pastry pizzas), **Cultureshock** (Sri Lankan cuisine), the **Burger Bus** (most ingredients are sourced from local food suppliers and growers), and **Don Paco's Taco Truck** (serving traditional Mexican staples, as well as handmade tamales on Wednesday at Micheltorena and San Andreas Streets, Mon through Fri 8 to 11 p.m.

THE PALMS $
701 Linden Ave., Carpinteria
(805) 684-3811
www.thepalmsrestaurant.com

This popular, informal Carpinteria hangout has been family owned and operated for some 40 years. Barbecue your own steak on the grill if you wish, or ask the chef to do it for you. You can also order fresh seafood and serve yourself from the salad bar. Ever had deep-fried croutons? Are you turned on by raw slabs of beef? Do you not mind if the carpet looks like it hasn't been changed since the place opened or if the atmosphere is more church meeting hall for a Sunday potluck than fancy-schmancy dining room? If so, then this is your place. Park yourself by one of the 2 fireplaces, order a beer, and chat with the locals. The Palms offers a full slate of traditional American food, including burgers, steaks, and fresh seafood. It's open for dinner 7 evenings a week and has a cocktail lounge with live music Thursday through Saturday.

PARADISE CAFE $$
702 Anacapa St., Santa Barbara
(805) 962-4416
www.paradisecafe.com

Many a local resident and visitor have wined and dined at this casual, quintessential Santa Barbara restaurant since 1983. It occupies a converted house on the corner of Anacapa and Ortega Streets, just a block from State Street.

The Paradise is best known for its tasty meats and burgers, but it also serves a pleasantly spicy black bean soup. You can order from an extensive list of Santa Barbara County wines, including its own Paradise Chardonnay, made by the Qupé winery. When the weather's warm, most people prefer to eat outside amid the tropical flowers. The separate bar area draws a hip singles crowd. The Paradise Cafe is open for lunch and dinner daily and also for breakfast on Sun.

ROY $$
7 W. Carrillo St., Santa Barbara
(805) 966-5636

If you just wandered by Roy, tucked amid shops on Carrillo Street downtown, you'd never think this unpretentious restaurant and bar serves some of the most delicious and best-value food in Santa Barbara. The owner and chef, Roy Gandy, has been surprising locals and visitors for more than 15 years with his creative concoctions made with fresh organic produce from local farmers' markets. Roy is also a favorite late-night dining spot. Bold, modern art leaps off the walls in the funky midnight-blue dining room, where you can slide into a banquette and order one of the best-value prix-fixe dinners in town. Entrees come with warm homemade bread, soup, and a tasty salad of mixed greens topped with the house dressing. The desserts are wonderful, too. Add a great list of wines and ales, a

funky bar, and you've got yourself a fabulous night out at a bargain price. Roy is open until midnight for dinner 7 nights a week.

SEAGRASS $$$
30 E. Ortega St., Santa Barbara
(805) 963-1012
www.seagrassrestaurant.com

For starters, if you are a foodie, and an Insider, and on a budget, ask if they are offering the special prix-fixe meal (Sunday through Thursday). If not, or if it's a weekend, dig deep into your pocketbook and go for it. Chef Roberto Perez moved from Nevada City, leaving behind a loyal following (some of whom trek here) to build a new fan base for his gourmet California cuisine. Start with an oyster shooter with ginger or the beet salad that is as tasty as it is artfully presented. We also liked the vichyssoise with chives and truffle oil, Waygu cross rib with potato, and cream-braised root vegetables and maple syrup sauce, all topped off with tasty profiteroles with warm chocolate sauce poured over the top. The room is pretty and semiformal, the music is jazz. All in all, a lovely spot for a special occasion or just darn fine food any day of the week. If you build it, they will come.

STELLA MARE'S $$-$$$
50 Los Patos Way, Montecito
(805) 969-6705
www.stellamares.com

Stella Mare's scores top points for its evocative French country ambience and fresh seasonal wine country cuisine cooked on a wood-burning grill. This upscale bistro-style restaurant and bar in a historic (1872) Victorian house overlooks the tranquil Andree Clark Bird Refuge and is a popular venue for special events—many bridal showers and wedding receptions take place here.

You can choose a seat in the gorgeous dining room, on the vine-draped patio, or in the stunning solarium, which floods with sunlight during the day and flickers with candlelight in the evening. People rave about the braised lamb shanks, grilled pork tenderloin, and fresh local fish, as well as the homemade pastas and desserts. After dinner, you can sink into one of the overstuffed, shabby chic lounges by the fire and sip a coffee. Stella Mare's offers live jazz on Wednesday nights. The restaurant is open for lunch and dinner Tues through Sun and serves an excellent brunch on Sat and Sun.

STONEHOUSE RESTAURANT $$$$
900 San Ysidro Ln., Montecito
(805) 969-4100
www.sanysidroranch.com

The rustic look of the small stone house (formerly a citrus packinghouse) nestled on the grounds of the San Ysidro Ranch (see the Accommodations chapter) belies its refined interior. Crisp table settings, Persian rugs, antiques, and original art infuse a sense of easy elegance into the dining room, and the food is every bit as impeccable as the decor. Chef Jamie West is back in the kitchen after a few years away, combining fresh, organic ranch-grown herbs, fruit, and vegetables with flavorful seasonings and adding influences from around the world.

Desserts are as appealing as the entrees, and the wine list shines. The Stonehouse has received many culinary awards over the years, including a *Wine Spectator* Award of Excellence, the James Beard Foundation 10th Anniversary Award, and a Distinguished Restaurants of America Award. This is also one of the most expensive restaurants in Santa Barbara, so be prepared when the tab arrives. The Stonehouse is open for dinner

daily. This is one of the few places in town where you really should dress for dinner. More casual is the Plow and Angel Bistro downstairs. The restaurant recently opened for lunch 2 days a week.

THE TEE-OFF RESTAURANT AND LOUNGE $$
3627 State St., Santa Barbara
(805) 687-1616
www.teeoffsb.com

The Tee-off (a golf theme is carried throughout) has been at this upper State Street location for about 50 years. It has an old-fashioned steak house ambience, with plush booths and red leather bar stools. The menu fits the theme, with steak, prime rib (a favorite), chops, chicken, and seafood topping the list. It's the perfect place to unwind after a game of golf, so order up a martini and a big juicy steak and enjoy. The Tee-off is open for dinner nightly.

TUPELO JUNCTION CAFE $$
1218 State St., Santa Barbara
(805) 899-3100
www.tupelojunction.com

Bon Appetit said Tupelo Junction Cafe, a Southern-style American restaurant, represents the "funky side" of Santa Barbara by pouring its coffee into country-style crockery mugs, mixing its mimosas in mason jars, and decorating with colorful fruit-crate labels. Amy Scott, proprietor, is the mastermind behind this restaurant, and she pulls it off, shall we say, with a Southern flair. Start your day with a buttermilk biscuit slathered in gravy or Mom's pumpkin-oatmeal waffle top with caramelized bananas, candied pecans, and maple syrup. For lunch maybe it's a deep-dish cheddar and Gouda mac 'n' cheese you're hankering for, or an apple wood–smoked bacon and fried green tomato BLT. Dinner still says "Southern home cooking," with entrees of blackened molasses organic salmon and fried chicken salad with corn bread. Bring on the crawdads! Breakfast, lunch, and dinner are served on time every day. Momma would be proud.

WINE CASK $$$$
813 Anacapa St., Santa Barbara
(805) 966-9463, (800) 436-9463
www.winecask.com

If you're a wine and food connoisseur, you'll be right at home at the Wine Cask, one of Santa Barbara's most popular restaurants. Local bottles comprise nearly half of the 20-page wine list, and the experienced waiters will happily recommend the best wine to complement your meal. Wander through the fountain courtyard, and you'll enter the dramatic dining room, which exudes a warm and elegant European ambience, with a baronial fireplace crackling on one side and antique hand-painted beams overhead. You can also dine alfresco on the stone patio—a lovely spot on warm summer days.

The food is fresh, locally sourced, and outstanding. Depending on the season, you can choose from grilled Kobe beef top sirloin, organic king salmon, or fresh local sea bass. Owners Doug Margerum and Mitchell Sjerven (of Bouchon) continue to preserve the Santa Barbara fine-dining experience enjoyed by locals and visitor for over a quarter of a century. The Wine Cask is open for lunch Mon through Fri and dinner Mon through Sat. Make sure you stop at the adjacent Margerum Wine Company Tasting Room, where you'll find a selection of imported wines to complement those of Santa Barbara County.

> **i** Dining alone? Check out the chef's table at the Wine Cask and meet other gourmands for a farmers' market–inspired dinner. The chef will even come out and chat.

ZOOKERS CAFE & JUICE BAR $$
5404 Carpinteria Ave., Carpinteria
(805) 684-8893
www.zookerscafe.com

Cute and cozy Zookers Cafe & Juice Bar was the first to add some zing to Carp's sleepy restaurant scene. This popular little neighborhood nook is a locals' favorite, serving affordable California cuisine (with a hint of granola). Wedged into an uninspiring strip mall, Zookers is unpretentious and laid-back. You can perch at a rustic wooden table in the dining room, or on one of the small patios in front or back. Zookers uses only fresh local organic greens for its flavorful salads and will gladly substitute tofu for chicken. In fact, the menu lists many mouthwatering meatless options. In addition to gourmet sandwiches, salads, quiche, and pasta, the seasonal menu includes turkey meat loaf, chicken breast stuffed with sage and prosciutto, cioppino, and seafood tostada. Daily specials of fresh fish, lamb, and pork broaden the already excellent selection. Cap your meal with a homemade dessert and a local bottle from the wine list (most are available by the glass), and you'll know what the buzz is all about. Zookers serves lunch and dinner Mon through Sat (closed Sun).

BREWPUBS

SANTA BARBARA BREWING
** COMPANY** $$
510 State St., Santa Barbara
(805) 730-1040
www.sbbrewco.com

Primarily known for its great selection of microbrewed beers (including Santa Barbara Blonde, Rincon Red, and Pacific Pale Ale), the Santa Barbara Brewing Company is a convivial place to hang out and enjoy some great food as well. Burgers, pizza, pasta, steak, and seafood are on the bill of fare (everyone loves the garlic rosemary fries), and there's a kids' menu with fish-and-chips, grilled cheese sandwiches, and other child-friendly foods. In addition to a wide choice of beers and ales, there's a full wine list. The Brewing Company is open for lunch and dinner daily and features a happy hour Mon through Fri from 3 to 6 p.m.

i **Don't feel like going out, but still yearning for tantalizing food? Call Restaurant Connection, Santa Barbara's "Original Restaurant Delivery Service," which picks up at over 35 restaurants and delivers meals right to your door. Call (805) 687-9753, or visit them online at www.restaurant connectionsb.com.**

CAJUN

THE PALACE GRILL $$–$$$
8 E. Cota St., Santa Barbara
(805) 963-5000
www.palacegrill.com
The good times roll in a big way every evening of the week at the Palace, which is consistently named one of the best Cajun restaurants in California. It's been written up in *Gourmet, Bon Appetit, Los Angeles* magazine, and many other publications. The colorful, lively Bourbon Street atmosphere provides a perfect complement to the spicy food. When Ronald Reagan was president and visited his nearby ranch, the Secret

Service and press corps reportedly ate regularly at the Palace. We've also heard of people driving for 5 hours just to eat here. The Palace actually offers a mix of New Orleans, Creole, and pasta dishes, plus steak, fish, and chicken dishes for those who prefer more subtle, less spicy seasonings. All meals are served by a waitstaff that works as a well-oiled team. Fresh seafood, typically redfish, crawfish, and prawns, is flown in direct from New Orleans.

Jazzing up the mouthwatering menu are Cajun crawfish popcorn (one of our favorites), blackened redfish or ahi tuna, Louisiana soft-shell crabs, gumbos, crawfish crab cakes, and oysters Rockefeller. Quench your thirst with a pepper martini, or just head for the self-service wine bar. For dessert, save room for the sinful bread pudding soufflé (which you need to order before dinner because it takes a while to prepare) or the Key lime pie made with real Florida Key limes.

The Palace Grill is open for lunch and dinner 7 days a week. Dinner reservations are accepted for Sun through Thurs, but on Fri and Sat nights they're taken for the first seating only (5:30 p.m.)—after that, it's first come, first served. Without reservations, plan on a wait of an hour or longer during prime dinner hours. The time usually passes quickly, though, while you're chatting with the interesting people in line, watching the magician who entertains on busy nights, and listening to the jazz musicians who often play here.

If you don't want to search for a parking place, take advantage of the Palace's valet parking. Just pull up to the front door (between State and Anacapa Streets) and ask for the service.

CHINESE

MADAM LU $–$$
3524 State St., Santa Barbara
(805) 898-9289, (805) 898-9220
www.madamlu.com

Whether you order to go, have food delivered, or dine in at the upper State Street restaurant, everyone will find something they like from the extensive menu. But we are creatures of habit here: Order C5—the fish fillet in crispy bean sauce served with snow pea sprouts—and we guarantee you won't be disappointed. All-you-can-eat daily lunch buffet ($9.95) is served from 11 a.m. to 2:30 p.m. There's also a small sister restaurant, Mama Wu (415 N. Miplas St.; 805-966-1088), if you are at the other end of town.

SHANGHAI CHINESE
RESTAURANT $–$$
830 N. Milpas St., Santa Barbara
(805) 962-7833
www.shanghaisbca.net

A family favorite for years, Shanghai lends credence to the saying "Don't judge a book by its cover." In fact, this hole-in-the-wall, set in a strip mall in a less-upscale part of town, is popular with vegetarians who go for the tofu-as-meat dishes, which are just as extensive as the regular menu. Shanghai serves up the standard Chinese fare—with meat or fake meat—in a way that tastes anything but standard. The hot-and-sour soup and mu shu pork are family favorites. (Be sure to ask for an extra plum sauce for the pork.) Celebrities and famed directors from Montecito all make this their haunt. Just look at the wall or ask for the books of birthday celebration pictures, and you're sure to see a recognizable face. Shanghai is open for lunch every day except Tues

and Sun, and it serves up dinner every day except Tues.

FRENCH

PACIFIC CREPES $
705 Anacapa St., Santa Barbara
(805) 882-1123

From the first friendly "Bonjour" to the last decadent bite, we love this delightful little French creperie. You can't beat the prices here, plus you can polish your French and feel as if you've popped over to Brittany for a bite to eat. Sit out on the sunny, pink-hued patio, or dine inside amid antique French posters and Breton-style blue and gold linens. The menu features authentic French-style omelets and buckwheat crepes (called galettes in Brittany) with your choice of fillings. You can choose any combination of meat, eggs, vegetables, smoked salmon, and hard-to-find imported French cheeses, including Reblochon and Roquefort. Pacific Crepes is open for breakfast, lunch and dinner 3 days a week. Open Fri and Sat from 8 a.m. to 11 p.m. and Sun from 8 a.m. to 9 p.m. A French conversation group meets here every Sun at 5:30 p.m. if you want to practice your _français_.

✳PETIT VALENTIEN $$
1114 State St. in La Arcada, Santa
Barbara
(805) 966-0222

We love this cozy little restaurant tucked into La Arcada for many reasons, including the fair prices for the very tasty fare. You can make a meal of the reasonably priced ($6–$9) starters, soup du jour, or salads that include pâtés de campagne; semi-boneless quail served with figs, grapes, and olives; a tasty Caesar; or _haricot vert_ salad. Or go for entrees (under $20) that include Kobe beef or pan-seared duck breast in a blood plum sauce. Leave enough room for the flourless chocolate cake, the lightest piece of heaven you may ever sink your lips into. Open for lunch Mon through Fri and dinner 7 nights a week. The chef-owner may be a man of few words, but he sings in the kitchen. The restaurant was named for a character in one of the Three Colors Trilogy (*Blue, White,* and *Red*) (1993–94) by the late, great Polish director Krzysztof Kieslowski who "adapted" the three French ideals—liberty, equality, fraternity—into three thought-provoking, modern-day dramas about people who cope with personal losses and tragedies. (Irène Jacob played a model named Valentine in *Red,* in case you are wondering).

RESTAURANT MIMOSA $$
714 State St., Santa Barbara
(805) 963-2272

Restaurant Mimosa is an old, local favorite that serves delicious French food at affordable prices. They recently moved from an unremarkable uptown location to the more active downtown. Patrons are known to celebrate special occasions here with their friends and relatives. The service is usually excellent, and though casual attire is fine here, you can also dress up and still feel quite comfortable. A balance between classic and country cooking styles, the "French casual" cuisine features meat, chicken, and seafood dishes.

INDIAN

SPICE AVENUE $
1027 State St., Santa Barbara
(805) 965-6004
www.spiceavenuesb.com

In a great location amid State Street shopping venues, Spice Avenue serves up East London/British–style Indian cuisine and has one of the best dinner buffet bargains in town. On Wednesday night, for $12.95 per person, you can heap your plate with all-you-can-eat curries, biryanis, and other Indian delights—including dessert. The daily lunch buffet is $7.95. Fragrant aromas lure you through the perfect people-watching terrace into a warm and exotic dining room adorned with spice-colored Indian fabrics, gold-framed prints, and potted palms. The buffet is a great way to sample a variety of dishes, and vegetarians will find plenty of meatless options. Order some naan to mop up all the sauces, quench your thirst with a mango lassi, or sip a little self-serve Burgundy, a chilled Chablis, or imported beer, and you'll be in dining nirvana. Spice Avenue is open for lunch and dinner (and takeout) daily.

i You want to shop, but he wants to eat? If you want to shop and your mate is hungry for tasty East Indian food, head to India House (418 State St., Santa Barbara; 805-962-5070), an Indian restaurant within a huge, fun shop selling everything from cotton kurtas and silk saris to bangles and *bindis.*

ITALIAN

CA'DARIO $$–$$$
37 E. Victoria St., Santa Barbara
(805) 884-9419
www.cadario.net

Ca'Dario is a self-proclaimed "unpretentious Italian neighborhood restaurant filled with aroma, clever waiters, good friends, and

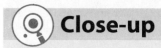 **Close-up**

Best Breakfasts

Need some serious sustenance to kick-start your day? Below is a list of some of our favorite breakfast nooks. Turn up in your shorts and flip-flops, refuel with some fresh-brewed java, and chow down on good old-fashioned breakfast grub for only a few bucks.

Breakwater Restaurant. 109 Harbor Way, Santa Barbara; (805) 965-1557. Gaze out at bobbing boats over bacon and eggs at this harborside cafe. You can order all the classics here, bask on the sunny deck, then burn some calories strolling along the breakwater.

East Beach Grill. 1188 E. Cabrillo Blvd., Santa Barbara; (805) 965-8805. Grab a table on the boardwalk, order the multigrain pancakes, and watch the beautiful bodies bronzing on the beach. Get there early, though—tables fill up fast.

Eladio's. 1 State St., Santa Barbara; (805) 963-4466; www.harborviewinnsb.com. Part of the Harbor View Inn, Eladio's offers a delicious start to your day while people-watching at this location across from Stearns Wharf.

Esau's Cafe. 507 Linden Ave., Carpinteria, (805) 684-1070. We love the humongous portions, the surf-movies projected on a couple of big flat-screen TVs, the outdoor and sidewalk-fringed tables, and the supercool and friendly vibe at this Carp favorite.

The Montecito Coffee Shop. 1498 E. Valley Rd., Montecito; (805) 969-6250. The Montecito Coffee Shop has been providing a simple breakfast menu to residents for over 60 years. This is a true locals' hangout.

Sambo's on the Beach. 216 W. Cabrillo Blvd., Santa Barbara; (805) 965-3269; www.sambosrestaurant.com. This is the original and last-standing Sambo's, founded in 1957. Big stacks of pancakes are made from scratch, and over the years some healthy alternatives have been added, including turkey sausages. Portions are generous, and so are the crowds. Be prepared to wait.

Shoreline Beach Cafe. 801 Shoreline Dr., Santa Barbara; (805) 568-0064. Smack-dab on beautiful Leadbetter Beach, this is the only restaurant in Santa Barbara where you can dig your toes in the sand while you dine. Savor the seascape and start your day with a breakfast burrito or Shoreline omelet stuffed with shrimp and salsa fresca.

Summerland Beach Cafe. 2294 Lillie Ave., Summerland; (805) 969-1019; www .summerlandbeachcafe.com. Sleepyheads can order breakfast all day at this colorful old Victorian house. Pick a table on the sunny porch and feast on omelets, Belgian waffles, and huevos rancheros.

rowdy conversation." In other words, you can expect a lively atmosphere and some really good food. In fact, we know locals who wouldn't go anywhere else for authentic Italian cuisine. Experienced Chef Dario Furlati whips up succulent dishes—osso buco

con risotto (braised veal shank with saffron arborio rice) and *sella d'agnello* (grilled rack of lamb basted with garlic, olive oil, and fine herbs), to name a few. The daily special and the fresh fish of the day, available at market price, are other great options. We adore the pumpkin ravioli in a browned-butter sage sauce. The wine list is excellent and heavy with Italian wines, and the service is attentive. The restaurant is open for lunch Mon through Sat and for dinner daily.

EMILIO'S RISTORANTE AND BAR $$
324 W. Cabrillo Blvd., Santa Barbara
(805) 966-4426
www.emilios-restaurant.com
Cozy and convivial, Emilio's, located on Cabrillo Boulevard across from the beach, serves a seasonal menu of delicious European country–style food using fresh organic vegetables and herbs. The appetizers and entrees are supplemented by both Italian and Santa Barbara County wines, and the bar serves everything from drink-of-the-moment martinis to grappas, vodkas, and scotches. Breads, raviolis, and gnocchi are made on-site, and paella is a specialty. Open for dinner nightly, Emilio's is usually crowded. Watch for appetizer specials and enjoy a bite and glass of vino at the bar.

GIANFRANCO'S TRATTORIA $$
666 Linden Avenue, Carpinteria
(805) 684-0720
This family-owned and family-run Italian trattoria—the name is an amalgam of Giovanni, the chef; Anna, his mother; and her husband Franco, who runs the till—is a delightful and welcoming lunch and dinner spot. Don't be fooled by the tiny storefront: There is also a delightful patio with a fountain in the back. Everything that comes out of the tiny kitchen is delicious, but a few favorites are the lobster ravioli and veal Milanese. Beautiful desserts of a more Parisian bent, courtesy of the chef's classically trained sister, presented for selection on a tray add the perfect ending. Popular on weekends; be sure to make reservations.

✳OLIO E LIMONE RISTORANTE $$$
11 W. Victoria St., Ste. 17, Santa Barbara
(805) 899-2699
www.olioelimone.com
Owned and operated by Chef Alberto Morello and his wife, Elaine, Olio e Limone serves up an imaginative menu of authentic Italian dishes—including a sprinkling of Sicilian specialties. This is one of our favorite Italian restaurants in town—and there are many. Along with Bouchon (see p. 56), this sophisticated little eatery is one of a few culinary gems to sprout up in this part of town. The restaurant lies just around the corner from the Arlington Center for the Performing Arts and is often buzzing with the symphony crowd, which comes here to dine before performances. Tucked in a tiny space on Victoria Street, Olio e Limone feels like a cozy Florentine trattoria. Tables are set skirt by skirt, and passersby can peek in through the row of windows facing the street. The food is bright and fresh and bursting with flavor. Among the pasta dishes, you'll find surprises like the ribbon pasta with morel mushrooms, asparagus, and cream, and the house-made duck ravioli. Olio e Limone has a full bar and is open for dinner daily and lunch Mon through Sat.

OLIO PIZZERIA $$–$$$
11 W. Victoria, Ste. 21, Santa Barbara
(805) 899-2699
This popular pizza shop–wine bar around the corner and under the same ownership as Olio e Limone serves up Napolitano pizzas (traditionally soft in the middle) from the wood-burning oven, and little dishes of imported *salumi* and cheeses as well as panini and salads in a more casual and lively atmosphere. If you are lucky, you might get the brown pizza plate, which translates to

pizza on the house. Or you might just order the carbonara pizza with an egg in the center and have egg on your face!

PANE E VINO $$$
1482 E. Valley Rd., Montecito
(805) 969-9274
We (along with practically everyone else in Santa Barbara) love the intimate atmosphere, charm, and high-quality meals at this small, authentic Italian trattoria. It's in the back of a shopping plaza parking lot in Montecito's Upper Village, but don't let the location fool you: This place is a popular little gem. It's also a favorite with local and visiting celebrities.

Choose a table in the bustling interior or outside on the vine-draped, heated patio. Most of the waiters are Italian, and the Italian music that plays in the background adds an aura of romance. The menu features rustic, Northern Italian foods: pasta, seafood, veal chops, and meats (including rabbit and duck). We favor the branzino (sea bass) when available, a tasty fish if ever there was one. Pane e Vino is open for lunch (Mon through Sat) and dinner Mon through Sun.

PASCUCCI $
729 State St., Santa Barbara
(805) 963-8123
www.pascuccirestaurant.com
The lively, contemporary atmosphere, good food at unbelievably affordable prices (at least for downtown Santa Barbara), and convenience of Pascucci make it one of the most popular eateries in the Paseo Nuevo shopping area. It offers delicious pasta, soups, salads, sandwiches, appetizers, and pizzas—and many items are under $10. In fact, it often scores awards in local newspaper polls for offering the "Best Meal under $10." This is

a great place to stop in for some sustenance after a busy day of shopping. The garlic dinner rolls are addictive. You can dine in the cozy interior, perch at the bar, people-watch on the street-side patio, or order a glass of Chianti and relax on a comfortable sofa by the fireplace. Pascucci is open for lunch and dinner daily.

> **i** In your hotel room and want a pizza delivered? Call Pizza Mizza (805-564-3900) for a thin-crust gourmet pizza (thick on request) or go to www.pizzamizza.com.

VIA VAI TRATTORIA & PIZZERIA $$
1483 E. Valley Rd., #20, Montecito
(805) 565-9393
An offshoot of Pane e Vino, Via Vai in the Montecito Village shopping center offers a variety of authentic Northern Italian dishes, with an emphasis on pizza and pasta. These are our favorite thin-crust pizzas in town; order the one topped with arugula and prosciutto and you've got salad and entree in one fell swoop. You'll also find everything from *pizze capricciosa* to *farfalle al salmone e piselli* and *salsiccia con polenta* on the menu. The grilled meats and seafood are just as tasty. You can dine in the bright dining room or on the outdoor heated patio. Dress is casual here, and the restaurant is popular with local Montecitans. Via Vai is open daily for lunch and dinner.

JAPANESE

ARIGATO SUSHI $$
1225 State St., Santa Barbara
(805) 965-6074
In the heart of downtown, opposite the Granada Theater, trendy Arigato is still rolling

out some of the freshest and best sushi in town. Voted the favorite Japanese sushi restaurant in a local poll, Arigato is best known for its wild combination rolls with equally wild names: California Sunset, Rock 'n' Roll, Swinging Roll, Wiki Wiki Roll, Wipeout Roll, and Sea Eel Goes Hollywood, to name a few. Can't choose? Get the Whatever Roll, and your chef will prepare his favorite for the day. You can also get excellent soft-shell crab tempura and other traditional Japanese dishes. You can perch at the sushi bar, sit downstairs, or dine alfresco on the patio out front. The place is nearly always packed with young (20s and 30s), chic-looking diners who love the sake bombs. The beverage list also offers more than 20 different types of hot or cold sake, imported Japanese beers, and some excellent wines—including the fruity plum wine. Arigato is open for dinner daily. Get there early if you can—the restaurant doesn't take reservations.

i For the latest restaurant news, check out www.santabarbara.com for tips from John Dickson, "the Restaurant Guy." His online Santa Barbara restaurant guide also notes top-rated restaurants. John is a man-about-town who also oversees the North Pole telephone line during Christmas holidays—due to a close phone-number glitch!

SAKANA $$
1046 Coast Village Rd., Montecito
(805) 565-2014
This sushi place tucked into the back corner of a Montecito shopping mall has seized the attention of the discerning Santa Barbara sushi crowd because of its artistic flair for culinary creations, but prices are higher than elsewhere. Cozy up to the bar or settle into one of the white linen-draped tables. Try the ahi carpaccio that melts in your mouth or the yellowtail melt. Sakana is open Tues through Fri for lunch and Tues through Sun for dinner. The restaurant is closed on Mon.

i Hankering for late-night sushi? Open until midnight Sun through Thurs and until 1 a.m. on the weekends is Santa Barbara's only late-night sushi bar Edomasa, located at 2710 De la Vina St., Santa Barbara, (805) 687-0210.

SUSHI-TERI $–$$
1013 Bath St., Santa Barbara
(805) 963-1250
www.sushiteri.com
We like the Japanese-country feeling of all the Sushi-Teri restaurants as well as the fair prices, especially at lunch. Tempura, fresh sushi, teriyaki, all the usual fare—and tempura green tea or red bean ice cream for dessert, too! With several locations—downtown, Carpinteria (970 Linden Ave., 805-745-1314), and Goleta (5745 Calle Real, 805-964-9909)—one should be near at hand.

MEXICAN

CAFE DEL SOL $$
30 Los Patos Way, Santa Barbara
(805) 969-3947
Cafe del Sol, in a pretty setting just across from the bird refuge, is an old Montecito favorite. Since 1965, this upscale Mexican eatery has attracted a loyal clientele of well-heeled locals who come here for the earthy ambience and friendly bar. You can dine on the sunny wraparound patio, in the evocative split-level dining room, or join the crowd of lively locals sipping cocktails at the bar.

Order up a bowl of fresh guacamole, then kick-start your meal with a margarita. The menu offers a wide range of options. The food is reasonably priced, and the restaurant is always humming with lively conversation. Cafe del Sol serves up lunch and dinner daily as well as Sunday brunch.

CARLITOS CAFE Y CANTINA $$
1324 State St., Santa Barbara
(805) 962-7117

The big brother of Cava (listed next), Carlitos Cafe y Cantina serves the same sort of upscale Mexican and Southwestern specialties as it's Montecito sibling. Fresh, homemade corn tortillas, carnes cooked over an open-fire grill, and fresh chiles and spices combine to make all of Carlitos' dishes a sensation.

Carlitos has a full bar, including a large selection of 100 percent Blue Agave tequilas with the requisite list of imaginative margaritas. Eat on the patio if it's a sunny day and enjoy the bubbling fountain and live entertainment that is offered nightly. This is a fun place to bring a group. Kids can keep busy with crayons at the table. Carlitos is open for lunch and dinner daily and for breakfast on Sun.

CAVA RESTAURANT AND BAR $$$
1212 Coast Village Rd., Montecito
(805) 969-8500
www.cavarestaurant.com

"Cava," the more sophisticated little brother of Carlitos Cafe y Cantina (see previous entry), dishes up creative Mexican and Spanish cuisine in a cozy spot on Coast Village Road. Choose a table on the small patio (there's a bit of traffic noise), or snuggle up inside, where a Santa Fe–style fireplace invites you to linger over cocktails. Your friendly waiter will bring a complimentary basket of chips and fabulous salsa (all salsas are made fresh every day) for dipping while you peruse the menu. Tip: Ask for the *quemada salsa*, a roasted pepper salsa, in addition to their zesty bean salsa. Entree portions are generous and are handcrafted with the bold flavors of Nuevo Latin cuisine. (All dishes are served with rice and beans.) Try the hearty posole soup or the Cava fajitas platter. For dessert, we loved the Besito de Cava, a chocolate torte with Patron XO coffee sauce and raspberry puree, topped with whipped cream. The restaurant is quite kid-friendly, with brown paper and crayons on the tables to keep little hands busy. Cava is open for lunch and dinner daily and also serves brunch on weekends.

LA SUPER-RICA TAQUERIA $
622 N. Milpas St., Santa Barbara
(805) 963-4940
No credit cards

This small, unassuming taco stand with a canopied patio serves up some of Santa Barbara's most popular Mexican cuisine. After earning a master's degree in Spanish linguistics at UCSB in the late 1970s, owner Isidoro Gonzalez decided to abandon academia and venture into the restaurant business. First, though, he went to Mexico to collect regional recipes from relatives and other chefs—recipes that still form the basis of his 20-item chalkboard menu.

When you place your order, you have a full view of the tiny kitchen, where you can watch the cooks roll out tortillas from fresh dough and toss sizzling steaks, chicken breasts, pork, and veggies onto the grill.

In addition to various tacos and quesadillas, Super-Rica serves up roasted pasilla chile stuffed with cheese and served with pork (the Super-Rica Especial), melted cheese with bacon cooked in Mexicanware (the Tocino Especial), and cup-shaped corn tortillas filled with chicken, cheese, and avocado (Sopes de Pollo). Drinks include sodas, Mexican beer, and horchata, a popular Mexican rice beverage. Thanks to rave reviews and glowing write-ups in *Sunset, the Los Angeles Times,* and other publications, Super-Rica has achieved widespread notoriety. During prime dining hours, the line of people waiting to order nearly always stretches out the door and down the street. Patio dining is humble, to say the least.

The restaurant is open Thurs to Tues for lunch and every night but Wed for dinner. Dine early or late if you want to avoid a 15-minute wait in the order line.

✳LOS AGAVES $–$$
600 N. Milpas St., Santa Barbara
(805) 564-2626
What's not to love about this bustling Mexican restaurant, beginning with the hardworking owner Carlos Luna, who seems to be permanently affixed to the counter where you order your food. This is our favorite Mexican food in town (and yes, La Super-Rica is just a few blocks away). The specialty of the house is the Molcajete—your choice of one meat or seafood, or go for "Sea and Earth": shrimp, chicken, and steak (or just one, if you prefer) served with Mexican cheese, green onions, avocado and homemade salsa in a traditional *molcajete,* the stone bowls used for grinding spices or making guacamole and salsas (like a mortar and pestle). But everything is excellent here, beginning with the fresh, hot chips and great selection of salsa at the salsa bar to the chiles rellenos and homemade *sopes* to the *rajas con queso* and homemade tamales,

all washed down with delicious homemade horchata, a traditional cinnamon rice drink. Got a hangover? *Menudo* is served on Sunday. Need we say more?

LOS ARROYOS $–$$
14 W. Figueroa St., Santa Barbara
(805) 962-5541
www.losarroyos.net
Good, reasonably priced, authentic Southern California–style Mexican food (the type that this author grew up on) that includes great chiles rellenos and reasonably priced combination plates that are popular with families as well as couples and solo diners. The Montecito location (1280 Coast Village Rd., 805-969-9059) often has lovely live music on the patio, and if you are on your own, there's an outdoor counter with stools offering a view of the action on Coast Village Road. Old-time Insiders affectionately know the area as the "Bermuda Triangle," as many a lass has been lost at night after too many cocktails across the street at Lucky's or perhaps even muchos margaritas here at Los Arroyos. Full bar.

RUDY'S $
305 W. Montecito St., Santa Barbara
(805) 899-3152
Rudy's is particularly famous for its great burritos, flautas, chimichangas, chiles rellenos, and tamales. It also has great burgers and some of the best *sopes* in town. It's a great place to stop for a quick lunch or dinner before a movie or to just call up and order takeout. Rudy's is open for lunch and dinner daily. The long list of Rudy's locations attests to the popularity of its food. Additional locations are at 811 State St., Santa Barbara (805-564-8677); 3613½ State St., Santa Barbara (805-563-2232); 5680 Calle Real, Goleta

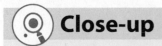

Close-up

The Locavore Movement

A fast-growing food trend has hit most of Santa Barbara's fine restaurants. Started by a group of affectionately nicknamed "locavares" in San Francisco (www.locavores .com), this concept involves eating only locally grown or harvested foods from within a 100-mile radius of your hometown. The values behind this trend are ones of health, conservation, and economics. If the produce hasn't been picked green and then spent days traveling across the United States, it retains more body-loving vitamins and minerals. Local produce doesn't carry the cost of bicoastal or international transportation, a cost we all know is growing bigger by the day. Buying local also supports the local agricultural economy and, in Santa Barbara, the fishing community, too.

Santa Barbara restaurant proprietors Mitchell Sjerven of Bouchon and John Downey of Downey's, as well as many other top chefs and restaurateurs, are dedicated to providing menus that are "freshly Santa Barbara." In Santa Barbara, their task is much easier than in most towns. Farmers' markets occur 6 days a week, fishermen bring the catch of the day in the harbor, and the Santa Ynez Valley is bursting at the seams with local wines.

It's not just restaurateurs that are trying to follow this trend. Many Insiders are dedicating themselves to eating local by visiting farmers' markets or by accessing the organic sections of many markets, such as Lazy Acres.

(805-681-0766); and 1001 Casitas Pass Rd., Carpinteria (805-684-7839).

MIDDLE EASTERN & GREEK

ZAYTOON $$
209 E. Canon Perdido, Santa Barbara
(805) 963-1293
www.zaytoon.com

Very popular with young and old hipsters alike, Zaytoon serves delicious Middle Eastern fare in the sedate dining room or on the patio that features not only outdoor fireplaces, but also hookahs for groups wanting to partake in an after-dinner group smoke. The vegetarian appetizer platter is big enough for two to share (you can make a meal of it), but the lamb kebab and other entrees are so tasty, you should forge ahead. The restaurant also has a very tasty Lebanese

red wine by the glass and a good selection of Santa Barbara County wines. The waitstaff is delightful. Open for dinner and lunch.

i Greek treat: Fridays only! Grab a house-made gyro from Metropolus (216 E. Yanonali St., Santa Barbara; 805-899-2300; www.metrofinefoods .com), a great specialty foods market and gourmet deli a bit off the beaten track, but not far from the waterfront beach and parks.

SPANISH

CADIZ $$
509 State St., Santa Barbara
(805) 770-2760

This lower State Street newcomer had tongues wagging from the moment it opened the

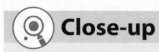

Close-up

Sweet Tooth Delights

If you find yourself hankering for a little sugar fix, we've got the cure. Locally made ice cream (including organic and flavors like strawberry sourced from local organic farmers), artisan chocolates, and the ever-popular cupcake are close at hand.

One of the most whimsical spots is **Whodelicious.** Here Dr. Seuss meets Willy Wonka in this fun paean to the cupcake. Located at 811 State St., Santa Barbara, (805) 966-2253 in the Paseo Nuevo shopping mall. For more information go to www .whodelicious.com.

La Bella Rosa Bakery, 1411 San Andreas St., Santa Barbara, (805) 966-9660. Try the traditional Mexican pastries (*elostito, chilindrina,* and *bigote*) or cupcakes or delicioso tres leches cake. You can also pick up tamales or masa (corn meal dough to make tamales) or grab a *torta* (tri-tip sandwich) for the hungry, non–sweet tooth in your crowd. Amazing hours: Mon through Sat 5:30 a.m. to 8 p.m., Sun 5:30 a.m. to 2 p.m.

Crushcakes & Cafe, 1315 Anacapa St., Santa Barbara, (805) 963-3752, and 4945 Carpinteria Ave., Carpintera, (805) 684-4300, www.crushcakes.com. Organic and gluten-free cupcakes, also serves breakfast all day. The vegetable goat-cheese muffins (not too sweet) are our fav.

Jeannine's Bakery is popular for their lemon bars, low-fat strawberry scones, and delicious cakes that are a favorite with locals for special occasions. Four locations: 1253 Coast Village Rd., Montecito, (805) 969-7878; downtown: 15 E. Figueroa St., Santa Barbara, (805) 687-8701; upper State: 3607 State St., Santa Barbara, (805) 687-8701.

The best croissants for miles around (including chocolate-filled and almond varieties), in addition to éclairs, a dozen flavors of macaroons, and other French pastries can be found at **Renaud's Patesserie & Bistro.** Be sure to try their long cinnamon-hazelnut twists (which we are especially fond of). For those of us who need more sustenance between macaroons, breakfast or lunch is offered at either of the two locations in Santa Barbara. Uptown: Loreto Plaza at 3315 State St., (805) 569-2400; Downtown: Arlington Plaza at 1324 State St., (805) 892-2800. Visit them online at www.renaudsbakery.com.

doors in the spring of 2011. The stunning Moroccan/Spanish–style interior is dimly lit, has an inviting bar, patio tables facing State Street, and music (too loud for this diner's taste), making this the new hip dining spot of the year. Small tasty tapas and main dishes are artfully prepared by Chef John Petitt (formerly of the Wine Cask and Seagrass, where he received a 29 out of 30 rating from Zagat).

Favorite tapa dishes include the flash-cooked alpine salmon and the shaved-artichoke salad with an anchovy dressing; the saffron risotto tapa is also loved among foodies. Many ingredients are sourced from the farmers' market, which occurs right out front on Tuesday afternoon and evening. Prices seem reasonable but can add up quickly, especially if you order one of the $15 specialty cocktail drinks such

For decades, **McConnell's Ice Cream** (201 W. Mission St., Santa Barbara; 805-569-2323; www.mcconnells.com) was the only game in town, and the company's reputation has spread far and wide ever since they were founded in 1949. With one store on the Westside for fresh scoops, pints, and sundaes, their scrape-the-butter-off-the-roof-of-your mouth concoctions (a rich 17 percent milk fat) makes McConnell's some of the richest, densest commercially available ice creams. Flavors include all the usual suspects, plus favs like island coconut, macadamia nut, chocolate burnt almond, and Elberta peach, but the Mission Street store also has frozen yogurt in flavors like maple sugar and strawberry tart. Pints are also sold to grocery stores up and down the California coast, including Vons, Gelson's Super Market, Whole Foods Market, Bristol Farms, and many other places. In recent years, several very fine ice cream and gelato purveyors have joined the scene.

Spoon (1222 State St.; 805-962-1838) is one of our favorite stops for a cold, sweet treat. Friendly, cheerful owner Erin Casey is generous with tasting samples, and we think this is the best gelato in town. Conveniently located near the Granada Theatre (perfect top-off to a concert) and not far from the Arlington, this tiny, friendly, no-frills gelato shop will gladly let you taste before settling on one, or two, or maybe even three flavors.

Rori's Artisanal Creamery makes some amazing organic ice cream, and the flavors are stupendous. Choose from serious dark chocolate (72 percent), creamy vanilla bean, Stumptown espresso, NY strawberry cheesecake (with graham cracker–crust garnish), malted milk ball (a fav), salted caramel, root beer float, peanut butter and jelly, lemon curd (with poppy seed garnish), milk chocolate chunk, fresh mint patty, and Roman's Dairy-Free Chocolate Coconut. Available at, Gelson's Market, Jeannine's on Figueroa, Simply Pies, Lazy Acres, Whole Foods and GardenMarket on Santa Claus Lane. In Los Olivos, Los Olivos Grocery carries Rori's.

Here's the Scoop (1187 Coast Village Rd., Montecito; 805-969-7020) was one of the first not only to bring gelato to our 'hood but to make their own using ingredients from some of our favorite farmers, like Tom Shepard's organic strawberry flavor. Sample the pistachio, Savannah honey with almonds, and panna cotta with caramel cream, but the sorbets—like mango—rock. Yum. What more can we say?

as the Palermo (similar to a manhattan but with vanilla-pod twist added). Open for lunch, happy hour, and dinner Tues through Sun.

THAI

YOUR CHOICE   **$$**
3404 State St., Santa Barbara
(805) 569-3730
www.yourchoicethairestaurant.com

Your Choice is a favorite uptown Thai restaurant. The spacious, contemporary dining room is always filled with the alluring aromas of coconut, lemongrass, and other savory Thai ingredients. The long menu features all sorts of appetizers, soups, salads, curries, seafood, beef, chicken, noodle, and rice dishes (the pad thai and the hot-and-sour soups are fantastic). Your Choice serves dinner every day and lunch Tues through Sun.

YOUR PLACE $$
22-A N. Milpas St., Santa Barbara
(805) 966-5151, (805) 965-9397

Your Place is Santa Barbara's oldest Thai restaurant, and it's regularly voted the best Thai restaurant in town in local polls. The kitschy dining room is a treat in itself—you can gaze at the giant fish tank and the authentic Thai decorations while feasting on mouthwatering plates of exotic foods. Choose from more than 200 authentic Thai dishes, from satay and panang curry to coconut ice cream.

The restaurant sits right on Milpas Street, just a few blocks north of the freeway. It's open for lunch and dinner Tues through Sun (closed Mon).

ZEN YAI $$
425 State St., Santa Barbara
(805) 957-1193

For Thai food with gourmet flair, Zen Yai delivers. The atmosphere is different than any other Thai places in town: dark, sultry, and hip. Favorite dishes include pumpkin curry, noodle dishes, and seafood soups and entrees. Open for lunch and dinner; lunch served Tues through Fri, dinner Tues through Sun. Closed Mon.

THE BLUE OWL AT ZEN YAI $
425 State St., Santa Barbara
(805) 705-0991

The spot opens for late night/after-hours barhoppers and night owls in need of some noshing; the Blue Owl at Zen Yai has different ownership but the same location as the main Zen Yai. Dishes served from 11:30 p.m. until 2:30 a.m. include steam buns brushed in duck fat then grilled, short-rib fried rice, Thai basil cheeseburgers, and red curry shrimp rolls. The Blue Owl tri-tip sandwich, with pickled veggies and oyster-chili mayo

on a grilled crusty roll, is the top seller. Open Thurs through Sat.

VEGETARIAN & VEGAN FARE

THE NATURAL CAFE $
508 State St., Santa Barbara
(805) 962-9494
www.thenaturalcafe.com

The Natural Cafe serves up great-tasting health food for vegetarians and health-conscious carnivores alike (you won't find red meat here, just turkey and chicken). In past local polls, the cafe scored awards for best veggie burger and best health food. Pick a table, scan the extensive menu, and line up at the cash register to order your meal. When it's ready, one of the super-friendly, helpful staffers will deliver it to your table. There's something for everyone here: fish, chicken, pasta, vegetarian entrees, a kids' menu, a complete juice bar, beer, local wines, and desserts. Additional locations are at 361 Hitchcock Way, Santa Barbara (805-563-1163), and 5892 Hollister Ave., Goleta (805-692-2363). All locations of the Natural Cafe are open for lunch and dinner every day.

SOJOURNER $
134 E. Canon Perdido St.
Santa Barbara
(805) 965-7922
www.sojournercafe.com

Voted "Best Spot to Dine Alone" in past local newspaper polls, Sojourner has served up natural food in a cozy, relaxed setting since 1978. It's a stone's throw from the Old Presidio (across the street), just 2 blocks east of State Street. The menu includes mostly vegetarian dishes: soups, sandwiches, salads, pastas, polenta cakes, crispy tofu and onions, vegetarian stir-fry, and lasagna. The desserts are excellent: Berry cobblers in the summer (go ahead—add a scoop of ice cream) and the daily vegan cookie are popular favorites.

For a protein pickup, try the Sojburger, a vegetarian protein patty with melted cheese, guacamole, sour cream, and sprouts. Beverages to complement your meal include juices, smoothies, chai, Yogi tea, and vegan shakes. Sojourner also has an espresso bar and serves beer and local wines. The "Soj" is open daily for lunch and dinner.

i Would you like to "get fresh" on the American Riveria? Ask for the complimentary culinary travel planner, *Sip and Savor,* highlighting Santa Barbara County's culinary attractions, cooking classes, and locally grown produce. Call (800) 676-1266 or log on to www.santabarbarafresh.com to order yours.

SPIRITLAND BISTRO $$
230 E. Victoria St., Santa Barbara
(805) 966-7759
www.spiritlandbistro.com
This small restaurant maximizes its limited space with its big sophistication. Crisp yellow linens on carefully laid-out tables and an attentive, if not slightly flirtatious, waitstaff create an ambience of elegance that bespeaks a four-star restaurant rather than

one that claims offerings of organic global cuisine. Chef Jessica Hsian's mantra is "Creative, flavorful, and pure," and she hits the note just right with offerings of authentic ethnic cuisine. Try the Asian five-spice and sesame-crusted organic free-range chicken, the Hawaiian macadamia nut–crusted sea bass, or the vegan Greek moussaka. The smells alone will send you around the world. Of special note: If you're allergic to milk or wheat or a practicing vegan, Spiritland Bistro has a meal for you, which is often not the case when people with special dietary needs are dining out.

VIETNAMESE

SAIGON $–$$
318 N. Milpas, Santa Barbara
(805) 966-0916
Everything we've had here has been super tasty, from the soups to spring rolls, the delicious curries, pho, and even Vietnamese sandwiches on a baguette if you ask. There are three locations—the original on Milpas; downtown (1230 State St., 805-966-0909); and uptown in Five Points Plaza (3897 State St., 805-964-0909). Vegetarian menu offers soy meat and tofu options. Good for takeout if you prefer quiet dining to rather large, open, noisy cafeteria-like settings. Lunch and dinner 7 days a week.

NIGHTLIFE

When the sun goes down, Santa Barbara nightlife ignites. The afterglow from spending a day at the beach or on the water converts to social energy—and you'll discover most of it centered between Stearns Wharf and the 1300 block of State Street. Even people who live in Goleta, Carpinteria, and Montecito head for downtown Santa Barbara just to be at the heart of the action.

Most dance clubs and bars catering to the younger crowd are located between the 300 and 600 blocks of State Street. As you walk north from there and approach the "arts and culture district" that extends to the 1300 block, you'll find more restaurants, a few bars, theaters, and coffeehouses along the way. Santa Barbara's cultural events calendar is busy every month of the year (see the Arts chapter for a broad overview of your many choices).

OVERVIEW

In this chapter we've included some of the most popular nightspots in the area. We begin with our favorite bars by geographic area. Then we list a few places according to their specialties: sports bars, dance clubs, billiards, coffeehouses, and movie theaters.

BARS & LOUNGES

Downtown/Beachside Santa Barbara

BARRA LOS ARCOS
Doubletree Hotel
633 E. Cabrillo Blvd., Santa Barbara
(805) 564-4333
www.fpdtr.com
The Doubletree is one of Santa Barbara's tourist and convention hotels, and its Barra Los Arcos matches the casual, yet sophisticated character of the rest of the hotel. The bar offers a full range of drinks and light music. Many hotel guests come to this soothing spot to wind down after a busy day of sightseeing or business meetings.

BISTRO ELEVEN ELEVEN
Hyatt Santa Barbara
1111 E. Cabrillo Blvd., Santa Barbara
(805) 730-1111
Bistro Eleven Eleven is a casual-to-slightly-dressy restaurant and bar at the Hyatt Santa Barbara (formerly the Mar Monte). You can dine and sip locally brewed beer while watching the sunset over the Pacific. Happy hour is 5 to 7 p.m. seven days a week.

✳BLUE AGAVE
20 E. Cota St., Santa Barbara
(805) 899-4694
www.blueagavesb.com

We've noticed more than a few Hollywood celebrities popping into this small, 2-story restaurant/bar with soft lights, contemporary decor, and a romantically hip ambience. This is a great spot to take a first date. On weekends the place is packed with chic singles and couples in their late 20s, 30s, and 40s. You can choose from various types of margaritas (Blue Agave has an extensive tequila selection) as well as excellent martinis. If you don't like standing, we suggest you go early for dinner—especially if you have a date—so you can snuggle up in one of the coveted booths or on a cozy couch by the fireplace upstairs.

i To find out what's happening on any given night, check the "Pop, Rock & Jazz" or "The Week" sections of the *Santa Barbara Independent* (a free weekly paper that comes out on Thursday) or *Scene* magazine in the *Santa Barbara News-Press* (included in the Friday edition).

CADIZ
509 State Street, Santa Barbara
(805) 770-2760
www.cadizsb.com

This newcomer is a lively "oasis" due to the Spanish/Moroccan–style interior. Serving tapas and entrees, you can cozy up to the bar or sink into the large lounge-seat section in the back of the restaurant if you are a big groups. Open until 1:30 a.m. on the weekends. Happy hour is 5 to 6:30 p.m. Tuesday through Friday (closed Mon). All tapas are $7 each; select wines, including a sparkling Spanish cava by the glass are $5; specialty cocktails that are usually $12 to $10 are $7 during happy hour. Beers are $3 to $5.

DARGAN'S IRISH PUB & RESTAURANT
18 E. Ortega, Santa Barbara
(805) 568-0702
www.dargans.com

Owned and run by some affable Irishmen, this bright, cheery, traditional Irish pub is one of our favorite bars in Santa Barbara. You can wander in here any night of the week and usually find a lively crowd chatting over a few pints and shooting some pool. We've also noticed people pouring in here after special events. This is the kind of place where anyone can wander in and feel perfectly comfortable; where the classic, foot-tappin' tunes are loud enough to enliven the crowd but not so loud that they drown out conversation. You can come here and play a game of darts with your buds, kick back with a Guinness stout by the fireplace, and warm your belly with some hearty Irish stew. For easy access to Dargan's, park in Lot 10 on East Ortega.

EL PASEO RESTAURANT
10 El Paseo, Santa Barbara
(805) 962-6050
www.elpaseorestaurant.com

In a historic building originally constructed in 1827 by one of Santa Barbara's founding fathers, El Paseo scores our vote as one of the most evocative spots to sip a margarita. The restaurant and bar are drenched in the spirit of Santa Barbara's Old Spanish Days, and the place gets packed during Fiesta with locals who come here to crack confetti-filled *cascarones* and dance on the tables. On warm summer evenings, the retractable roof rolls back, and romance hangs heavy in the air. Settle down in a high-back chair by the fountain, slurp some margaritas under the stars, and you'll be howling at the moon in no time. Happy hour is Mon through Fri from

4 to 6 p.m. Appetizers are half off (they used to be free in the good ol' days).

ℹ️ If you've overindulged, call Rose Cab (805-564-2600), Yellow Cab (805-964-1111), or Gold Cab (805-685-9797).

INTERMEZZO
813 Anacapa St., Santa Barbara
(805) 966-9463
www.winecask.com

The acclaimed Wine Cask Restaurant (which has a more upper-crust ambience) opened this relaxed, next-door bistro in 1997. It caters to the late-night crowd and offers bistro-style dining, a full bar, and fine cigars, which you can smoke on the patio. This is the type of place you go to before or after a concert or theater performance. Order a gourmet cheese platter or tasty flatbread, curl up on a leather couch, and sip a port by the crackling fire. Great wines from the "on tap" wine system—no corks, no bottles, but reusable kegs. Open nightly from 4 p.m.

THE JAMES JOYCE
513 State St., Santa Barbara
(805) 962-2688
www.jamesjoyce.com

In this cozy bar, you can order a pint of Guinness just as Joyce's Bloom would have done in 1904 Dublin. The James Joyce is a very popular, traditional Irish pub with a stone fireplace and a good selection of Irish whiskeys, single-malt scotches, and cigars. It serves up a heartwarming Irish coffee, too. Come here to shoot some pool, spark up the jukebox, play darts, or relax and chat with your buddies. The James Joyce also hosts live Dixieland jazz provided by the popular

Ulysses Jasz band some nights of the week as well as karaoke nights. Call for details.

JOE'S CAFE
536 State St., Santa Barbara
(805) 966-4638
www.joescafesb.com

Joe's has been around forever (since 1928) and is said to be the longest running restaurant and bar in Santa Barbara. As a restaurant, it delivers mom-and-pop-style steak, seafood, and Italian meals to your table. The bar, however, is another animal. The bartenders are known to pour the strongest cocktails in town, so the bar is nearly always packed. Joe's is also a popular meeting place for native Santa Barbarans who come here to catch up with old friends, spin some tunes on the jukebox, and prime themselves for a night on the town.

MILK AND HONEY
30 W. Anapamu St., Santa Barbara
(805) 275-4232
www.milknhoneytapas.com

This tapas bar (small bites) provides a tasty start for your night on the town. Though a bit pricier than other bars, Milk and Honey's cocktails are worth the cost. The lounge's modern, sultry decor is seductively inviting. Vintage black-and-white cartoons are screened above the bar, and rotating artwork lines the walls. They make a mean mojito and are open until midnight.

THE PRESS ROOM
15 E. Ortega St., Santa Barbara
(805) 963-8121
www.pressroomsb.com

The Press Room, named for its location next to the *News-Press* building, is where local bartenders head as soon as they're off work.

This small, cozy Brit-owned bar has a European feel and a great selection of beers. You'll find more than a dozen brews on tap here, including Guinness and West Bombardier. Best of all, the Press Room opens at all hours of the morning for big international football matches. It's popular with locals and foreigners and a great little spot to chat about sports

ROY
7 W. Carrillo St., Santa Barbara
(805) 966-5636
www.restaurantroy.com

Roy is one of the few downtown restaurants that serves meals late in the evening (until midnight). It also offers late-night entertainment occasionally, featuring original compositions by folk, jazz, rock, and blues musicians. The food is delicious and inexpensive. Drinks are a bit less of a deal, but they're still affordable. Roy has a full bar, beer, wine, and coffee. Get here early if you plan to eat on the weekend.

SOHO
1221 State St., Santa Barbara
(805) 962-7776
www.sohosb.com

If you enjoy live music and want to get away from the hustle and bustle of lower State Street, chances are you'll love SOhO. Buzzing with a mainly 30-something crowd, SOhO is a casual restaurant serving California cuisine and a loft-style bar up on the second floor of the Victoria Court shopping arcade. The site is ideal for all types of performances and dancing, with high ceilings, rows of windows, red brick walls (like those in a Soho loft), and an outdoor patio/deck. Live music fills the restaurant every night of the week. The musical variety ranges from blues, jazz, folk, funk, and reggae to rhythm and

blues and rock 'n' roll. Many of the bands and entertainers are local talent.

The music usually starts at 7:30 or 8 p.m. during the week, and on Monday night you can enjoy live jazz from 6 to 10 p.m. The Santa Barbara Jazz Society also holds events here on Sunday afternoons (check the SOhO schedule for info). Weekend nights heat up with dance music. If you want to make sure to get a good seat (or any seat at all when popular bands are playing), we suggest you eat dinner here first, but food is not the motivating factor for a trip to SOhO.

VELVET JONES
423 State Street, Santa Barbara
(805) 965-8676
www.velvet-jones.com

Velvet Jones is a smaller live-music destination that's worth checking out. One of the more intimate venues, Velvet Jones is still large enough to pack a crowd when big acts perform. Genres of bands vary from metal to pop and nearly everything in between. There's a comedy night most Tuesdays as well.

Wine with a View

Go ahead and feel like a millionaire aboard your sleek yacht: Grab a spot at a small table on the deck overlooking the Pacific at **Deep Sea Tasting Room** (805-618-1185; www.deepseawines.com), located on the second-story structure on the east side of Stearns Wharf. Try a flight or go for a glass of your favorite juice of the grape and watch the sunset over the sea. You might just think you're on your way to the South Pacific. Open 7 days a week from noon to 8 p.m.

WILDCAT LOUNGE
15 W. Ortega St., Santa Barbara
(805) 962-7970
www.wildcatlounge.com
This old locals' favorite still attracts a flock of artsy college grads and hip 20-somethings. The dimly lit '50s decor is saturated in deep red and black, with a few prized plush booths and a spacious smoking patio out back. You can also play pool, but you need to get here early to score a coveted table. Call for a schedule of events, which usually includes live local and national touring acts and social nights with various drink specials. Every Sunday is Gay Night, and some Sunday nights even feature a drag show. Call for details.

Midtown/Upper State Street Area

HARRY'S PLAZA CAFE
3313B State St., Santa Barbara
(805) 687-7910
www.harryssb.com
Everyone's wild about Harry's, an uptown version of downtown Joe's—a traditional, family-style restaurant with big booths and long tables. Like Joe's, it's a Santa Barbara institution. It's always lively and packed with locals, mostly age 30 and older. Be forewarned: The bartenders serve very strong drinks that pack a mighty punch.

Goleta

BEACHSIDE BAR-CAFE
5905 Sandspit Rd., Goleta
(805) 964-7881
www.beachside-barcafe.com
In a superb seaside location on Goleta Beach, this is a perfect spot for sunset drinks. Order up some oysters at the raw bar, relax in the contemporary dining room, or pick a popular spot on the glass-enclosed patio and lose yourself in the ocean views. Heat lamps and a well-stoked fire will keep you warm when the sea breeze picks up. The wine list spotlights local bottles, and the full bar has beers on tap and specializes in tropical cocktails. After your drinks, you can cap off the evening with a romantic, moonlit stroll along the pier. Come early on weekends, or you may have to wait.

The dress code—no shirt, no shoes, no service—is enforced.

To get here, take US 101 to the UCSB off-ramp (CA 217) and drive for about a mile to the Sandspit Road exit. Go left, then turn right into the Goleta Beach parking lot and veer left—you can't miss it.

ELEPHANT BAR
521 Firestone Rd., Goleta
(805) 964-0779
www.elephantbar.com
Elephant Bar is a lively, safari-style restaurant just off Hollister Avenue near the airport. It serves a varied menu for lunch and dinner, but at night most people come here for the action-packed bar scene and the jumbo-size drinks, like the African Queen Martini and the Jungle Colada.

MERCURY LOUNGE
5871 Hollister Ave., Goleta
(805) 967-0907
Warm, welcoming, and casual, this neighborhood retro '50s lounge is a local favorite. The Mercury serves a great range of beers and wines, including microbrews and imports. The affable owner will also let you bring in food from nearby restaurants. You can hang out and play pool, sip a cold beer on the outdoor patio, and meet some of the loyal regulars.

OLD TOWN TAVERN
261 Orange Ave., Goleta
(805) 967-2403
This lively karaoke bar is one of the popular spots for college students, especially on Wednesday nights. All levels of singing are welcome (you can be an off-key chanteuse, but as long as you appear to be enjoying yourself, the audience will love you). Step right up, as most patron are too busy dancing, playing pool, or chatting and drinking to pay much attention to any vocal gaffs.

Montecito

＊LUCKY'S
1270 Coast Village Rd., Montecito
(805) 565-7540
www.luckys-steakhouse.com
Owned by the founder of Lucky Brand jeans, this swank cocktail bar and steak house on affluent Coast Village Road draws an upper-crust crowd of chic, well-coiffed folks and moneyed Montecitans. Just look for the parade of posh cars at the valet parking. Its name speaks for itself. You can perch at the sleek bar, sip a Cosmopolitan, and gaze at the old black-and-white photos of movie stars on the walls. Lucky's has its own wine cellar and plasma TV for sporting events.

TY LOUNGE
1260 Channel Dr., Montecito
(805) 969-2261
www.fourseasons.com/santabarbara
The Ty Lounge at the posh Four Seasons Resort The Biltmore Santa Barbara is popular with locals as well as hotel guests. Known for the cozy fireplace in winter and popular outdoor seating for summer cocktails with a sunset view, the bar has given up on live bands and now provides a DJ on most Friday and Saturday nights throughout the

year. Light fare can be ordered, and specialty cocktails and wines by the glass are on the menu.

Carpinteria

CORK TREE CELLARS WINE BAR & BISTRO
910 Linden Ave., Carpinteria
(805) 684-1400
Great wines by the glass and a totally fun wine flight served on a wooden board—and you get to vote for your favorite. Stay for dinner as well; the food is good and reasonably priced. It's fun on Thursday afternoon/evening farmers' market day in Carp to sit outdoors and watch the action on the street.

THE PALMS
701 Linden Ave., Carpinteria
(805) 684-3811
www.thepalmsrestaurant.com
The casual Palms restaurant has long held the title of Carpinteria's main local hangout. The cocktail lounge brings in live music Friday and Saturday. Expect anything from rock 'n' roll and country music to covers of classic '60s and '70s tunes. Try the popular Tim's Titanic cocktail with Malibu rum and Midori, and if you feel like dancing, just get up and boogie on the large dance floor.

SLY'S
686 Linden Ave., Carpinteria
(805) 684-6666
When James Sly, the longtime chef at Lucky's in Montecito, decided to open his own high-end steak house in the town of Carpinteria, he knew that a bar and bar–dining area were de rigueur. Even if you can't afford dinner here, pop in for a predinner cocktail while waiting for your reservation at other nearby restaurants such as Giovanni's or the Siam

Elephant Thai Restaurant. Mrs. Lemon Jelly, a local restaurant blogger, thinks they make the best cocktails in Santa Barbara.

Summerland

THE NUGGET
2315 Lillie Ave., Summerland
(805) 969-6135

Saddle up to the long bar in this eatery where everyone is friendly. The Nugget has hosted everyone from local billionaires to Presidents Bill Clinton and Ronald Reagan. The cowboy atmosphere and their spicy Bloody Marys are legendary. Monday nights are popular with the Montecito crowd who like to "slum it" and kick "off" their heels, so to speak, over martinis and burgers. Best french fries in town.

i   Need an affordable designated driver? Bill's Bus (805-284-BILL; www.billsbus.com) transports college students between Isla Vista and downtown Santa Barbara Tues, Thurs, Fri, and Sat from 8:30 p.m. until 2 a.m. Call or check the website for details.

Up the Mountain

COLD SPRING TAVERN
5955 Stagecoach Rd., Santa Barbara
(805) 967-0066
www.coldspringtavern.com

For a real adventure, drive up CA 154 about 20 minutes from Santa Barbara to Cold Spring Tavern. The rustic 1865 cabin in the woods was once a stop on the main stagecoach route. Today it offers excellent food (fish, game, pastas, chili, and steaks), as well as a range of wines, beers, and mixed drinks. You'll always find a colorful crowd

here—everyone from bikers and ranchers to wine-tasting tourists. The tavern has live music Friday, Saturday, and Sunday (afternoons or evenings; check the schedule). A tip: Designate a driver when you go here—CA 154 has only two lanes in most places and is very curvy.

SPORTS BARS & BREWPUBS

O'MALLEY'S
523 State St., Santa Barbara
(805) 564-8904

O'Malley's has been around for ages. It's in the heart of the downtown bar district and flaunts the requisite overhead TVs and sports memorabilia on the walls. This is the kind of boozy bar blaring loud rock where you can dress down and play up (and check the score of your big game if you can muster the concentration). If you want a quieter spot to sit and chat, head upstairs to the cozy lounge. A DJ spins tunes usually Thursday, Friday, and Saturday nights.

SANTA BARBARA BREWING COMPANY
501 State St., Santa Barbara
(805) 730-1040
www.sbbrewco.com

The bright and cheery "BrewCo" is the only combination microbrewery/restaurant in Santa Barbara County. It's a classy, American-style brewpub with 10 large TVs in the front room and 13 in the back, broadcasting all major college and professional sporting events. Locals and travelers of all ages come here to meet with friends and drink fresh-brewed beer while watching the big game. This is also a great spot for a casual lunch any day of the week. You can wash down some hearty traditional American fare with a variety of homemade ales and lagers, such

Craft Beer Craze

Beer has taken a step or two up the social ladder. Local brewers carefully concoct the perfect balances of flavors, textures, styles, and finishes right on their premises, and you can drop in for a tasting.

- **Island Brewing Company,** 5049 6th St., Carpinteria; (805) 745-8272; www.islandbrewingcompany.com
- **Telegraph Brewery,** 416 N. Salsipuedes St., (805) 963-5018, www.telegraphbrewing.com
- **Corks n' Crowns,** 32 Anacapa St. (805) 845-8600; www.corksandcrowns.com
- **Union Ale,** 214 State St.; (805) 845-8243; www.unionale.com
- **The Brewhouse,** 229 W. Montecito St.; (805) 884-4664; www.brewhousesb.com
- **Santa Barbara Brewing Company,** 501 State St.; (805) 730-1040; www.sbbrewco.com
- **Hollister Brewing Company** 6980 Marketplace Dr.; (805) 968-2810; www.hollisterbrewco.com
- **Firestone-Walker Brewery's Taproom Restaurant** 620 McMurray Rd.; (805) 686-1557; www.firestonewalker.com

as Santa Barbara Blonde, Rincon Red, Pacific Pale Ale, and State Street Stout.

DANCE CLUBS

EOS
500 E. Anacapa St., Santa Barbara
(805) 564-2410
www.eoslounge.com
Pulling off a balmy, Mediterranean feel with lots of room to dance or hang out on the outdoor patio, Eos club is right off of State Street but easy to spot thanks to their signature spotlight on the exterior wall. Dance the night away and then sign up for the Eos wine tour as well.

THE SAND BAR
514 State St., Santa Barbara
(805) 966-1388
www.sandbarsb.com
The Sand Bar is a casual restaurant, bar, and dance spot with a beach theme. You can sit indoors or on the lush outdoor patio and dance until you drop—or until the bar closes. Live reggae jams on Tuesday nights, and other nights it's funk, jazz, or blues. Happy hour is 4 to 7 p.m. Tues through Sun.

TONIC
634 State St., Santa Barbara
(805) 897-1800
www.tonicsb.com
Tonic doesn't have the most inspiring outside appearance (during the day you'll likely

walk past it without realizing), but once inside it is easy to get into the party mood with one of the larger dance floors and sound systems in Santa Barbara. Less lounge and more bar/dance club, Tonic has a few coveted booths inside and on the large outdoor patio and bar where you can take a break from all that dancing to catch your breath under the stars.

WILDCAT LOUNGE
15 W. Ortega St., Santa Barbara
(805) 962-7970
www.wildcatlounge.com
Wildcat has a good-size dance floor and DJs spinning tunes almost every night, as well as live local and national touring acts and social nights with various drink specials; Sunday is Gay Night. This locals' favorite still attracts a flock of artsy college grads and hip 20-somethings, including Santa Barbara native Katy Perry when in she's in town. The dimly lit '50s decor is saturated in deep red and black, with a few plush booths and a spacious smoking patio out back. You can also play pool, but you need to get here early to score the coveted pool table.

BILLIARDS

DON Q FAMILY BILLIARD CENTER
1128 Chapala St., Santa Barbara
(805) 966-0915
Don Q is Santa Barbara's largest pool hall. It attracts billiards fans of all ages and serves beer to players 21 and older, as well as chips and sodas. Kids can play with video and pinball games if they don't want to play pool. Don Q has a room full of excellent tables, including tournament and carom tables. Open from noon to 2 a.m. every day.

ZODO'S BOWLING & BEYOND
5925 Calle Real, Goleta
(805) 967-0128
zodos.com
Besides the bowling, Zodo's is probably the most-happening place to go on Wednesday's College Night, as well as other nights of the week. Besides a fun night bowling with friends or family, enjoy Zodo's fully stocked bar, food menu, and happy hour.

COFFEEHOUSES

Santa Barbara has a thriving coffeehouse culture. Cafes serve as the main social hubs for many locals seeking alternatives to the bar scene. It's easy to find Starbucks, Peet's, and other chain coffee shops: They're strategically located up and down State Street as well as in Montecito and Carpinteria. Summerland has a locally owned hangout.

✳CAFE LUNA
2354 Lillie Ave., Summerland
(805) 695-8780
This popular neighborhood coffeehouse in Summerland serves great specialty coffee drinks and croissants from Renaud's (best French bakery in town) and offers free wireless Internet amid friendly patrons and hosts. It also serves simple lunch dishes, and you might even spot actor Billy Baldwin, a regular. Cafe Luna fires up the outdoor wood-buring pizza oven Thurs through Sun evenings, has live music on the weekends, and serve wines by the glass.

CAFE ZOMA
918 State St., Santa Barbara
(805) 965-5593
One of the few cafes to have outdoor seating on the sunny side of the street, Cafe Zoma also

has plenty of seating and a stone fireplace. Offering pastries, sandwiches, soups, and salads, this cafe is a great place to stop, refill, and maybe do a little people-watching. The music is always low enough to have a conversation, and they offer free wireless Internet.

CAJE
948 Embarcadero del Norte, Isla Vista
(805) 845-4612
If you are in the college town of Isla Vista, checking out the UCSB campus, stop in at this cafe. CAJE serves fresh fruit smoothies, teas, espresso, and coffee drinks in a modern "chill" setting. Outdoor seating, with patio heaters for chilly days, makes it the perfect spot in IV to do your homework or check e-mail (they have free wireless Internet).

COFFEE CAT
1201 Anacapa St., Santa Barbara
(805) 962-7164
The Coffee Cat is where you'll likely find wannabe screenwriters (or students doing their homework perhaps) hogging the coveted booths near the windows while writing their great American novel. Also, due to Coffee Cat's location across from the Santa Barbara County Courthouse and county administration buildings, the suits are known to grab their java jolt here. Coffee Cat offers a good, no-rush atmosphere and comfortable seating options, as well as smoothies and other noshes.

THE FRENCH PRESS
1101 State St., Santa Barbara
(805) 963-2721
The French Press is a light and airy downtown cafe with a devoted local following, for good reason: This coffeehouse uses all fresh ingredients in their drinks and pastries,

and it also brews fair-traded coffee. Decor is simple and inviting, with indoor and outdoor seating.

SANTA BARBARA ROASTING COMPANY
321 Motor Way, Santa Barbara
(805) 962-0320
www.sbcoffee.com
Insiders call this large coffeehouse/coffee-roasting company and its sister store "RoCo." It reminds us of the cozy coffeehouses where we used to meet friends and pretend to study when we were in college. RoCo is usually open until 11 p.m. daily.

MOVIE THEATERS

Moviegoing is one of Santa Barbara's favorite pastimes. Every day of the week you can choose from a wide range of new-release films shown in the afternoons, evenings, and sometimes in the mornings as well. Metropolitan Theatres owns all the theaters in the Santa Barbara area. You can call the Metropolitan Theatres Movie Hotline (877-789-6684) or visit the website at www.metrotheatres.com for locations and showtime information for all the following cinemas. If a theater also has a direct number, we've listed it.

Santa Barbara

ARLINGTON CENTER FOR THE PERFORMING ARTS
1317 State St., Santa Barbara
(805) 963-4408

FIESTA 5
916 State St., Santa Barbara

METRO 4
618 State St., Santa Barbara

NIGHTLIFE

PASEO NUEVO
8 W. De la Guerra Place (in the Paseo
Nuevo Mall), Santa Barbara

PLAZA DE ORO
371 Hitchcock Way, Santa Barbara

RIVIERA THEATRE
2044 Alameda Padre Serra,
Santa Barbara

i Take a trip back in time at the West Winds Santa Barbara Drive-In movie theater. The audio comes through your FM radio, so there are no clunky speaker boxes to attach to your window. Call (805) 964-9050 or go to www.westwinddi.com for info. Located at 907 S. Kellogg Dr. in Goleta.

Goleta

CAMINO REAL CINEMAS
Camino Real Marketplace, Hollister
Avenue and Stork Road, Goleta

FAIRVIEW THEATRE
225 N. Fairview Ave., Goleta

SHOPPING

The Santa Barbara shopping scene has changed considerably over the years. With high rents on State Street, many locally owned boutiques and stores have given way to chains and out-of-town ownership. In this section, we have highlighted our unique locally owned businesses that provide great shopping experiences. We hope you will support them.

The area also has some fabulous antiques shopping. You'll find a concentration of stores in Summerland and Carpinteria brimming with treasures from the past.

Perhaps what best defines shopping in Santa Barbara is the experience itself. Strolling the sunny outdoor paseos amid palms and fountains, people-watching at a sidewalk cafe, and sampling luscious local fruits at our friendly farmers' markets are all part of the Santa Barbara shopping experience. It's a browser's paradise.

OVERVIEW

In this chapter, we first give you an overview of the region's main shopping areas. Then we take you on a brief tour of major shopping malls and arcades and share a list of home-grown stores that are unique to the area. Finally, we depart from our usual geographic listing format to point out a few of the most popular specialty stores by category—from bookstores to surf wear to women's clothing. All stores are open daily unless otherwise noted.

If you're on a mission, take this book with you to save time. Need help making a selection? Ask one of our friendly shopkeepers. Most love to chat with customers and are happy to point out one-of-a-kind treasures. Finally, a few words of advice before you head out: Pace yourself, make sure you take time to stop and enjoy the scenery, and buy something special so you'll remember Santa Barbara long after you return home. Happy shopping!

SHOPPING AREAS

Santa Barbara

For the quintessential Santa Barbara shopping experience, head downtown to **State Street.** You'll find most stores concentrated on or near lower State Street, between the beginning of State Street at Stearns Wharf and the 1400 block. Popular palm-lined **Paseo Nuevo Mall** (651 State St.), in the heart of the downtown shopping district, is a great place to start your shopping marathon. It's the largest outdoor mall in this area, parking is plentiful in the underground parking structure (enter from Chapala), and from here you can stroll up and down State Street, browsing as you go.

While you're wandering, keep an eye out for the hidden paseos, or brick-paved shopping arcades, tucked back off State Street. *Paseo* comes from the Spanish word for "passage," and these cobbled shopping corridors will lead you to some delightful locally owned specialty shops and courtyard cafes. **Historic El Paseo** lies across State Street from Paseo Nuevo and Victoria Court, and the charming **La Arcada Court** shopping arcades sit at the upper end of the district between the 1100 and 1200 blocks. You can read more about these paseos in the Shopping Malls & Arcades section. To access the State Street shopping district, park in any of the city lots along Anacapa and Chapala Streets. Before you head downtown, you might also want to check out the Santa Barbara Downtown Organization website at **www.santabarbaradowntown.com** for a list of shops and services in the area as well as printable maps of the downtown shopping district and parking lot locations.

On upper State Street, which starts at about the 3000 block and continues through the 4000 block, you'll find a long stretch of shops, services, and businesses. **La Cumbre Plaza,** another outdoor mall adorned with palms and fountains, is the main magnet in this area—it occupies the entire 3800 block of State Street.

You'll also find several strip malls here, as well as a few shopping centers anchored by supermarkets: **Five Points** (across from La Cumbre Plaza on the 3900 block of State Street), **Loreto Plaza** (at the intersection of Las Positas Road and State Street), and **Ralph's** (near the intersection of State Street and Alamar Avenue, between State and De la Vina Streets).

Goleta

Loads of stores, specialty shops, and services line both sides of **Calle Real** between Patterson and Fairview Avenues, considered the downtown area of Goleta. The main strip mall in the area is the remodeled **Calle Real Center,** with nearly 50 merchants. These include Patty Montana (unique women's clothing), gift shops, the wholesaler chain store Trader Joe's, and restaurants such as Outback Steakhouse. Parking is plentiful along the strip that fronts the stores.

The **Camino Real Marketplace**—the largest shopping mall and discount center on the South Coast—opened in 1999 at the intersection of Hollister Avenue and Storke Road. (See the Shopping Malls & Arcades section of this chapter for a detailed description.)

Montecito

The upscale shopping area of **Coast Village Road** lies parallel to US 101 between Hot Springs and Olive Mill Roads. You'll find a mix of galleries, high-end home stores, gift shops, and chic boutiques along here, as well as some popular restaurants. You can park in the designated lane fronting the stores. At the Hot Springs Road intersection, you'll find a large shopping center with a Vons grocery store and drugstore, a health food store, and other specialty shops.

Montecito Village, or what the locals call "the Upper Village" at the intersection of San Ysidro and East Valley Roads, is a collection of exclusive boutiques, specialty shops, antiques stores, restaurants, a fine jewelry store, a terrific bookstore, a grocery store, and the post office. Keep your eyes open if you're hoping to run into a film star or celebrity. Since many of them live nearby, this is where you're most likely to find one grabbing a cup of coffee, a newspaper, or a bite to eat, often at Pierre La Fond or Via Vai Restaurant. If you are lucky, you'll catch Jonathon Winters regaling folks at the local sandwich shop or see Oprah shopping.

(Q) Close-up

Santa Claus Lane

For more than half a century, people were greeted by an odd sight while passing through Carpinteria: a 22-foot Santa Claus atop a chimney, surrounded by a Christmas-themed spread of shops and eateries. This seemingly bizarre fixture was considered one of the most charming landmarks of Santa Barbara from 1950 until 2003, when the beloved Santa Claus of **Santa Claus Lane** was sadly (in many people's minds) relocated to Oxnard. In its prime, the papier-mâché statue sat above Santa's Candy Kitchen, which delighted families with all sorts of Christmas treats, from gingerbread cookies to peanut brittle. Children adored this icon, as well as other features of Santa Claus Lane, including the village train rides and shops like Santa's Toyland and Santa's Trading Post.

Santa Claus Lane has evolved into a wide array of shops and restaurants, like the **Garden Market** (3811 Santa Claus Ln., Carpinteria, 805-745-5505; www.thegardenmarkets .com), which serves fresh, organic food daily in a lovely garden setting amid flora and fountains. **The Artful Angler** (3817 Santa Claus Ln., Carpinteria, 805-566-5900; www .artfulangler.com), a full-service fly-fishing shop, carries everything for the avid fisherperson. The lane is also home to favorites like the **Padaro Beach Grill** (3765 Santa Claus Ln., Carpinteria) and **A-Frame Surf Shop** (3785 Santa Claus Ln., Carpinteria, 805-684-8803; www.aframesurf.com), as well as **SALT** (3717 Santa Claus Ln., Carpinteria, 805-684-1655), a great women's clothing and swimwear store.

Santa Claus Lane is known for its beach that lies just across the railroad tracks at the entrance (take care when crossing). When the tide is low, you can go for a stroll in either direction. Heading west along exclusive Padaro Lane beach, you can gaze at the mega-million-dollar beach houses that dot the coast, and you may even spot actor Kevin Costner surfing or walking the beach below his pad!

Carpinteria & Summerland

These two seaside enclaves south of Santa Barbara are best known for their quaint shops and friendly, small-town feel. Summerland is home to the popular **Bikini Factory** and **Indian Summers** boutique, and it's also a haven for antiques shopping. You'll find most of the stores concentrated along **Lillie Avenue** and **Ortega Hill Road,** and many are housed in colorful Victorian cottages. In Carpinteria you'll find some great surf shops, small boutiques, and local stores filled with antiques, collectibles, and gifts for the home and garden. Most shops are located in the business district, which consists of several blocks radiating south, east, and west from the intersection of Linden and Carpinteria Avenues. You'll also find a couple of strip malls off Casitas Pass Road, between US 101 and Carpinteria Avenue. Parking is usually plentiful and easy to find.

SHOPPING MALLS & ARCADES

Downtown

EL PASEO
800 block of State Street, Santa Barbara
Historic El Paseo was reportedly California's first shopping center. It was built in the

1920s on the site of a historic residence that belonged to one of Santa Barbara's original Spanish families. Stroll through the cool courtyards with their fountains, tiles, and wrought-iron gates, and you'll feel as though you're in an old Spanish village. Once a breathtaking locale of elite shops, El Paseo now comprises 2 restaurants, a bar-cafe, 2 wine tasting bars, an antiques store, 2 jewelry stores, and a plethora of investment firms and local business offices.

LA ARCADA COURT
1114 State St., Santa Barbara
www.laarcadasantabarbara.com
You'll know you're at the entrance to beautiful La Arcada Court when you see a giant clock on a pedestal in front of a broad, tiled walkway about a half block from the Museum of Art. The Spanish-Mediterranean ambience takes you back in time and makes you forget the hustle and bustle of adjacent State Street. Wander the cool paved corridors, and you'll find art galleries, specialty shops, and coffee shops. In fact, the arcade is somewhat of a gallery in itself. Whimsical sculptures and life-size bronzes provide fun photo opportunities, and the sounds of bubbling fountains fill the air. Visit the old-fashioned barbershop, or browse the stores for top-of-the-line children's clothing, consigned women's clothing, contemporary furniture, and one-of-a-kind gifts.

PASEO NUEVO
651 State St., Santa Barbara
(805) 963-7147
www.paseonuevoshopping.com
Pretty palm-lined Paseo Nuevo is the star of the Santa Barbara shopping scene. Built in 1990, this stunning outdoor mall occupies 2 full city blocks in the heart of downtown near many of the most popular restaurants, cafes, clubs, and bookstores. Palms, fountains, and tropical flowers adorn the brick-paved courtyards, where shoppers dine alfresco and stroll in the sunshine. Nordstrom and Macy's anchor the mall, and in between you'll find more than 50 shops and restaurants, a 5-screen movie theater, the Contemporary Arts Forum gallery, and the Center Stage Theater (see the Arts chapter for descriptions of the latter two). During the summer months and holiday seasons, you can enjoy live jazz, carolers, and other entertainment while you browse the shops.

Paseo Nuevo merchants include well-known chains (Victoria's Secret, Gap, Bebe, Banana Republic, and See's Candy), as well as a few that are unique to Santa Barbara and/or Southern California (Angl, Room Magic by Karen Andrea). You'll find plenty of parking underneath and adjacent to the mall (enter on Chapala Street) as well as in the city lots on Anacapa and Chapala Streets.

VICTORIA COURT
1200 block of State Street, Santa Barbara
(805) 965-2216
Locals like the small-scale, cozy ambience of the 2-story collection of shops and restaurants at Victoria Court. The SOhO nightclub is upstairs, and a changing panoply of boutiques are down below. At last glance, Lola, a delightful resale women's clothing store, took residence as well as a new restaurant, Scarlett Begonia, named for the owner's daughter.

Uptown

LA CUMBRE PLAZA
3853 State St., Santa Barbara
(805) 687-6458
www.shoplacumbre.com

La Cumbre Plaza is a convenient one-stop shopping venue. It's 3.5 miles north of downtown Santa Barbara, between US 101 and State Street, bordered by Hope Avenue and La Cumbre Road. Completed in 1967, this complex was our only large-scale mall before Paseo Nuevo was built in 1990. Amble along the lovely outdoor walkway with its tiled fountains and colorful flowers. La Cumbre also attracts fewer tourists than State Street, so it tends to be less crowded, but parking can sometimes be a challenge.

Macy's and Sears department stores anchor the north and south sides of La Cumbre Plaza. In between you'll find well-known chain stores such as Williams-Sonoma, J. Crew, Tiffany & Co., BCBG Max Azria and Pottery Barn.

Goleta

CAMINO REAL MARKETPLACE
Hollister Avenue and Storke Road, Goleta
(805) 685-3458
www.caminorealmarketplace.com
The biggest shopping attraction in Goleta is the Camino Real Marketplace, which opened in 1999. Located at the Hollister Avenue/ Storke Road intersection, this sprawling "big box" mall introduced the first conglomeration of discount retail outlets to the region. With 83 acres and 3,000 parking spaces, it's also the most diverse shopping center on the South Coast. Though some residents wince at the increased traffic and loss of open space, most shoppers appreciate the discounted wares now available in our notoriously high-priced region. In addition to well-known stores such as Best Buy, Costco, Staples, Home Depot, and Ross Dress for Less, the mall includes restaurants such as Kahuna Grill and Holdren's Steak House and a multiplex theater

UNIQUE SANTA BARBARA STORES

GAME SEEKER
537 State St., Santa Barbara
(805) 564-6611
www.boardgamesrfun.com
On a family road trip and need a little distraction? Stop by Game Seeker, located next door to Hotel Santa Barbara. Game Seeker stocks an immense amount/dizzying array of games, puzzles, and toys—everything to keep your brood entertained. Game Seeker has games for all age levels from toddler to adult, as well as classic games, high-end versions of traditional games, strategy games, active games, and of course, travel-ready games, perfect for those long car trips.

IMAGINE
11 W. Canon Perdido, Santa Barbara
(805) 899-3700
This pair of wonderfully imaginative emporiums peddles a variety of uniquely artistic items as far ranging as toys and gifts to furnishings. Find everything from clothing you won't find elsewhere to home accessories and decorations, cool jewelry, gifts for men and under $5 knickknacks. Sale staffers are super helpful and friendly, too. Imagine's second location is in Montecito at 1470 E. Valley Rd. (805-695-0220).

JEDLICKA'S SADDLERY
2605 De la Vina St., Santa Barbara
(805) 687-0747, (800) 681-0747
www.jedlickas.com
Bring out the wrangler in you with Jedlicka's, renowned for its cowboy boots and hats.

Started by George (Jed) Jedlicka in 1932, this Western store provides "everything for you and your horse." This is where real ranchers outfit themselves. You'll have a great time looking through the authentic Western clothes, belt buckles, Stetson hats, custom-made saddles, and riding equipment for men, women, and children. Jedlicka's is closed Sun.

LEWIS & CLARK
1116 State St., Santa Barbara
(805) 962-6034
www.lewisandclarkltd.com
Locally owned for 30 years, Lewis & Clark is packed chockablock full of sweet treasures. Within its cottage feel (loose bricks clack quietly underfoot), are china, books, vintage linens, and inexpensive jewelry. You could while away an entire afternoon investigating every corner of this gem of a store, and it's especially festive and appropriate for special holiday shopping such as Easter and Christmas. A second location is in Montecito at 1286 Coast Village Rd. (805-969-7177).

MAGELLAN'S
3317A State St. (in Loreto Plaza)
(805) 568-5402
www.magellans.com
America's leading source for travel supplies is headquartered in Santa Barbara, and we love this showroom where you can view all the unique travel products featured in Magellan's catalogs, from alarm clocks and luggage to rain gear and water filters. If you are a traveler, it's hard to leave this place empty-handed. More than luggage, there's very stylish lightweight clothing, super comfortable and lightweight shoes, teensy-weensy keychain backpacks, and more, more, more.

Access the website for great web specials and travel advice.

i If you want to send a little bit of Santa Barbara home or as a gift, Santa Barbara Gift Baskets (805-965-1245, www.sbgiftbaskets.com) can put together a panoply of locally produced gourmet foods, wines, and gifts, including the "Fiesta Bucket" and "Little Bit of Santa Barbara."

PRANA
1200 State St., Santa Barbara
(805) 564-1007
www.prana.com/sbo
Walk in from the adjoining Santa Barbara Outfitters store and leave the busy active-wear atmosphere behind. Santa Barbara Outfitters has partnered with the yoga and outdoor apparel line, PrAna, to create a relaxed and soothing shop with all the apparel, shoes, and a small amount of home accessories to add balance and peace to your life. PrAna has indoor bike racks for the environment-conscious cruiser and offers free yoga classes every week.

SANTA BARBARA MUSEUM OF ART
1130 State St., Santa Barbara
(805) 884-6454
www.sbmastore.net
The Santa Barbara Art Museum Store sells aesthetically pleasing goods. You can find beautiful pottery, dishes, paper wares, home accessories, jewelry, goofy cameras, and more; there is even a section for children with toys and other fun stuff. You can also page through books about art and artists, purchase cards made by local artists, or just admire all the simply cool things on display. Like most art museum gift shops, this is also

a good stop for purchasing beautiful post-cards to send back home.

SANTA BARBARA OUTFITTERS
1200 State St., Santa Barbara
(805) 564-1007
www.sboutfitters.com
Santa Barbara Outfitters is "SB's year-round playground." Locally owned and operated, it carries everything needed to get out and partake in Santa Barbara's natural wonders. Originally better known for its adventure programs (including mountain biking, river rafting, hiking, backpacking, and trips to the Channel Islands), locals now turn to the huge store for their athletic needs. Name the sport, and you'll find the equipment or apparel required. The store has an indoor climbing wall, which is open 7 days a week and is the perfect place to let your kids (or yourself!) test their adventurous spirit. Be sure to check out their online store.

ANTIQUES

Santa Barbara and its neighboring city, Summerland, have a variety of old Victorians brimming with antiques that lure people from far and wide. Take a walk down the quaint streets of yesteryear—Brinkerhoff Avenue in Santa Barbara and Lillie Avenue in Summerland—where you're sure to discover the perfect antique.

ANTIQUE ALLEY
706 State St., Santa Barbara
(805) 962-3944
This antiques collective is jam-packed with all kinds of collectibles and bric-a-brac. The aisles resemble a giant estate sale, with antique furniture, estate jewelry, china,

glassware, pottery, fine art, paintings, prints, and vintage clothes.

JUST FOLK
2346 Lillie Ave., Summerland
(805) 969-7118
www.justfolk,com
When television-producer friends Marcy Carsey (*The Cosby Show*) and Susan Braewald discovered their penchant for American folk and outsider art, they joined forces to build a delightful, award-winning, 2-story showroom in Summerland that exhibits and sells first-rate American antiques and art. Worth a visit, even if you cannot afford the goods.

Flea Markets

Treasure hunting? There are early-bird flea markets (7 a.m. to 7:30 p.m.) at **Earl Warren Showgrounds** (check the website www.earlwarrenshowgrounds.com for days and time), and **Santa Barbara High School** has a Saturday flea market from 7 a.m. to 1 p.m. **Carpinteria Historical Museum Flea Market** (956 Maple Ave., Carpinteria, 805-684-3112) takes place the last Saturday of the month from 8 a.m. to 3 p.m.

But the mother of all flea markets in the area occurs five to six times annually about 30 minutes south at the **Ventura County Fairgrounds Seaside Park,** put on by R. G. Canning Shows. Check the website for dates and info: www.rgcshows.com/Ventura.aspx.

MEDITERRANEE
2500 Lillie Ave., Summerland
(805) 695-0910
www.mediterraneeantiques.com
South American and European antiques, fine art, and a dizzying array of garden fountains and furnishings fill the 12,000-square-foot house-turned-showroom and gardens of Carolina Pierpont's delightful gallery. Known to love a party, Carolina often hosts popular open houses complete with dancing Brazilian girls and plenty of good food and drink.

MICHAEL HASKELL ANTIQUES
539 San Ysidro Rd., Montecito
(805) 565-1121
www.michaelhaskell.com
One of Santa Barbara's most highly respected antiques dealers, Michael Haskell is not only a Santa Barbara native, but he has a local surf spot named for him. Specializing in Spanish Colonial furnishings, art, and santos as well as 18th- and 19th-century Italian pieces, he and his son Eric also have a fine antique reproduction line of lighting, iron, and furnishings.

SUMMERHILL ANTIQUES
2280 Lillie Ave., Summerland
(805) 969-3366
Summerhill was established in 1977 as seaside Summerland's first antiques store. Browse this chock-a-block shop filled with world-class antiques from around the globe and then wander down the block in either direction to a myriad of other fine antiques shops and boutiques.

SUMMERLAND ANTIQUE COLLECTIVE
2192 Ortega Hill Rd., Summerland
(805) 565-3189)
www.summerlandantiquecollective.com

Many booths stocked by 26 different dealers and a constantly changing inventory make this a fun stop on your antiques road show trail. Just about everything old under the sun and then some.

THE TREASURE HOUSE
1070 Fairway Rd., Montecito
(805) 969-1744
www.musicacademy.org/about-us/ treasure-house
Set on the Music Academy of the West campus, this consignment shop sells "antiques and fabulous things" to benefit the Music Academy of the West. You'll find everything from antiques, china, linens, and silver to furniture and paintings here. The Treasure House also gladly accepts donations. Open noon to 3 p.m. Tues through Sat.

BOOKSTORES

BENNETT'S EDUCATIONAL MATERIALS
Magnolia Shopping Center
5130 Hollister Ave., Santa Barbara
(805) 964-8998
www.BennettsEducational.com
Parents, teachers, and anyone looking for quality books, toys, and school supplies will love this store, which has been in business in Santa Barbara since 1972. Bennett's sells a diverse range of children's books, workbooks, teaching resources, developmental toys, posters, and puzzles with an emphasis on educational items. The preschool section is particularly strong. Pop in and have a look. You're sure to find something fun and fascinating for your little ones.

THE BOOK DEN
15 E. Anapamu St., Santa Barbara
(805) 962-3321
www.bookden.com
The Book Den, founded in 1902, is Santa Barbara's oldest and best-stocked bookstore, with tens of thousands of new, used, and out-of-print books (mostly used). Consistently voted "Best Used Bookstore" in a local poll, this popular store also provides online out-of-print search services. The titles encompass a wide range of subjects, including California history and architecture and books in foreign languages. You can browse the virtual shelves at the website or wander in and look for yourself. To find the store, just walk across the street from the Museum of Art. Since the closing of Borders and Barnes & Noble, The Book Den now also carries a good selection of new releases and best sellers and hosts book signings for local authors.

CHAUCER'S BOOKS
Loreto Plaza
3321 State St., Santa Barbara
(805) 682-6787
www.chaucer.booksense.com
Insider bibliophiles rank Chaucer's as the best independent bookstore in town. It has a huge selection of titles—all stacked sky-high on shelves, floors, and any available space in the relatively small quarters. Chaucer's has extremely knowledgeable staff, an incredibly diverse selection of books, an outstanding children's section, and regular book signings by famous authors. The store is in Loreto Plaza, at the intersection of Las Positas Road and State Street.

FRONT PAGE
5737 Calle Real, Goleta
(805) 967-0733
This small bookstore offers a great selection of magazines, newspapers, popular paperbacks, current best sellers, maps, cards, and stationery. You'll also find postcards and a few children's titles.

ISLA VISTA BOOKSTORE
6553 Pardall Rd., Santa Barbara
(805) 968-3600
www.ivbooks.com
Conveniently situated just down the road from UCSB, Isla Vista Bookstore is a complete off-campus college store. It primarily sells used textbooks and educational paperbacks but also offers clothing, art, and school supplies.

i Left Coast Books is a combo used bookstore/art gallery/literary oasis in Old Town Goleta run by a Simon Taylor, a very cool former NYC art critic and curator. The space is located at 5877 Hollister Ave. in Goleta. For more information, visit www.leftcoastbooks.us. Open Wed through Sat 11 a.m. to 6 p.m.

LOST HORIZON BOOKSTORE
703 Anacapa St., Santa Barbara
(805) 962-4606
Lost Horizon buys, sells, and appraises single copies and entire libraries of antiquarian books and maps. It has hundreds of books on the fine and decorative arts, monographs on artists, pencil-signed prints, paintings, and photographs.

METRO ENTERTAINMENT
6 W. Anapamu St., Santa Barbara
(805) 963-2168
www.metroautographs.com
Kids clamor to go to Metro, which has every type of comic book published. It carries a full line of them, including Japanese anime, children's, and independent. It also has games, toys, and TV and movie merchandise and memorabilia.

PACIFICA GRADUATE INSTITUTE
BOOKSTORE
801 Ladera Ln., Montecito
(805) 879-7327
www.pacifica.edu/bookstore.html
The Pacifica Graduate Institute Bookstore carries titles related to psychology, mythology, religion, and philosophy in ancient cultures. The store also stocks CDs, DVDs, cards, videos, drums, images, and jewelry. For more information on the institute, see the Education & Child Care chapter.

PAPERBACK ALLEY USED BOOKS
5840 Hollister Ave., Goleta
(805) 967-1051
For more than 25 years, Paperback Alley has bought and sold thousands of fiction and nonfiction books, mostly paperbacks. You're bound to find something you like at an affordable price.

PARADISE FOUND
17 E. Anapamu St., Santa Barbara
(805) 564-3573
www.paradise-found.net
If you're into metaphysics, you'll find paradise here in the form of metaphysical books, gifts, jewelry, incense, tapes, compact discs, and astrology charts. Listen to music, and savor the incense. An on-site intuitive reader or astrologer is often on hand. Call for an appointment.

READ 'N POST
1046-B Coast Village Rd., Montecito
(805) 969-1148
An entire wall of the Read 'N Post is devoted to magazines of all types and sizes, including an abundant collection of French magazines. The store also carries a wide selection of newspapers, maps, and paperbacks. Buy a magazine or paper, drop off your mail (there's a post office here), then head next door to Starbucks for a cup of coffee—that's what many Montecitans do every day.

i The Montecito Public Library (as well as other public libraries) sell gently used donated books for a song. The money helps support the library.

TECOLOTE BOOK SHOP
1470 E. Valley Rd., Montecito
(805) 969-4977
When it first opened for business in 1925, Tecolote was a carriage-trade bookstore—the staff would bring books to the carriage to show the customers. Today the small, intimate Tecolote remains a favorite bookstore among Insiders. Choose from a diverse selection of books, and pay extra attention to the many unusual art and coffee-table books, especially those on Montecito and Santa Barbara history.

Tecolote sits on the edge of a green lawn with a fountain in Montecito's Upper Village, an ideal spot to rest, read, and regroup. It is also the site of the best book signings in the area. Don't be surprised to see local authors such as T. C. Boyle, Fanny Flagg, Jonathan Winters, and other local celebs, including Drew Barrymore and local author

Barnaby Conrad (as well as this book author), both signing and attending the fun celebrations of the written word. They are so old-fashioned that there's no website, but Mary Sheldon and her staff are always there to recommend books and lend a helping hand.

THE TRAVEL STORE OF SANTA BARBARA
12 W. Anapamu St., Santa Barbara
(805) 963-4438, (888) PAC-TRAV
www.sbtravelstore.com

Pacific Travelers offers one-stop shopping for travel books, luggage, clothing, gifts, and accessories, but it's probably best known for its excellent maps. Whether you're headed to Antarctica, Italy, or Mozambique, you can order a map of your destination here. The expert staff will help you find everything you need.

UCSB BOOKSTORE
University Center
UCSB, Santa Barbara
(805) 893-3271
www.bookstore.ucsb.edu

Conveniently located on campus in the University Center, the UCSB Bookstore buzzes with students, teachers, and faculty members, and it's also open to the public. The store specializes in academic support materials, but you can also stock up on computer software, greeting cards, UCSB sweatshirts, gifts, and school and office supplies.

VEDANTA BOOK SHOP (SARADA CONVENT BOOKS)
925 Ladera Ln., Montecito
(805) 969-5697
www.vedanta.org

Part of the Vedanta Temple, this religious bookstore offers an impressive variety of books covering all major religions, including Buddhism, Hinduism, Native American religions, Islam, and Sufism. You'll also find a huge selection of deity statues, for example, Kuan Yin (a goddess of compassion), Buddha, traditional Christian statues, santos, and angels and gift items, such as jewelry and incense. Parking is free, and this most tranquil spot may be the closet thing to shopping nirvana, as you can meditate in the adjacent Vedanta Temple as well as enjoy some spectacular views.

CLOTHING

ANGEL
1221 Coast Village Rd., Montecito
(805) 565-1599
www.wendyfoster.com

At Angel, the younger and hipper sister store of Wendy Foster, you'll find a hand-picked selection of cool clothes and accessories from small designer labels. Montecito darlings shop here for special events, but the store stocks everything from bikinis, jeans, and trendy sportswear to chic evening dresses and accessories.

BONITA
2330 Lillie Ave., Summerland
(805) 565-3848
www.bonitasummerland.com

This upscale Summerland "gypset style" boutique features chic clothing (from Anna Sui to Odd Molly) for gals with gypsy souls. Cool accessories, designer lingerie by Elle McPherson and Stella McCartney, unique jewelry, and gifts round out the items carefully selected by owner Rita Villa.

DIANI
1324 State St., Ste. B, Santa Barbara
(805) 966-3114
www.dianiboutique.com
Caroline Diani displays a collection of sleek and timeless designer clothing in this soothing showroom of sea grass, potted palms, and blond woods. Inspired by her time in Kenya, the collections accent classic, understated style and include European and American labels.

DIANI SHOES
1324 State St., Ste. H, Santa Barbara
(877) 342-6474
Right around the corner from the main boutique is Diani Shoes, which, as the manager says, "is like stepping into someone's closet and picking out the perfect thing." This tiny store is filled with seasonal "exclusives." This is the place for the woman in search of must-haves.

The Ultimate Garage Sale

Shoppers come from far and wide to scout out Santa Barbara's garage sales. But the granddaddy of all the sales in the **Annual May Madness Sale** held at the Music Academy of the West grounds in early May for more than 30 years. Great used clothing, furniture, bric-a-brac, antiques, and other odds and ends are for sale. Get there early to get a good spot in line. For info, check www.music academy.org or phone (805) 969-4726. All proceeds support the Music Academy.

INDIAN SUMMERS
2275 Ortega Hill Rd., Summerland
(805) 969-1162
www.indiansummersboutique.com
This tiny gem of a boutique appeals to women of all ages looking for stylish, comfortable casual wear. The store carries collections from well-established and new designers, including James Perse and JW Los Angeles, and T-shirts from Michael Stars. You'll also find handcrafted jewelry and other accessories, such as hats, shoes, leather totes, and purses. The store is closed Mon.

LOVEBIRD
7 E. De la Guerra, Santa Barbara
(805) 568-3800
www.lovebirdsb.com
Lovebird's clothes have a charming, ageless appeal, and the prices are great as well. A favorite among locals, women of all generations can discover something to purchase at this teensy boutique. In addition to apparel, bags, and shoes, artwork and cards by local artist Erika Carter are squeezed in. Lovebird is owned by a local jewelry designer whose lovely handmade designs—earrings, charms, rings, and necklaces—are crafted by a team of women in Bali. Look for the metal bowl filled with bags of jewelry on sale for great discount prices. An additional location is at 535 State St. (805-560-9900).

TAKAPUNA
428 E. Haley St., Santa Barbara
(805) 963-4848
www.takapuna.com
Men's bespoke suits speak to you? Check out the very cool custom designs and Clacton and Frinton line at Takapuna, the go-to store for custom-fitted clothing and suits (including bespoke) for men and women, as well as

a varied assortment of cool gifts and accessories. A wee bit off the beaten path of State Street, Takapuna is well worth the trek.

THE TERRITORY AHEAD
515 State St., Santa Barbara
(805) 962-5558, ext. 181
www.territoryahead.com

Many people know about this high-quality clothing company through its popular mail-order catalog. But here in Santa Barbara—the home of the Territory Ahead—you can try on and buy clothes and accessories in the flagship store. Territory Ahead designs and develops casual yet classy men's and women's clothing and accessories made from high-quality natural-fiber fabrics and materials. These are the clothes you might wear while on safari or strolling the streets of Shanghai. For bigger savings, visit the Territory Ahead Outlet a few blocks away, at 400 State St. (See the Outlet Stores section toward the end of this chapter for details.)

WENDY FOSTER
833 State St., Santa Barbara
(805) 966-2276
www.wendyfoster.com

The clothes in this upscale boutique reflect Santa Barbara's casually elegant style. The store stocks sportswear as well as dressier outfits from small labels—clothing you can't usually find in other shops. It's very expensive, but the quality is high, and the subdued colors and classic designs seem to stay in style. If you can't decide on a purchase, buy a gift certificate and give the gift of guilt-free shopping. Don't be surprised to see Meg Ryan or other Hollywood celebs popping in to see what Wendy's got in store. A second location is at 516 San Ysidro Rd. (805-565-1506).

YELLOWSTONE CLOTHING INC.
527 State St., Santa Barbara
(805) 963-9609

One of the best places to find vintage clothing on State Street, Yellowstone is popular with the younger crowd for its funky, eclectic, and chill atmosphere and selection. In addition to '40s dresses, vintage Hawaiian shirts, and other funky finery for men and women, there's jewelry, sunglasses, and shoes.

FARMERS' MARKETS

SANTA BARBARA CERTIFIED FARMERS' MARKET ASSOCIATION
232 Anacapa St., Ste. 1A
(805) 962-5354
www.sbfarmersmarket.org

Sunset magazine selected the Santa Barbara farmers' market as one of the "Top 10 Farmers' Markets in the West." It was started in 1973 by a handful of Santa Barbara growers who sold their produce at the Mission Rose Gardens. Now it's a nonprofit association with more than 140 growers.

We love shopping at the farmers' markets every week for our fruits and vegetables (many are organic or not sprayed with pesticides), flowers, nuts, eggs, honey, cheese, and plants. They're also fun places to browse and people-watch. Bring lots of change and small bills as well as sacks or baskets for all your purchases.

The association currently sponsors the following local markets:

- **Downtown Santa Barbara Market** (the largest and most popular one) is at the corner of Santa Barbara and Cota Streets and is open Sat from 8:30 a.m. to 12:30 p.m.

- **Camino Real Marketplace,** at the corner of Storke Road and Hollister Avenue in Goleta, is open Sun from 10 a.m. to 2 p.m.
- **Old Town Santa Barbara Market,** in the 500 and 600 blocks of State Street, is open Tues from 3 to 6:30 p.m. (4 to 7:30 p.m. during the summer).
- **Harding School** (1625 Robbins St.) Wed from 3 to 6:30 p.m.; in **Solvang** (Copenhagen Drive and 1st Street) Wed from 2:30 to 6 p.m. (2:30 to 6:30 p.m. in the summer)
- **Camino Real Center** (7004 Marketplace Dr.) Thurs from 3 to 6 p.m.
- **Carpinteria Market,** in the 800 block of Linden Avenue, is open Thurs from 3 to 6 p.m. (3 to 6:30 p.m. during the summer).
- **Montecito Market** is in the 1100 and 1200 blocks of Coast Village Road and is open from Fri 8 to 11:15 a.m.

i If you're heading out to the farmers' market, take a big basket or canvas bag. If you don't have one, there is usually a street vendor selling beautiful baskets from Africa to make your shopping more pleasurable.

SANTA BARBARA FISHERMEN'S MARKET
Santa Barbara Harbor (in front of Brophy Bros. on the Navy Pier)
(805) 965-9564
www.sbfish.com
You can't get fish much fresher than this unless you catch it yourself. The market is usually held every Sat from 7:30 to 11:30 a.m. You can buy only whole fish, so be prepared to feed a crowd or freeze what you don't eat. Take your fish to the adjacent Fish Market (run by the same association) at 117-F

Harbor Way, and they'll fillet your fish so it's ready to cook. If you're not an early bird or if it happens to be a day of the week other than Saturday, you can still purchase the association's fresh fish at the aforementioned Fish Market, which is open daily.

GARDENING SUPPLY

GALLUP & STRIBLING ORCHIDS
3450 Via Real, Carpinteria
(805) 684-9842, (805) 684-1998
www.americanorchids.com
Gallup & Stribling Orchids is one of the world's largest wholesale orchid growers, but everyone is welcome to buy these tropical blooms in their excellent visitor center. Set on 48 acres in the foothills of Carpinteria, the nursery specializes in growing cymbidiums and phalaenopsis as cut flowers and potted plants. The visitor center displays many of the farm's prized specimens and a huge selection of these outrageously ravishing blooms.

GARDEN MARKET
3811 Santa Claus Ln., Carpinteria
(805) 745-5505
www.thegardenmarket.com
From the front, Garden Market resembles a fruit market, with its baskets of avocados, papayas, and mangoes, but wander in and you'll find a cute little cafe, delightful gifts, and a courtyard nursery. Looking for a gift for the gardener in your life? Take a peek in the gardening shed out back, where you'll find books, gloves, accessories, and gift baskets.

ISLAND VIEW NURSERY
3376 Foothill Rd., Carpinteria
(805) 684-0324
www.islandviewnursery.com

Nestled in the Carpinteria foothills, Island View Nursery is a gardener's paradise—unique, with distinctive garden and flora. The Arrangement Bar is the perfect stop for creating the most perfect arrangements. The outdoor gardens are equally inspirational. Wander the winding pathways, and you'll discover an abundant selection of succulents, bamboo, colorful annuals, and perennials in a gorgeous garden setting adorned with pottery and hand-carved statues, fountains, and garden art. Specializing in tropicals, Island View has a reputation among landscape designers and architects for unique, hard-to-find plants including bamboos, exotic palms, and cycads. The retail location is a fantastic place to buy unusual gifts or gather some ideas for a tropical home makeover.

i Santa Barbara is one of the nation's leading producers of orchids. If you'd like to tour an orchid-growing estate or buy a rare specimen, visit www.sborchidshow.com for information on growers, a history of orchid growing in the region, and the International Orchid Show.

SANTA BARBARA BOTANIC GARDEN
1212 Mission Canyon Rd., Santa Barbara
(805) 682-4726, ext. 127
www.sbbg.org
The Garden Growers Nursery at the Botanic Garden is a great source for native California and unusual drought-tolerant Mediterranean plants. It's staffed by volunteers from 10 a.m. to 3 p.m. daily and is open on a self-serve basis during the garden hours (see Attractions). You can also shop for books, crafts, gift items, cards, and posters at the Garden Shop, which is open daily during Botanic Garden hours.

SANTA BARBARA ORCHID ESTATE
1250 Orchid Dr., Goleta
(805) 967-1284
www.sborchid.com
One of the world's largest collections of orchids is shown at the 5-acre Orchid Estate, home of a vast selection of cymbidiums. A stroll through the grounds will surprise and delight the senses. You can purchase orchid plants and bulbs as well as cut flowers, and all can be shipped anywhere in the United States.

SEASIDE GARDENS
3700 Via Real, Carpinteria
(805) 684-6001
www.seaside-gardens.com
Stroll this 3-acre botanical wonderland and wander through garden displays of plants from around the world. The gardens were designed by local landscape designers and include Asian, Australian, California native, Central/South American, grassland, Mediterranean, native wetland bioswale, perennial/cottage, South African, succulent, and tropical themes. Can't make it there? For a virtual tour, visit the website.

JEWELRY

BRYANT & SONS, LTD.
812 State St., Santa Barbara
(805) 963-1179
www.bryantandsons.com
For more than 45 years, Bryant and Sons, Ltd., has been bedazzling Santa Barbara men and women as well as tourists. Located in the historic El Paseo, the original fine jewelry store carries fine watches from Rolex, Patek

Philippe, and Cartier. With a team of a dozen experts, whether you are looking for an engagement ring, a drop-dead gorgeous pair of emerald earrings, a string of pearls or even a piece of fine crystal, this is a most civilized place to drop your cash. A second location is in Montecito at 1482 E. Valley Rd., #37 (805-565-4411).

33 JEWELS
814 State St., Santa Barbara
(805) 957-9100
www.33jewels.com
Located in a small, welcoming store in the El Paseo shopping alley, 33 Jewels is filled with fine earrings, necklaces, rings, and other jewelry items, including estate jewelry. Be sure to pop upstairs, if vintage costume jewely rocks your boat.

OUTLET STORES

ITALIAN POTTERY OUTLET
929 State St., Santa Barbara
(805) 564-7655
www.italianpottery.com
The Italian Pottery Outlet offers the largest selection of Italian ceramics in the western United States. You can buy all sorts of pottery firsts and seconds, from Sicilian folk art to classic designs, for up to 50 percent off retail prices. The store also carries other gift items from Italy.

THE TERRITORY AHEAD OUTLET STORE
400 State St., Santa Barbara
(805) 962-5558, ext. 185
This outlet store carries discontinued and discounted clothing and accessories—the same stuff you see in Territory's regular store a block up State Street, only a few months

later and a lot cheaper. Expect discounts of 30 to 80 percent. Some of their best sellers are seconds sold at cost—especially leather goods, such as shoes and jackets. See the store description in the Clothing section earlier in this chapter.

SKATEBOARDS

CHURCH OF SKATAN
26 E. Gutierrez St., Santa Barbara
(805) 899-1586
If you're obsessed with skateboarding, you'll be totally at home in this unusual shop housed in a building that was once a real church. It provides top-quality equipment for hard-core skateboarders, including a large selection of shoes.

SURF & BEACHWEAR

If you want to look like a Santa Barbara Insider, you should wear the proper attire: shorts, T-shirts, sandals, bathing suits, hats, and sunglasses. Go to any of these shops and ask the staff for guidance—they'll be glad to deck you out in Santa Barbara style.

A-FRAME SURF SHOP
3785 Santa Claus Ln.
Carpinteria
(805) 684-8803
www.aframesurfshop.com
Run by two local brothers, this surf shop opened in 1999 on Santa Claus Lane. Heading for the waves and need some equipment? You can rent surfboards, body boards, wet suits, fins, and skim boards here, and surfing lessons are available year-round. The store also sells short boards from local designers such as Progressive and Clyde Beatty Jr., as well as some hard-to-find smaller lines of surf and beachwear for men,

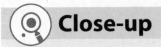

Close-up

A Garden of Eden for Organic Shopping

If you're hunting for organic products here in Santa Barbara, you'll find an array of excellent health food stores and fruit and vegetable stands. Here are a few of our favorites:

For convenient one-stop shopping, go to **Lazy Acres Market,** at 302 Meigs Rd. (near the intersection of Cliff Drive) in Santa Barbara (805-564-4410; www.lazyacres .com). Lazy Acres carries high-quality organic produce, grains, and dairy products, as well as all-natural (haven't been pumped with hormones or antibiotics) fish, poultry, and meats, a deli counter, a bakery, gourmet treats, and all the usual things you would expect at a supermarket.

Whole Foods, at 3761 State St. in Santa Barbara (805-837-6959; www.wholefoods market.com) features just about everything under the sun from organic produce to deli items and cheeses—well, the sky's the limit and hopefully your credit card has a high one, as this market is referred to as "whole wallet."

Lassen's Health Foods, at 5154 Hollister Ave. in Goleta's Magnolia Shopping Center (805-683-7696; www.lassens.com), and **Tri-County Produce Co.,** at 335 S. Milpas St. in Santa Barbara (805-965-4558; www.tricountyproduce.com), also offer a range of organic and natural products.

Weekly farmers' markets are great places to find fresh organic produce (see the Farmers' Markets section of this chapter). You can also stop in at the following stands—most are open daily: **Fairview Gardens Farms,** 598 N. Fairview Ave., Goleta (805-967-7369; www.fairviewgardens.org; many local residents invest in harvest "shares" of produce from mid-March through mid-November); **Lane Farms Green Stand,** 308 Walnut Ln., off Hollister Avenue, Goleta (805-964-3773); **Lane Farms–San Marcos Gardens,** 4950 Hollister Ave., Goleta (805-964-0424); and **Mesa Produce,** 1905 Cliff Dr., Santa Barbara (805-962-1645).

women, and children. You'll also find a large selection of Hawaiian shirts.

THE BEACH HOUSE
10 State St., Santa Barbara
(805) 963-1281
www.surfnwear.com

Local teenagers love the Beach House, as do the young-at-heart. Santa Barbara's quintessential beach store sells long and short surfboards, boogie boards, beachwear, and accessories. If you want to learn more about surfing, check out the books, videos, and antique surfboards. The store also runs a

great summer surf camp (Santa Barbara Surf Adventures) for kids. (See the Kidstuff chapter.)

THE BIKINI FACTORY
2275 B Ortega Hill Rd., Summerland
(805) 969-2887
www.bikinifactory.com

The Bikini Factory is a funky little store just off the freeway exit in Summerland that has been saving women from the bathing suit blues for more than three decades. It has a fantastic selection of swimsuits and casual clothes for all ages and sizes. You can mix and match bikini tops and bottoms, and customize your own bathing suit.

CHANNEL ISLANDS SURFBOARDS
36 Anacapa St., Santa Barbara
(805) 966-7213
www.cisurfboards.com
The classic surf store specializes in high-performance short boards, but you can find a huge variety of surfboards here, all designed by Al Merrick, one of the best board designers and shapers in the surfing industry. You can also choose from a good selection of wet suits, shirts, shorts, sun-dresses, and sandals.

SURF COUNTRY
Calle Real Center
5668 Calle Real, Goleta
(805) 683-4450
www.surfcountry.net
Surf Country is a complete surf and skate shop, with a great selection of surfboards, wet suits, skateboards, and beachwear for children and adults. You'll also find clothes, watches, sunglasses, hats, and accessories, and the staff is happy to dispense information about the best surf and beach spots. Surf Country rents soft and hard surfboards and body boards; wet suits and surfing lessons are also available.

UNIQUE GIFTS & HOUSEWARES

MAISON K
1159 Coast Village Rd., Montecito
(805) 969-1676
www.maisonkinc.com
We love just about everything that boutique owner Kimberly Phillips (the "K" in Maison K) discovers on her travels and in her universe

for this delightful, 2-story emporium. There are itsy-bitsy affordable gifts as well as wonderful one-of-a-kind pieces of antique furniture, photographs, yummy cashmere shawls, and unique jewelry. You might find a hat from Peru, a pillow from Morocco, or a pair of pumps from Paris—always a surprise!

i Feeling crafty? Loop and Leaf (536 Brinkerhoff Ave., 805-845-4696, www.loopandleaf.com) stocks artisan yarns and knitting supplies. There are private knitting and crocheting lessons and group seminars range from "Knitting 101" to more advanced classes.

PLUM GOODS
909 State St., Santa Barbara
(805) 845-3900
www.plumgoodsstore.com
Plum Goods is chock-full of goodness. This store celebrates natural, funky, and eco-friendly products that look good and function well, too: home accessories, tableware, pottery, cards, bags, textiles, and more items to inspire healthy, natural living.

UPSTAIRS AT PIERRE LA FOND
516 San Ysidro Rd., Montecito
(805) 565-1503
www.upstairsatpierrelafond.com
Everyone loves this upstairs housewares and gift shop above Pierre La Fond deli and the Wendy Foster shops in Montecito. There are coffee-table art books, baby clothing and toys, fine bedding, unique pottery, and even lingerie, candles, scents, and more. Always lots of pretty items to tempt, all selected and displayed with the greatest care and in best of taste.

ATTRACTIONS

Santa Barbarans love showing visitors around their beautiful home. When you come here, you'll see why. For such a relatively small town, Santa Barbara offers an amazing diversity of things to see and do. Explore the region, and you'll discover nationally acclaimed museums, wildlife sanctuaries, stunning gardens, fascinating historical sights, informative tours, and an exciting lineup of ocean adventures. Look around you. Chances are many of your fellow explorers are locals who unabashedly proclaim that they'd rather spend their vacation discovering their own city than jet off to some exotic locale.

Of course, the locals have "been there, done that," but they know that new exhibits, expansions, and upgrades make Santa Barbara attractions worth visiting again and again. That being said, even longtime residents are often surprised to discover new pockets that seem to have slipped off their radar. The continual changing and upgrading of existing attractions are why many Santa Barbarans are happy to spend their vacations at home.

If you're a history buff, you'll be pleased to know that most of the city's historical sights lie within a short stroll from each other in the downtown area. You can explore them in a couple of hours by taking the self-guided Red Tile Walking Tour (see the Close-up in this chapter), which begins at the County Courthouse, one of Santa Barbara's most famous landmarks.

If you're more interested in some seaside fun, head for Stearns Wharf and the Santa Barbara Harbor, where you can go for a stroll in the crisp sea air, grab some fresh seafood, and browse the specialty shops.

SANTA BARBARA

Cultural Attractions

ARLINGTON CENTER FOR THE PERFORMING ARTS
1317 State St., Santa Barbara
(805) 963-4408
The Arlington Center is one of Santa Barbara's most beloved performance venues, and both its name and its location speak volumes about Santa Barbara history. In 1875 the tony Arlington Hotel occupied the current site

of the Arlington Center. The hotel was a magnet for the rich and famous of the day, including several presidents, movie stars, military heroes, and foreign guests.

In 1909 a fire of undetermined origin burned the hotel to the ground. A "new" Arlington was built on the site, but it never quite lived up to the original and was razed in 1925. In 1931 Fox West Coast Theatres built an impressive Moorish-style movie palace on the site. That historic structure is now occupied by the Arlington Center for the Performing Arts.

The seats on the main floor of the elaborate theater provide the illusion of being under an open sky in the central courtyard of a Spanish village. Slanted tile roofs, arched doorways, and balconies surround the perimeter, and above the rooftops are mountain vistas and twinkling stars arranged as they might appear in the night sky. So realistic is this scene that Santa Barbarans have often been able to convince a newcomer that this is indeed an outdoor theater-under-the-stars.

These days, in addition to featuring first-run films, the Arlington hosts a plethora of special events, including lectures and concerts from the Arts & Lecture Series, as well as special award events as part of the Santa Barbara International Film Festival. No formal tours are offered, and the theater is open regularly to the public only during the screening of movies or other public events. Plan to go early so you can explore a bit before the lights go down.

KARPELES MANUSCRIPT LIBRARY
   MUSEUM
21 W. Anapamu St., Santa Barbara
(805) 962-5322
www.rain.org/~karpeles
A small museum dedicated to historical documents, the Karpeles has a significant collection of rare manuscripts and original documents. Discover works from authors such as H. G. Wells, Mark Twain, Sir Arthur Conan Doyle, and John Steinbeck. In addition, the Karpeles has historical documents from the fields of history, music, science, and art, including works by Einstein, Darwin, and Newton. Since the Karpeles family's

acquisitions are rather staggering, exhibits change periodically, so you may see new documents each time you visit. Occasionally, the museum hosts special events such as the Great Women in History exhibit. The museum is open Wed through Sun from 10 a.m. to 4 p.m. Admission and all special events are free. You can read more about the museum in the Arts chapter.

✳SANTA BARBARA MUSEUM OF ART
1130 State St., Santa Barbara
(805) 963-4364
www.sbmuseart.org
One of the top 10 regional museums in the country, the Santa Barbara Museum of Art has permanent collections of Asian, American, and European art, including works by such well-known artists as Thomas Eakins, Claude Monet, Marc Chagall, Pablo Picasso, and Georgia O'Keeffe. See the chapter on the Arts for more details.

Historic Places & Historical Museums

CARRIAGE & WESTERN ART MUSEUM
129 Castillo St., Santa Barbara
(805) 962-2353
www.carriagemuseum.org
When Santa Barbara's historic carriages and stagecoaches are not making their annual appearance in the Old Spanish Days parade (see our Annual Events chapter), they're housed at this museum, which contains one of the most extensive collections of antique carriages in the country. You'll see a variety of horse-drawn carriages (sans the horses, of course), many owned by early Santa Barbara families and restored by the museum. The museum also houses an impressive collection of saddles, a horse-drawn fire truck, an antique hearse, and an old wine-cask cart. The Carriage Museum is open daily from 9

a.m. to 3 p.m. for self-guided tours. Docent tours are available without reservations on the third Sun of every month from 1 to 4 p.m. Admission is free, but a donation to the nonprofit museum is appreciated.

EL PASEO & CASA DE LA GUERRA
15 E. De la Guerra St., Santa Barbara
(805) 965-0093
www.sbthp.org
Spanish Colonial Revival–style architecture is shown off beautifully in El Paseo, a small shopping complex (reportedly California's first "shopping center") built in the 1920s around the historic de la Guerra adobe, Casa de la Guerra. The adobe was built between 1819 and 1826 by José de la Guerra y Noriega, who was, at the time, commander of El Presidio de Santa Barbara. De la Guerra and his wife, Doña María Antonia, raised 12 children here, and the house was the social center of Santa Barbara for years.

The wedding reception of the de la Guerras' daughter Anita took place at Casa de la Guerra in 1836 and was described in Richard Henry Dana's book, *Two Years Before the Mast*. In 1998 the Santa Barbara Trust for Historic Preservation restored the adobe house and opened an evocative little museum here filled with furniture and artifacts from the era and featuring rotating exhibits. You can visit the museum from noon to 4 p.m. Thurs through Sun. Admission is $3 for adults; children 16 and under are free.

Today you can feel the history as you stroll El Paseo. Once filled with shops and galleries, El Paseo now houses mostly offices and restaurants. It's a fabulous spot for lunch. You can relax in the old world courtyard, sip a margarita at El Paseo restaurant, and imagine the Spanish dons and doñas mingling at the casa more than two centuries ago.

Browsing is free anytime at El Paseo. The main entrance is on the 800 block of State Street, but you can also access it from De la Guerra and Anacapa Streets.

EL PRESIDIO DE SANTA BARBARA STATE HISTORIC PARK
123 E. Canon Perdido St., Santa Barbara
(805) 965-0093
www.sbthp.org
Sitting incongruously in the middle of bustling downtown Santa Barbara is a nearly block-long complex of stark adobe buildings that represent the city's beginnings. Founded in 1782 by Lieutenant José Francisco de Ortega, the Royal Presidio was the last military outpost of the Spanish Empire in the New World.

An ongoing restoration process by the Santa Barbara Trust for Historic Preservation has preserved the spirit of the place. The bell tower that was destroyed by an earthquake in the 19th century was replaced, along with two huge bells, one of which is believed to be the original Presidio Bell rung by Father Junipero Serra at the first mass said here in 1782. (See the History chapter for more information.) The careful restoration makes it easy to imagine the Spanish padres sitting in their sparsely furnished quarters or Santa Barbarans of 200 years ago worshipping in the Presidio Chapel, reconstructed on its original foundations.

Also of note here is El Cuartel, the guard's house. It's the oldest building in Santa Barbara and the second oldest in the state of California.

Visits to the site are self-guided, although groups may call to arrange a docent-led tour. A 15-minute slide show is well worth seeing, and a scale model of the Presidio offers a detailed look at life in Spanish California. The Presidio is open every day from 10:30 a.m. to

4:30 p.m. Admission is $3 for adults; children under 16 are free.

Digging Up History

The rear courtyard of El Presidio has become an archaeological dig. Students from the Cal Poly–San Luis Obispo Continuing Education Program and board members from the Santa Barbara Historic Trust joined together for investigations that have already uncovered artifacts from Santa Barbara's Chinese, Spanish, and American periods. You can participate in history yourself by learning how to make adobe bricks. Call El Presidio at (805) 965-0093 for more information.

FERNALD MANSION
414 W. Montecito St., Santa Barbara
(805) 966-1601
www.santabarbaramuseum.com
Next door to the Trussell-Winchester Adobe (see p. 115), the 14-room Fernald Mansion is one of only a few Victorian homes preserved in Santa Barbara. An example of the traditional Queen Anne–style Victorian, the gabled "gingerbread" mansion was built in 1826 by local lawman Judge Charles Fernald for his wife, Hannah.

The mansion was originally located on lower Santa Barbara Street but was moved to the Montecito Street address, where it is now a museum operated by the Santa Barbara Historical Museum. The Fernald family's furnishings and personal effects are of interest, as are the hand-carved ornamentation, staircase, and wainscoting.

Guided tours are offered every Sat at 1 and 2 p.m. Group tours are available by appointment. Admission is $5 for adults and $1 for children under 12. The mansion is not wheelchair accessible.

*LOBERO THEATRE
33 E. Canon Perdido St., Santa Barbara
(805) 963-0761
www.lobero.com
Located in the heart of the downtown historic district, the Lobero Theatre is California's longest continuously operating theater. Offering an intimate and beautiful setting, the Lobero's wide variety of programming attracts audiences from every cultural background and all walks of life—from youth to adults, from jazz lovers to ballet enthusiasts. Recently the Lobero has been named one of *DownBeat* magazine's "Best Places to See Jazz," worldwide. Originally founded in 1873 and rebuilt in 1924, the Lobero Theatre is recognized as one of Santa Barbara's architectural jewels and a state and city landmark. From its earliest days, the Lobero has been Santa Barbara's grand stage for both community and professional performances. Today the Lobero is the home stage for the major local performing arts organizations and dance schools, and acts as a meeting space for corporate, nonprofit, and social groups. More than 70,000 people attend performances at the Lobero annually, traveling from throughout California, the United States, and the world.

*OLD MISSION SANTA BARBARA
2201 Laguna St., Santa Barbara
(805) 682-4713
www.sbmission.org
Known as the "Queen of the Missions" for its beauty and hilltop setting, Old Mission

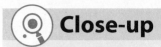

Close-up

Adaptable Adobe

When you're exploring Santa Barbara's famous architectural landmarks, you'll come across the word *adobe* (ah-DOH-bee)—adobe buildings, adobe bricks, adobe clay. In fact, adobe makes up a large part of Santa Barbara's foundation. Not only is this humble, hard-packed clay one of the region's dominant soils, but it was also one of the city's first building materials, and volunteers are adapting the original recipe to restore historic landmarks today.

Mud buildings may seem primitive to us, but they made perfect sense for the Spanish and Mexican settlers—environmentally and economically. Instead of chopping down trees for lumber or using expensive materials, the settlers simply scooped up the earth beneath them, mixed it with straw and water, then shaped the mixture into large blocks using wooden molds. After the bricks baked in the scorching sun, the settlers used them to build Santa Barbara's first houses, forts, and churches. The adobes, as they are called, were extremely energy efficient. Fortified with thick, 2- to 5-foot (0.6- to 1.5-meter) walls, they adapted beautifully to the temperature extremes of the arid climate, staying cool in summer and warm in winter.

Today, adobe bricks are still made by hand in Santa Barbara, using much the same methods the Spanish and Mexican settlers applied more than two centuries ago. Each year, volunteers get down and dirty during Adobe Days, making bricks to restore the structures at El Presidio de Santa Barbara State Historic Park (see the write-up in this chapter). The volunteers still use the traditional recipe—mud, straw, and water—but they adapt it slightly by adding a bucket of emulsified asphalt to help waterproof the bricks. Hardworking volunteers have made every brick used to restore these historic buildings for the last 25 years, re-creating Santa Barbara's rich history for all of us to enjoy.

To visit some of the city's historic adobes, take the self-guided Red Tile Walking Tour (see the other Close-up in this chapter). If you would like to take part in Adobe Days, call the Santa Barbara Trust for Historic Preservation at (805) 965-0093.

Santa Barbara was the 10th of California's 21 missions founded by Franciscan friars and is the only one that has been continuously occupied by the Franciscan order since its founding.

Dedicated on December 16, 1786, the mission complex has undergone many changes since its humble beginnings as a small chapel and living quarters for missionaries and Chumash Indians. In December 1812, a major earthquake nearly leveled the chapel and surrounding buildings. The present pink sandstone church—with one bell tower—was constructed around the old chapel and dedicated in 1820. The second bell tower was added more than a decade later.

In 1925 the mission suffered the shock of another major earthquake, and the towers and living quarters had to be repaired and reinforced. The building remained intact until the years following World War II, when deterioration called for complete reconstruction of the mission facade, which was done in the early 1950s. In future years, the mission will undergo further restoration as the soft stone and adobe bricks crumble with age.

Visit the mission today, and its graceful beauty will instantly impress you. Reportedly inspired by a drawing of a church designed by the Roman architect M. Vitruvius Polion in the first century BC, Mission Santa Barbara has strongly influenced the architectural style of the city. As you wander through the grounds, notice the thick adobe walls, red-tile roof, and open courtyards, features that are echoed in many of Santa Barbara's other public buildings. Inside, rooms are preserved in the style of the 1700s, with artifacts and displays relating to early mission life.

The self-guided tour includes 8 museum rooms, the cloister gardens, the chapel, the cemetery, and the beautiful Moorish fountain and courtyard. You can also view a 20-minute video on mission history. Docent-led group tours must be arranged in advance. A gift shop near the entrance sells religious items and educational materials on Santa Barbara and the California missions. For a moment of quiet reflection after your tour, wander down to the beautiful Mission Rose Gardens. You can also explore the ruins of the old Mission aqueduct built by the Chumash in 1806—just wander across the street from the church. Mission Santa Barbara is open 7 days a week from 9 a.m. to 5 p.m. Tour hours are 9 a.m. to 4:30 p.m. daily; $5 for adults, $4 for seniors, $1 for youth 6 to 15, and children under 6 are free.

PAINTED CAVE
Off CA 154 on Painted Cave Road, Santa Barbara

This ancient, 22-foot (6.7-meter)-deep cave preserves brightly colored pre-Columbian pictographs inscribed by the Chumash, Santa Barbara's first residents. Unfortunately, unscrupulous marauders removed the cave's other Stone Age artifacts in the 1870s, including arrowheads, axes, and baskets. The rock paintings remain intact, now protected by a locked iron gate.

The cave is on the edge of the road, 2 miles past the intersection of San Marcos Road and Old San Marcos Road, and you have to look carefully or you'll drive right by. Watch for the sign on Painted Cave Road if you're coming from East Camino Cielo Road. There is parking space for only 2 cars. The road is steep, so drive carefully.

i *Adobe* is the Spanish word for a sun-dried brick and for the clay soil used to make these bricks. Santa Barbara's best-known historical adobe dwelling is Casa de la Guerra in El Paseo.

✴SANTA BARBARA COUNTY COURTHOUSE
1100 Anacapa St., at Anapamu Street, Santa Barbara
(805) 962-6464
www.santabarbaracourthouse.org

Hundreds of historic courthouses grace this fair country, but it would be difficult to find another as stunning—both inside and out—as the Santa Barbara County Courthouse, a magnificent Spanish-Moorish structure that is one of the most photographed buildings in the nation. In 2003 it was declared a state historic landmark, and it's now well on its way to becoming a national landmark.

Completed in 1929 (fortuitously, just before the stock market crash), the ornate structure features hand-painted ceilings, a spiral staircase, wrought-iron chandeliers, imported tiles, carved doors, and beautiful historical murals depicting early California history and Chumash life.

Outside, spacious lawns and swaying palm trees surround the building, set off by a beautiful sunken garden, which serves as an evocative venue for many weddings, community events, and concerts. In the words of Charles H. Cheney, who in 1929 wrote the preface to *Californian Architecture in Santa Barbara*, "romance ran riot" in the courthouse, an assessment that was not altogether a compliment, as Cheney deemed it too large and overdone to "belong" to what he viewed as the low-key, intimate style of the city.

Still, Cheney acknowledged the "extraordinary number of intriguing bits of design" found both inside and outside the structure, and it is these unique features that continue to draw visitors more than 80 years after the building was completed.

Free hour-long guided tours are offered Mon through Sat at 2 p.m., with an additional 10:30 a.m. tour on Mon, Tues, and Fri, or you can wander around on your own. Be sure to go to the top of the clock tower, which affords a panoramic view of the city. The courthouse is open weekdays 8 a.m. to 5 p.m. and weekends 10 a.m. to 5 p.m., but the doors close to new visitors at 4:45 p.m. Admission is free.

✴SANTA BARBARA HISTORICAL MUSEUM
136 E. De la Guerra St., Santa Barbara
(805) 966-1601
www.santabarbaramuseum.com
Art, textiles, furniture, clothing, and other artifacts from Santa Barbara's rich, multicultural past have been preserved in this complex of adobe structures under the auspices of the Santa Barbara Historical Museum. Step back in time as you view the collected remnants of the area's Spanish, Mexican, and American periods, or stroll the inner courtyard, which seems far removed from the busy streets that surround the museum and adjacent historical adobes (including Casa Covarrubias, constructed in 1817). You can browse on your own (all exhibits are carefully labeled) or book a guided tour.

The Gledhill Library, on the museum grounds, houses an impressive collection of books, maps, and photographs chronicling Santa Barbara's history. It's open to the public 10 a.m. to 4 p.m. Tues through Fri, and 10 a.m. to 1 p.m. the first Sat of the month. (An hourly library research fee applies if you are not a member of the Historical Museum.)

The museum is open Tues through Sat from 10 a.m. to 5 p.m., and Sun from noon to 5 p.m. It offers free, guided tours on Sat at 2 p.m., and during the summer on Sun at 2 p.m. also. Admission is free, but a donation is appreciated. If you can't find a parking space on the adjacent street, watch for the small driveway next to the museum on De la Guerra Street; you'll find more parking in back.

i *Paseo* comes from the Spanish *paso*, which means "a step" and *pasear*, "to take a stroll." In Santa Barbara, it refers to the quaint Spanish-style promenades and courtyards linking downtown streets.

TRUSSELL-WINCHESTER ADOBE
412 W. Montecito St., Santa Barbara
(805) 966-1601
www.santabarbaramuseum.com
In 1853 the side-wheel steamer *Winfield Scott* sank off Anacapa Island. The ship's captain, Horatio Trussell, salvaged a ridge pole from its mast as well as other useful timber and brass and used the objects, along

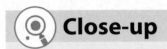

Close-up

Red Tile Walking Tour

If you're interested in Santa Barbara's famous architecture and fascinating history, we highly recommend the Red Tile Walking Tour. Named for the color of the roof tiles on many of Santa Barbara's downtown buildings, this self-guided tour takes you to some of the city's most important historic landmarks. Strolling around Santa Barbara in the sunshine on this 12-block tour is the best way to appreciate the city.

• Start your tour at the **Santa Barbara County Courthouse (1)** (1100 Anacapa St.; 805-962-6464). If you time it right, you can join a free hour-long guided tour starting in the Mural Room offered Mon through Sat at 2 p.m. with an additional 10:30 a.m. tour on Mon, Tues, and Fri. Don't miss the view from the clock tower.

• Cross Anacapa Street to the **Santa Barbara Public Library (2)** (40 E. Anapamu St.; 805-962-7653). Here you can view art exhibitions at the Faulkner Gallery Mon through Thurs from 10 a.m. to 9 p.m., Fri and Sat from 10 a.m. to 5:30 p.m., and Sun from 1 to 5 p.m.

• Continue down Anapamu Street to the **Santa Barbara Museum of Art (3)** (1130 State St.; 805-963-4364; www.sbmuseart.org). One of the top 10 regional museums in the country, the museum displays Asian, American, and European treasures spanning more than 4,000 years. Don't miss the acclaimed *Portrait of Mexico Today* (1932), the only intact mural in the United States by renowned Mexican artist David Alfaro Siqueiros. You'll see it at the front entry steps.

• Stroll a half block south on State Street and enter charming **La Arcada Court (4)** (1114 State St.) with a 16-foot (5-meter) clock at the entrance. This quaint Spanish paseo and courtyard are filled with fountains, shops, cafe-style restaurants, and a series of life-size bronze statuary that provide great photo ops.

• Wander south on State Street to Carrillo Street, then turn east toward the mountains to the **Hill-Carrillo Adobe (5)** (11 E. Carrillo St., 805-963-1873), dating from 1826. The first city council met here in 1850. It is now used by local nonprofits for meetings and events, but you can admire the building from the outside.

• Return to State Street and walk south 2 blocks to **El Paseo (6)** (11–19 E. De la Guerra St.). Built in the 1920s around historic Casa de la Guerra, this "Street in Spain" was reportedly California's first shopping complex. As you stroll along the cobbled flower-lined passageway, notice the graceful details of the Spanish Colonial Revival architecture. El Paseo Restaurant here is a great spot to sip a margarita. Across the street from El Paseo, you'll find palm-lined **Paseo Nuevo (7)** Mall, packed with specialty shops and sidewalk cafes.

• Continue through the passageway of El Paseo and enter the courtyard of **Casa de la Guerra (8)** (15 E. De la Guerra St., 805-966-6961). Built between 1819 and 1826, the adobe was originally home to José de la Guerra y Noriega, commander of El Presidio de Santa Barbara, and it was the social center of Santa Barbara for years. Across the street, framed by date palms, is **De la Guerra Plaza (9),** site of the annual Fiesta downtown marketplace. Adjacent you'll see the Spanish Revival *Santa Barbara News-Press* building and City Hall.

• Turn left on De la Guerra Street, head toward the mountains to Anacapa Street, and you'll see the 1849 **Oreña Adobes (10)** (2729 E. De la Guerra St.). Look for the plaque on the corner of De la Guerra and Anacapa Streets.

• Cross Anacapa Street and follow the hibiscus trees half a block down De la Guerra Street to **Presidio Avenue (11)**, the oldest street in Santa Barbara. At the corner, look for the plaque commemorating the guard's house built around the 1840s. If you enter the garden, you'll see a tranquil koi pond and elephant fountain.

• Return the way you came and cross De la Guerra Street to the **Santiago de la Guerra Adobe (12)** (110 E. De la Guerra St.), one of the city's oldest structures. Next door, you'll find another historic home, the 1830 **Lugo Adobe (13)** (114 E. De la Guerra St.) tucked in the pastel-hued courtyard of Meridian Studios.

• Stroll toward the mountains to the corner of De la Guerra and Santa Barbara Streets and visit the **Santa Barbara Historical Museum (14)** (136 E. De la Guerra St.; 805-966-1601; www.santabarbaramuseum.com), where you'll see artifacts from Santa Barbara's multicultural past. The museum is open Tues through Sat 10 a.m. to 5 p.m., and Sunday noon to 5 p.m. All exhibits are carefully labeled for self-guided tours.

• Turn right at the corner of De la Guerra and Santa Barbara Streets just past the Historical Museum, where you'll find 1817 **Casa Covarrubias (15)** (136 E. De la Guerra St.; 805-966-1601) and the adjoining historic adobe. The peaceful oak-shaded courtyard graced by a fountain is a popular venue for special events.

• Leave the way you came, cross De la Guerra Street, and stroll up Santa Barbara Street to the pink-painted **Rochin Adobe (16)** (820 Santa Barbara St.), made of salvaged bricks from the ruins of structures built against the south east Presidio walls.

• Continue north along Santa Barbara Street to Canon Perdido Street. At the corner is **El Presidio de Santa Barbara State Historic Park (17)** (123 E. Canon Perdido St.; 805-965-0093; www.sbthp.org), site of the Presidio's founding in 1782. You can view a 15-minute slide show and take a self-guided tour of the Presidio every day from 10:30 a.m. to 4:30 p.m.

• Follow Canon Perdido Street toward State Street, where you'll find the reconstructed Presidio Chapel, the Canedo Adobe, and **El Cuartel (18),** all part of the Presidio barracks. Once the family home of the soldier entrusted with guarding the Presidio gate, El Cuartel is the oldest existing adobe in Santa Barbara and the second oldest in California.

• At the southeast corner of Canon Perdido and Anacapa Streets, you'll see the **Post Office (19)** (836 Anacapa St.), a mix of contemporary Federalist and Art Deco styles with a Monterey Revival wood-shingle roof.

• On the northwest corner is the **Lobero Theatre (20)** (33 E. Canon Perdido St.; 805-963-0761; www.lobero.com). Founded in 1873 by opera enthusiast Jose Lobero, this state historic landmark is California's oldest continuously operating theater. Continue north along Anacapa Street back to the Santa Barbara County Courthouse.

Courtesy of the Santa Barbara Car Free project and the Santa Barbara Chamber of Commerce.

with adobe bricks, in the construction of this home, built in 1854. Later Dr. Robert F. Winchester, a local physician, occupied the home until his death in 1932.

Now under the auspices of the Santa Barbara Historical Museum, the home is a small museum that includes period furnishings and other items used by the Trussell and Winchester families. The museum welcomes visitors for guided tours every Sat at 1 and 2 p.m. If you would like to arrange a group tour at another time, call the Historical Society at the listed number to make a reservation. Admission is $5 for adults and $1 for children under 12.

Local Landmarks & Outdoor Attractions

MORETON BAY FIG TREE
Chapala Street at US 101, Santa Barbara
The Moreton Bay Fig Tree (and yes, everyone in Santa Barbara knows exactly which tree you are talking about when you say "the" Moreton Bay Fig Tree) was planted on July 4, 1876, by a young girl who had been given the seedling by a sailor fresh off the boat from Australia. A year later, when the girl moved away, she gave the little tree to a friend, who transplanted it to its current location. The rest, as they say, is history.

The tree is now huge (some say it is the largest specimen of *Ficus macrophylla* in the country), and it has had quite a life here in the fertile soil of Santa Barbara. In the 1930s the tree was nearly cut down to make way for a gas station until the legendary Pearl Chase (an incredibly influential advocate and leader for the preservation of key sites) put a stop to that nonsense.

In 1961 the Parks Department measured the tree and announced that more than 16,000 people could stand in the shade

beneath the 21,000 square feet covered by its outstretched branches. In the 1970s it was a home of sorts to the city's homeless people, who camped on the lawn until they were finally evicted. In 1982 it was declared a city landmark. Now its trunk is about 12.5 feet in diameter, and counting!

In recent years, the venerable tree underwent special treatment to ensure that it continues to flourish. Both the Santa Barbara Parks Department and the Historic Landmark Commission approved the installation of a chain barrier to keep people at a distance (branches have been broken by climbing children, and people have carved their initials in the trunk). Interpretive signs tell you about the tree and politely ask that you admire it from afar.

The Moreton Bay Fig Tree is always open, and admission is free.

SANTA BARBARA HARBOR AND BREAKWATER
Entrance at Harbor Way, off Cabrillo Boulevard, west of Castillo Street, Santa Barbara
We think Santa Barbara Harbor is a must-see attraction. In the 1920s Santa Barbara businessman Max Fleischmann funded its construction because he wanted a safe haven for his 250-foot yacht, the *Haida*. Tucked inside a protective breakwater, it's a great spot for a relaxing stroll, and you can't beat the salty ambience and stunning views of the mountains and sea. More than 1,000 boats bob in the slips here—from tiny rowboats to large luxury yachts. Paddling around in a kayak is a great way to explore the area, and you can rent them right on Harbor Way (see the Beaches & Watersports chapter.) Keep an eye out for harbor seals and sea lions. The breakwater, constructed in

1924, is paved and wide enough to accommodate you, your friends, and a baby stroller, so go for a walk (but watch out during rough seas).

At the east end of the harbor is SEA Landing, where the *Condor Express* departs for whale-watching excursions and Truth Aquatics' boats anchor (see the Beaches & Watersports chapter). The harbor is open every day, and there is no admission price for exploring.

✳STEARNS WHARF
State Street and Cabrillo Boulevard, Santa Barbara
www.stearnswharf.org
When Santa Barbara lumberman John Stearns completed his namesake pier in 1872, he could hardly have imagined that more than 100 years later it would be the most visited landmark in town. For decades after its completion (it was then the longest deep-water pier between Los Angeles and San Francisco), the wharf was used for loading and unloading freight and passengers, but in 1941 the Harbor Restaurant was built, marking the beginning of the wharf's transition into a tourist attraction. Today its seaside location, restaurants, shops, and festive atmosphere draw visitors by the thousands.

We love the clickity-clack sound as we slowly drive out on this wonderful old wooden pier. Limited parking (including valet parking) is available on the wharf itself, or you can park in the nearby public lots on Cabrillo Boulevard and walk the 0.5-mile (1 kilometer) to the end of the pier. Many restaurants will validate your parking ticket, if you stay over the free limit.

As you enter, check out the Dolphin Fountain, formally known as the Santa Barbara Bicentennial Friendship Fountain, which was created by local artist Bud Bottoms in 1982 under the sponsorship of the Santa Barbara/Puerto Vallarta Sister City Committee. A replica of the fountain adorns each of Santa Barbara's sister cities, including Puerto Vallarta, Mexico; Toba, Japan; and Yalta, Ukraine.

Continuing on, you'll find several popular seafood restaurants (Santa Barbara Shellfish is one of our favorites) and shops selling confections, souvenirs, and sportswear. The water taxi *Lil' Toot* departs from the pier, and you can do a little wine tasting here. Stearns Wharf is always open, and admission is free.

Natural Attractions & Science Museums

SANTA BARBARA BOTANIC GARDEN
1212 Mission Canyon Rd., Santa Barbara
(805) 682-4726
www.sbbg.org
In 1926, rather than see a pristine Santa Barbara canyon turned into a housing development, Anna Blaksley Bliss snapped up the land and declared it a botanical preserve in memory of her father, Henry Blaksley.

Today the 78 acres that make up the Santa Barbara Botanic Garden provide a superb setting for the study of native California flora. More than 5 miles of trails meander along the banks of upper Mission Creek and through the garden's meadows and canyons, which are planted with wildflowers, cacti, oak, sycamore trees, and more than 1,000 species of rare and indigenous plants. There's an entire section devoted to flora found on the Santa Barbara Channel Islands, as well as a forest of redwood trees and display areas on the California desert and mountains.

The Botanic Garden is open 9 a.m. to 6 p.m. Mar through Oct, and 9 a.m. to 5 p.m.

Nov to Feb. Admission is $8 for adults; $6 for seniors 60 and older and for teens 13 through 17 and students with current ID; and $4 for children ages 2 through 12. Children younger than 2 are admitted free.

SANTA BARBARA MARITIME MUSEUM
113 Harbor Way, Ste. 190, Santa Barbara Harbor, Santa Barbara
(805) 962-8404
www.sbmm.org

The Santa Barbara Maritime Museum offers interactive exhibits for the whole family. The museum features the California coast's diverse maritime history, including the Honda Point disaster, the US Navy's largest peacetime shipwreck; a working periscope; model ships; a sportfishing exhibit that allows all ages to land the big one, hard-hat diving equipment; antique instruments; rare artifacts; and historical photos. A treasure map activity for young children includes prizes from a treasure chest. The museum's 86-seat Munger Theater presents feature films and documentaries such as James Cameron's *Ghost of the Abyss* and *Aliens of the Deep,* and the Coast Guard film *On Wings of Eagles.* Surf films are shown on Saturday.

After your visit, browse the gift shop for maps, nautical books, clothing, toys, and gifts. The museum is closed Wed, but it's open every other day except major holidays from 10 a.m. to 6 p.m. during the summer (from Memorial Day to Labor Day) and from 10 a.m. to 5 p.m. during the rest of the year. Note that admission is free on the third Thursday of every month. Admission is $7 for adults; $4 for seniors, students, and kids ages 6 to 17; and $2 for children ages 1 to 5; children under 1 and members are free. Also visit the fourth-floor visitor center and savor the great views.

SANTA BARBARA MUSEUM OF NATURAL HISTORY
2559 Puesta del Sol Rd., Santa Barbara
(805) 682-4711
www.sbnature.org

Located just beyond the old mission building, the Santa Barbara Museum of Natural History is uniquely nestled in nature. Founded in 1916 as the first museum in Santa Barbara, this charming Spanish-style structure is set on 11 acres along the banks of Mission Creek. The museum features exhibit halls dedicated to the study of California and Santa Barbara County natural history, including astronomy, birds and eggs, geology, insects, mammals, marine biology, Native Americans, paleontology, and antique manuscripts and natural history art.

Your adventure begins outside the entrance, where the magnificent 73-foot (22-meter) skeleton of a blue whale provides a perfect photo op. Pass through the entrance into a quaint courtyard, then follow the signs to the areas that interest you most. Plan ahead and bring a picnic to enjoy under the majestic oak trees along Mission Creek.

The museum is a treasure trove of Chumash artifacts (don't miss the baskets and the full-scale model of a Chumash canoe) and features small but impressive exhibits on mammals, birds, insects, gems and minerals, plants, and marine life. Adults and kids love to push the button of the famous generational rattlesnake exhibit to make the tail rattle. Grandparents, too, remember pushing this same button as children and enjoy bringing their grandchildren to the museum to experience this memorable thrill.

In addition to its many permanent attractions, the museum offers a dynamic schedule of special exhibits and events for the whole family (see the Kidstuff chapter for details on activities of interest to children).

The Gladwin Planetarium, located in this museum, features a changing lineup of programs reflecting the seasonal skies or other cosmic events. On the second Sat of every month from dusk to 10 p.m., the museum hosts the Star Party and invites you to bring the whole family to survey the night sky through high-powered telescopes. (*Tip:* Bring a jacket just in case.) The museum's gift shop sells books, jewelry, and lots of cool stuff for kids.

The museum is open 10 a.m. to 5 p.m. daily (except Thanksgiving Day, Christmas Day, New Year's Day, and the last Saturday in June for the annual Santa Barbara Wine Festival). Museum general admission is $10 for adults; $7 for seniors and teens, and $6 for children; summer admission may differ. On the third Sunday of the month (except in June, July, and August) admission is free to all. Planetarium tickets are $4 per person with museum admission. Get the SB Nature Pass and visit the museum and the Ty Warner Sea Center for one low price. Parking is free.

i A walk along the breakwater at the Santa Barbara Harbor is a welcome diversion for Santa Barbara residents and visitors alike. Be careful, however, when the surf is high. More than one unsuspecting person has been doused when waves crashed over the wall. (The waves aren't dangerous—just wet and cold.)

SANTA BARBARA ZOO
500 Niños Dr., Santa Barbara
(805) 926-5339, (805) 962-6310,
recorded information
www.sbzoo.org

Zoos and kids seem made for each other (and indeed, this one is amply discussed in the Kidstuff chapter), but the Santa Barbara Zoo is such a charming place that we think it's worth a visit whether you have the kids in tow or not. To begin with, there's a fabulous ocean view from its grassy hilltop, which is believed to have once been the site of a Chumash camp.

Long after the Chumash were gone, a grand mansion was built on the hill and was the centerpiece of a 16-acre estate. John Beale erected the original in 1896, but after his death in 1914, his widow Lillian married John Child, and the property became known as the Child Estate. After Mr. Child's death, the land was presented to the Santa Barbara Foundation, which in turn transferred management to the Child Estate Foundation.

In 1962 the land was cleared, making way for the very humble Child Estate Zoo, which opened in August 1963. A llama, two sheep, a goat, a turkey, and a pair of spider monkeys were the only inhabitants of the new zoo, but the community had a vision of what the zoo could become and set about making it a reality. In 1972 the zoo joined the Association of Zoos and Aquariums (AZA) and has continued its development in keeping with the AZA's goals and objectives. In 1981 the zoo was accredited by the AZA—a status it currently maintains.

Over the years, Santa Barbara's zoo has added an impressive number of new animals and exhibits, and it continues to be dedicated to preserving a high-quality environment for both visitors and the zoo's permanent residents. More than 600 animals currently reside at the zoo, which attracts more than a half-million visitors every year, many of them longtime Santa Barbarans who go back often to see what's new.

The newest exhibit is California Trails, which features endangered or threatened species from the Golden State. California condors are the centerpiece of the $7.5 million complex—the largest in the zoo's history. Numbering only 22 in 1982, these huge scavengers have made a comeback, thanks to captive breeding, and over 100 now fly free and breed in the wild. Zoo volunteers monitor condor nests in the nearby Sespe Condor Sanctuary. The zoo's 4 juvenile condors are joined by an adult "mentor bird." Also on view: wee Channel Island foxes, found only on the islands seen from the zoo's hilltop; desert tortoises; bald eagles; and local reptiles and amphibians. Other highlights are Asian elephants Sujatha and Little Mac, 2 bachelor lowland gorillas, a family of active Asian small-clawed otters, a flock of Humboldt penguins, and a Masai giraffe calf, born in early 2011.

You can easily "do the zoo" in a few hours, but if you have kids, you may want to make a day of it. And a stop at the new Explore Store is a must. The zoo is open every day (except Christmas) from 10 a.m. to 5 p.m., with ticket sales ending at 4 p.m. Admission is $12 for adults, and $10 for children ages 2 through 12 and seniors 65 and older; children under 2 are free. Parking is $5 per vehicle.

TY WARNER SEA CENTER
211 Stearns Wharf, Santa Barbara
(805) 687-4711
The sea center is owned and operated by the Santa Barbara Museum of Natural History, so ask about the SB Nature Pass and visit both for one low price. When you enter the 2-story glass foyer, a life-size 39-foot (12-meter) model of a California gray whale and her calf greets you. This interactive and downright fun sea center makes for a pleasant and educational expedition, where adults and children get hands-on, close encounters with sea creatures like sharks, sea stars, crabs, and more. Visitors can do marine science and be an oceanographer for a day. Plus children love crawling through the 1,500-gallon (5,600-liter) surge tank to get a real-life peek at the power of the ocean from the inside out. Open daily from 10 a.m. to 5 p.m. (except Thanksgiving Day, Christmas Day, and New Year's Day). General admission is $8 for adults; $6 for seniors and teens, and $5 for children. Summer admission may differ. Parking on Stearns Wharf is free for the first 90 minutes with ticket validation.

GOLETA

RANCHO LA PATERA & STOW HOUSE
304 N. Los Carneros Rd., Goleta
(805) 681-7216
www.goletahistory.org
Rancho La Patera offers guided tours of the Stow House, overviews in the Visitor Interpretive Center, and hands-on exhibits in the Cavelleto History Education Center. The Stow House, a restored Carpenter Gothic home built in the 1870s, is one of the oldest homes in Goleta and is filled with furniture, clothing, kitchenware, and other items from the period. Its interior is especially charming when adorned for Christmas. A blacksmith's shop and other small outbuildings have also been preserved.

The grounds are lovely, with various exotic plantings and a wide expanse of shaded lawn that is often used for special events such as weddings, an annual old-fashioned Fourth of July celebration, and other community events. Lake Los Carneros, a small artificial lake east of the house, is a popular site for walking or birding. Visit Sat and Sun from 1 to 4 p.m.

Admission is $8; children under 12 are free. The historic Stow House is open for guided tours at 2 and 3 p.m.

SOUTH COAST RAILROAD MUSEUM & GOLETA DEPOT
300 N. Los Carneros Rd., Goleta
(805) 964-3540
www.goletadepot.org
The Goleta Depot, built in 1901, has been restored on this site, adjacent to the Stow House (see above). The museum is very small but includes railroad memorabilia, photos, and an extensive model railroad. Movies are screened in the theater room. You can send a telegraph or climb aboard the real caboose displayed on tracks outside.

A big draw is the miniature train that circles the grounds and offers rides Wed and Fri between 2 and 3:45 p.m. and Sat and Sun between 1:15 and 3:45 p.m. (see the Kidstuff chapter for details on train rides at the museum). A small museum shop sells gifts and educational materials with a railroad theme. The museum is open 1 to 4 p.m. Fri through Sun. Admission is free, but donations are requested.

MONTECITO

✳CASA DEL HERRERO
1387 E. Valley Rd., Montecito
(805) 565-5653
www.casadelherrero.com
Casa del Herrero (1925) is one of Santa Barbara's most underrated attractions. Listed in the National Register of Historic Places, this stunning home was designed by acclaimed architect George Washington Smith on a beautiful 11-acre estate in Montecito. Still under original ownership, it's one of the finest examples of Spanish Colonial Revival architecture and is now preserved as a museum. Inside you'll see an amazing collection of 13th- to 18th-century Spanish furnishings, decorative arts, extensive Mediterranean tile work, and other colorful architectural details, including a ceiling from a 15th-century convent. The 90-minute tour of the casa also includes a visit through the elaborate Moorish garden and adjacent workshop, where you can view an array of silversmith tools. Tours are available from Feb through Nov, Wed and Sat at 10 a.m. and 2 p.m. Reservations are essential, and a fee of $15 per person is payable when you reserve your space.

✳GANNA WALSKA LOTUSLAND
695 Ashley Rd., Montecito
(805) 969-9990
www.lotusland.org
Lotusland is a Santa Barbara gem. You have to do some planning in order see it, but you will never forget your visit. Overseen by the Ganna Walska Lotusland Foundation, the 37-acre estate is named for the sacred Indian lotus, which was planted there in the early 1890s by nurseryman R. Kinton Stevens.

In 1941 the estate was purchased by well-known Polish opera singer Madame Ganna Walska, who shaped Lotusland into what it is today: a series of breathtaking theme gardens filled with rare botanical specimens that delight the eye and renew the spirit.

Your 2-hour guided tour will take you through an imaginative Theatre Garden displaying 16th-century German and Viennese sculptures of dwarves and hunchbacks; the delightful Blue Garden, planted with blue fescue, blue Atlas cedars, and blue Mexican fan palms; a breathtaking Aloe Garden, with its centerpiece Shell Pond lined with abalone and South Sea Island giant clam shells; a forest of dragon trees from the Canary Islands; a serene Japanese Garden; and the second-finest collection of rare cycads in the world, including 11 of the 12 genres.

Other highlights include a working horticultural clock, a 12th-century baptismal font, and topiary, fern, palm, and succulent gardens. This is far more than an interesting tour for garden buffs; it is an invitation to the fascinating world of Madame Walska and her botanical wonders. Don't miss it. Tours are conducted Wed through Sat at 10 a.m. and 1:30 p.m. from mid-February to mid-November.

Reservations can be made up to a year in advance; call between 9 a.m. and noon Mon through Fri to book. The reservation office is open year-round. Admission is $35 for adults, $10 for children ages 5 to 18, and $5 for children under 5.

CARPINTERIA

CARPINTERIA HARBOR SEAL COLONY
Below Carpinteria Bluffs
Carpinteria is home to one of only two publicly accessible harbor seal colonies in Southern California. To see these fascinating creatures, hike a half mile (1 kilometer) down the spectacular bluff-top trail at the southern end of Bailard Avenue. You'll see the viewing area perched on a bluff just before the Venoco pier.

CARPINTERIA VALLEY MUSEUM OF
   HISTORY
956 Maple Ave., Carpinteria
(805) 684-3112
www.carpinteriahistoricalmuseum.org
Although it may not have the glamour of Santa Barbara, Carpinteria is a delightful little city with deep historical roots. Its small museum depicts the lives of Carpinteria's earliest residents, with exhibits on the Chumash, the city's pioneer families, and its agricultural history. Furniture, clothing, farm tools, and other historical artifacts are on display, along with exhibits on oil production, an early 20th-century schoolhouse, and a quilt depicting local historical events. The museum is open 1 to 4 p.m. Tues through Sat. Admission is by donation.

SIGHTSEEING TOURS

ARCHITECTURAL FOUNDATION OF
   SANTA BARBARA WALKING TOURS
(805) 965-6307
www.afsb.org
These educational 2-hour walking tours are one of the best sightseeing deals in town. For a $10 donation per person (children under 12 are free), trained docents from the Architectural Foundation will guide you through the hidden courtyards and original adobes of downtown Santa Barbara, pointing out distinctive architectural features and sharing historical tidbits. The Sabado (Saturday) tour leaves from the steps of City Hall, De la Guerra Plaza, at 10 a.m. Along the way, you'll visit the historic De la Guerra Adobe, El Paseo, and some of Santa Barbara's earliest buildings as you explore the architectural legacy of the Spanish and Mexican settlers. You'll also learn about the giants of Santa Barbara design. The Domingo (Sunday) tour departs from the entrance of the public library at 10 a.m. This tour explores Santa Barbara's downtown art and architecture, as it was reborn after the 1925 earthquake. Reservations are only required for private groups and the physically challenged. Rain cancels all tours.

CAPTAIN JACK'S TOURS
(805) 564-1819
www.captainjackstours.com
Offering some 20 different tours—ranging from $50 wine or beer tours to tours on Segways (motorized human scooters), as well as helicopter, sailing, horseback riding, and even double tandem sky-diving tours—Captain Jack seems to have a tour for everyone. The most popular tours tend to be the wine country or the Heaven on Earth kayak and horseback-riding combo, but the Top Deck tour takes it all in and includes kayaking, horseback riding, and wine tasting ($250 per person or two for $400). Rates start at $35.

CLOUD CLIMBERS JEEP & WINE TOURS
(805) 646-3200
www.ccjeeps.com
Looking for a wilder kind of wine country tour? Cloud Climbers picks you up from your doorstep in a 5- to 7-passenger canopy-covered Jeep for 6-hour backcountry safaris to four of the region's best wineries for tasting. Along the way, explore rugged mountain trails; learn about winemaking, local history, flora, and fauna; and pass by the former Reagan Ranch. Tours include a made-to-order picnic lunch in a lovely setting, custom routing and winery selections based on guests' wine preferences, a logo wine glass, tasting fees, and a professional guide. Awarded "Best Adventure Tour of California 2010" and known as Santa Barbara's original backcountry wine tasting tour, Cloud Climbers has earned a great reputation and is perfect if you're looking for a little adventure and hate being cooped up in a crowded coach. This tour starts at 10 a.m. Tour prices start at $89.

LAND & SEA TOURS

ABOARD THE LAND SHARK
(805) 683-7600
www.thelandshark.net
Amphibious land-and-sea tours depart daily, weather permitting, from 10 E. Cabrillo (next to the Dolphin Fountain at Stearns Wharf) for informative, exciting, and relaxing 90-minute narrated tours that weave their way in the open-air Land Shark through the streets of downtown Santa Barbara before submerging into the Pacific for a nice float on the water. Arrive 15 minutes before departure, and it's wise to bring a jacket or sweater. November 1 through April 30 departures at noon and 2 p.m.; May 1 to October 30 departures at noon, 2 p.m., and 4 p.m. Adults $25; $10 for children under 10. Cash and credit cards accepted.

PERSONAL TOURS LTD.
PO Box 60109, Santa Barbara, CA 93160
(805) 685-0552
www.personaltoursltd.com
You get just what you'd expect from this well-established Santa Barbara company, which offers affordable, in-depth, private tours with a personal touch. All tours are custom designed to match your special interests. You can focus on Santa Barbara's estates and gardens, natural history, fine arts, real estate, or photography, or explore the hot shopping spots. If you're not sure what you want to see, call and chat with the friendly staff, and they'll happily recommend an itinerary to fit your time limitations and budget. Tours are priced according to the duration of the trip and the vehicle used but range from $105 for a basic tour in your own car to $375 for a basic coach tour. You can also choose from sedans, convertibles,

custom vans, and minibuses. Charter tours to out-of-town attractions, such as Hearst Castle, Big Sur, and Los Angeles events, are also available, and international language tours can be arranged with advance notice. Vehicles are equipped for the physically challenged, and all tours require reservations in advance.

SANTA BARBARA OLD TOWN TROLLEY
22 State St., Santa Barbara
(805) 965-0353
www.sbtrolley.com
Hop aboard the 30-passenger Santa Barbara Trolley for a 90-minute narrated tour of Santa Barbara City and all the major tourist attractions.

This is an affordable way to see the sights in a day, and it offers some flexibility so it's a great option if you have the kids in tow. The trolley tour includes 14 attractions, such as beautiful Butterfly Beach in Montecito, the Moreton Bay Fig Tree, and Santa Barbara County Courthouse. The only scheduled stop included in the 90-minute tour is at Mission Santa Barbara, where you can leave the trolley and stretch your legs for 15 minutes. If you want to spend more time at the other attractions, you can hop off anywhere along the route and explore on your own, then hop aboard again when another trolley comes by. The tours run daily every hour between 10 a.m. and 4 p.m. from Stearns Wharf. Admission is $19

for adults and teens, and $9 for children 12 and younger.

SPENCER'S LIMOUSINE & TOURS
(805) 884-9700
www.spencerslimo.com
Take a peek at gated movie-star estates on a celebrity tour of Montecito, explore the city's architectural gems, or visit top attractions on a Santa Barbara City tour, all in the comfort of a plush limousine or Lincoln Town Car. Voted one of the top tour companies by local newspaper polls, Spencer's Limousine & Tours customizes all its tours based on your special interests. Spencer Winston, a docent for the Santa Barbara Historical Museum and avid historian, spices his narration with hot little tidbits along the way. Tours can be customized. Call for prices.

SPITFIRE AVIATION
300 Moffett Place, Santa Barbara
(805) 967-4373
www.flyspitfire.com
Unique to Santa Barbara, this touring company lets you see the city and environs from the sky, where you can really appreciate the area's dramatic topography. Board a 4-seat Cessna at the Santa Barbara Airport for your tour, and you're up, up, and away! Lasting just over an hour, the excursion includes an aerial view of Santa Barbara, the coastline, the Santa Ynez Valley, and the mountains.

KIDSTUFF

Santa Barbara is a kid's paradise. From an amazing zoo to a beachside skateboard park and free weekend festivals (see the Annual Events chapter), there are plenty of diversions for younger visitors that their parents will also enjoy. Families can even design an entire vacation just exploring the many free, distinctly different beaches and parks.

In this chapter, you'll find information about Santa Barbara kids' favorite haunts and activities. Many of these also appear in more complete detail in other chapters, for example, Beaches & Watersports, Recreation, the Arts, and Attractions. In these cases, we provide a brief description tailored for kids in this chapter and refer you to the appropriate chapter for other details.

WHAT'S HAPPENING IN SANTA BARBARA

Several publications have listings of the many daily, weekly, ongoing, and special events for kids in the Santa Barbara area. The *Santa Barbara Independent,* a free weekly paper available at newsstands all over the county, also lists events for kids. *Santa Barbara Family Life* (www.sbfamilylife.com), a free monthly magazine, includes articles, parenting tips, book and software reviews, a calendar of events, discount coupons, and a section just for kids. You can find it at grocery stores, bookstores, the library, and many other places frequented by families. Look up http://sbparent.com for everything happening with parents and kids in the area.

> **i** Looking for a babysitter? Check out www.mummysdayoff.com or call (805) 570-6171. They pet-sit as well.

After you've done your prep work, you're ready to explore. Take this manual along—it has lots of tips about where to go and what to do.

ART FOR KIDS

ADDERLEY SCHOOL
Santa Barbara Youth Ensemble
319-A Anacapa St., Santa Barbara
(805) 899-3680
www.adderleyschool.com
The Adderley School is associated with the Santa Barbara Youth Ensemble and prides itself in putting the child's heart and soul before anything else. The caliber of performances and production of this group are phenomenal. Outstanding musicals with Broadway-worthy sets, a live orchestra, and super costumes showcase many young, breathtaking performers whom we suspect

are the stars of tomorrow. In spring 2010, the youth ensemble brought *How to Succeed in Business Without Really Trying* to the Lobero Theatre, home to the school's productions, and in spring 2011 they performed the classic *West Side Story*, which received rave reviews. Don't miss the next production provided by this tour de force in performing arts.

ART FROM SCRAP
302 E. Cota St., Santa Barbara
(805) 884-0459
www.artfromscrap.org

Art from Scrap is a fun place where children and adults can transform springs, foam rubber, plastic neon-colored squigglies, yarn, paper, and all sorts of industrial doodads into works of art. Art from Scrap promotes conservation and reuse of discarded materials through hands-on exploration. Regional businesses and manufacturers donate materials. Art from Scrap Fun Workshops have varying themes and are offered every Sat from 10 a.m. to noon. The cost is $8 per person. Art from Scrap's office and retail store are open Tues, Wed, and Fri from 10 a.m. to 2 p.m., Thurs 10 a.m. to 6 p.m., and Sat 10 a.m. to 3 p.m.

i Drop your kids (ages 7 and up) off at Art from Scrap on Saturday mornings from 10 a.m. to noon while you shop for fresh fruits and veggies at the nearby farmers' market.·

SANTA BARBARA MUSEUM OF ART
Ridley-Tree Education Center at the McCormick House
1600 Santa Barbara St., Santa Barbara
(805) 962-1661
www.sbmuseart.org

Young Michelangelos will revel in the inspired classes taught at the Ridley-Tree Education Center. SBMA's ArtVenture camps cover sculpture, painting, drawing, collage, and architecture in full-day programs, from 9 a.m. to 3 p.m. Ceramics programs are half-day camps (9 a.m. to noon) with the option to stay for regular camp programs for an extra fee. Call for more details and information, or download the brochure from the Santa Barbara Museum website at www .sbma.net/kidsfamilies.

GETTING WET & WILD

When the weather's warm (which is often), Santa Barbara kids like to cool off down by the ocean or in one of our many community pools.

Favorite Beaches

Most young Insiders hang out at the beach a lot. You'll always find a pack of them boogie-boarding and surfing at beaches every day during the summer and on warm-weather weekends the rest of the year. The following are their favorite beach haunts (see the Beaches & Watersports chapter for detailed descriptions). Lifeguards are generally on duty at these beaches daily from early or mid-June until Labor Day.

Santa Barbara
ARROYO BURRO BEACH
2981 Cliff Dr., Santa Barbara
(805) 687-3714
www.sbparks.org

This is the place to find Insider kids, who call it "Henry's" (spelled Hendry's) beach. Even when the surf's not up, dozens of children float around in wet suits, hoping for a swell. Parents like to hang out at the Boathouse

Restaurant, which has great atmosphere and good grub. It's also a great beach for tide pooling when the tide is low, and you can reserve a group area here for birthday parties.

> Before you take the kids to a park or beach, check out www.sbparks .org and www.sbparksandrecreation.com for information on facilities, directions, and maps.

EAST BEACH/CABRILLO PAVILION BATHHOUSE
E. Cabrillo Boulevard near Niños Drive, Santa Barbara
(805) 897-2680
www.sbparksandrecreation.com
Although East Beach isn't the best beach for surfing and boogie-boarding, you can't beat the services and activities. There's a playground, snack shop/restaurant, bathrooms, showers, and volleyball courts. You can rent boogie boards, beach chairs, volleyballs, and more at the bathhouse.

LEADBETTER BEACH
Shoreline and Loma Alta Drives, Santa Barbara
(805) 897-2680
www.sbparksandrecreation.com
"Leds" is a broad stretch of sandy beach between the yacht harbor and Shoreline Park. Since it's a favorite local sailboarding spot, you can watch the sailboards and catamarans ply the waves while you're digging for crabs and building sand castles.

If you don't want to picnic, you can order great food at the Shoreline Beach Cafe, with tables either right in the sand or just above on the patio. The waves near the point

are often ideal for pint-size surfers: not too big, but big enough for fun boogie-board and surf rides. Picnic and barbecue areas, restrooms, and outdoor showers are also available here.

Goleta
GOLETA BEACH COUNTY PARK
5986 Sandspit Rd., Goleta
(805) 967-1300
www.sbparks.org
This 29-acre county park is very popular with local families. It lies right near the entrance to UCSB and offers boating, fishing, restrooms, a playground, horseshoes, volleyball courts, and picnic and barbecue areas on a grassy expanse under a stretch of palm trees. Paved bicycle trails twist through the park, and you can fish off the Goleta Pier and munch on snacks from the snack bar. The popular Beachside Bar-Cafe, located on the beach inside the park, provides excellent food and views in a casual atmosphere.

Summerland
LOOKOUT PARK/SUMMERLAND BEACH
2297 Finney Rd., Summerland
(805) 568-2460
www.sbparks.org
You'll find this scenic little park and beach access tucked between US 101 and the ocean, near the Summerland exit. The park provides spectacular cliff-top views over the sheltered beach to the distant Channel Islands. Romp in the playground and picnic at tables on the bluffs above the beach. When you're ready for a swim or a stroll along the shore, just head down the path to the beach. The park has barbecue facilities, restrooms, and on-site parking.

Carpinteria
CARPINTERIA CITY BEACH
End of Linden Avenue, Carpinteria
(805) 684-5405
www.carpinteria.ca.us
This is billed as the "world's safest beach." That's because the natural reef breakwater along the shore tames large waves and eliminates riptides. The gently sloping shore and mild waves make swimming conditions ideal. In summertime, a small store on the beach rents beach equipment and raises funds for youth recreation. Bring your kayak or paddleboard and launch at Ash Avenue. Carpinteria Beach has lifeguards each day throughout the summer.

CARPINTERIA STATE BEACH
Entrance at Linden Avenue near
6th Street, Carpinteria
(805) 684-2811
www.parks.ca.gov
One of the most popular parks in California's state park system, this beautiful 48-acre stretch of coast is right next to City Beach. You'll find day-use and camping facilities here and a visitor center with natural history exhibits and nature programs. It's a fantastic place to explore tide pools, watch birds, swim, fish, hike, picnic, and splash around. Keep an eye out for sea lions and dolphins, and you can view harbor seals thronging on the beach at the nearby rookery. (See Carpinteria Harbor Seal Colony in Walk on the Wild Side later in this chapter.) The park also has an excellent swimming beach and a fairly good area for surfing. For camping information, read the Camping section in the Recreation chapter.

Surf & Boogie-Board Lessons

If you want to learn to surf or boogie-board or just improve your skills, we recommend you take lessons from the experts. They'll teach you about safety, surf etiquette, and a whole lot more. See the Beaches & Watersports chapter for information on renting or buying boards, wet suits, and other equipment.

Carpinteria
A-FRAME SURF SHOP
3785 Santa Claus Ln., Carpinteria
(805) 684-8803
www.aframesurfshop.com
Surf's up at this popular Santa Claus Lane surf shop where surfing and standup paddleboard lessons are available year-round. Lessons prices range for $65-$90 person and all you need to bring is a towel, water bottle, and the cool dudes who teach take care of the rest.

Santa Barbara
SURF HAPPENS SURF SCHOOL
(805) 966-3613
www.surfhappens.com
Surf Happens offers private or group instruction and runs popular year-round surf camps for kids (see the Summer Camps section), as well as after-school instruction and Saturday surf clinics with lessons, contests, and prizes. Instruction focuses on strengthening the fundamentals of surfing techniques and improving both mental and physical fitness. Lessons usually take place at Santa Claus Lane Beach in Carpinteria or Leadbetter Point in Santa Barbara and cost about $60 per hour, depending on the number of kids in the group. All equipment is available for rental from Surf Happens.

Goleta
SURF COUNTRY
109 B S. Fairview, Goleta
(805) 683-4450
www.surfcountry.net
Sign up for Surf Country's lessons and learn to paddle a board, maneuver it quickly, gain balance, read a wave, and surf as safely as possible. A 90-minute lesson costs $85 for an individual and $75 per person for three or more people. The shop supplies the surfboard, wax, leash, and wet suit. Surf Country offers lessons by appointment for all levels, from beginner to advanced.

Swimming Pools

If you're looking for a cool spot on a hot day, you can head to one of Santa Barbara's clean, safe community pools. Lifeguards are always on duty. The listings here are all outdoor pools. Several private indoor heated pools, however, are open for day use with limited hours. The Santa Barbara YMCA (805-687-7727; www.ciymca.org) charges $20 for nonmember day use of the heated indoor pool and $10 if you're accompanied by a member. Call for hours. Several private organizations also offer swim instruction for infants and children in warm indoor pools year-round. Call Santa Barbara Aquatics (805-967-4456), Santa Barbara YMCA (805-687-7727; www.ciymca.org), or Wendy Fereday Swim School (805-964-7818; www.feredayswimschool.com).

Santa Barbara
LOS BAÑOS DEL MAR POOL
401 Shoreline Dr., Santa Barbara
(805) 966-6110
Built in 1914, this historic 50-meter pool is on the waterfront next to West Beach at the harbor (where Castillo Street ends). Open year-round for adult lap swimming, and from mid-June to mid-August, the pool is open for recreational swimming Mon through Sat from 1:15 to 5 p.m. and weekdays from 2:15 to 3:45 p.m. Fees are $4 for adults and teens, $1 for children 18 and younger. Parking is available in the harbor lot and on the street. (See the Recreation chapter for information on other Los Baños programs.)

OAK PARK WADING POOL
Oak Park, Alamar, and Junipero Avenues, Santa Barbara
(805) 966-6110
A fountain sits in the middle of this large, sparkling pool. You can splash and float here if you're 7 or younger. The pool is open noon to 5 p.m. daily from the second week of June through the middle of August; in May to mid-June and from Labor Day to the end of September, it's open from 2 to 5 p.m. on weekdays and 11 a.m. to 5 p.m. on weekends. Bathing suits are required, and children who are not toilet trained must use a non-disposable swim diaper. Admission is free.

WEST BEACH WADING POOL
401 Shoreline Dr., Santa Barbara
(805) 966-6110
This spacious 18-inch-deep pool sits right next to the "big" pool complex, Los Baños del Mar. It's open to kids 7 and younger weekdays only from July 5 to the middle of August, from noon to 4 p.m. Bathing suits are required, and children who are not toilet trained must use a non-disposable swim diaper. Park in the harbor lot or on the street. Admission is free.

Goleta

UNIVERSITY OF CALIFORNIA AT SANTA BARBARA CAMPUS, GOLETA

(805) 893-7616

www.recreation.ucsb.edu/aquatics

UCSB opens its gorgeous outdoor pool complex to the public (including potty-trained children) everyday during summer weeks. It includes a 50-meter pool, a diving pool, plus an additional lap pool with a shallow area for kids. Trained lifeguards on duty for all hours; swim lessons also available. Daily fees: $12 for adults, $6 for children; save money with summer family memberships. See website for hours.

Carpinteria

CARPINTERIA COMMUNITY SWIMMING POOL

5305 Carpinteria Ave., Carpinteria

(805) 566-2417

This outdoor pool is in a beautiful setting and offers swimming, exercise classes, and youth programming. Call the pool for the latest schedule and price information.

WALK ON THE WILD SIDE

Santa Barbara isn't just inhabited by people—lots of exotic animals, plants, and other natural wonders live here, too. Following are some of the best places to see, touch, feel, and experience all these things for yourself.

Santa Barbara

SANTA BARBARA BOTANIC GARDEN

1212 Mission Canyon Rd., Santa Barbara

(805) 682-4726

www.sbbg.org

The Botanic Garden is much more than a collection of plants and flowers—it's a great place to dive headlong into the world of nature. Walk (or run) along the 5.5 miles of trails, and you'll discover a redwood grove, meadows, canyons, a historic dam, a Japanese tea house, and a creek.

There's a picnic area and a gift shop filled with books, games, and interesting items for kids as well as adults. The Botanic Garden also sponsors workshops and special events for children throughout the year. Call and ask for the Education Department for details, or visit the website. (Also see the Attractions chapter for additional details, hours, and admission fees.)

SANTA BARBARA MUSEUM OF NATURAL HISTORY

2559 Puesta del Sol Rd., Santa Barbara

(805) 682-4711

www.sbnature.org

See a live tarantula, walk beneath a giant blue whale skeleton, and learn all about the Chumash, the Native Americans who lived in the Santa Barbara region for thousands of years. This museum has lots of exhibits on birds, marine life, mammals (including grizzly bears, coyote, and deer), shells, and lizards. Explore the wonders of the universe in the museum's Gladwin Planetarium, which has regular shows throughout the year. Star Parties are held the second Sat of every month from 8 to 10 p.m.

Be sure to stroll over to the creek and the picnic areas in the Museum Backyard. It's a great place to hang out and watch squirrels, birds, and lizards in action. On your way out, you have to leave through the museum gift shop—a perfect time to ask for a souvenir from Mom and Dad.

The museum offers after-school and weekend workshops for kids and adults throughout the year. Call or visit the website for details. See the Attractions chapter for a full museum description, including hours and admission prices.

SANTA BARBARA ZOO
500 Niños Dr., Santa Barbara
(805) 962-5339
(805) 926-6310 (recorded information)
www.sbzoo.org

Get up-close and personal with lions, gorillas, elephants, penguins, and other animals. Considered the finest small zoo in California, the Santa Barbara Zoo is as wild as Santa Barbara gets. It's also one of the best places for kids to spend free time on fair-weather days. Lots of Insider kids go there at least once a week year-round and attend a week or two of Zoo Camp in the summer (see the Summer Camps section later in this chapter).

Once part of a grand estate, the beautifully landscaped grounds include palm gardens, exotic plants, and an expansive hilltop knoll overlooking the ocean. More than 600 animals representing 160 species live amid the lush gardens—gibbons, otters, monkeys, toucans, flamingos, meerkats, and giraffes, to name just a few. Most exhibits have low enclosures and windows or open space, so shorter visitors (even toddlers and babies in strollers) can easily see and interact with the animals. Don't miss the crooked-neck giraffe, the Cats of Africa exhibit, and the gorillas.

You can see nearly all the animals in an hour or two, but you'll probably want to spend at least a half-day just enjoying the grounds. Take a spin on the handmade Dentzel miniature carousel—you can ride on a sea serpent, unicorn, horse, pig, frog, rabbit, or fish. It's for kids only (sorry, Mom and Pop!) and costs $1, weather permitting, Wed through Sun from 11 a.m. to 2 p.m. You can also hop aboard one of the miniature C. P. Huntington trains that circle the zoo. Train ticket prices are adults, $4, $3.25 for members; kids ages 2 to 12, $3.50, $2.75 for members; kidlets under 2 are free. From the train you can see animals, behind-the-scenes areas, and the adjacent Andree Clark Bird Refuge.

If you're bursting with energy, head up to the new Kallman Play Area with its Anthill just made for sliding down (bring some cardboard for a faster ride). When your own tummy growls, spread out a picnic lunch on the grassy hilltop or grab a taco from the new eatery, the Wave. Or you can buy salads, sandwiches, burgers, corn dogs, and other all-American (traditional amusement park) fare at a restaurant at the zoo entrance.

Don't leave without browsing the gift shop, which has everything from African artifacts, puzzles, books, and games to jewelry, clothing, and exotic stuffed animals. The new Explore Store sells all-things green, from handbags made from recycled pop-tops to travel guides describing local hikes.

The zoo offers fun workshops for kids, adults, and families year-round. One of the more popular kids' workshops is the Zoo Snooze, an overnight adventure where you learn all about animal nightlife. Another is the award-winning Zoo Camp, held in the summer and during both spring and winter breaks.

For information on workshops, visit the website, or call (805) 962-5339 and ask for the Education Office.

i Taking the gang to the zoo? Rent a wagon for $7, pop the kids and your bags inside, and you can whiz around the exhibits with ease.

TY WARNER SEA CENTER
211 Stearns Wharf, Santa Barbara
(805) 962-2526
www.sbnature.org/seacenter
"What's in all that water anyway?" Find out at the Ty Warner Sea Center. Be an oceanographer for a day by taking water samples and analyzing them through video magnifiers, or learn about ongoing scientific research and try to beat the computers by giving the right answer. The live tide-pool tanks are a favorite, offering a close-up view and hands-on experience with ocean creatures. The video theater presents an engaging and awe-inspiring documentary on the wonders of our own Santa Barbara Channels. This is truly a fun way to spend a morning or afternoon.

Don't forget to get a lip-sticking cotton candy or melt-in-your-mouth ice cream on Stearns Wharf on the way out, or an ocean-themed souvenir from the gift shop.

Goleta

ELLWOOD GROVE MONARCH BUTTERFLY ROOSTING SITE
End of Coronado Street, Goleta
This dense eucalyptus grove is one of several places along the California coast that attract wintering monarch butterflies. The black-and-orange butterflies usually start to arrive in October, and you can see them hanging from the trees and fluttering about. Peak butterfly-watching season is November to February.

The grove is in the Santa Barbara Shores neighborhood near the Winchester Canyon exit of US 101. To find it, drive along Coronado Street from Hollister Avenue toward the ocean. This will dead-end at the eucalyptus grove. Park on the street and follow the trail to the right about 100 yards. Look up in the trees—you can't miss them!

WILDERNESS YOUTH PROJECT
5386-D Hollister Ave., Goleta
(805) 964-8096
www.wyp.org
Nature is the greatest teacher, and nothing exemplifies this more than the Wilderness Youth Project. After-school, summer, and weekend programs for kids ages 3 to 17 have kids learning what's in the wilds of nature. Ever heard of the elderberry? Did you know it can be used to help the common cold or flu? Or how about a plantain (like a banana) salve? Wilderness Youth Project kids know it as the "Band-aid" plant because it's great for bee stings, cuts, and poison oak. Check out the website for full program details and costs.

Carpinteria

CARPINTERIA BLUFFS NATURE PRESERVE
Parking at the south end of Bailard Avenue
(805) 684-5405
Back in the year 2000, the community purchased 53 acres of oceanfront bluff-top property to preserve as public open space and habitat in perpetuity. Explore the stunning views of the Pacific Ocean and the tranquil open space. The preserve features several miles of trails and vista points for viewing the ocean and the Channel Islands and overlooks the harbor seal rookery.

CARPINTERIA HARBOR SEAL COLONY
Carpinteria Bluffs
End of Bailard Avenue, Carpinteria
Want to see a real wild seal colony? Well, you're in luck, because Carpinteria is home to one of only two publicly accessible harbor seal rookeries in California. Best of all, the rookery is tucked in a cove below the

beautiful Carpinteria bluffs—a fantastic place to hike and look for other wildlife, too. The best time to visit is from December 1 to May 31, when the seals haul out on land to rest, give birth, and nurse their pups. From January to May, volunteers are there to answer your questions. Visit from late February to April, and you might even be lucky enough to see a chubby little seal pup coming into the world.

To find the rookery, take the Bailard Freeway exit in Carpinteria, turn right, and park in the lot at the end of the street near the hot dog stand. Follow the path to the right along the ocean, and you'll see breathtaking views of Rincon Point to the east and the Channel Islands to the south. Watch for red-tailed hawks. They hover here looking for ground squirrels and gophers. But don't get too close to the edge; it's very steep.

About 0.5 mile (1 kilometer) down the track, you'll see the viewing area just before the pier. Dogs scare the seals, so if you happen to be walking one, tie it up before you enter the area. Shhh! Be very quiet. Creep up to the railing slowly, and you should be able to spot the seals way down on the beach below. Look for some in the water and on the rock. See how well their big, blubbery bodies blend with their natural surroundings?

SALT MARSH NATURE PARK
Ash Avenue
Carpinteria
This 8-acre Salt Marsh Nature Park with trails through a restored tidal wetland is a great place to bird-watch or just take a leisurely stroll and enjoy the views.

North of Santa Barbara

CACHUMA LAKE
CA 154, 20 miles northwest of
Santa Barbara
(805) 686-5054
www.sbparks.org
Take a cruise on Cachuma Lake and spot bald eagles, deer, and other animals. Park naturalists lead 2-hour guided Eagle and Wildlife Cruise tours year-round. Winter trips focus on bald eagles and other migratory birds; spring and summer trips enjoy sightings of nesting hawks, fawns, wildflowers, and an occasional bobcat. You can also hike, bike, boat, fish, kayak, and canoe. If tent or RV camping is not your thing, there are yurts and even comfy new cabins. See the Parks and Recreation chapters for a detailed description of the lake.

LIL' ORPHAN HAMMIES
PO Box 924, Solvang 93464
(805) 693-9953
www.lilorphanhammies.org
This little piggy went to Solvang to see the potbellied pig rescue and sanctuary. This 5-acre pig "pen" rescues, adopts, boards, and takes long-term care of potbellied pigs. Tours are offered to school-aged children.

OSTRICH LAND
610 E. CA 246, Solvang
(805) 686-9696
www.ostrichland.com
What is the world's largest bird? The ostrich, and there are plenty of them at Ostrich Land. Quick—how many toes do they have? Did you guess two? You're right. All other birds have three or four. Feeding the birds is allowed for a small fee per sack. The bowl of feed is put on a finger-saving dustpan. Just lift the dustpan to the ostrich's mouth and

watch the feed be gobbled down. Seeing ostriches in action can be quite a sight, as they can run up to speeds of 40 miles an hour. On this 33-acre breeding farm, the 50 or so ostriches can really kick it into action. Fifteen emus, the largest bird native to Australia, also call Ostrich Land home. Look for the small roadside shop selling fresh eggs, meat, feathers, and egg art. Open daily 10 a.m. to 6 p.m. Admission is $4 for ages 13 and above, and $1 for ages 12 and younger.

QUICKSILVER MINIATURE HORSE RANCH
1555 Alamo Pintado Rd., Solvang
(805) 686-4002
www.syv.com/qsminis/
Kids can hardly believe their eyes when they see these little horses that were originally bred in Europe as pets for royalty. Patient and gentle, miniature horses are sometimes no bigger than a large dog. Aleck and Louise Stribling have been breeding these cute-as-a-button horses for years on their 20-acre high-tech training facility. Please note: The ranch doesn't offer rides in carts or petting pens. Open daily 10 a.m. to 3 p.m. Admission is free. Tours are available only by appointment. For tours of 20 or more, the cost is $3 per person.

"RETURN TO FREEDOM" AMERICAN WILD HORSE SANCTUARY
PO Box 926, Lompoc, CA 93438
(805) 737-9246
www.returntofreedom.org
Meet Spirit, the horse who inspired Dream Works' animated movie *Spirit: Stallion of the Cimarron*, at this nonprofit sanctuary for wild horses. It was schoolchildren, in the 1950s, who initially convinced government officials to enact laws protecting wild horses through

a letter campaign they developed at the urging of Velma Johnson, known as "Wild Horse Annie." Now children can see the results of their predecessors' work at the sanctuary. The Children Living History Tours give a firsthand look at wild horse behavior for $20 per adult and $10 for children under 12. The sanctuary officially declares August Youth Month, which includes a volunteer day and an overnight camp experience. For future ranch hands, there's Kid's Day at the Ranch, where children learn about the day-to-day operations of managing a horse and burro ranch. If you want to roll up your sleeves, pitch some hay, and also pitch in, there's the Youth Volunteer Weekends, where everyone helps around the ranch, then gathers around the campfire for late-night stories. The next morning, bright-eyed and bushy-tailed and with a feeling of satisfaction, everyone breaks down camp and heads home. Call for the available dates and pricing.

WIGGLE MODE

You've got the wiggles and you just can't sit still any longer. What's a kid to do? Luckily, there are many places in Santa Barbara where kids can run around and expend excess energy. Here are a few safe, fun ways to shake your sillies out and develop your motor skills.

Indoor Play

KINDERMUSIK WITH KATHY AND FRIENDS
SB Dance Arts
1 N. Calle Cesar Chavez, Ste. 100,
Santa Barbara
(805) 884-4009
www.kindermusikwithkathy.com

Kindermusik is extremely popular with Santa Barbara parents and their children. The director, Kathy Hayden, a music and movement specialist, is a former Gymboree owner as well as preschool, kindergarten, and first-grade teacher who shares her passion for music with children from 3 months to 9 years. Depending on the age group, the sessions involve creative dance, instrument exploration, piano, ukulele, xylophones, singing, Kinder Choir, and storytelling through music. Classes range from about $180 for a 12-week program for infants to $230 for young children. Materials for the classes, such as books, CDs, and instruments, incur an extra charge. Classes are also held at the Carpinteria Women's Club, 1059 Vallecito; and at Maravilla Senior Living in Goleta, 5486 Calle Real.

MY GYM SANTA BARBARA
3888 State St., Santa Barbara
(805) 563-7336
www.mygym.com
Bury yourself in a sea of plastic balls, clamber over padded obstacles, swing from the trapeze, bounce on the trampoline, watch puppet shows, dance, sing, jiggle, wiggle, and just go crazy. In 2003 this colorful, music-filled children's gym opened a location in Santa Barbara, opposite La Cumbre Shopping Mall, and it's filled with active little Insider kids ages 7 weeks to 11 years old.

Playgrounds

The Parks chapter provides complete details on the area's best parks. Here, though, we'd like to point out a few of the local kids' favorite playgrounds. They're all in Santa Barbara, and they all have safe, modern play structures plus unique atmospheres that spark your imagination. Romp on!

CHASE PALM PARK SHIPWRECK PLAYGROUND
Cabrillo Boulevard, between Santa Barbara Street and Calle Cesar Chavez, Santa Barbara
(805) 564-5418
www.sbparksandrecreation.com
Designed for toddlers through 12-year-olds, this amazing playground opened in May 1998, replete with spouting whales, a shipwreck village, talking tubes, and bridges. The 15,000-square-foot (1,394-square-meter) playground represents Santa Barbara, from the Santa Ynez Mountains (represented by a tall back wall) all the way to the Channel Islands.

Beneath the mountains stretches a cityscape—a series of arched facades adorned with Spanish/Mexican details. From the spongy "shore," a pier juts out in the sandy "ocean." A ramp leads to one of the coolest play structures around—a ship that appears to have crashed on rubber-coated rock.

Cross another couple of bridges and you come to an island—a mounded area with a deck and pole like Robinson Crusoe's. In the sand area, you can ride statues of whales, dolphins, and other sea creatures, as well as a spring-mounted raft and buoy.

Toddlers can make sand castles and dig around in a contained area shaped like breaking waves. Water mists sprinkle the sand (and any kids sitting nearby) every few minutes, timed by embedded computer chips. The playground also has picnic areas and restrooms.

KIDS' WORLD
Alameda Park, corner of Micheltorena and Garden Streets, Santa Barbara
(805) 564-5418
www.sbparksandrecreation.com

Sit on a shark, ride a whale, hide in the turrets of a magic castle, and race across suspension bridges. This one-of-a-kind playground is 8,000 square feet of pure fun. It was designed by Santa Barbara children and constructed by community volunteers in 1993.

Very young children can scramble around in the toddler area, which has pint-size swings, slides, and climbing equipment. Older, more agile kids can tear through tunnels, slip through slides, swing on ropes, and generally have the time of their lives. (Be sure to wear brightly colored clothes so Mom and Dad can spot you between the wooden castle slats.) Just across the street, at Alice Keck Park Memorial Garden, you can watch koi circle the pond and count the turtles basking in the sun.

OAK PARK PLAYGROUND
300 W. Alamar Ave. at Junipero Street, Santa Barbara
(805) 564-5418
www.sbparksandrecreation.com
"Take me to the oak tree park!" Santa Barbara children make this request all the time. It has 2 great playgrounds—one perfect for toddlers and small children and another for the agile and daring. During the summer months, kids 7 and younger can cool off in the wading pool (see the Swimming Pools section earlier in this chapter). It has restrooms, shady picnic sites, and convenient parking in the lot or on the street.

SHORELINE PARK PLAYGROUND
Shoreline Drive and San Rafael Avenue, Santa Barbara
(805) 564-5418
www.sbparksandrecreation.com
This small playground, near the parking lot and restrooms at the west end of Shoreline Park, is ideal for younger children. It's where Insiders take their little ones to practice riding trikes and two-wheelers. From here you can take in fantastic views of the ocean and the Channel Islands. At certain times of year you can spot whales, and throughout the year you can often watch the schools of dolphins that regularly play nearby.

STEVENS PARK
258 Canon Dr., Santa Barbara
(805) 564-5418
www.sbparksandrecreation.com
Twenty-five-acre Stevens Park lies at the entrance to the foothills near the intersection of San Roque and Foothill Roads. Here you can picnic, go on short nature walks, and hike along creek-side and canyon trails. It has swings and 2 play structures (one for toddlers and one for older kids), restrooms, barbecue and picnic areas, and on-site parking.

TAR PITS PARK
East end of Carpinteria State Beach
The Chumash built their canoes and boats here and caulked the planks with natural asphalt. You can see gooey black stuff oozing down the cliffs, plus lots of sea creatures on the reef. To get here, take Concha Loma to Calle Ocho. Park and walk over the railroad tracks to the lookout point. Walk down the steps to reach the beach. Make sure you wear old shoes and swimsuits—the natural asphalt can really stick to them.

Skating & Skateboarding

The best places to in-line skate or skateboard are along the Cabrillo Bike Path or Skater's Point Skate Park (see the listing below). You can rent equipment at a number of beachside locations—see the Recreation chapter for details. No one's allowed to skate or skateboard on any public street or on many city sidewalks or public ways in the downtown and beach area. When you see signs with pictures of skates and skateboards with a big line painted through them, you'll know you're in a restricted area. When you rent or buy equipment, ask for information on prohibited areas.

SANTA BARBARA HOCKEY ASSOCIATION
In-line Hockey Rink
Earl Warren Showgrounds, 3400 Calle Real, Santa Barbara
(805) 564-2035
www.sbhockey.com
The nonprofit Santa Barbara Hockey Association runs this huge in-line hockey rink at Earl Warren Showgrounds, reputedly one of the best in Southern California. Kids of all ages can skate at open sessions during the daytime on weekdays or at the popular Saturday night session. The association also organizes hockey leagues for kids age 5 to 17 for all levels, from beginners to advanced. You'll have to bring your own equipment, and you might want to pack some snacks and drinks. To find the rink, enter Earl Warren Showgrounds through Gate C off Calle Real.

i One of our favorite family activities is cycling along the beachfront on the Cabrillo Bike Path. Rent a family-size surrey and pedal together. Along the way, you can explore Andree Clark Bird Refuge, watch the pelicans on Stearns Wharf, and look for seals at the Santa Barbara Harbor. (For bike rentals, see the Recreation chapter.)

SKATER'S POINT SKATE PARK
Chase Palm Park
236 E. Cabrillo Blvd. (near Stearns Wharf), Santa Barbara
(805) 897-2650
www.sbparksandrecreation.com
Completed in 2000, this waterfront skate park is a popular hub for Santa Barbara's skating community. You can't beat the location. It's right on the beachfront. Head toward Stearns Wharf, and you'll see it on the east side. Kids of all ages flock here to ride the 14,200 square feet of ramps, bowls, ledges, pipes, and rails. While they're waiting, they can practice on Cabrillo Bike Path or watch all the action from the observation decks. The park is open daily from 8 a.m. to sunset. Inexperienced skaters are encouraged to try out the park before 11 a.m. on the weekends. Helmets and knee and elbow pads are required, and admittance is free.

Youth Sports

Santa Barbara offers countless opportunities for kids to participate in individual and team sports. The city's **Parks and Recreation Department** sponsors dozens of youth sports lessons and team programs for boys and girls; among them are aquatics, baseball, flag football, golf, softball, T-ball, tennis, track and field, and volleyball. Call (805) 564-5495 or (805) 564-5418 for information, or visit www.sbparksandrecreation.com.

The **Santa Barbara Family YMCA** (805-687-7727; www.ciymca.org) and the **Montecito Family YMCA** (805-969-3288; www.ciymca.org) also offer a range of youth sports programs. If you're interested in joining a sports league or would like private instruction, we recommend you call the **Page Youth Center** at (805) 967-8778 or visit www.pageyouthcenter.org. Popular youth sports include Little League, BMX motocross, football, roller hockey, soccer, swimming, diving, and water polo. A number of private organizations offer training and specialized instruction in gymnastics, martial arts, horseback riding, and tennis.

One club worth special mention is the **Santa Barbara Sea Shell Association** (www.sbssa.org), Santa Barbara's oldest youth sports club. It promotes the sport of sailing by teaching its members racing skills, seamanship, and the art of being a good sport.

THINKING MODE

Bookstores

CURIOUS CUP CHILDREN'S BOOKSTORE
929 Linden Ave., Carpinteria
(805) 220-6608
www.curiouscup.com
From babies to young adults and beyond, Curious Cup has something for your favorite bookworm. They offer a variety of multicultural and bilingual books, *manga,* used books, Spanish and English fiction books, cards, journals, games, and eclectic gifts for kids of all ages. In addition to the incredible variety of books, Curious Cup has a fabulous community room for book clubs, writing groups, seminars, and community events. Storytimes are also held weekly. If you're feeling curious, check out the website for more info.

Libraries

Nearly all branches of the **Santa Barbara Public Library** offer a weekly Preschool Story Time. They also sponsor many special events for children, for example, puppet and magic shows, films, and drumming workshops. You can pick up a monthly calendar of events at any branch. You can also check out videos and connect to the Internet at any branch.

If you have any questions or need help finding something, the experienced children's librarians are more than happy to help out. Hours vary by branch; call for information, or visit the library website at www.ci .santa-barbara.ca.us/departments/library. If the branch locations aren't convenient, you can always visit the Bookmobile, a huge traveling library that goes all over the city: to schools, shopping centers, retirement centers, and other locations throughout the community. Call the Goleta branch for schedules.

Preschool Story Time
SANTA BARBARA CENTRAL LIBRARY
40 E. Anapamu St., Santa Barbara
(805) 962-7653
10:30 a.m. Tues and Thurs

SANTA BARBARA EASTSIDE BRANCH
1102 E. Montecito St., Santa Barbara
(805) 963-3727
10:30 a.m. Wed, bilingual storytimes 10 and 10:30 a.m. Thurs

GOLETA BRANCH
500 N. Fairview Ave., Santa Barbara
(805) 964-7878
10:30 a.m. Wed and Thurs

MONTECITO BRANCH
1469 E. Valley Rd., Santa Barbara
(805) 969-5063
10:30 a.m. Thurs

CARPINTERIA BRANCH
5141 Carpinteria Ave., Santa Barbara
(805) 684-4314
10:30 a.m. Thurs

JUST PLAIN FUN

Goleta

**SOUTH COAST RAILROAD MUSEUM &
GOLETA DEPOT**
300 N. Los Carneros Rd., Goleta
(805) 964-3540
www.goletadepot.org
Hop aboard a miniature train, clamber through a real caboose, and check out cool train artifacts from long ago. Built in 1901, the Victorian Goleta Depot is a historical landmark as well as a fun place to picnic and hang out. It's located at Lake Los Carneros County Park, right next to the historic Stow House (see the Attractions chapter). The museum is dedicated to the history and adventure of railroading, emphasizing American rural railroad stations.

The miniature train ride is by far the most popular attraction for children at the museum. It operates year-round on Wed and Fri through Sun. The rides are usually offered from 2 to 3:45 p.m. during the week and from 1 to 3:45 p.m. on weekends.

It costs $1 for a single ride, $1.50 for two rides, and $2 for three rides. Ticket prices are usually higher during special events at Easter, Christmas, and other holiday times. Infants aren't allowed on the train; you have to be able to get on and off by yourself and be at least 34 inches tall. Parents may ride with their children.

Other popular attractions include an extensive HO-scale model railroad exhibit, working railroad communications and signaling equipment, a bay-window caboose, a station yard track, and a gift shop with train history–related gifts for all ages. On the third Saturday of every month, you can ride a handcar around the grounds. A minimum height of 48 inches is required.

The museum is open Fri through Sun 1 to 4 p.m. Admission is free, but donations are suggested.

HUNGER MODE

Since Santa Barbara is such a laid-back place, many restaurants have children's menus, crayons, and comfortable seating for wiggly bodies. We want to tell you about a couple of our favorites—places where the food is great, kids won't get bored, and parents can relax, too.

LONGBOARDS GRILL
210 Stearns Wharf, Santa Barbara
(805) 963-3311
Perched high on Stearns Wharf overlooking the water, Longboards is a great hangout for little Insider surfer dudes and gals. It's also a great spot for Mom and Dad to sip a beer and watch the sunset. Relax on the ocean-view outdoor deck, or choose a surfboard-shaped table inside. While you wait for your meal, you can munch on free peanuts (throw the shells on the floor), check out the surfing memorabilia, watch videos of monster waves and wipeouts, or just gaze out at the ocean through the panoramic windows. The children's menu includes favorites such as grilled cheese sandwiches, corn dogs, mini burgers, and chicken tenders with fries. After the meal, well-behaved kids can pick a toy from the treasure chest as a special treat.

PADARO BEACH GRILL
3765 Santa Claus Ln., Carpinteria
(805) 566-3900
www.padarobeachgrill.com
Bordering popular Santa Claus Beach, this friendly outdoor restaurant is a hands-down Insider family favorite. You can't beat the setting. Picnic tables dot nearly half an acre of beachfront lawn centered by a huge sandbox and play area packed with toys. While the kids are digging around in the sand, Mom and Dad can relax with a glass of wine and a burger. The lawn is separated from the beach by fenced-off train tracks, so the kids can't go wandering off the property, and they have plenty of room to run around. Padaro Beach Grill is open daily for lunch and dinner until 8 p.m. on Sun through Thurs and 9 p.m. on Fri and Sat. Brunch is served on the weekends. Call for seasonal hours. Pooches are welcome on the street side of the lawn, but they must be leashed.

SILVERGREENS
791 Chapala St., Santa Barbara
(805) 962-8500
www.silvergreens.com
Since it was founded in 1995, Silvergreens has offered a wide array of delicious and healthy food to adults and children alike. They are constantly introducing unique menu items, from their Green Fries appetizer to the more recent Hummus Delight sandwich. The kids menu includes classic entrees such as cheeseburgers and fettucine Alfredo, and kids can choose from side orders like watermelon wedges, hand-cut french fries, or carrots. Open daily until 10 p.m. A second location is in Isla Vista at 900 Embarcadero del Mar (805-961-1700); it delivers after 5 p.m. and is open until 1 a.m. on weekdays and 2 a.m. on weekends.

WOODY'S BODACIOUS BARBECUE
5112 Hollister Ave., Goleta
(805) 967-3775
www.woodysbbq.com
Voted "Best Barbecue Restaurant" in a local poll for more than 25 years in a row, Woody's is a fun place to take the kids. The rugged Wild West decor (you wash your hands in a bathtub in the center of the room) and great kid's menu of dino ribs, chicken strips, hamburgers, and hot dogs are sure to be a hit with the young ones. Moms and dads will love the prices and the portions. The huge servings of succulent barbecue chicken, baby back ribs, and oak-smoked prime rib and duckling will satisfy even the hungriest of bellies. Vegetarians can graze at the salad bar. Woody's is open for lunch and dinner daily.

SUMMER CAMPS

The hardest task facing Santa Barbara kids every summer is deciding which camps to attend. Santa Barbara has dozens of day camps and a few overnight camps in the area. Some are general summer camps that typically offer arts and crafts, sports, and activities. Others focus on a particular theme or sport, for example, music, arts, sailing, basketball, or aquatic activities.

Your best bet for choosing a camp is to pick up a regional camp guide. The *Santa Barbara Independent* publishes an excellent summer camp/youth activity guide every spring. Another excellent resource is the City of Santa Barbara's *Parks & Recreation Activity Guide* (spring/summer issue). You can view the latest issue online at www.sbparksandrecreation.com, or call (805) 564-5418. The following camps are the most popular among Insider kids. Happy camping!

Santa Barbara

CHANNEL ISLANDS OUTFITTERS (PADDLE SPORTS CENTER) YOUTH ADVENTURE CAMP
(805) 899-3010

For 9- to 16-year-olds, this camp for young adventurers teaches them about sustainability and managing their impact on the environment. Surfing, boogie-boarding, sea kayaking, astronomy, rock climbing, wilderness survival basics, Channel Islands National Park visits, and camping are all part of the weekly adventures. Sessions 1 and 2 are for 9- to 12-year-olds and last for 2 weeks; the cost is $990. Session 3, for 13- to 16-year-olds, lasts 2 weeks and the cost is $1,200. Call for more information.

SANTA BARBARA FAMILY YMCA
36 Hitchcock Way, Santa Barbara
(805) 687-7727
www.ciymca.org

The Santa Barbara Family YMCA has offered an affordable day camp for years. Activities typically include field trips, games, swimming, arts and crafts, drama, music, and sports. Day camp serves children entering kindergarten through 9th grade. Fees are $155 a week. Financial assistance is available. Registration forms and information can be found online at www.ciymca.org.

SANTA BARBARA SURF ADVENTURES
10 State St., Santa Barbara
(805) 963-1281
www.santabarbarasurfadventures.com

Run out of the Beach House in Santa Barbara, this popular 1-week summer surf camp is geared to first-time and beginner surfers who want to brush up on their surfing skills. Classes, taught by professional lifeguards and experienced longtime Santa Barbara surfers, also cover beach safety, first aid, and marine biology. One-week Leadbetter Beach camps start at about $290 and include a soft surfboard, wet suit, camp T-shirt, and lunch from Shoreline Cafe. One-week travel camps cost about $330.

SHOWSTOPPERS THEATRE PRODUCTIONS
(805) 314-1221
http://showstopperstheatreproductions .com

ShowStoppers offers summer performance workshops for kids ages 7 through 14. Participants acquire musical theater skills through practical workshops where they learn to perform in a musical production. Call for more information.

SURF HAPPENS SURF SCHOOL
1117 Las Olas Ave., Santa Barbara
(805) 966-3613
www.surfhappens.com

Each summer Surf Happens operates 13 weeks of surf camps beginning mid-June and running until early September The camps teach fundamental movements, introduce surf etiquette, and help students overcome fear of the water. The series includes summer sleepover camps at El Capitán, travel camps when more advanced surfers scout the coast for the best waves of the day, international camps at surfing hot spots around the world, and day camps at Santa Claus Lane Beach. Call for details.

YOUTH SAILING/KAYAKING CAMP
Santa Barbara Sailing Center
(805) 962-2826, (800) 350-9090
www.sbsail.com
The Santa Barbara Sailing Center has offered these popular camps since 1962. Kids ages 7 to 15 can "learn the ropes" at the sailing camp and can practice paddling at the kayaking camp. The weeklong sessions (Mon through Fri) include 20 hours of hands-on instruction and are offered from mid-June to the end of August. Kayaking sessions are held from 8:30 a.m. to 12:30 p.m. Sailing sessions meet in the afternoons from 1 to 5 p.m. Sessions cost $175.

ZOO CAMP
Santa Barbara Zoo
500 Niños Dr., Santa Barbara
(805) 962-5339
www.santabarbarazoo.org
Zoo Camp is regularly voted the "Best Kids' Camp in Santa Barbara" in local newspaper polls. It's open to all kids from ages 3 to 12. Campers are grouped by age or grade; group size ranges from 6 to 12 kids, with 1 counselor and 2 to 4 counselors-in-training per group.

Each weeklong session (Mon through Fri, 9 a.m. to 2 p.m. or 8 a.m. to 5 p.m. for the extended stay) focuses on a particular theme, for example, habitats, diversity, or conservation. Themes are repeated every 2 weeks, and you can sign up for as many sessions as you like. Each week's activities revolve around the theme of the week and include animal encounters, group play, behind-the-scenes visits, games, stories, educational activities, and art projects. Contact the zoo for information on zoo camp fees and scholarships.

Goleta

THE FIRST TEE CENTRAL COAST
6034 Hollister Ave., Goleta
Administrative Office: PO Box 1611,
Summerland, CA 93067
(805) 684-2184
www.firstteecentralcoast.org
The First Tee Central Coast teaches more than just the game of golf to kids ages 11 to 17. It also teaches about the nine core values of honesty, integrity, sportsmanship, respect, confidence, responsibility, perseverance, courtesy, and good judgment and about maintaining a positive attitude, thinking through the consequences of decisions, and defining and setting goals. Held on public golf courses throughout Santa Barbara County, the local First Tee is located in Goleta at Twin Lakes Golf and Learning Center.

UNIVERSITY OF CALIFORNIA AT SANTA BARBARA SUMMER CAMPS
UCSB Campus, Goleta
(805) 893-3913
www.recreation.ucsb.edu
Since 1981, UCSB has provided excellent summer programs for local and visiting youth. The UCSB Day Camp is open to kids ages 5 through 14; it's led by UCSB coaches, local teachers, and students earning teaching credentials. The 1-week sessions introduce kids to various sports, games, and activities appropriate for the specific age group and skill level.

Typical activities include arts and crafts, gymnastics, swimming, field trips, beach days, archery, and sports. Groups are sorted into three divisions: Lower Camp (ages 5 through 6), Inter Camp (ages 7 through 10), and Upper Camp (ages 11 through 14). UCSB Day Camp costs between $125 and $140 a week.

UCSB coaches also run specialized volleyball and basketball camps for girls and boys (day and overnight). UCSB Ocean Camps offer 1-week surf and kayak sessions for boys and girls ages 9 through 15. Fees vary.

Montecito

MONTECITO FAMILY YMCA
591 Santa Rosa Ln., Montecito
(805) 969-3288
www.ciymca.org
Between 50 and 75 school-age kids attend the camp during each session. Each session has a theme and lasts 2 weeks. Typical activities include arts and crafts, swimming, barbecues, and field trips to local parks and beaches. The Y offers special activities such as bowling, bike trips, and visits to theme parks. Specialty camps such as tennis, swimming, and skating/blading are also available. Fees are $340 per session. Extended care is available if needed. Limited scholarships are available.

WESTMONT COLLEGE SPORTS CAMP
Westmont College
955 La Paz Rd., Montecito
(805) 565-6010
www.westmont.edu/sports/camps
Summer sports camps run by this Christian college are especially popular because camp leaders emphasize fun and help children develop confidence in their abilities. Kids from ages 5 through 14 can sign up for half-day programs in basketball, soccer, tennis, volleyball, track and field, archery, and general sports skills, or full-day sports camp for basketball, soccer, or baseball. Age groups vary depending on the sport. Half-day sessions cost $225; full-day sessions,

$250. Sessions last 1 week. Visit the website for online registration.

Special Needs

CAMP WHEEZ
Sansum Clinic
PO Box 1200, Santa Barbara, CA 93102
(805) 681-7897
www.sansumclinic.org
Camp Wheez is a day camp for elementary schoolchildren, ages 6 to 12, with chronic asthma, providing them with a camp experience designed for their special needs. It is free of charge and open to the community. Application in advance is required.

HAPPY ADVENTURE SUMMER CAMP
Cornerstone House
(805) 684-5840
www.cornerstonehouse.org
This 20-year-old day camp offers 2 weeks of summer activities for developmentally disabled youth ages 5 to 18. It's run by Cornerstone House, a nonprofit. Call (805) 680-2538 for more details.

ESPECIALLY FOR TEENS

BOXTALES THEATRE TRAINING
(805) 962-1142
www.boxtales.org
Learn to be a thespian with this fun-loving theater group, BOXTALES. The 3-week summer intensive teaches acting, movement, storytelling, acro-yoga, mime, music, characterization, and collaboration. The camp stimulates minds, encourages teamwork, builds character, and develops self-esteem. There's a $750 fee; the program is for ages 9 through 13.

JUNIOR LIFEGUARD PROGRAM
Santa Barbara Parks and Recreation
Cabrillo Bathhouse
1118 E. Cabrillo Blvd., Santa Barbara
(805) 897-2680
www.sbparksandrecreation.com
www.santabarbaraca.gov/summerfun/
jr_lifeguards.htm

Youth from ages 9 through 17 get into the swim of things with the Parks and Recreation Department's summer Junior Lifeguard Program. One of the coveted summer programs, it means something in Santa Barbara to say you're a junior lifeguard. Learn how to tower guard, rescue, and offer first aid and CPR. An overview of oceanography and marine biology is also taught. Check out the application process online, or call for more information. A tryout period before the summer is required.

TWELVE35 CENTER
1235 Chapala St., Santa Barbara
(805) 882-1235
www.sbpal.org

The Santa Barbara Police Activities League (PAL) has partnered with the city's Parks and Recreation Department to sponsor programming for local youth ages 12 to 19. Activities are planned by the teens themselves and include sports tournaments, drug-free and tobacco-free dances with DJs and live bands, special classes, field trips, teen-produced TV shows, murals, and conferences. The fee for each activity varies. Other teen activities are coordinated by Neighborhood & Outreach Services of the Parks and Recreation Department and include a culinary arts program, the Santa Barbara Arts Alliance, and a job apprenticeship program. Call (805) 963-7567 for more information.

SANTA BARBARA WINE COUNTRY

Once a sleepy little enclave on the other side of the mountain, the Santa Ynez Valley is recognized internationally for its premium wine production. The demand has been so great that a million-plus cases of reds and whites are produced each year. Production yields over $360 million a year—one-third of which comes from the grapes alone.

Within 45 minutes of leaving downtown Santa Barbara, you'll land smack-dab in the heart of one of California's premier wine regions.

The North County (which is how most Santa Barbarans refer to the region on the north side of the Santa Ynez Mountain range) is a tranquil and beautiful area, with scenic roads that wind through rolling, oak-studded valleys and mountains. Reminiscent of old rural California, it's home to ranchers, farmers, and, in recent years, more than a few celebrities escaping the glare of Hollywood.

Agriculture dominates the North County scene, and much of Santa Barbara County's produce originates here. Strawberries and broccoli almost always rank in the top three of the county's most valuable cash crops. The other top crop is wine grapes.

FROM MISSIONS TO MAVERICKS

Santa Barbara County's winemaking and grape-growing history spans more than 200 years. It started in 1782, when Father Junipero Serra carried grapevines from Mexico all the way to Santa Barbara. Mission Santa Barbara maintained several vineyards, and there was even a winery on Santa Cruz Island. Justinian Caire planted 150 acres with imported French grape slips and shipped his wines up the coast to San Francisco for bottling.

By the 1920s, wine grapes grew on about 250 acres of land until Prohibition effectively shut down all winery operations in the area. It took more than 30 years for the industry to rebound. But it did so with a vengeance.

In the early 1960s, researchers at the University of California at Davis discovered that the unusual geography, topography, and climate of the Santa Barbara County region held great promise for growing wine grapes. This substantiated the suspicions of several winemaking pioneers, who were already scoping out the region for places to plunk their vines.

Time for a geography lesson. By now, you're probably used to hearing about the unusual east–west orientation of the Santa Barbara coastline. Well, the Santa Ynez and San Rafael mountain ranges also run east–west. In fact, they are the only mountain ranges running in this direction (most run

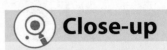

Close-up

What's in a Name

Ever looked at bottles of wine from Santa Barbara County and wondered about the different regions on the labels? These appellations, also known as American Viticultural Areas (AVAs), can divulge much about the character of the wine you are about to drink. If a label says "Santa Ynez Valley," this means at least 85 percent of the grapes were grown in that federally recognized region. It's a guarantee of geographic origin. Once you know a bit about the growing conditions in these areas, you'll have a richer appreciation for the differences in climate and soils that create the flavor of the wine. California has 69 appellations, four of which belong to Santa Barbara County. We've described these four AVAs briefly below so you can impress your friends next time you buy a bottle.

Happy Canyon—The newest appellation, designated as an official American Viticultural Area (AVA) by the Trade and Tax Bureau in November of 2009, Happy Canyon is the smallest AVA in Santa Barbara County. Nestled in a peaceful corner with verdant hillside vineyards, abundant sunshine and oak-studded grasslands make it one of the area's most picturesque viticultural areas. The 23,941-acre wine-growing region, located in the easternmost part of the Santa Ynez Valley, is recognized for its unique microclimate and its ability to produce top quality Bordeaux varietals. It lies north and west of Cachuma Lake and is home to six major vineyards: Cimarone, Grassini, Happy Canyon Vineyard, McGinley, Star Lane, and Vogelzang Vineyards. The area's warm climate, geography, and soil composition distinguish it from other growing regions in Santa Barbara County. With mid-morning fog burn-off and average summertime temperatures in the low 90s, Happy Canyon's warm microclimate is the perfect home for Bordeaux varietals like Cabernet Sauvignon, Merlot, Cabernet Franc, Sauvignon Blanc, Malbec, and Petit Verdot as well as many Rhône varietals. The soil, a mixture of loam and clay loam with interspersed cobbles, is high in mineral levels while low in nutrients, resulting in small vines and very low grape yields—a circumstance that results in concentrated flavors and excellent *terroir* expression.

Santa Maria Valley—This funnel-shaped region in the northern part of Santa Barbara County has a cool climate, thanks to its prevailing ocean winds, and enjoys one of the longest growing seasons of any viticultural area in the world. The area's well-drained soils range from sandy loam to clay loam, and its cool temperatures make it one of California's best AVAs for Pinot Noir and Chardonnay. Rhône varietals also thrive here, showing great clarity and depth of fruit.

Santa Rita Hills—In 2001 the Bureau of Alcohol, Tobacco, and Firearms approved this AVA to differentiate wines made from grapes grown in the cooler western edge of the Santa Ynez Valley. Conditions here mirror those found in Reims in Champagne, France. Morning fog is frequent, winds are strong, and soils typically contain less clay and more calcium than those in the eastern Santa Ynez Valley. World-class Pinot Noir and Chardonnay are produced in this region, which encompasses most of the vineyards lying west of US 101.

Santa Ynez Valley—Lying predominantly east of US 101, this region is generally warmer than the Santa Rita Hills area with well-drained soils ranging from sandy loams and clay loams to shaly and silty clay loams. The area primarily produces high-quality Cabernet Sauvignon, Cabernet Franc, Merlot, Syrah, Grenache, and Sauvignon Blanc.

north–south) along the entire West Coast of North America (except in parts of Alaska). Another unusual geographical feature of Santa Barbara County is that the valleys between these local mountains run perpendicular to the coast, sucking cool ocean breezes and fog inland during late afternoon and evening. The result: hot sunny days and cool nights—perfect conditions for growing wine grapes.

The region is basically a grower's paradise: All the classic grape varieties thrive here, thanks to the numerous microclimates and the long, cool growing season. The region is far enough south to avoid the early winter storms that sometimes threaten late harvests up north. And since the winters are usually temperate, bud break on the vines occurs much earlier than up north. The grapes here hang on the vines longer, which allows them to develop rich, intense, concentrated flavors.

In 1962 Pierre Lafond established Santa Barbara Winery, the first commercial winery in Santa Barbara County since Prohibition. Stearns Wharf Vintners followed suit in 1965. The 1970s gave birth to several more fledgling wineries, including Firestone Vineyard (the first winery to produce and release wine made from fruit in Santa Barbara County), Rancho Sisquoc Winery, Zaca Mesa Winery, and the Brander Vineyard.

By the 1980s, the buzz about Santa Barbara's viticultural promise lured more winemakers to the region, and the industry's roots were firmly entrenched in local soil. Today you can tour more than 80 wineries (however, there are more than 197 federally bonded winery licensees) in Santa Barbara County. The vast majority are small operations, run by families or individuals, rather than large corporations.

GREAT GRAPES

More than 60 varieties of grapes are perfectly planted in Santa Barbara County. The top three grape varietals are Chardonnay, Pinot Noir, and Syrah, in that order. Nearly everyone here grows and produces Chardonnay. Santa Barbara County has also been singled out for producing world-class Pinot Noir—a fragile, delicate varietal that requires not only ideal growing conditions, but also careful management. Other popular Santa Barbara County wines include Sauvignon Blanc, Merlot, Cabernet Sauvignon, and Pinot Grigio.

While great grapes form the basis of great wines, they wouldn't amount to much without the expertise of an experienced winemaker. The winemakers of Santa Barbara County have earned a reputation in the wine world not only as wizards in the technical sense but also as creative innovators who aren't afraid to experiment with new methods and varietals. Here, you'll notice some unique and intriguing blends that you won't find anywhere else.

Santa Barbara County wines have earned great respect in the wine world and won numerous awards in regional, national, and international competitions. Once you taste them, you'll be raving, too.

WINE COUNTRY INFORMATION

SANTA BARBARA COUNTY VINTNERS' ASSOCIATION
(805) 688-0881, (800) 218-0881
www.sbcountywines.com
The Santa Barbara County Vintners' Association is a nonprofit organization founded in 1983. It supports and promotes Santa Barbara County as a premium wine-producing and wine grape–growing region. It also strives to enhance the position of Santa Barbara County

wines in the world marketplace. Current members include more than 110 wineries, 25 independent vineyards, and several vineyard consultant/management companies.

The Vintners' Association sponsors festivals, seminars, and tastings and provides information to the media and consumers. Call or visit the association's website for specific information about wineries and events and to request a current Santa Barbara County wine country map.

i Want mini tastes of wine and tapas, too? Avant Wine & Tapas (35 Industrial Way, Buellton; 805-686-9400; www.avantwines.com) offers tastings beginning at 75 cents (up to $4 for 1-, 3-, or 6-ounce pours). It's located upstairs in an off-the-beaten-track warehouse where several local winemakers craft their vintages.

TOURING & TASTING THROUGH WINE COUNTRY

Santa Barbara wine country is not Napa, but we think that's a blessing. It's not nearly as touristy or crowded, and we think the wines rank up there with the best. When you go touring here, you can relax and enjoy gorgeous scenery and outstanding wines without the crowds and the hype. Many wineries welcome visitors year-round, most on a daily basis and others at least on weekends.

Tasting rooms range from cozy spaces in historic farmhouses and rustic cabins to spacious, contemporary buildings. You can try the wines and buy a few bottles (or cases) to bring home, and at some wineries you can sample and purchase gourmet foods, such as pasta sauces, salsas, grapeseed oils, and other winery products.

Several wineries offer tours of the wine-making facilities and/or caves, and one or two will take you through the vineyards at certain times of year. Reservations for tasting and tours are usually required for groups of 10 or more—you'll need to call ahead and make an appointment.

Most Santa Barbara County wineries lie along three scenic wine routes: the **Santa Ynez Valley Wine Trail,** the **Foxen Canyon Wine Trail,** and **Santa Rita Hills** loop, which runs into the Lompoc Wine Ghetto, which now boasts a dozen tasting rooms (see the Wineries section of this chapter). You can also visit a few tasting rooms in Los Olivos and the Danish village of Solvang. If you can't make it out to the wine country, don't worry. You'll find tasting rooms in Santa Barbara by the beach and downtown.

In this chapter, we give you an overview of most of the area's main tasting rooms. We also let you know about a few of our favorite hotels, inns, and restaurants in Santa Barbara wine country. If you'd like someone to guide you through the wine country—and do all the driving—we recommend a few tour companies.

i In the summer, when it's foggy and cool on the coast, it's usually hot and sunny in the wine country. So if you're heading to the valley for a day of wine tasting, dress in cool, light clothing. But bring a light sweater. It cools off at night.

HOW TO GET THERE

Before heading out on your wine-tasting adventure, be sure to get an up-to-date wine touring map featuring all Vintners' Association member wineries, restaurants, lodgings, wine shops, and touring services. The association is adding members all the time, and it produces a map you can pick up at winery tasting rooms, visitor centers, restaurants, and hotels throughout Santa Barbara County or by calling the Vintners' Association at (805) 688-0881 or (800) 218-0881. You can also view a PDF version of the map online at www.sbcountrywines.com. (Check the website for information updates.)

From Santa Barbara, you have two travel options. The first (and our favorite) is the "scenic" or "mountain" route along CA 154 (San Marcos Pass), which drops dramatically into the Santa Ynez Valley. Drive carefully. The road twists and turns over mountain passes and can be a little tricky—especially on wet or foggy days. From downtown Santa Barbara, take US 101 to the State Street/CA 154 exit and take CA 154 up the mountain. As you descend, you'll see spectacular views of the Santa Ynez Mountains, the Los Padres National Forest, and Cachuma Lake.

About 40 minutes after leaving Santa Barbara, you'll arrive at the point where CA 154 intersects with CA 246. Turn left to visit historic Santa Ynez or the Danish village of Solvang, or continue on about 5 miles to charming Los Olivos. All are great points to stock up on picnic items and gas before you head out on the wine trails.

The second option is the coastal route, which offers great views of some of the last remaining unspoiled tracts of coastline in California. Drive north along US 101 about 45 miles to CA 246 in Buellton. Head west if you want to visit the wineries in the Santa Rita Hills region. Otherwise head east. We suggest you begin your tour by stopping at the historic town of Santa Ynez about 10 miles east of US 101. From there it's a short drive to many of the wineries on the Santa

Ynez Valley Wine Trail. If you're planning to take the Foxen Canyon Wine Trail, you should continue driving north on US 101 past Buellton, up to the CA 154 turnoff. Turn right and head east a few miles to Foxen Canyon Road.

TOURS & TRANSPORTATION SERVICES

Taking an escorted tour is a great way to cruise through wine country. Just sit back, relax, and sample wine without worrying about driving.

BREAKAWAY TOURS AND EVENT PLANNING
3463 State St., Ste. 141, Santa Barbara
(805) 783-2929, (800) 799-7657
www.breakaway-tours.com
Specializing in seriously fun and educational tours, Breakaway Tour guides really know their stuff. Much more than someone just driving you to your destination, the guides are passionate about wine—so passionate that they'll share information about the grape-growing region and teach you how to read a wine label. Breakaway gives you the best kind of break away—they do all the planning. Call for tour details and prices.

i For a contrast in scenery, take the mountain route on the way to the wine country and the coastal route on the return journey (or vice versa).

CLOUD CLIMBERS JEEP & WINE TOURS
(805) 646-3200
www.ccjeeps.com
Cloud Climbers specializes in sightseeing adventures in custom open-air Jeeps. Professionally guided excursions celebrate the

SANTA BARBARA WINE COUNTRY

history, flavors, and magical beauty of Ojai. Winding country roads, dirt trails, secret gardens, challenging-to-get-to exclusive vistas, local olive oil sampling and wine tasting included. Cloud Climbers provides a picturesque and engaging Jeep excursion that is memorable and refreshing. Daily, morning, and afternoon departures; tour prices start at $89.

PERSONAL TOURS LTD.
PO Box 60109, Santa Barbara, CA 93160
(805) 685-0552
www.personaltoursltd.com

This excellent local company will customize a wine country tour to suit your needs. All tours are narrated, so you'll learn some interesting tidbits about the vineyards, celebrity ranch estates, and other attractions in the area. Vehicles range from sedans, convertibles, and custom vans to minibuses and motor coaches with restrooms. The company also provides driver-guide service in your own car or rental. Call for prices.

SANTA BARBARA WINE COUNTRY CYCLING TOURS
3640 Sagunto St., Santa Ynez
(805) 686-9490, (888) 557-8687
www.winecountrycycling.com

Imagine escaping to the wine country on two wheels instead of four. Santa Barbara Wine Country Cycling Tours is an innovative touring company that offers half-day or full-day guided tours. Half-day tours are $75 per person or $60 per person for four or more. If you add in lunch, it's $125 per person or $110 per person for four or more. Full-day tours are $150 per person and, for four or more, $125 per person. Self-guided tours are $35 for a half day and $45 for a full day.

Rates are cheaper if you BYOB (bring your own bike).

> **i** Heading out for a day of wine tasting? Appoint a designated driver before you begin the tour and take a bottle of water. Sipping wines in the sun all day can leave you feeling dehydrated.

SPENCER'S LIMOUSINE & TOURS
(805) 884-9700
www.spencerslimo.com

Regularly voted one of the top Santa Barbara tour companies in local polls, Spencer's offers wine tours in the comfort of a plush limousine or Lincoln Town Car. Spencer is an avid historian, so you can expect fascinating narration along the way. Tours are customized to suit your taste in wines and places of interest and include tastings at 6 different wineries. You'll find a lunch menu in the car, and Spencer will pick up your gourmet selection at a local Italian deli on the way so you can picnic at one of the wineries. Tours range from 5 to 8 hours. Call for prices.

SUPERRIDE SHUTTLE & TOURS
(805) 683-9636, (800) 977-1123
www.SuperRide.net

SuperRide specializes in customized narrated tours of Santa Barbara County wineries and attractions. This means you and your group will be the only clients on the tour, and the company will pick you up at your hotel and take you to the wineries of your choice. If you're not sure where to go, ask SuperRide to suggest an itinerary based on your special interests. Depending on the size of your group, you can choose from a Lincoln Town Car, passenger van, minibus, or luxury coach. All tours include a gourmet picnic lunch and as much bottled water as you need. Make sure you book at least 24 hours in advance.

SUSTAINABLE VINE WINE TOURS
3981 La Colina Rd., Santa Barbara
(805) 698-3911
www.sustainablevine.com
We like the notion behind these 6-hour, behind-the-scenes tours in vans that run on biodiesel fuel. Take an inside look at organic and biodynamic winemaking. Itineraries vary but could include a visit to Demetria Winery, lunch with the owners of Ampelos Cellars, and a fine finish at Alma Rosa Winery & Vineyards, run by eco-minded wine pioneers Richard and Thekla Sanford. The cost is $125, including tastings, lunch, and transportation to and from the Santa Barbara area; reservations required.

WINE'EDVENTURES
(805) 965-9463
www.welovewines.com
If you want to feel as though you've learned something about wine before you start sipping, these narrated tours are an excellent choice. The owner, Dusty Rhodes, was involved in wine-country tours in Napa and Sonoma for more than 20 years before establishing WINE'edVENTURES in 1999. At the moment, they are the only company in Santa Barbara running daily tours to the wine country. Hop aboard the 24-passenger air-conditioned minicoach, and you'll learn all about wine-country history, stagecoach trails, Prohibition, wine lingo, and local tidbits. The Deluxe Excursion costs $105 per person and includes visits to 4 wineries, tasting fees, an oversized wineglass, a wine production tour, and a picnic lunch.

i The Santa Barbara County Vintners' Association has created an app for the iPhone and Android for touring wine country that shows winery hours and directions, as well as other tidbits of helpful information.

THE WINERIES

Now that you're familiar with the area, you're ready to start your wine-tasting tour. Following are brief descriptions of the main wine trails and the wineries along them in alphabetical order, including tasting room hours. Most charge a nominal tasting fee (usually $5 to $10 per person, for 5 to 8 tastings). Some also offer you the chance to taste special reserve wines for a fee.

It's best to devote at least a day to each trail, or a weekend in Los Olivos or Solvang, so you can take your time tasting, relaxing, and taking in the views. Also, you should eat a bit before each session and remember to drink lots of water—wine can dehydrate you quickly, especially in warm weather. Take a picnic, because once you're on your wine safari, you won't find vittles on the wine trail.

Foxen Canyon Wine Trail

One of the most popular and bucolic wine trails winds along Foxen Canyon and connects two wine-growing regions: the Santa Ynez Valley and the Santa Maria Valley. The trail begins on Foxen Canyon Road, just north of Los Olivos. From there, the road twists and turns through 20 miles of gently rolling hills and vineyards until it reaches Santa Maria, the northernmost area of the county. Each winery along the way is as distinctive as their varietals. For a comprehensive listing of all of the wineries along the trail, visit the Foxen Canyon Wine Trail Association's website at

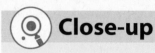

Close-up

Tasting in Los Olivos

Los Olivos is a quaint, historic town at the north end of the Santa Ynez Valley Wine Trail and near the beginning of the Foxen Canyon Wine Trail. It's a great place to stop for a snack or a meal or to shop for high-quality art at its famous galleries.

The downtown area covers just a few square blocks, so you can park your car and walk wherever you need to go. You can taste an array of local premium wines right in town at tasting rooms on Grand Avenue, the main street in Los Olivos. Some of the rooms offer wines made by wineries without visitor facilities, and several are part of the Santa Ynez Valley Wine Trail.

There are 20 independent tasting rooms that give you the chance to sample various local wines. They include Longoria, Consilience, Qupé, Verdad, Coghlan, Carissa, and many others. Just wander the streets of this quaint town and make your own favorite discoveries. Some of the establishments we suggest include the **Los Olivos Tasting Room** (2905 Grand Ave., Los Olivos; 805-688-7265), **Los Olivos Wine Merchant** (2879 Grand Ave., Los Olivos; 805-688-7265) and **BiN 2860 International Wine Shop** (2860 Grand Ave., Los Olivos; 805-688-7788).

www.foxencanyonwinetrail.com. This is the perfect route to follow if you want to feel as though you've stepped back in time—and escape the worries of your workaday week.

CAMBRIA WINERY AND VINEYARD
5475 Chardonnay Ln., Santa Maria
(805) 937-8091, (888) 339-9463
www.cambriawines.com

From its name, many people assume this winery is located in the coastal town of Cambria. Actually, Cambria Winery is located about 12 miles east of downtown Santa Maria, at the base of Tepusquet Canyon, a former Chumash encampment.

This was the original vineyard in the area, and as Tepusquet Vineyard it produced top-quality wine grapes from the early 1970s to the mid-1980s. Katherine's Chardonnay, Julia's Pinot Noir, Tepusquet Syrah, and other flagship wines make up 90 percent of production.

The winery tasting room is open 10 a.m. to 5 p.m. Sat and Sun and weekdays by appointment.

COSTA DE ORO WINERY
1331 S. Nicholson Ave., Santa Maria
(805) 922-1468
www.cdowinery.com

This tasting room showcases Costa de Oro's award-winning wines, along with Gold Coast produce and gourmet food selections. Gary Burk, winemaker, made his way into the wine business through the music business, but that's a whole other story. He struck the right chord with his winemaking, having received 90 points or higher from *Wine Spectator* and *Wine & Spirits* magazines. His wines have also appeared in the top 100 lists in respected wine magazines. Wine accolades include winning "Best of Show" at both the Orange County and Santa Barbara County fairs.

COTTONWOOD CANYON VINEYARD & WINERY
3940 Dominion Rd., Santa Maria
(805) 937-8463
www.cottonwoodcanyon.com
Cottonwood Canyon is a small ultra-premium winery specializing in Estate Chardonnay, Pinot Noir, and Syrah. The Beko family founded it in 1988, and you can sample their wines here in the vineyard tasting room.

The winery sits on a hilltop overlooking the valley, and the picnic area boasts fantastic views of the northern end of the Foxen Canyon Wine Trail. Tours of the wine caves, which are dug into the hillside, are offered on Sat and Sun at 11 a.m. and 1 and 3 p.m., midweek by appointment only. The tasting room is open from 10 a.m. to 5 p.m. Sun through Thurs and 10 a.m. to 6 p.m. Fri and Sat.

CURTIS WINERY
5249 Foxen Canyon Rd., Los Olivos
(805) 686-8999
www.curtiswinery.com
Curtis Winery opened in April 1998 right next door to Firestone (see subsequent listing). Winemaker Chuck Carlson selects hand-picked grapes from estate vineyards and various Santa Barbara County vintners with a focus on the Rhône varietals.

Sheltered by oaks in a cool, white adobe, the tasting room is usually set with at least one Viognier, a Viognier blend, a Heritage rosé, a Syrah, and a Syrah blend. Curtis is also producing small lots of wine in a gravity-flow facility. The winery is open for tours, tasting, and sales from 10 a.m. to 5 p.m. daily, and you'll find some shaded picnic tables near the tasting room.

FESS PARKER WINERY & VINEYARD
6200 Foxen Canyon Rd., Los Olivos
(805) 688-1545, (800) 841-1104
www.fessparker.com
Fess Parker (aka Davy Crockett) and his family own this large, contemporary winery. Fess, the founding visionary who passed away in 2010, turned the reins over to his son and daughter. In fact his son, Eli Parker, is the winemaker. The vast tasting room is set amid 700 acres of vineyards, lawns, manicured rose gardens, and winery facilities. Step inside and you can browse the antiques and Hollywood memorabilia or relax by the massive stone fireplace.

Several of Fess Parker's Syrahs, a Pinot Noir, and a Chardonnay scored over 90 on Robert Parker's list. The gift shop offers gourmet items, signature winery merchandise, picnic snacks, and Davy Crockett and Daniel Boone items, including Fess's trademark coonskin caps and coonskin bottle toppers. Tastings and sales are available from 10 a.m. to 5 p.m. daily.

FIRESTONE VINEYARD
5000 Zaca Station Rd., Los Olivos
(805) 688-3940, ext. 31
www.firestonewine.com
Founded in 1972, Firestone is the oldest estate winery in the county. It sits atop a secluded mesa overlooking the valley and vineyards and is best known for its excellent Chardonnay. The winery also makes award-winning Cabernet Sauvignon, Merlot, Syrah, Sauvignon Blanc, and Riesling.

You can picnic in a secluded courtyard or in a picnic area on the hillside overlooking the scenic valley below. Firestone is open for tours, tasting, and sales from 10 a.m. to 5 p.m. daily. Tours are at 11:15 a.m. and 1:15

and 3:15 p.m. Don't miss the vineyard tours during harvest time.

i Fill up your gas tank before you drive the Foxen Canyon Wine Trail. You won't find any services along the way, and it can take up to an hour just to drive along this winding road, so make sure you leave enough time to visit the final winery on your list before they cork the bottles.

FOXEN VINEYARD
7200 and 7600 Foxen Canyon Rd., Santa Maria
(805) 937-4251
www.foxenvineyard.com

Foxen Vineyard's small, rustic winery and tasting room are in a 100-year-old-plus converted barn and other historic buildings right off the side of the road. Foxen makes small amounts of handcrafted Chenin Blanc, Chardonnay, Pinot Noir, Cabernet Sauvignon, Cabernet Franc, Merlot, Syrah, Viognier, and Sangiovese using traditional French methods. It's open for tasting and sales 11 a.m. to 4 p.m. daily.

KOEHLER WINERY
5360 Foxen Canyon Rd., Los Olivos
(805) 693-8384
www.koehlerwinery.com

In 1997 Peter Koehler purchased this property, hired winemaker Doug Scott, and decided to use the high-quality grapes grown on the 30-year-old vines to make his own wines. Cabernet Sauvignon, Chardonnay, Sauvignon Blanc, Riesling, Syrah, Sangiovese, Grenache, and Viognier all flourish on this 100-acre estate, and you can sample some of the wines in the tasting room from 10 a.m. to 5 p.m. daily. The shaded picnic tables are a pretty spot to enjoy lunch.

✳RANCHO SISQUOC WINERY
6600 Foxen Canyon Rd., Santa Maria
(805) 934-4332
www.ranchosisquoc.com

This rustic winery on a 37,000-acre cattle ranch uses only the finest grapes from its 308-acre estate vineyard—one of the oldest in the county. When you arrive at Rancho Sisquoc, you really feel like you're out on a homestead in the Old West—there's nothing around for miles except pastures, vineyards, and a few ranches and farms. The picnic tables on a grassy area are a great spot to relax and eat.

In the tasting room, you can sample various Rancho Sisquoc wines, such as Sauvignon Blanc, Chardonnay, Sylvaner, Riesling, Merlot, Cabernet Sauvignon, and a Meritage blend. The Rancho Sisquoc tasting room is open from 10 a.m. to 4 p.m. daily. Keep an eye out for the redwood chapel at the entrance, which is also featured on the wine label. In 1966 it became the first official landmark in Santa Barbara County, and in 1975 it was dedicated as a State Historical Landmark.

San Ramon Chapel

The San Ramon Chapel and cemetery is a very special redwood chapel at the entrance to Rancho Sisquoc (and featured on the wine label). In 1879, the chapel was placed under the patronage of Saint Raymond Nonnatus (San Ramon), patron of agriculture and farming, by Bishop Francis Mora. In 1966, the chapel became the first historical landmark in Santa Barbara County.

ZACA MESA WINERY
6905 Foxen Canyon Rd., Los Olivos
(805) 688-9339, (800) 350-7972
www.zacamesa.com

Spanish settlers called this area *la zaca mesa* (the restful place), and the name truly fits the bill. This is one of our favorite wineries, not just for its fantastic estate-bottled wines but also for the gorgeous natural setting—an unobtrusive, environmentally correct building that blends perfectly with the surroundings.

The 750-acre property includes 240 acres of mesa vineyards, tranquil dirt roads, nature trails, herb gardens, and native landscaping. You can picnic at tables in the grassy courtyard picnic area or up on the nature trails.

Established in 1972, Zaca Mesa produces about 30,000 cases of wine a year with an emphasis on Rhône varietals, including Viognier, Syrah, and Roussanne. The winery is known as a trendsetter because of its unique blends of Rhône varietals, including the Z Cuvée, a blend of Grenache, Mourvedre, Syrah, Cinsant, and Counoise.

Zaca Mesa is open for tasting from 10 a.m. to 4 p.m. daily, with extended hours (from 10 a.m. to 5 p.m.) on weekends during summer.

Accommodations
FESS PARKER WINE COUNTRY INN
& SPA
2860 Grand Ave., Los Olivos
(805) 688-7788
www.fessparker.com

Tucked behind olive trees on the main street in Los Olivos, this posh bed-and-breakfast-style hotel has beautifully appointed rooms, a pool, a spa, and a fleet of bicycles for your use. Fess Parker (aka Davy Crockett) purchased the hotel in the summer of 1998 and remodeled it to reflect a wine country theme. Fess's wife, Marcella, infused a personal touch by decorating each room differently. Some are bright and airy, with potted palms and light color schemes; others are warm and cozy. All the rooms have antique furnishings, gas fireplaces, down comforters, TVs in armoires, wet bars, hair dryers, and plush robes. One room in the complex across the street is equipped with a Jacuzzi tub. If you really want to pamper yourself, go to the spa for all sorts of rejuvenating facial, body, and massage therapies. The resort also offers meeting space with audiovisual equipment. Room rates start at $300 per night during weekdays and $495 on weekends, including in-room continental breakfast and nightly wine and cheese reception.

Restaurants
LOS OLIVOS CAFE
2879 Grand Ave., Los Olivos
(805) 688-7265
www.losolivoscafe.com

On the main street in the heart of Los Olivos, this cute Mediterranean-style cafe is a popular spot with the locals. Featured in a scene in the movie *Sideways,* what was a thriving cafe is now a virtual hot spot. Sautéed wild king fillet of salmon on a warm spinach salad is a must, and so is the deliciously decadent Chocolate Scream. If you're planning a picnic lunch, you can order food to go. Los Olivos Cafe is open for lunch and dinner daily.

Santa Ynez Valley Wine Trail

The Santa Ynez Valley Wine Trail winds through the southern end of Santa Barbara wine country, where most of the population lives. You'll see horse farms and orchards, historic towns, and the quaint Danish village of Solvang.

The trail is a loop that takes you to all the major wineries in the Santa Ynez Valley. You can start in Buellton, then head over to Santa Ynez, go up to Los Olivos, and wind back through historic Ballard to Solvang. Or follow the route in reverse.

Either direction you take, you can spend a day (or longer) stopping at the premium wineries along the trail.

THE BRANDER VINEYARD
2401 Refugio Rd., Los Olivos
(805) 688-2455, (800) 970-9979
www.brander.com

Suffused with Old World charm, the Brander Vineyard was established in 1975 by Argentinean-born Fred Brander, and it has always been acclaimed as a top producer of premium Sauvignon Blanc. Along with the Sauvignon Blanc, Brander makes a Bouchet (a blend of red Bordeaux varietals), Merlot, and Cabernet Sauvignon. Its sister winery, Domaine Santa Barbara, produces Chardonnay, Pinot Gris, Cabernet-Syrah, and Pinot Noir, and you can taste these wines at Brander. Housed in a small, pink European-style chateau, the tasting room is open daily from 11 a.m. to 5 p.m. during the summer and from 11 a.m. to 4 p.m. the rest of the year.

BRIDLEWOOD ESTATE WINERY
3555 Roblar Ave., Santa Ynez
(805) 688-9000
www.bridlewoodwinery.com

Surfer boy/winemaker David Hopkins is as mellow as his wine. He insists he blends for "character and balance," not the AVA (American Viticultural Areas) label, and we believe him. Under the red-tile roof of this elegant and stately winery, you'll feel a world away from all that matters. After a few sips of the tasting room pour, you'll feel it even decidedly more so. A recent excellent vintage—Blend 175 (Syrah, Cab, Zin, Grenache, and Viognier)—was named because it took 174 blends before Hopkins got something that was up to his standards. Bridlewood is the quintessential wine-tasting experience. The tasting room is open from 10 a.m. to 5 p.m. daily.

i The term *estate winery* means the winery grows it own fruit to make the wines rather than purchasing it from other vineyards. This gives the vintner greater control over the winemaking process from the vine to the bottle.

BUTTONWOOD FARM WINERY
1500 Alamo Pintado Rd., Solvang
(805) 688-3032
www.buttonwoodwinery.com

We love Buttonwood for its wines and the family vibe here, but also for special summer events like the "Red, White, and Blues" festival, farm dinner in mid-August. The organic produce sold in the tasting room is worth the trip as well: In summer they offer delicious, organic, farm-fresh peaches.

*THE GAINEY VINEYARD
3950 E. CA 246, Santa Ynez
(805) 688-0558
www.gaineyvineyard.com

Run by the father-son team of Daniel J. and Daniel H. Gainey, this is one of only a few wineries in Santa Barbara County to own vineyards in both warm and cool microclimates: one for top-quality Bordeaux varietals and the other for Burgundian varietals. It produces about 18,000 cases annually. Varietals include Sauvignon Blanc, Chardonnay, Riesling, Merlot, Pinot Noir, and Cabernet Franc.

Rising at the end of a long drive lined with pepper trees, the beautiful Spanish-style tasting facility was built in 1984. Within its cool tiled interior, you can taste and purchase the wines and buy delicious tapenades, pasta, gourmet vinegars, and bread dippers. Be sure to pick up some of the complimentary gourmet recipe sheets near the counter. If you're looking for a place to eat lunch, you can relax and dine at picnic tables overlooking the vineyards. Each year the winery hosts an extensive program of events, including cooking classes, outdoor concerts, winemaker dinners, and an annual harvest "crush party." The tasting room is open 10 a.m. to 5 p.m. daily (last tasting at 4:30 p.m.). Free tours begin at 11 a.m. and 1, 2, and 3 p.m.

KALYRA WINERY
343 N. Refugio Rd., Santa Ynez
(805) 693-8864
www.kalyrawinery.com

Fact: Santa Barbara County is home to one of the few wine regions in the world with easy access to great surf breaks. What does this have to do with making wine, you may ask? It's what lured Aussie-born winemaker Mike Brown to Santa Barbara County to pursue his passion for crafting fabulous quaffs (with a little surfing on the side). With more than 20 years of winemaking experience under his belt in both California and Australia, Mike opened the Kalyra Winery and tasting room in 2002 with his younger brother Martin. *Kalyra* is a translation from an Australian aboriginal language meaning

"a wild and pleasant place," and you'll find the tasting room fits this description well. Aboriginal art adorns the walls, Aussie salsas are set out for tasting, and the friendly staff and great tunes enhance the lively ambience. The winery produces a Sauvignon Blanc and Chardonnay, but it's best known for its dessert wines, including a tawny port, orange muscat, and black muscat. You can also taste wines under the M. Brown label here, including an excellent Australian Shiraz and Riesling. The tasting room is open from 10 a.m. to 5 p.m. daily, and you can enjoy a picnic lunch on the scenic deck or at the tables on the lawn.

SUNSTONE VINEYARDS AND WINERY
125 Refugio Rd., Santa Ynez
(805) 688-9463, (800) 313-9463
www.sunstonewinery.com

Sunstone's name comes from its sun-colored stone embankment overlooking the Santa Ynez River Valley, and it's one of the most beautiful wineries and tasting rooms in the area. Completed in 1993, the spacious, Provençal-style facility offers an elegant tasting bar, stone floors, an arbored porch, beautiful landscaping with French lavender and rosemary, a courtyard with umbrella tables, and a unique stone cave dug into the hillside and packed with French oak barrels filled with aging wines. You can also purchase gourmet pasta sauces, vinegars, and grilling oils from the display in the rustic tasting room.

The winery uses only organically grown grapes. Its signature wine is Merlot, but it also makes excellent Cabernet Sauvignon, Syrah, Viognier, Sauvignon Blanc, Chardonnay, and Muscat Canelli. The tasting room is open from 10 a.m. to 4 p.m. every day.

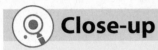

Close-up

The Urban Wine Trail

It seems like every time we turn around, a new wine-tasting room has been added to **Santa Barbara's Urban Wine Trail** (www.urbanwinetrailsb.com). This makes it easy-peasy to go wine tasting for some of the county's finest varietals without trekking 40 minutes via automobile (or taking a potentially expensive wine tour) to the Santa Ynez Valley. You can do this trail by foot—or even enlist a local wine tour company to drive you around if you plan on tasting at a few (or more) tasting rooms. Remember, those six to eight tastings per stop add up quickly, so we recommend you sniff, swirl, sip, and spit if you plan on tasting at more than one or two stops on the trail.

The Urban Wine Trail, at this writing, has more than a dozen wine-tasting rooms (and growing) in the heart of downtown, near the waterfront, and in industrial areas, including a section affectionately dubbed "the Funk Zone." There's even an outpost in Summerland (although you will need to drive, bike, or bus from downtown).

Pick up a trail map, complete with wine lingo and a place to make notes from the visitor center or at any of the wineries. Better yet, check the website or mobile app for news and updates. Days and hours vary, and some tasting rooms are open by appointment only, so check your Urban Wine Trail map or app before heading out on your wine safari. And be sure to enlist a designated driver.

Like we said, new tasting rooms keep cropping up like spring wildflowers. Here's some of the highlights:

- **Kalyra.** 212 State St.; (805) 965-8606; www.kalyrawinery.com

- **Oreana.** 205 Anacapa St.; (805) 962-5857; www.oreanawinery.com

- **Santa Barbara Winery.** 202 Anacapa St.; (805) 963-3633; www.sbwinery.com

- **Cottonwood.** 24 Anacapa St., Ste. 1A; (805) 963-1221; www.cottonwoodcanyon.com

Accommodations

SANTA YNEZ INN
3627 Sagunto St., Santa Ynez
(805) 688-5588, (800) 643-5774
www.santaynezinn.com

This $2 million Victorian-style boutique hotel in the Old West town of Santa Ynez is a fresh choice for visitors seeking luxury accommodations in the wine country. The elegant 2-story inn offers 20 plush guest rooms and suites, a fitness facility with sauna, an outdoor heated whirlpool and sundeck,

meeting rooms, catering facilities, and extensive gardens. Each room is uniquely decorated. Expect antique furnishings, queen- or king-size beds, TVs with DVD/CD entertainment systems, coffeemakers, hair dryers, robes, and thoughtful touches such as fresh-cut flowers. Some rooms also come with gas fireplaces, balconies or patios, double steam showers, and whirlpool tubs. Rates range from $200 to $400 per night and include a full gourmet breakfast, evening wine, hors d'oeuvres, and desserts.

- **Kunin Wines.** 28 Anacapa St.; (805) 963-9633; www.kuninwines.com
- **Municipal Winemakers.** 22 Anacapa St.; (805) 931-6864; www.municipal winemakers.com
- **Margerum Tasting Room.** 813 Anacapa St., downtown; (805) 966-9463; www .margerumwinecompany.com
- **Au Bon Climat.** 813 Anacapa St., next door to Margerum; (805) 845-8435 www .aubonclimat.com
- **Carr.** 414 N. Salsipuedes St.; (805) 965-7985; www.carrwinery.com
- **Jaffurs.** 819 E. Montecito St.; (805) 962-7003; www.jaffurswine.com (appointment required)
- **Summerland Winery.** 2330 Lillie Ave., Summerland; (805) 565-9463; www.sum merlandwine.com

If you're getting hungry by now, or it's around lunch or dinner time, you don't have to go far from Margerum or Au Bon Climat tasting rooms. Within Margerum are **Wine Cask Restaurant** and its bistro, **Intermezzo Bar and Cafe.** Enjoy the historic atmosphere of the restaurant, which is housed in the antiquarian El Paseo building, as you have a lunch of farmers' market–fresh soups and salads, filet mignon enchiladas, or flatbreads with delectable toppings including lamb, preserved peppers, and a variety of elegant cheeses. It'll be hard to choose from all the delicious options if you visit at dinner: crispy-skin salmon; a duck cassoulet "trio" (duck leg confit, braised pork cheek, and Farpoint Ranch sausage), as well as an array of steaks, chicken, scallops, and pork, all treated with care. Pair these incredible dining options with an excellent wine, and Wine Cask will leave you contentedly sighing. It's a perfect note to end on after a great day of great wine.

Restaurants
THE HITCHING POST II
406 E. CA 246, Buellton
(805) 688-0676
www.hitchingpost2.com

Where do local and visiting vintners head when they want a great Santa Maria–style steak, interesting company, and robust wines all in one place? The Hitching Post II, a casual cowboy-style steak house and bar, is at the top of the list. Choose the cut and size of steak you'd like (all are from midwestern

corn-fed beef, and nearly all are certified Angus), and the cook will grill it to perfection over an open fire of red oak. Reviewers also rave about the wine list, which features Santa Barbara County wines, of course, including those made by the owner/chef/winemaker, Frank Ostini.

Complete steak dinners include a fresh vegetable tray, choice of soup or bay shrimp cocktail; organic mixed green salad; choice of rice pilaf, baked potato, or french fries; salsa; and garlic bread. Prices vary by the steak's size and type. You can also order combination meals of steak with quail, shrimp, or duck.

Don't worry if you're not a beef eater—the menu also features pork ribs and chops, seafood, quail, turkey, ostrich, and various other entrees. You can even order a children's meal of steak or chicken for $8.

✳TRATTORIA GRAPPOLO
3687 C Sagunto St., Santa Ynez
(805) 688-6899
www.trattoriagrappolo.com
Using fresh local ingredients, Chef Leonardo Curti whips up delicious Italian cuisine at this family-run local favorite. Popular dishes are the *rollino* appetizers (pizza crust wrapped around smoked mozzarella and radicchio topped with fresh tomatoes) and entrees such as the cioppino and tortelloni (homemade ravioli stuffed with spinach and ricotta cheese in a butter sage sauce). Locals love to sit inside and chat with the friendly staff or perch at the wine bar inside and watch the chef work his magic, but you can also sit outside on the patio. The restaurant serves beer and a large selection of wines from around the world. Trattoria Grappolo is open every day for dinner and Tues through Sun for lunch. Reservations are recommended.

i Tequila time? Check out the margarita specials at Dos Carlitos Restaurant, 3544 Sagunto St., Santa Ynez, (805-688-0033) for a change of pace. Great chips and salsas, fresh guacamole, and a Mexican menu soak up your cocktails.

THE VINEYARD HOUSE
3631 Sagunto St., Santa Ynez
(805) 688-2886
www.thevineyardhouse.com

Next door to the elegant Santa Ynez Inn, tucked in a beautiful old Victorian house, Vineyard House serves hearty American and international cuisine, using fresh produce from local farmers and herbs straight from the garden. You can dine inside or on the romantic outdoor deck. Lunch dishes include salads, burgers, pastas, and sandwiches. The dinner menu offers a choice of meat, fish, chicken, and pasta entrees. The Vineyard House is open daily for lunch and dinner. It's closed on Tues.

Santa Rita Hills Loop

Home to some of Santa Barbara's winemaking visionaries, this cooler region of the Santa Ynez Valley is tucked behind the coastal mountains. The cooler microclimate here produces world-class Pinot Noir and Chardonnay. You can drive along a scenic 34-mile (55-kilometer) loop to explore the area and visit some of the wineries. Along the way, the road carves through wide-open countryside rimmed by rugged mountains, and you'll see some of the most unspoiled scenery in the Santa Barbara Wine Country. Starting from US 101, you can either take Santa Rosa Road west and loop back on CA 246 or vice versa. Although Mosby Winery isn't technically in the Santa Rita Hills AVA, you have to drive right by it when you take Santa Rosa Road, so we've included it in this section.

You can begin or end your Santa Rita Hills loop in Buellton and visit two tasting rooms: **Casa Cassara,** 291 Valley Station; (805) 688-8691; www.ccwinery.com, and **Cold Heaven Urban Tasting Room,** 92 A 2nd St. (805) 686-1343; www.coldheaven cellars.com.

ALMA ROSA WINERY & VINEYARDS
7250 Santa Rosa Rd., Buellton
(805) 688-9090
www.almarosawinery.com
The indefatigable Richard Sanford (along with his delightful wife, Thekla) is an icon in the world of wine. A near-native of the valley, Sanford came here 35 years ago to create wines that would rival France. His pioneering paid off. With the first planting of Pinot Noir vines, Sanford became successful and established quite a reputation. Perhaps Sanford's greatest feat is still yet to come with this new venture of winemaking combined with organic farming and sustainable agriculture methods. Continuing in his renowned tradition, Sanford is still putting out the most excellent of Pinot Noirs and Chardonnays. The tasting room, one famously featured in the movie *Sideways,* is open daily from 11 a.m. to 4 p.m.

BABCOCK WINERY & VINEYARDS
5175 E. CA 246, Lompoc
(805) 736-1455
www.babcockwinery.com
Dentist Walt Babcock and wife, Mona, established this winery in 1984, and son Bryan has been making highly lauded premium, handcrafted wines ever since. The *Los Angeles Times* named him one of the "10 Best Winemakers of the Year." Babcock is known for its Chardonnay, Pinot Noir, Syrah, Gewürztraminer, and Pinot Grigio, making it one "taste test" you really shouldn't miss. The Babcock tasting room is open daily from 10:30 a.m. to 4 p.m.

FOLEY ESTATES VINEYARD & WINERY
6121 E. CA 246, Lompoc
(805) 737-6222
www.foleywines.com

How does William Foley II, the founder and CEO of Fidelity National Finance Corporation, have enough time to be a vintner? Who knows, but Foley's passion for wine drove him to purchase the former J. Carey Cellars in 1997. He promptly changed the name to Lincourt, a combination of the names of his two daughters. In 1998 he purchased Rancho Santa Rosa and planted 230 acres of Pinot Noir, Chardonnay, and Syrah. He named that venture Foley Estates. Visit the unbelievably huge tasting room and event center there. It's as impressive as the wine. Open daily from 10 a.m. to 5 p.m.

LAFOND WINERY & VINEYARDS
6855 Santa Rosa Rd., Buellton
(805) 688-7921
www.lafondwinery.com
French-Canadian-born Pierre Lafond founded Santa Barbara's first post-Prohibition winery, Santa Barbara Winery, in 1962 (see the Urban Wine Trail Close-up in this chapter) and is one of the valley's viticultural pioneers. In 2001 he opened this new estate winery and vineyard to visitors, specializing in vineyard-designated Pinot Noir, Syrah, and Chardonnay. You can sample the wines daily from 10 a.m. to 5 p.m. in the tasting room designed by Lafond himself (who also happens to be an architect). From here you can see all the working areas of the winery. Bring lunch and picnic at tables on the lawn.

MELVILLE VINEYARDS AND WINERY
5185 E. CA 246, Lompoc
(805) 735-7030
www.melvillewinery.com
At the northern end of the Santa Rita Hills loop near Babcock Vineyards, Melville is a relatively young estate winery, specializing

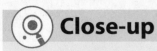

Close-up

Stop in Solvang

If you want to sample wines and soak up some Danish culture at the same time, stop by Solvang while you're in the wine country. In recent years several tasting rooms have popped up amid the windmills and pastry shops. Following are two Insider favorites.

Lucas & Lewellen Vineyards. 1645 Copenhagen Dr., Solvang; (805) 686-9336, (888) 777-6663; www.llwine.com. In 1996 veteran viticulturalist Louis Lucas and Judge Royce Lewellen teamed up with winemaker Dan Gehrs to focus on making fine, food-friendly wines at affordable prices. The results are drawing accolades. Visit their huge tasting room in downtown Solvang, where you can sample wine under three different labels. The namesake label features Rhône, Bordeaux, and Burgundy varietals; the Mandolina label offers award-winning Italian varietals such as Dolcetto, Barbera, Nebbiolo, Pinot Grigio, and Rosato; and the Virgin label includes an unwooded Sauvignon Blanc and Chardonnay. Lucas & Lewellen is also the only winery producing champagne and one of the few producing Cabernet Sauvignon. The tasting room is open from 11 a.m. to 5:30 p.m. daily. You can also purchase clothing, wine accessories, and ceramics.

Presidio Winery Tasting Room. 1603 Copenhagen Dr., #1, Solvang; (805) 693-8585, (888) 930-9463; www.presidiowinery.com. Founded in 1991, Presidio Winery produces premium handcrafted Pinot Noir (the signature wine), barrel-fermented Chardonnay, Merlot, and late harvest Zinfandel, as well as a few wines that are only available in the tasting room, such as a Chenin Blanc and Syrah. The tasting room opened in 2003 on the corner of Mission Drive and Atterdag Street in downtown Solvang and is open from 11 a.m. to 6 p.m. daily. Feel free to ask questions—the friendly staff encourages your curiosity. You can also purchase wine gifts and accessories, clothing, and gourmet food items.

---

in Pinot Noir, Chardonnay, and Syrah. Set in a gorgeous Mediterranean-style villa surrounded by poplar trees, oaks, and sprawling vineyards, the winery eschews competitions but wins high praise for its wines. It's a beautiful winery to visit and at which to enjoy a picnic on the patio and lawn. You can sample the wines—including some limited bottlings from the small lot collection available only through the tasting room—Mon through Fri from 11 a.m. to 3 p.m. and Sat through Sun from 11 a.m. to 4 p.m.

MOSBY WINERY
9496 Santa Rosa Rd., Buellton
(805) 688-2415, (800) 70-MOSBY
www.mosbywines.com

Although Mosby Winery isn't technically in the Santa Rita Hills AVA, it lies just off US 101, and you can easily pop in here on your way to the other wineries in the region. This 46-acre vineyard and winery was once part of the old Rancho de la Vega land grant and has been owned and operated by Bill and Jeri Mosby since 1975. The rustic, restored 1860s carriage house now serves as the tasting room. No other Santa Barbara County winery produces as many Italian varietals or brandies as Mosby.

It's mainly known for its Pinot Grigio, Sangiovese, and brandies, which include Grappa di Traminer (from estate-grown Traminer), Distillato di Prugne Selvaggie (made from wild Pacific plums), and Acqua di Lampone (made from Oregon raspberries). It's also one of the few wineries in the country to produce Teroldego and Cortese. Mosby also produces an award-winning Dolcetto, a dry, medium-body red wine. The tasting room is open Mon through Fri 10 a.m. to 4 p.m. and Sat through Sun 10 a.m. to 5 p.m.

i If you have time while you're exploring the Santa Rita Hills region, visit La Purisima Mission (805-733-3713; www.lapurisimamission.org), the most fully restored of all California's missions, near the Lompoc end of the Santa Rita Hills loop.

SANFORD WINERY
5010 Santa Rosa Rd., Lompoc
(805) 688-3300, (800) 426-9463
(toll-free in California only)

Sanford is a little farther out than some of the others, but we think it's worth the drive for the breathtaking scenery and rich historic ambience. In 1971, Sanford was the first winery to plant Pinot Noir on what is now the Terlato family's famous Sanford & Benedict Vineyard in the heart of the Santa Rita Hills appellation. The winery is on the neighboring vineyard known as Rancho La Rinconada, which was part of an 1845 Spanish land grant. Look carefully for the sign on the left side of the road; the driveway leads between two blocks of grapevines up to the tasting room. They specialize in making world-class Chardonnays and Pinot Noirs. Surrounded by drought-tolerant native California plants, the tasting room and winery are beautiful buildings built in the California Mission style with adobe bricks and Spanish tile roofs. The tasting room and adjoining picnic facilities are open daily from 11 a.m. to 4 p.m. Tours of the adobe winery are available on weekends or by appointment.

DAY TRIPS

With all the people coming to Santa Barbara to escape the rigors of big-city life, you wouldn't think Santa Barbarans would be looking for a getaway of their own. The fact is, even we enjoy a change of scenery every now and then. There are basically two choices for a day trip or getaway out of Santa Barbara: drive north to the Santa Ynez Valley or drive south to the tranquil Ojai Valley.

If you head north on US 101 (which will eventually take you to San Francisco), you're basically eschewing the big city and looking for some peace and quiet in northern Santa Barbara County or in the little beach towns that dot the coast between here and Monterey. We'll give you a peek at the charming Danish town of Solvang and environs in the Santa Ynez Valley.

Traveling south on US 101 will take you to Los Angeles, where you'll find all the sights and entertainment you've come to expect from a large cosmopolitan city. But most people run away from L.A. to Santa Barbara, not the other way around. The artsy and rural town of Ojai, an off-the-beaten-path destination south of Santa Barbara with a bohemian feel, is a 45-minute drive inland.

HEADING NORTH

Solvang

Solvang, one of the most popular day trip destinations with Santa Barbarans, is just a 45-minute drive up the coast. From either US 101 or CA 154, take CA 246 into the heart of this self-proclaimed "Danish Capital of America."

Here you can get a good look at Danish-style architecture (including windmills), check out the **Hans Christian Andersen Museum** at 1680 Mission Dr. (805-688-2052; www.solvangca.com/museum) and the charming **Elverhoj Museum of History & Art** at 1624 Elverhoj Way (805-686-1211; www.elverhoj.org).

The specialty and gift shops are fabulous, and the art galleries and antiques stores make browsing irresistible. All of these attractions draw hordes of tourists, so plan to wade through the crowds at this Disney-esque Danish town, especially on weekends and during the summer. If you really want to get a taste of Denmark, visit during the Danish Days celebration in September (see the Annual Events chapter).

Solvang is particularly charming when decorated for Christmas (see the Winterfest listing in the Annual Events chapter), which is a great time to shop and pick up some incredible Danish pastries to tempt Santa. (First you have to get them home without devouring them—quite a challenge for most of us.) Summertime brings the **Pacific Conservatory of the Performing Arts Theaterfest** (805-922-8313; www.pcpa.org), the Central Coast's professional resident theater company, and several productions are staged in the city's outdoor **Festival Theatre** each season from June through October.

i Allow yourself to be seduced by the smell of *aebleskiver,* small, round Danish pancakes smothered in raspberry jam with a dusting of powdered sugar. Try one of Arne's famous *aebleskiver* sold from a small window at the Solvang Restaurant (1672 Copenhagen Dr.) or even purchase a pan to make your own at home.

Golfers will love the beautiful **River Course at the Alisal** (805-688-6042; www.rivercourse.com), a public 18-hole championship course on the banks of the Santa Ynez River near the exclusive 10,000-acre **Alisal Guest Ranch and Resort,** at 1054 Alisal Rd. (805-688-6411, 800-4-ALISAL from outside the 805 area code; www.alisal.com).

You'll find the city's recent face-lift has changed Solvang's former hotel names, like the Vagabond Inn and Chimney Sweep Inn, to upscale names, like the **Wine Valley Inn and Cottages** (1564 Copenhagen Dr., Solvang; 805-688-2111, 800-824-6444; www.winevalleyinn.com) and **Hadsten House Inn and Spa** (1450 Mission Dr., Solvang; 805-688-3210, 800-457-5373; www.hadstenhouse.com), a sure reaction to the influx of trendy tourists. Contact the **Solvang Conference and Visitors Bureau,** at the corner of Mission Drive and CA 246 (805-688-6144, 800-468-6765; www.solvangusa.com) for information.

You can also explore the nearby wineries and sample wines at the tasting rooms in downtown Solvang (see the Santa Barbara Wine Country chapter).

Accommodations
✳THE ALISAL GUEST RANCH AND RESORT
1054 Alisal Rd., Solvang
(805) 688-6411, (800) 4-ALISAL (from outside the 805 area code)
www.alisal.com
This exclusive 10,000-acre resort and working cattle ranch has 73 comfortable California ranch–style cottages, studios, and suites, each with a wood-burning fireplace. Voted one of the "50 Best Dude Ranches in the West" by *Sunset* magazine, this popular resort has been pampering guests—many of them loyal returnees—since 1946. The resort has hosted an impressive list of celebrities ever since Clark Gable and Lady Ashley exchanged vows here back in 1949 in the original library. Today, it is a favorite hideaway for active couples and families who enjoy all the cozy comforts of home but want to remain incommunicado for a while—all the rooms are telephone- and television-free. The room rate ranges from $495 to $650 a night and includes breakfast and dinner. The resort offers an incredible array of recreational facilities, including 6 tennis courts; two 18-hole golf courses; a private 100-acre spring-fed lake for boating and fishing; guided horseback rides; a ropes course; and miles of spectacular nature trails. At certain times of the year, the resort offers the Round-Up Vacation package that includes unlimited horseback riding on scheduled trips, golf, tennis, and fishing.

Dining in the Ranch Room is reserved for guests, and you'll have to dress up in the evening—dinners are formal, and men require a jacket. The Alisal's River Grill overlooking the public course is open to the public for breakfast, lunch, and dinner, and the Ranch Grill on the private golf course serves breakfast and lunch.

Cachuma Lake

Want a little more nature? Check out **Cachuma Lake Eagle and Wildlife Cruises.** You'll spend 2 hours cruising Cachuma Lake in a 30-passenger pontoon boat. A Santa Barbara County park naturalist navigates you through the wilds while regaling you with stories. Cruises are available on Fri, Sat, and Sun year-round. Call (805) 686-5050 for departure times and more information, or check out the website at www.cachuma.com.

HAMLET INN
1532 Mission Dr., Solvang
(805) 688-4413
www.thehamletinn.com
Brought to you by the same hip owners of the Presdio Motel in Santa Barbara, this newcomer offers some edge to the "new Solvang." The Hamlet Inn is decorated with Danish Modern furnishings and modern amenities such as Vers iPod docking stations. It's located in the midst of downtown Solvang within walking distance to shops, wine-tasting rooms, restaurants, the Elverhoj Museum, PCPA Theaterfest, Hans Christian Anderson Museum, and a short drive to world-class golf courses and wineries. Complimentary bicycles are perfect for getting

around town. Lounge chairs, a gazebo, and a bocce ball court add to the fun.

MIRABELLE INN AND RESTAURANT
409 1st St., Solvang
(805) 688-1703
www.solvangstorybook.com
This small, quaint inn situated in the heart of Solvang is the closest thing to a combination European-style inn and fine dining establishment in the region. Run by veteran restaurateur and innkeeper Brigitte Guehr (she also owns the Meadowlark Inn), Mirabelle Inn's beautifully decorated rooms feature antiques, fireplaces, four-poster beds, and Jacuzzi tub. Full breakfast, turn-down service, wine and appetizers in the evening, robes, DVDs, and spa services make this inn a fine choice for solace and romance in Solvang.

The intimate, romantic restaurant under the fine command of Chef Norbert Schulz seats 30, both indoors and on a lovely front patio. Try the chef's tasting menu; *foie gras,* grilled lamb, sea bass, and other entrees are superb, as is the wine list, but be sure to save room for one of the fine house-made desserts, like the cinnamon ice cream or gingerbread cake served with lingonberry ice cream.

SOLVANG GARDEN INN
293 Alisal Rd., Solvang
(888) 688-4404
www.solvanggardens.com
We are rather fond of this small, charming, and very inexpensive inn located just at the edge of downtown Solvang on the road that leads to Alisal Ranch. The affable owner, Paul Navratil and his wife, Diana, have gone to great lengths to convert what was once a nondescript motel into a welcoming lodging with beautiful gardens at the

entrance and a secret garden tucked into the back. Accommodations, each different and decorated in an antique-y style, range from single- and double-bed rooms with showers and/or shower-tub combos. Continental breakfast includes a pastry treat from one of the local bakeries, and the friendly staff—or Paul himself—will direct you to the good life and attractions in the area.

Restaurants
CECCO RISTORANTE
475 1st St., Solvang
(805) 688-8880
www.ceccoristorante.com
This pizzeria-trattoria from chef-owner David Cecchin has some mighty tasty offerings. You can eat outside on the patio and watch the tourists pass by, inside in one of the dining rooms, or grab a seat at the counter with a view of the wood-burning pizza oven. We love the calamari, the salads, and, of course, the pizza. Nice mix of valley wines and imports from Italy. Open for lunch and dinner.

ROOT 246
420 Alisal Rd., Solvang
(805) 686-8681
www.root-246.com
James Beard Award–winning Chef Bradley Ogden brings his culinary artistry to this elegant and popular culinary destination in the Hotel Corque, both owned by the Santa Ynez Band of Chumash Indians. If you don't feel like splurging on the $36 ciopinno with lobster pasta or $45 chili-cocoa-rubbed filet, go for the market prix fixe, a 3-course dinner priced at $29 that might feature an organic romaine Caesar salad with garlic-Parmesan croutons, Yankee pot roast, heirloom root vegetables, potato puree, and

warm chocolate cake with vanilla ice cream for dessert.

Lompoc

Just a hop, skip, and jump from Solvang (3 miles to the east on CA 246 to be exact), is the **Chumash Casino** (800-248-6274; www.chumashcasino.com), operated by the local Chumash tribe. Touted as "the best place to play from L.A. to the Bay," the casino has become a gambling and entertainment hot spot, offering a large range of gaming options and big-name entertainment.

Five miles northwest of Solvang is **Lompoc** (correctly pronounced LOM-poke), where flower seeds are a blooming business. More than 15 miles of private flower fields bloom in the summer, including wide expanses of sweet peas, lavender, marigolds, calendula, and larkspur. You can get a map of the flower fields from the **Lompoc Valley Chamber of Commerce** at 111 S. I St. (805-736-4567, 800-240-0999; www.lompoc .com). Also in Lompoc, along CA 246, is **La Purisima Mission State Historic Park** (805-733-3713; www.lapurisimamission.org). La Purisima was the 11th of the 21 Spanish missions built in what became California. All of the main buildings are filled with furniture and other artifacts. Candlelight tours, concerts, and crafts are just some of the activities here.

In downtown Lompoc, it's hard to miss the dozens of murals depicting the city's culture and history. You can drive by and admire them, or call the Chamber of Commerce for information on walking tours.

But the big news here is the **Lompoc Wine Ghetto** (www.lompocghetto.com), a cluster of more than a dozen tasting rooms in a nondescript industrial park. From A to Z (Ampelo to Zotovich and many fine winemakers in between, including Longoria, Palmina, and Fiddlehead), this destination is for the true oenophile. What the location lacks in atmosphere (no shaded picnic tables here), it more than makes up for in fab vintages. The Lompoc Wine Ghetto is located at the intersection of 9th Street and Industrial Way in Lompoc, check the website for more information.

The Lompoc Valley is the "Gateway to the Santa Rita Hills Wine Country." Established in 2001, the Santa Rita Hills AVA is actually a sub-appellation of the Santa Ynez Valley AVA. See the Santa Rita Hills Loop section in the Santa Barbara Wine Country chapter for more information.

Also here is **Vandenberg Air Force Base** (www.vandenberg.af.mil), where missile launches often light up the sky. Public tours are offered the second Wed of each month. Two-week advanced reservations are required. There is a 9:45 a.m. check-in. For up-to-date information, call (805) 606-3595. The base's main gate is at the end of CA 1.

HEADING SOUTH

Ojai

Ever heard of the 1930s film *Lost Horizon*? Well, if you have, you can be in Shangri-la within 45 minutes of leaving downtown Santa Barbara. The famous movie was filmed in **Ojai** (pronounced OH-hi), a lush valley surrounded by vast groves of orange trees, the majestic **Topa Topa Mountains,** and millions of acres of **Los Padres National Forest** lands.

It's one of the most scenic spots in all of California (besides Santa Barbara, of course) and an ideal destination for a day trip, but the temperature can be mighty different:

very hot in the summer and quite cold in winter months.

Ojai (population 7,800) is a laid-back destination where you can golf on championship courses, pamper yourself with an enticing array of spa treatments, shop for quality artwork, and even take a spiritual journey. But it's also a Shangri-la for artists and for outdoor-recreation and nature lovers. You can hike along hundreds of miles of trails and go mountain biking, horseback riding, boating, fishing, and camping. Ojai is home to a number of unique centers of philosophy and spirituality—in fact, it's a New Age capital of sorts.

For visitor information, contact the **Ojai Visitors Bureau** at (888) OJAI NOW or visit www.ojaivisitors.com.

To get to Ojai, just drive south from Santa Barbara about 12 miles to Carpinteria. At the Ventura/Santa Barbara County line, you'll see an exit for CA 150. If the road is open (mudslides sometimes close this scenic country road during the winter months), you can take it all the way to Ojai, about 20 miles to the southeast (just follow the signs).

An alternate route is to drive 20 or so miles to Ventura, then take the CA 33/Ojai exit and head up to the mountains for 11 miles. Along the way you pass through a few small towns: Casitas Springs, Oak View, and Mira Monte. The road forks just a mile or two before downtown Ojai. Just keep heading east. The road will become a combination of CA 33 and CA 150 for a while.

Just before you reach downtown Ojai, you'll come to another major intersection: the "Y." This is where CA 33 turns to continue its trek over the mountains to the northwest. To reach downtown, though, you should veer right and stay on CA 150 heading east. We recommend you stop in at the

Ojai Valley Chamber of Commerce, at 201 S. Signal (805-646-8126; www.ojaichamber .org), where you'll find maps and tons of information on accommodations, restaurants, special events, things to see and do, shopping, and art galleries.

It's fun to walk around the small, quaint town of Ojai. Many people drive hundreds of miles just to poke around the galleries and boutiques.

The Arts

Ceramicists know Ojai as the home of the now-deceased bohemian artist, craftsperson, and writer Beatrice Wood (her motto was "young men and chocolates") as well as Vivicka and Otto Heino.

Visit the incredibly art-worthy **Beatrice Wood Center for the Arts** at 8560 Ojai-Santa Paula Rd. (805-646-3381; www.beatricewood .com). It's open Fri, Sat, and Sun from 11 a.m. to 5 p.m. and by appointment other days.

For information on local artists and events, contact **Ojai Studio Artists** (www .ojaistudioartists.org). They have a self-guided art studio tour every fall that is a fabulous way to meet some of the wonderful artistic talent that resides in the valley and peek inside their studios.

i Be sure to browse at Bart's Books, which sets out more than 100,000 used books on tree-shaded patios. It's located 1 block north of Ojai Avenue on the corner of Cañada and Matilija Streets (805-646-3755). Bart's is closed Mon.

The **Ojai Valley Museum,** 130 W. Ojai Ave. (805-640-1390; www.ojaivalleymuseum .org), is a fun place to explore if you're interested in finding out about the colorful local history. Admission is $3 for adults and $1 for children 6 to 18. Children under 6 are free. Hours are 1 to 4 p.m. Mon through Thurs, and 10 a.m. to 4 p.m. on Sat. Guided tours are available on Wed.

Getting Around

It's easy to get around Ojai—just hop aboard the air-conditioned, wheelchair-accessible **Ojai Trolley Service,** which traverses the valley's main strip Mon through Fri from 7:08 a.m. to 5:53 p.m., and Sat and Sunday from 9:08 a.m. to 4:53 p.m. The 1-hour town ride costs 50 cents, and if you're 65 or older or younger than 2, you ride free. The trolley stops near most of the hotels, motels, restaurants, and shops. Note that it does not operate on major holidays.

Festivals & Events

Ojai offers a jam-packed year-round calendar of events, and many visitors arrange their trips to coincide with them. A few major events include the **Ojai Music Festival** (www.ojai festival.org), a renowned series of classical music concerts that occurs in June. The **Ojai Wine Festival** (www.ojaiwinefestival.com), an afternoon also on the same June weekend that you can spend tasting wines, sampling cuisine from Ojai Valley restaurants, and browsing through displays of works by local and regional artists and artisans,

Theater 150, Ojai's professional theatre company (316 E. Matilija St., Ojai; 805-646-4300; www.theater150.org) features the works of local playwrights, and there's even an annual **Ojai Film Festival** (www.ojaifilm festival.com).

Fifteen-acre **Libbey Park,** in the center of town, is the site of many special events. The park includes the newly refurbished Libbey Bowl (where most performances take place), picnic areas, tennis courts, and a playground.

The Great Outdoors

If you've come to Ojai to enjoy the great outdoors, there are many options. The scenic 9-mile (14.5-kilometer) **Ojai Valley Trail** has wide pathways for horseback riding, biking, walking, and jogging. It links Ventura's **Foster Park** (7 miles north of Ventura near Casitas Springs) to Ojai's **Soule Park,** at the eastern edge of town, so you can park your car at Foster Park and ride your bike to Ojai, if you wish. Dogs are allowed on leashes only. Ask for a trail map at the Chamber of Commerce.

You can rent bikes at **Bicycles of Ojai,** 108 Cañada St. (805-646-7736). **Project Ride** (445 W. Roblar St.; 805-798-5193) also rents bikes and does awesome Ojai tours.

Hiking in the mountains near Ojai can be sheer bliss—the vistas from the peaks over the valley, ocean, and islands below are spectacular. At the **Ojai Ranger Station,** 1190 E. Ojai Ave. (805-646-4348), you can pick up free maps of dozens of backcountry hiking and mountain-bike trails in the **Los Padres National Forest.** Note that the ranger station is closed on weekends. To make camping reservations, call (877) 444-6777, or visit www.reserveusa.com. Adventure Passes are required if you want to park in the Los Padres National Forest. You can purchase them at the ranger station. A day pass costs $5; an annual pass is $30.

Hoping for a few hours trolling for trout in a beautiful lake? Head for the **Lake Casitas Recreation Area,** 11311 Santa Ana Rd., just 5 miles southwest of Ojai. In 1984 the Olympic rowing and canoeing events were held here. You can rent boats (805-649-2233, 805-649-1122 for reservations; www.lakecasitas.info) and fish for bass, catfish, trout, and crappie

from sunrise to sunset. There's also a lakeside cafe, **Lake Casitas Snack Bar** (805) 649-2514. You can get your entrance fee waived if you eat there and have your receipt stamped (but you're given a time limit, so it's definitely an eat-and-run situation). There's nothing fancy at this order-at-the-counter spot, but the views are peaceful.

i Giddy-Up! Horses and equestrian trails abound in Ojai. Western Trail Rides (805-640-8635; www.west erntrailrides.org) offers guided trail rides ($60 per person per hour) for one or two people (maximum) and lessons. Ojai on Horseback (805-509-3991; www .ojaionhorseback.com) also offers trail rides.

If golf is your game, you can tee off at the legendary par-70 PGA course at the **Ojai Valley Inn & Spa,** 905 Country Club Rd. (805-646-1111, 888-697-8780; www.ojai resort.com), or the **Soule Park Golf Course,** an 18-hole, par-72 public course at 1033 E. Ojai Ave. (805-646-5633; www.soulepark .com).

Spa & Spirituality

Ojai is where Insiders go for an ultimate pampering experience—for a birthday, wedding, or anniversary treat, or just for a massive dose of R & R. The most exclusive, Five Diamond spa is the **Spa Ojai,** at the Ojai Valley Inn & Spa, 905 Country Club Rd. (805-646-1111, 888-697-8780; www.ojairesort.com).

Rated as one of the best spas in the country, Spa Ojai offers innovative treatments and programs for creativity, self-discovery, and fitness. Step inside and you'll find 28 treatment areas (some with fireplaces), a cardiovascular fitness center, a weight room, 2 pools, an art studio, and a hair and nail salon. Take your pick of massages, body treatments, facials, and fitness programs in an elegant setting.

Another famous spot is **the Oaks at Ojai,** a residential health spa where you can check in to lose pounds and inches and indulge in facials, body scrubs, and paraffin treatments. It was voted one of *Travel & Leisure*'s "10 Best Destination Spas." It's at 122 E. Ojai Ave. (800-753-6257; www .oaksspa.com).

Anyone interested in philosophy and spiritual traditions may want to check out a couple of renowned centers located here. The **Krishnamurti Library,** at 1070 McAndrew Rd. (805-646-4948; www.kfa.org), has a comprehensive collection of the writings and tapes of philosopher J. Krishnamurti. Open Wed through Sat 1 to 5 p.m. Closed Mon and Tues. You can also slumber peacefully in Krishnamurti's former guesthouse, a 1910 farmhouse, and cottages at the **Pepper Tree Retreat** (805-646-4773, 877-355-5986; www.peppertreeretreat.com), which provides a tranquil haven at the east end of town. Rates are $99 to $169 per night and include a vegetarian buffet breakfast.

The **Krotona Institute of Theosophy,** at 46 Krotona Hill (CA 33 at Hermosa Road; 805-646-2653), includes a library, bookstore, and school of theosophy. The public is invited to check out the institute's beautiful grounds—a 115-acre wooded estate with Spanish-style buildings, lily ponds, and magnificent views. The Krotona Institute is open daily; call for hours.

For one of the most beautiful views in the valley, visit **Meditation Mount,** at 10340 Reeves Rd. (805-646-5508; www.med itation.com), home to Meditation Groups Inc., a nonprofit organization dedicated to improving life on this planet for everyone through meditation. You are invited to stop by the complex and meditation room between 10 a.m. and sunset daily.

Accommodations

Although you can easily return to Santa Barbara (it's just 45 minutes away), you might be tempted to overnight in Shangri-la. For accommodation arrangements, contact the Ojai Valley Chamber of Commerce (805-646-8126; www.ojaichamber.org) for an Ojai Valley area accommodations guide.

THE BLUE IGUANA INN
11794 N. Ventura Ave., Ojai
(805) 646-5277
www.blueiguanainn.com
The Blue Iguana Inn is an affordable, artsy place to hang your hat and explore. This Southwestern-style villa is right on CA 33, 2 miles west of downtown Ojai. It has single rooms, 1- and 2-bedroom suites, and 2-bedroom bungalows. Room rates start at $99 and go up to $229 for a 2-bedroom bungalow.

EMERALD IGUANA INN
110 Pauline St., Ojai
(805) 646-5277
www.emeraldiguana.com
The Blue Iguana's sister property is a bit more upscale and private and also has a small pool. The Emerald Iguana has more of a Bali-feel to it and features charming, vibrant paintings by "Ojai Living Treasure" Nancy Whitman.

THE OAKS AT OJAI
122 E. Ojai Ave., Ojai
(800) 753-6257
www.oaksspa.com

A slightly more affordable accommodations option is the Oaks at Ojai, a resident fitness spa. It has 46 rooms, including cottages and a main lodge plus a pool. It also offers massages, facials, and a hair and nail salon.

✳ OJAI VALLEY INN & SPA
905 Country Club Rd., Ojai
(805) 646-1111; (888) 697-8780
www.ojairesort.com
If you're looking for a luxurious resort, you can't go wrong by choosing Ojai's most famous hotel: the Ojai Valley Inn & Spa. It's a full-service, 220-acre luxury resort with spectacular views, 304 deluxe guest rooms and suites, an 18-hole championship golf course (site of many Senior PGA events), and 2 heated swimming pools, including a 60-foot (18-meter) lap pool. The inn offers tons of activities—tennis, swimming, hiking, biking, and Jeep tours—along with a children's program, a golf academy, and a fitness center. The Spa Ojai has a huge range of services. Call for rates.

✳ RIVER CLIFF BUNGALOW
Directions/address given upon booking
(805) 646-5277
www.vacationrentalsojai.com
For a truly special Ojai experience, book a few nights at this 1-bedroom, 2-bath rental bungalow with living room, a sitting room, fireplace, Japanese soaking tub, and fully stocked kitchen. The bungalow is set on a 20-acre nature and botanical preserve. A long deck overlooks Santa Ana Creek, and guests awaken to the sounds of birdsong and the waters rushing by (depending on the season). You can dine on the patio, explore, or picnic in the botanical gardens and you may think you are a million miles away, but in fact it's just a 10-minute drive to downtown Ojai for supplies. Rates range from $250 to $385 a night, and all proceeds from the rental are used to maintain the gardens under the auspices of the nonprofit Conservation Endowment Fund.

Restaurants
If all the beautiful scenery, spirituality, and spa treatments make you hungry, Ojai has a great selection of restaurants that range from the ultimate gourmet experience to excellent taco stands and pizza parlors. You can pick up a detailed restaurant list from the Chamber of Commerce.

BOCCALI'S RESTAURANT
3277 Ojai–Santa Paula Rd., Ojai
(805) 646-6116
www.boccalis.com
This is a casual local's favorite. The owners use fresh-picked produce from their nearby ranch for the pizza and pasta dishes. On a warm day, the oak-shaded outdoor patio is a serene spot to sit and gaze out over the orchards. Boccali's is open every day for dinner and Wed through Sun for lunch.

FEAST BISTRO
254 E. Ojai Ave., Ojai
(805) 640-7987
www.feastofojai.com
Our favorite place to dine in downtown Ojai is Feast Bistro. This tiny, chef-owned restaurant in the arcade has an open kitchen and patio dining in the rear, and the farm-fresh creative cuisine is top-notch.

✳ OJAI VALLEY INN & SPA
905 Country Club Rd., Ojai
(805) 646-1111, (888) 697-8780
www.ojairesort.com

Ojai Valley Inn & Spa has several that are tonier dining venues than most in town. Jimmy's Pub is popular with the golf crowd and boasts a casual atmosphere with a wood-burning brick pizza oven and a myriad of draft beers and Central Coast wine offerings. It's open daily from 11 a.m. to 11 p.m. Maravilla, the inn's upscale award-winning restaurant, highlights the region's fresh foods in a beautiful setting. Maravilla opens daily at 5:30 p.m. under the command of Executive Chef Chad Minton. For lunch, the Oak Grill overlooks the verdant green garden, California oaks, and the herb garden is open during summer months.

THE RANCH HOUSE
S. Lomita Street, PO Box 458, Ojai 93024
(805) 646-2360
www.theranchhouse.com
The Ranch House offers gourmet dining in a gorgeous garden setting with meandering streams. It's open for dinner Tues through Sun and for brunch on Sunday (closed Mon). We prefer the ambience to the cuisine (they seem to be resting on their laurels) but always stop in to purchase their homemade breads that are sold out of the kitchen door.

ANNUAL EVENTS

Santa Barbara loves a party. No matter what month of the year, you'll find enough galas, fund-raisers, benefits, ethnic festivals, and celebrations to keep you busy every weekend. Luckily, the local press does a great job of publishing calendar listings, so you can look ahead and pick and choose events that appeal to you.

As you glance through our list, you'll notice that many events are related to the local agricultural bounty. For example, there's the Santa Barbara International Orchid Show (March), the Lompoc Flower Festival (June), the California Lemon Festival (October), the California Avocado Festival (also in October), and a host of festivals and parties celebrating the local winemaking industry.

A colorful lineup of ethnic festivals also graces the list. Many of these have become Santa Barbara perennial favorites mostly because they are fun, free, offer fabulous food, and have a delightful international flavor. Many of the fund-raisers involving wine and wine tasting are expensive. Although you might think $50 or more is a bit steep for a few hours of sipping wine and eating hors d'oeuvres, these events are extremely popular with Santa Barbarans, and nobody minds the cost because the money goes to worthy causes (besides, you can fill up on excellent wine and hors d'oeuvres). If you can't afford fancy wine dinners, you'll find plenty of events to attend that are inexpensive and even free. In addition to the ethnic and agricultural festivals noted above, many family-oriented events offer free admission.

OVERVIEW

The following listings are in alphabetical order under each month. Unless indicated otherwise, admission to all events is free (although you'll probably have to pay for food and maybe some activities). Prices listed are correct as we go to press, but they have a tendency to creep up from year to year. The events that cost are always worth the money. Enjoy!

JANUARY

AIRSPORTS HANG GLIDING AND PARAGLIDING FESTIVAL
South side of Elings Park
Cliff Drive, Santa Barbara
(805) 965-3733
www.flyaboveall.com/newyear1.htm
If you're not into football, spend a pleasant New Year's Day afternoon observing experienced hang-glider and paraglider pilots maneuver their crafts down one of the oldest training hills in the country. This is a grassroots, low-key, no-frills festival. No rides

are given to the uninitiated; however, if you call ahead of time to make a reservation, you may be able to do a tandem ride.

For the best viewing, enter the park at the Cliff Drive entrance located on the north side of Cliff Drive. Bad weather cancels the festival, but if the weather holds, most gliders are launched between noon and 4 p.m. Organizers encourage a donation to the nonprofit Elings Park Foundation.

SANTA BARBARA INTERNATIONAL FILM FESTIVAL
Various locations, Santa Barbara
(805) 963-0023
www.sbiff.org
Usually held at the end of January and running into February, this local film festival, now in its second decade, has received worldwide acclaim for its diverse programming and screenings of more than 200 films from around the world. It has a strong local following, and enthusiastic fans, industry professionals, and celebrity guests take part in an exciting 11 days of screenings and other special events held all over town.

Independent films made in the United States and abroad are screened at local theaters, and workshops and symposiums focusing on films and filmmaking are held at various venues in the city. Many famous actors and film professionals (including actors such as Cate Blanchett, Leonardo di Caprio, Nicole Kidman, and directors such as Peter Jackson and James Cameron) are feted each year with awards. Other celebrities, including locals like Jeff Bridges and director Andy Davis, often join in the festivities, which include a star-studded opening night. You'll find schedules for all festival events on the website and at local hotels; you can also check listings in the local newspapers or call

to get on the mailing list. You can purchase special passes, which allow admission to all festival events, or you can buy mini-packs of film tickets. Get tickets early for the special events, as they often sell out ahead of time. For details, call or visit the website.

FEBRUARY

AMERICAN RIVIERA WINE AUCTION AND DINNER
Santa Barbara County Vintners' Association
PO Box 1558, Santa Ynez 93460
(805) 688-0881
www.sbcountywines.com
Tuxedos (and maybe even tails) are definitely in order for this exclusive wine auction that raises funds for the Santa Barbara–based nonprofit Direct Relief International. The multicourse gourmet dinner features celebrity chefs and wines that are perfectly married with the cuisine. Hosted at Santa Barbara's fanciest hotels (the venue has changed), there's always a bidding frenzy for the plethora of auction items. Ticket prices tend to be high; phone for information, but remember it's for a great cause: DRI helps people around the world after natural disasters, such as tsunamis, earthquakes, and nuclear power-plant meltdowns.

HARBOR SEALS BIRTHING
Carpinteria Bluffs
Bailard exit off US 101
In February and March, the harbor seals birth their adorable pups. This is one of only two places along the Southern California coastline that offers public access to the harbor seal colony. Take pictures, ooh and aah, but don't touch them or make loud noises. Barking dogs are especially forbidden, as

they can scare off the mother seals, which results in the abandonment of the pups. Harbor seals are federally protected, and any infringement on their colony results in a $10,000 fine.

MARCH

HOLISTIC LIVING EXPO
Sacred Productions
Earl Warren Showgrounds
US 101 at Las Positas Road
www.holisticlivingexpo.com
Make an interdimensional shift by attending the Holistic Living Expo. The metaphysical is ever-present in Santa Barbara, no more so than at this unique fair that offers spiritual readings, presentations, workshops, and speakers on healing the mind, body, and soul. Admission is $5 or $8 for two, $3 for seniors and teens. Children are free.

SANTA BARBARA INTERNATIONAL ORCHID SHOW
Earl Warren Showgrounds, US 101 and Las Positas, Santa Barbara
(805) 403-1533
www.sborchidshow.com
Santa Barbara produces more orchids than any other region of the country, and local growers introduce their finest blooms at this 3-day event, which is the longest-running orchid show in the state. The show features the largest collection of specimens brought in by more than 50 exhibitors from around the world. Booths are designed around each year's theme, and both commercial and private growers compete for the top awards.

A selection of blooming plants, corsages, supplies, commemorative pins, and limited-edition posters are on sale. In conjunction with the show, many local growers host open houses and greenhouse tours. Admission is $12 for adults; $10 for seniors 65 and older and students with ID; children 12 and under are admitted free. Buying tickets in advance saves you a few dollars.

APRIL

EASTER BUNNY EXPRESS
South Coast Railroad Museum
300 N. Los Carneros Rd., Goleta
(805) 964-3540
www.goletadepot.org
All aboard at Wabbit-Twacks Station for a trip around the South Coast Railroad Museum on a miniature train. Your ticket includes a visit to Harvey's House (for a cookie and beverage), Easter Bunnyville (to meet the Easter Bunny and get a surprise), Jack-Rabbit Junction (to enter a drawing), and What's Up Doc (for a souvenir)—an egg-cellent Easter adventure. Call for admission prices.

FOUNDING DAY
El Presidio de Santa Barbara
123 E. Canon Perdido St., Santa Barbara
(805) 965-0093
www.sbthp.org
The place where Santa Barbara began celebrates the city's birthday with a reenactment of the founding of the Presidio. Come down and take a look at Santa Barbara as it was once upon a time. Presidio and Chumash descendants usually ring the bells in the bell towers. Multicultural dance and music performances begin the festivities.

SANTA BARBARA COUNTY VINTNERS' FESTIVAL
Various locations, Santa Ynez Valley
(805) 688-0881
www.sbcountywines.com

Meet the region's vintners at this dynamic wine-and-dine festival. Wander around and taste delectable samples from local restaurants and catering companies. Local artists display their works, and live music provides the perfect accompaniment. This is truly considered by wine Insiders as the vintners' festival by, and for, the vintners. Call for admission prices and tickets.

SANTA BARBARA EARTH DAY FESTIVAL
Santa Barbara County Courthouse Sunken Gardens
(805) 963-0583
www.sbearthday.org
In 1969 an oil rig ruptured off the coast of Santa Barbara, spewing 200,000 gallons of crude oil into the sea. The spill devastated marine habitats and fueled an environmental movement that culminated in the designation of Earth Day in 1970. Hosted by the Community Environmental Council and University of California at Santa Barbara's Donald Bren School of Environmental Science and Management, the festival includes live music, the Green Car Show, Advanced Transportation Marketplace, and Energy Village. Kids will love the children's activities: The Children's Enchanted Forest features arts and crafts, musical performances, theater, storytelling, dancing, singing, instrument making and playing, face painting, and a marine touch tank.

SANTA BARBARA FAIR & EXPO
Earl Warren Showgrounds
US 101 and Las Positas, Santa Barbara
(805) 687-0766
www.earlwarren.com
Held in April, the city's annual Fair & Expo is 5 days (usually Wed through Sun) of fun with an old-fashioned county-fair ambience. Exhibits, crafts, art, games, animals, and carnival rides, along with live entertainment and food booths, are the hallmarks of this event.

A special area is dedicated to the younger set, offering puppet shows, jugglers, a petting zoo, and pony rides. Teenagers will enjoy the thrill rides, while smaller kids can find tamer fare at the Kiddie Carnival. A Junior Livestock competition occurs on Saturday afternoon, and there are special exhibits aimed at young adults. Tickets are $7 for adults, $5 for seniors 55 and older, and $3 for kids 6 through 12. Children 5 and under are admitted free, as are seniors on Saturday afternoons between noon and 4:30 p.m.

SANTA BARBARA KITE FESTIVAL
Santa Barbara City College
"Great Meadow"/West Campus Lawn
www.sbkitefest.com
The kite festival has been a tradition in Santa Barbara for over two decades. Held during National Kite Flying Month, this family affair is filled with high-flying events like tail chase and sports flying. From the teensiest models to the grandest affairs, this mellow event will tickle your fancy.

WHEELS AND WAVES CLASSIC CAR AND HOT ROD SHOW
De la Guerra and State Streets
(805) 964-0639
www.wheelsandwaves.com
State Street closes down to moving traffic and hosts 400 of the nation's finest hot rods and classics—no models built later than 1976. Rev up your engines for the live music, good drink, and tasty food. Who knows? Maybe your own personal favorite will win the prize.

MAY

BONSAI WEEKEND AT THE GARDEN
Santa Barbara Botanic Gardens
1212 Mission Canyon Rd., Santa Barbara
(805) 682-4726
www.sbbg.org
The art of miniature trees and landscapes is presented in this weekend of Japanese cultural activities hosted by the Santa Barbara Botanic Gardens and the Bonsai Club of Santa Barbara. Guided tours of the garden's Japanese Tea House, along with the teaching of an authentic Japanese tea ceremony, accentuate the weekend's activities. The event is free with botanic garden admission.

CHILDREN'S FESTIVAL
Alameda Park West
Micheltorena and Anacapa Streets,
Santa Barbara
(805) 965-1001
http://fsacares.org/support-fsa/events/
childrens-festival
You'll find free entertainment as well as a ton of fun stuff to do all day long at the Children's Festival. The most popular activity is the pony ride, which usually has a long line of would-be cowboys and cow gals waiting for their turn. There's also face painting, kids' crafts, carnival games, magicians, clowns, and Sportsworld, with games to test athletic skills in kids ages 6 and up. Food booths tempt you to splurge on a variety of treats. The festival is always held the Saturday after Mother's Day, with proceeds benefiting the Family Service Agency of Santa Barbara.

CINCO DE MAYO
Various locations, Santa Barbara
(805) 965-8581
www.cincodemayosb.com/
This celebration, marking the anniversary of the Mexican defeat of the French at the city of Puebla, has been taking place for more than two decades in Santa Barbara. Celebrate and enjoy the food booths and entertainment at De la Guerra Plaza (on De la Guerra between State and Anacapa Streets). Some activities are held on the day of Cinco de Mayo (May 5), while others are scheduled on the closest weekend. Check the newspaper or website, as times and events vary.

DOWNTOWN ART AND WINE TOUR
Downtown Organization
27-B E. De la Guerra St., Santa Barbara
(805) 962-2098, ext. 22
www.santabarbaradowntown.com
Sip a local red or a delicate white and nibble on tasty tidbits while touring the downtown art scene. An absolute sellout every year, the $50 tickets are definitely a prebuy must. Proceeds benefit such events as the Downtown Childrens' Holiday Parade.

*I MADONNARI
Mission Santa Barbara
Laguna and Los Olivos Streets,
Santa Barbara
(805) 964-4710, ext. 4411
www.imadonnarifestival.com
Held annually on Memorial Day weekend, I Madonnari is a charming Italian street-painting festival held in the Mission courtyard. More than 200 artists get down on their hands and knees to create colorful chalk masterpieces on the asphalt and cement. Spectators stroll the courtyard at their leisure, then walk down to the lawn, where an "Italian marketplace" features food booths and entertainment. After the festival is over, the street paintings remain, so you can browse later if you don't want to brave the festival crowds.

PEARL CHASE SOCIETY HISTORIC HOME TOURS
Various locations
(805) 961-3938
www.pearlchase.org
The historic home tour showcases up to 9 houses on a weekend in mid-May. Downtown, uptown, or winding through Montecito, tour beautiful homes you'd probably never be invited in to see, many designed by George Washington Smith, Mary Craig, and many other renowned architects of yesteryear who helped shape the look of Santa Barbara and Montecito. Tickets are around $55, but the tour is well worth the price of admission.

SEA FESTIVAL
Santa Barbara Harbor
www.sbmm.org
The Santa Barbara Maritime Museum's Annual Sea Festival takes place on a Saturday in May from 11 a.m. to 4 p.m. in and around the Santa Barbara Maritime Museum in the harbor. In the past, events have included touring the *Bill of Rights,* a visiting 115-foot tall ship, a yacht, and Coast Guard boats, hard-hat diving demonstrations, and arts and crafts activities.

STEELHEAD TROUT FESTIVAL
Stearns Wharf
(805) 963-0583, ext. 116
www.communityenvironmental council.org
It was over a decade ago that steelhead trout were declared an endangered species. What does Santa Barbara do when something's endangered? Raise money to help out, and in a creative way. This exuberant festival does just that with a steelhead sculpture art exhibit on State Street, a 5-kilometer fun-run mimicking the path of a steelhead trout, and live music and fun on Stearns Wharf. The giant fiberglass trouts, painted by local artists such as Rebecca Stebbins, are displayed on State Street after the festival.

WOMEN'S LITERARY FESTIVAL
Fess Parker's Doubletree Resort
633 E. Cabrillo Blvd., Santa Barbara
www.womensliteraryfestival.com
This annual conference presents the work of contemporary female authors from a variety of life experiences and backgrounds. The goal of this festival is to use literature as a means of increasing awareness of social diversity and to strengthen the community through mutual respect. The event hosts a variety of presentations given by distinguished women authors and is dedicated to promoting literacy, diversity, and social justice. The festival gives readers the chance to interact with the authors and learn about the stories they tell.

JUNE

LOMPOC FLOWER FESTIVAL
Various locations, Lompoc
(805) 735-8511
www.flowerfestival.org
The Lompoc Valley, known for its thriving flower seed industry, turns into splashes of vibrant color during June, July, and August. This self-proclaimed "greatest little free festival in the West" celebrates the valley's blooming harvest with a weekend's worth of arts and crafts, flower field tours, and—what festival would be without it?—lots of delicious food.

A parade features floats decorated with local flowers, a carnival offers rides and attractions for the whole family, and you'll find free entertainment at several local venues. The festival's highlight is the flower show, which has been judged one of the highest ranking shows in the state. More than 200 amateur flower arrangements and 500 specimens are on display, and there are arrangements by commercial growers and a children's section.

Other events held in conjunction with the festival include guided bus tours departing from Ryon Park and rolling past 1,000 acres of local flower fields, where you can buy seeds directly from farmers, and an arts and crafts show displaying the works of artists and artisans.

*MUSIC ACADEMY OF THE WEST SUMMER FESTIVAL
1070 Fairway Rd., Montecito
(805) 969-4726
www.musicacademy.org/festival
Every June through August, 140 gifted young classical singers and instrumentalists gather for 8 weeks to study and make music with accredited guest artists, conductors, and faculty. The festival features more than 175 musical events—concerts, recitals, vocal/concerto competitions, and even a full-staged opera—that occur daily, half of which are free of charge to attend. For more information and a complete schedule of events visit the website.

SANTA BARBARA WRITERS CONFERENCE
1111 E. Cabrillo Blvd., Santa Barbara
Info: 27 W. Anapamu St., Santa Barbara
(805) 568-1516
www.sbwriters.com
Smash through writer's block with a source of literary inspiration by indulging in this weeklong Santa Barbara Writers Conference. This internationally renowned event was founded by Barnaby and Mary Conrad and is now owned and run by Monte Schulz, a respected fiction author and son of Charles Schulz (of *Peanuts* fame and a featured conference speaker for many years). It is open to the public and includes workshops on biography, humor, nonfiction, fiction, screenwriting, poetry, science fiction, mysteries, children's books, and more. Such literary luminaries as T. C. Boyle, Jane Smiley, Pico Iyer, and Ray Bradbury have been guest speakers in the past.

A highlight of the conference is Agents and Editors Day, when writers are able to pitch their stories in 15 minutes or less to a bevy of nationally known agents and editors. Many budding authors have reveled in their success when an agent or editor has asked to have the full manuscript sent to him or her. But you must be an attendee to take part ($625 for the week, not including lodging). Fannie Flagg (*Fried Green Tomatoes at the Whistlestop Cafe*) credits SBWC with launching her writing career. Evening lectures in 2011, open to the public for a fee, featured authors such as Ray Bradbury, T. C. Boyle, Eric Puchner, and Simon Van Booy.

*SUMMER SOLSTICE CELEBRATION
State Street and Alameda Park,
Santa Barbara
(805) 965-3396
www.solsticeparade.com
The Summer Solstice Celebration, held at high noon on the Saturday nearest June 21, is when the city throws its distinguished past out the window and goes completely wacko. A whimsical theme is chosen for the parade each year, and participants walk, cycle, in-line skate, or use some other creative form of transportation (no motorized vehicles or live animals are allowed) up State Street dressed

in imaginative and colorful costumes that relate to the theme. (Well, actually, some people ignore the theme, using the occasion to parade around half-dressed and body-painted, or just half-dressed, period.) After the parade, the whole party moves up the block to Alameda Park for a free celebration with food, drink, and dance that continues for the rest of the afternoon.

This is Santa Barbara's largest single-day arts event, and it's about as wild and unpretentious a parade as you can get. Everyone has fun at Summer Solstice, and parade-watchers are often as wild and crazy as the participants. If you don't have a thing to wear or want to design your own float, sign up for the public workshop held in the weeks prior to the parade and make your own ensemble with the help of artists-in-residence.

i The Summer Solstice Parade is only half the fun. After the parade, head to Alameda Park for the wild free party with food, drink, and dance. And the partying has now been extended to 3 days of revelry!

ZOO BREW
Santa Barbara Zoo
500 Niños Dr., Santa Barbara
(805) 962-5339
Info: (805) 962-6310
"Drink Beer. Save Wild Life" is the theme for the Zoo Brew. This afternoon fund-raiser for the animals at the zoo features tastings from a whole herd of breweries from the Central Coast region and beyond. A DJ provides the music, and special animal encounters are featured. Ticket price ($45 to $65 at the door, if available) includes zoo admission, a commemorative tasting glass, and unlimited tastings from participating brewers. Special Zoo Brew food and merchandise is available for purchase. The first event sold out, so get your tickets early and roar!

JULY

GREEK FESTIVAL
Oak Park
300 W. Alamar Ave., Santa Barbara
(805) 683-4492
www.santabarbaragreekfestival.com
Always held the week before Fiesta (which can land it in late July or early August), the Greek Festival is far and away the favorite ethnic festival of Santa Barbarans. Who can resist the moussaka, shish kebab, and bak-lava, not to mention that infectious music? You'll be dancing like Zorba by the time you leave. It's great fun and always crowded. Admission is free.

INDEPENDENCE DAY PARADE AND CELEBRATION
(805) 284-5245
www.spiritof76sb.org
The grand march of this parade celebrating July 4 begins at 1 p.m. on the corner of Micheltorena and State Streets. It ends at Cota, where an exhibit of vintage military vehicles is on display. A free concert in the Santa Barbara County Courthouse Sunken Gardens takes places after the parade, beginning at 4 p.m.

There's also partying all day long at Chase Palm Park on the waterfront, then an explosion of fireworks at the end of the breakwater starting at 9 p.m. Reputed to be the largest fireworks display between Los Angeles and San Francisco, the fireworks are never disappointing. (**Note:** All personal fireworks are illegal in Santa Barbara.)

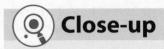 **Close-up**

A Trio of Summer Music Festivals

The arts scene, which includes music, theater, dance, and visual arts, is alive and well all year-round in Santa Barbara, but the music scene is especially vibrant when June busts out all over. Many music festivals offer events that are free of charge; others have reasonably priced tickets or bundle festival passes. These are just three of our Insider favorites, ranging from the internationally acclaimed Ojai Music Festival, an outdoor festival of modern classical music in nearby Ojai; free rock, blues, and jazz concerts in Chase Palm Park; and picnic concerts and performances at the Music Academy of the West.

Among the most prominent music institutions and establishments in Santa Barbara, the **Music Academy of the West** continues to foster engagement in music during its summer-school session and festival season. The **Music Academy of the West Summer Festival** began in 1947, and since then, each mid-June to about mid-August, 140 phenomenal young classical singers and instrumentalists come from around the world to study and perform with guest artists, conductors, and Academy faculties. Lasting only 8 weeks, the festival is composed of 200 events that tap into the realms of chamber, orchestral, and operatic music; from Bach to Beethoven to Rossini. All the while, the young performers learn from the best in featured master classes, which you can attend for a nominal fee. The festival takes place on campus at the beautiful Miraflores estate as well as at the Granada Theatre. We recommend you pack a picnic and then attend an indoor "picnic concert" in Hahn Hall—if you can nab a ticket. Most are scooped up by savvy, season ticket holders. Still, half of the events are free of charge. Call (805) 969-8787 or go to www.musicacademy.org for more information.

Also in the classical realm, but always with a modern twist, is the annual **Ojai Music Festival** that takes place over 4 days in mid-June. The festival features contemporary music as diverse as Purcell's and Ives's as well as premieres of work by living composers such as Osvoldo Golijov, John Adams, and Steve Macky, often accompanied by birdsong at the recently refurbished outdoor Libbey Bowl. The Ojai Music Festival, established in 1947, has seen the likes of 20th-century icons such as Igor Stravinsky, and in 2011 artistic director/new music champion Dawn Upshaw led the festival. For more information and tickets, go to www.ojaifestival.org or call (805) 646-2053.

Back in Santa Barbara, if you are looking for something with more of a boogie beat, shake your booty at one of the free outdoor concerts held at **Chase Palm Park.** A Santa Barbara tradition, these concerts sponsored by the Santa Barbara Parks & Recreation Department feature jazz, rock, country, and blues acts. Pack a picnic and be ready to move your feet! Concerts run from the beginning of July throughout the summer from 6 to 8:30 p.m. Be sure to arrive early to get a good spot and pack a picnic. No alcohol allowed. For concert schedule, call (805) 897-1946 or visit www.sbparksandrecreation.com.

PACIFIC PRIDE FESTIVAL
Leadbetter Beach
(805) 963-3636, ext. 111
www.pacificpridefestival.org
The only major lesbian-, gay-, transgendered-, and queer-pride celebration, this festival culminates a week-long Pride Week celebration meant to bring together the community.

SANTA BARBARA COUNTY FAIR
County Fairgrounds
937 S. Thornburg St., Santa Maria
(805) 925-8824
www.santamariafairpark.com
A local tradition for more than 110 years, the Santa Barbara County Fair is an old-fashioned kind of celebration. You'll find kids auctioning off livestock, displays of local agricultural bounty, exhibits galore, top-flight entertainment such as Kenny Loggins and Boyz II Men, dog and horse shows, and a popular carnival midway in addition to a plethora of food. Lots of fun is in store for the whole family. Preadmission is $5 for adults, $3 for children 6 to 11, $18 for carnival wrist bracelet (access to all rides), $15 for destruction derby (beat-up cars beating each other up even more until there's only one left), and $10 for general admission.

SANTA BARBARA NATIONAL
   HORSE SHOW
Earl Warren Showgrounds
US 101 and Las Positas, Santa Barbara
(805) 687-0766
www.earlwarren.com
This national horse show is a long and distinguished Santa Barbara tradition. The National Horse Show draws horses from eight western states and riders from around the world, making it one of the top

multibreed shows in the nation and the only one in the west to appear on the American Horse Shows Association's short list of "Major National and International Equestrian Competitions."

The 2-week-long show features Paso Fino horses, Morgans, Hackney Ponies, Roadsters, Tennessee Walking Horses, and Welsh ponies and cobs the first week and jumpers and hunters the second. Ages of the participants vary from 5 to 85, making this a decidedly family event. Even if you don't understand a thing about horse shows, the arena performances at this one are both entertaining and enjoyable.

SEMANA NAUTICA
Various locations, Santa Barbara, Goleta, and Carpinteria
www.semananautica.com
A full summer-sports festival that spans both sides of the July 4 holiday, Semana Nautica offers for your participation or observation just about every sport you can imagine, from beach volleyball to spearfishing tournaments. More than 30 events are scheduled at venues throughout the South County, including swimming, kayaking, in-line hockey, softball, cycling, and running. Get off that couch and start training! Schedules are available starting June 1. There is a small fee for participation in each event, but you can watch for free.

AUGUST

✳OLD SPANISH DAYS
Various locations, Santa Barbara
(805) 962-8101
www.oldspanishdays-fiesta.org
Old Spanish Days (the locals call it "Fiesta") is a quintessentially Santa Barbaran celebration.

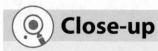 **Close-up**

The Spirit of Fiesta

Every year, on a warm summer night, thousands gather beneath the steps of Mission Santa Barbara. As the moon rises from the lavender peaks and the crowd falls silent, a proud señorita lights up the stage. She stands tall. Her gaze fixed, her chin up, she stretches her slender arms to the sky. Guitars strum a crisp glissando, and with a swirl of her skirt and a staccato of clicks from her heels, flamenco fills the air. This is Fiesta Pequeña, "Little Fiesta," a prelude to the annual 5-day **Old Spanish Days** celebration (**"Fiesta"** to the locals), and this beautiful señorita dances for all Santa Barbara. She is an ambassador picked for her passion and poise. She is the Spirit of Fiesta.

For many Santa Barbarans, Fiesta means a 5-day margarita fest. It means fat burritos in El Mercado, long bar lines, late nights, and cracking *cascarones* (confetti-filled eggs) on the heads of unsuspecting friends. Some think it's too commercialized, but to most Santa Barbarans, Fiesta is a proud tradition. It's one of the few times of the year when the community comes together to celebrate its diverse heritage regardless of social status, religion, or race.

Like the celebration today, the first modern-day Fiesta was spawned from a mix of history, art, and commerce. The descendants of the families who first settled in Santa Barbara in the 18th and 19th centuries wanted a way to preserve the gracious Old Spanish culture of the past. Old Spanish Days refers to the Rancho Period of the early 19th century, when Santa Barbara was an isolated patchwork of pueblos and ranches under first Mexican and then American rule. The spoken language, dress, and customs hailed from Spain, hence the name of the period. By all accounts, the residents of Santa Barbara during this time lived in harmony, and the spirit of charity and hospitality was strong. "Mi casa es su casa" (my home is your home) was the popular sentiment of the time. It was a life less hurried, when the arrival of visitors or the return of old friends and family prompted huge celebrations known as fiestas. The people on neighboring ranchos were invited to come meet the strangers passing through, learn the news of the day, and enjoy food, drink, and dance. It was a life of simplicity, generosity, and warmth—the sweet life. This romantic notion of the past hung heavy in the minds of the descendants of these Californios, as they were called. So in the early part of the 20th century, they organized special festivals such as La Primavera (the spring party) with colorful costumes, music, and dance to keep the spirit of the Old Spanish Days alive.

Against this background of nostalgia came the imminent opening of the new **Lobero Theatre.** It was 1924. The theater had just been restored, and civic leaders wanted to celebrate its debut with a gala event, something the whole community could enjoy. With this in mind, the Community Arts Association conceived an idea.

A distinguished annual tradition that began in 1924, the 5-day event is a colorful feast for the eyes, ears, and palate as residents and thousands of tourists celebrate the city's Spanish roots. Some of the most popular events are the 2 parades, El Desfile Histórico (the Historical Parade) and El Desfile de los Niños (the Children's Parade); Las Noches de

Why not organize a festival to mark the occasion? Representatives from Community Arts shared the idea with the merchants' association and received an enthusiastic response. For years, the business folk in town had dreamed of staging an annual summer festival to entertain and attract tourists in the relatively quiet warmer months. Celebrating the opening of the Lobero was the perfect occasion.

As a result of these mixed motivations, representatives from three diverse groups—art lovers, businesspeople, and descendants of early Spanish settlers—all came together and formed a committee to plan the celebration. Working side by side with a budget of only $5,000, they came up with many ideas of their own and decided to incorporate elements of La Primavera as well. They wanted the 5-day celebration to include food stalls, a western rodeo, activities for children, an arts and crafts fair, and free nightly performances of music, song, and dance. The committee also envisioned a large parade as a critical component of the celebration and enlisted Dwight Murphy, a noted horseman of Santa Barbara, to organize the event.

That first **Fiesta Parade** was a walking history book, albeit a romanticized version. Chumash, Spanish explorers, and soldiers marched down State Street reenacting important events from Santa Barbara's past. The arrival of the Spanish pioneers, the founding of the Presidio and the Mission, the raising of the Mexican flag, and the Gold Rush, among other events, were all represented in the parade. Golden palominos, saddled in silver, pulled the beautifully decorated floats. Spectators dressed in the colorful costumes of Old Spanish Days, and a spirit of unity prevailed. The festival was a huge success.

Today, the **Historical Parade** (El Desfiles Histórico) is one of the largest equestrian parades in the United States, and some of the elements of that original festival still survive. Visit Santa Barbara in the first week of August (when Fiesta traditionally takes place) and you can still enjoy the free nightly entertainment with costumes, song, and dance (known today as **Las Noches de Ronda**), a children's parade **(El Desfile de los Niños),** open-air marketplaces filled with the aromas of authentic Old Spanish Days cuisine **(El Mercado),** an arts and crafts show, and a western rodeo **(Competencia de los Vaqueros),** the same events that brought thousands of locals and visitors together over 80 years ago.

As you sit sipping your margarita, watching the beautiful señorita twirl across a moonlit stage, think of the true spirit of Fiesta. It's not just the costumes, the crowds, and confetti. It's a time-honored ritual that reflects the friendliness of the people of Santa Barbara. It's a time to share our history, culture, and traditions and the townspeople's love of music, art, and dance. But most importantly, it's the gracious spirit of old Santa Barbara passed from generation to generation, a spirit of tolerance, hospitality, and warmth. Viva La Fiesta!

Ronda, a free program of dance and music held every evening in the sunken gardens of the Santa Barbara County Courthouse; the 2 *mercados* (marketplaces), one in De la Guerra Plaza downtown and one at MacKenzie Park on upper State Street, where vendors sell everything from Mexican food to T-shirts; the Competencia de los Vaqueros, a stock horse show and rodeo held at Earl Warren Showgrounds; and Celebración de los Dignitarios, a fun-filled evening of wine and finger foods held hilltop at the Santa Barbara Zoo. A special feature is professional bull riding on Thursday night of Fiesta week at Earl Warren Showgrounds.

You haven't really done Santa Barbara until you've done Fiesta, so pour yourself a margarita, grab your castanets, and party! Oh, and watch out for those *cascarones*, decorated eggs filled with confetti that are sold on the street. You haven't been initiated into Fiesta until someone has cracked one over your head, spilling colorful confetti right into your hair, down 'your back, and into your clothes, your car, your house, and . . . well, you get the picture. Admission to most of the public events is free.

SANTA BARBARA TRIATHLON
Various locations
(805) 682-1634
www.santabarbaratriathlon.com
This is considered by many to be one of the most beautiful and most challenging triathlon courses in the country. Some 900 triathletes compete on the long course, which involves a 1-mile (1.6-kilometer) swim, a 34-mile (54.8-kilometer) bike race, and a 10-mile (16.1-kilometer) run. The women's-only sprint and coed sprint attract around 400 athletes competing in a 500-yard (457-meter) swim, a 6-mile (9.7-kilometer) bike race, and a 2-mile (3.2-kilometer) run. Want to get back in shape? Training for the Santa Barbara Triathlon is guaranteed to do it.

SEPTEMBER

ARTWALK
Santa Barbara Museum of
Natural History
2559 Puesta del Sol, Santa Barbara
(805) 682-4711
www.sbnature.org
Truly one of our favorite events and a major fund-raiser for the museum, the ARTwalk opens on Friday night with a reception, then proceeds with 2 days of art exhibitions and a juried fine arts show and sale. Paintings, jewelry, glass, photographs, and ceramics by more than 100 artists from California line the museum grounds. It's a beautiful weekend wandering through the Mission Creek outdoor setting while sipping a glass of Merlot and talking to the artists. Celebrity artists are featured each year in a special indoor show. Admission is $7, and $50 for the Friday night Artist and Patron Reception.

i Best warm summer night hangout during Fiesta: the Santa Barbara County Courthouse. Bring a blanket, a picnic dinner, and binoculars for a close-up view, and enjoy a (free!) evening of Spanish, Mexican, and Native American dance, music, and song.

DANISH DAYS
Various locations, Solvang
(800) 468-6765
www.solvangcc.com
It's almost as good as being in Denmark when you visit the annual Danish Days festival held in mid-September in Solvang. Folk dancing, music, parades, storytelling, demonstrations of Old World Danish crafts, and plenty of good food (we recommend the deliciously delectable *aebleskiver* smothered in raspberry jam and powdered sugar)

contribute to the charm of this weekend festival. Everyone dresses up in native costumes, and a roving beer wagon adds to the ambience. Even if you find ethnic festivals ho-hum, the *aebleskiver* alone make this one worth attending.

TASTE OF THE TOWN
Riviera Park and Gardens
2030 Alameda Park Serra, Santa Barbara
(805) 563-4685
www.tasteofthetownsantabarbara.com
Santa Barbarans love to eat and drink. The Arthritis Foundation joined the bandwagon by creating this sell-out event. Taste of the Town showcases the finest of Santa Barbara food, wine, and beer and appeals to culinary lovers. Bring your appetite and be ready to balance your food and wine plate while you stroll the pretty setting.

OCTOBER

CALIFORNIA AVOCADO FESTIVAL
Linden Avenue, Carpinteria
(805) 684-0038
www.avofest.com
The California Avocado Festival has grown into the South Coast's largest free family festival. Three days of fun celebrate the avocado in all its forms and are dedicated to enjoying all its attributes. The food court offers a variety of avocado concoctions while music and other entertainment add to the fun. There's a gigantic vat of guacamole (the world's largest purportedly), a "Best Guacamole" contest, a kids' block party featuring games and activities, and lots of shopping opportunities from local arts and crafts vendors. The Avocado Expo Tent supplies an educational slant, in case you feel the need to be a bit serious.

CALIFORNIA LEMON FESTIVAL AND GOLETA FALL CLASSIC CAR & STREET ROD SHOW
Storke and Phelps Roads, Goleta
(805) 967-2500 (Goleta Valley Chamber of Commerce)
www.lemonfestival.com
The California Lemon Festival has pucker power! Lemonade, lemon cakes, lemon bars, lemon tacos, and lemon meringue pies satiate your appetite at this 2-day event devoted to the citrus crop that's been the staple of Goleta's economy for years. Too bad lemon juice can't fill the tanks of the eye-catching assortment of classic cars and street rods. Pony rides, moon bounces, laser tag, and a petting zoo are just a few (and we mean only a very few) of the exciting activities. "Safety Street," a large gathering of safety professionals, is a big hit with the children. They can sit in a fire truck or take a peek into the back of an ambulance.

i If you have kids and fancy a taste of Fiesta but want to avoid the downtown crush, head to El Mercado del Norte at MacKenzie Park off Las Positas Road in Santa Barbara. You'll find the same food booths as well as live music and dance and a host of kid-friendly attractions, including a petting zoo, rides, and a miniature train.

CELEBRATION OF HARVEST
Santa Barbara County Vintners' Association
Rancho Sisquoc Winery, 6600 Foxen Canyon Rd., Santa Maria
(805) 688-0881
www.sbcountywines.com/festivals.htm
Local vintners celebrate the grape harvest at this fall festival held on the second Saturday

of October from 1 to 4 p.m. Similar to the Santa Barbara County Vintners' Festival held in April, the Celebration of Harvest features local wines, gourmet tastings from local restaurants, and a silent auction. Tickets go on sale at the end of July and must be purchased in advance from the Santa Barbara County Vintners' Association. For 18 of the past 20 years, the event has been held in the bucolic setting of Rancho Sisquoc.

EPICURE SB: A MONTH TO SAVOR SANTA BARBARA
www.epicuresb.com

This monthlong culinary celebration features some 100 events, including a variety of food and drink festivals, seasonal menus, cooking classes, art shows, book signings, and many other tasty treats. Come get a taste of the American Riviera by taking part in one—or 100—of these delicious culinary adventures.

SANTA BARBARA BEER FESTIVAL
Elings Park
1298 Las Positas Rd., Santa Barbara
www.sbbeerfestival.com

If artisan microbrews rock your boat, then check out this Oktoberfest celebration for the 21-plus crowd at Elings Park. Folksy, blusy and rock bands provide a soundtrack to your nosh on sausages and cheese and all the other tasty treats you would want to devour while appreciating your beer, making this fall event a delightful day in the park. Proceeds benefit Elings Park and the Santa Barbara Rugby Association, so there's sure to be some eye candy in the sports department as well on hand. Entrance fee is $45 advanced purchase, $55 at door, but designated drivers get in free.

SANTA BARBARA HARBOR AND SEAFOOD FESTIVAL
Santa Barbara Harbor
(805) 897-1962
www.harborfestival.org

Lobster, crab, mussels, clams—you name it. Whatever seafood you're hankering for, it's guaranteed fresh off the boats. Don't know a thing about cooking seafood? Demonstrators will show you how. There are also interactive maritime and children's activities, boat rides, and the most amazing of tall ships for everyone to see. This is one festival that will really "float your boat."

SOL FOOD FESTIVAL
Plaza de Vera Cruz
180 E. Cota St., Santa Barbara
www.solfoodfestival,com

This 1-day community-created festival raises awareness of the sustainable, organic, and local food systems of Santa Barbara County. Held on the first Saturday in October at Plaza de Vera Cruz, across the street from the Saturday farmers' market, naturally. Come celebrate a food system based on "the energy of the sun, rather than fossil fuel, that is healthier for our bodies, our environment, and our economy."

NOVEMBER

NEW NOISE SANTA BARBARA
(805) 845-1776
www.newnoisesb.org

The New Noise Music Foundation produces the annual New Noise Santa Barbara Music Conference & Festival that brings together over 100 music and tech industry speakers and artists to perform in venues throughout downtown Santa Barbara. The festival is an important addition to the Santa Barbara community, helping artists and entrepreneurs listen, learn, and connect with some of the brightest music and technology minds in the world.

SANTA BARBARA NATIONAL AMATEUR HORSE SHOW
Earl Warren Showgrounds
US 101 at Las Positas, Santa Barbara
(805) 687-0766
www.earlwarren.com
Always held around Thanksgiving (thus the nickname "Turkey Show"), this major event is an important training show for future Olympian equestrians. Junior and amateur riders compete in English and Western divisions. In addition to the equestrian highlights, turkey dinners are sponsored, and barns compete for the best-dressed Thanksgiving table.

DECEMBER

DOWNTOWN HOLIDAY PARADE
State Street, Santa Barbara
(805) 962-2098
www.santabarbaradowntown.com
Many local kids strut their stuff in this traditional holiday parade, with bands playing Christmas songs and a few floats, one carrying a smiling Santa Claus. It's no coincidence that this parade winds its way down State Street, where most of Santa Barbara's retail stores are located, so after the parade, browse the shops and spend some money. Christmas is coming, after all! The parade usually starts at 6:30 p.m. Every year a boy and a girl are chosen to be the Holiday Prince and Fairy based on their creativity and imagination expressed in an art contest, and they magically light the large Christmas tree to mark the official start of the holiday season and the Downtown Holiday Parade.

FOLK AND TRIBAL ARTS MARKETPLACE
Santa Barbara Museum of Natural History
2559 Puesta del Sol, Santa Barbara
(805) 682-4711
www.sbnature.org
You can shop the world in a weekend at this 3-day arts and crafts marketplace, which is usually held the first weekend in December in the museum's auditorium. It's the perfect place to find an unusual gift for the holidays, with booths featuring jewelry, baskets, clothing, art, and other objects from around the world. Highlights include textiles from Guatemala, carvings from Africa and Asia, and jewelry from India. Prices for the art and crafts range from as low as 50 cents up to $500 for more elaborate pieces. Admission is free.

THE *NUTCRACKER*
Arlington Theatre
1317 State St., Santa Barbara
(805) 963-4408
A Santa Barbara tradition for more than 20 years, the enchanting *Nutcracker* ballet is presented each December by the Santa Barbara Festival Ballet and the Santa Barbara Ballet Center, with celebrated guest artists and imaginative sets and costumes. Performances are usually on a Saturday and Sunday, with matinees both days and an evening performance on Saturday. Call for ticket prices.

PARADE OF LIGHTS AT THE HARBOR
The waterfront off Stearns Wharf, Santa Barbara
(805) 564-5531
www.santabarbara.ca.gov

This Yuletide evening parade features dozens of boats adorned with holiday lights and other festive decorations cruising around Stearns Wharf and the local waterfront. There's a theme chosen for the parade each year, and entries range from the whimsical to the elaborate. If swells are high, or blustery winds decide to blow in, the boats cruise around inside the harbor. Make sure you bundle up—it's chilly near (and on) the water.

i What are the best seasonal events in Santa Barbara? According to a local poll, Summer Solstice and Fiesta take the top honors for summer, while the Parade of Lights and the Downtown Holiday Parade are the winter favorites.

SANTA BARBARA TROLLEY
CHRISTMAS LIGHTS TOURS
Around town
(805) 965-0353
www.sbtrolley.com
All aboard for this magical Christmas tour of lights on the Santa Barbara trolley. It's true that many Santa Barbarans have holiday fever and overindulge in holiday lights. Some neighborhoods even hold contests for decorations. The Santa Barbara Trolley geniuses scope out the homes and create 90-minute tours showcasing the displays. This tour is guaranteed to wow. Call for prices.

WINTERFEST (SOLVANG)
Various locations, Solvang
(805) 688-6144, (800) 468-6765
The Danish town of Solvang is appealing at any time of year, but it's especially delightful when dressed up in twinkle lights for Christmas. The Winterfest celebration is marked by millions of lights adorning the downtown area, live entertainment, and special events. A tree-lighting ceremony kicks off the monthlong celebration. There's a Christmas Tree Walk led by Santa and Mrs. Claus, a Christmas parade, the Nativity Fest, and the Danish Christmas Celebration at the Elverhoj Museum of History and Art. Now that you're in the Christmas spirit, stop in at the city's many unique shops in search of that special gift—and don't forget to sample the fabulous Danish pastries and cookies.

THE ARTS

The Santa Barbara arts scene has been hopping since the 1870s. Spurred by reports of the glorious climate and gorgeous scenery, wealthy families from the East, South, and Midwest began moving here in droves in the late 1800s and the first half of the 20th century. Rather than do without the established opera houses, museums, theaters, and orchestras to which they were accustomed, they decided to bring world-class culture right here.

This tremendous local support continues to this day and is largely responsible for the big-city variety and quality of arts and culture in our relatively small community. We have our own symphony, two chamber orchestras, choral groups, a professional ballet company, and several theater companies presenting everything from Shakespeare and Broadway-style musicals to contemporary dramas and comedies. You can also explore several major art museums, a natural history museum, and a number of historical museums.

A great thing about Santa Barbara is that you don't have to travel far to enjoy performances by world-class artists. Instead, they come here, and they don't seem to need much convincing. Santa Barbara is a perfect stopover on a trip to Los Angeles or San Francisco. And who wouldn't want to hang out on the beach or stroll the streets of our beautiful town between performances?

The area's stimulating intellectual environment has attracted both emerging artists and those whose names are already internationally renowned. Just sit for a while in a downtown cafe and look around. You're bound to see budding photographers, screenplay writers, artists, and musicians. You might also run into one of our many resident celebrities, including film stars, directors, producers, and novelists.

OVERVIEW

While we couldn't possibly include everything related to the arts in this chapter, we've tried to give you a good idea of the depth and breadth of our cultural offerings. The chapter isn't arranged geographically because nearly all the groups and venues are in Santa Barbara.

To find out what's happening in Santa Barbara while you're here, we recommend you pick up any of the following publications. The *Santa Barbara Independent* is a free weekly newspaper that comes out every Thursday and includes a detailed events calendar for the entire week. It also has a popular arts section with reviews, information, and gallery listings. The *Santa Barbara News-Press* features a daily listings calendar. The Friday issue includes a special *Scene* magazine with a day-by-day events listing for the week as well as reviews and other arts information. *CASA,* a weekly arts-oriented real estate tabloid, covers local theater arts, and musical events.

ONE-STOP CULTURAL SHOPPING

Santa Barbara has a number of arts organizations and centers that sponsor a wide range of exhibits, events, programs, and activities throughout the year.

CABRILLO PAVILION ARTS CENTER
1118 E. Cabrillo Blvd., Santa Barbara
(805) 564-5418
**www.sbparksandrecreation.com/
beachfront**
On East Beach overlooking the sand and sea, the Cabrillo Arts Center presents a range of art exhibits at the pavilion and organizes a variety of fun classes and events at other sites around town, all sponsored by the Parks and Recreation Department. Visit the gallery at the Arts Center itself and you'll see a new exhibit each month by a local group or organization, such as the Santa Barbara Art Association and the Los Padres Watercolor Society. The center also presents special art exhibits coinciding with ethnic and cultural celebrations like African American, Hispanic, and Native American Heritage Months. The Arts Center gallery is open Mon through Fri 9 a.m. to 5 p.m. Admission is free. In July and August, you can attend free concerts hosted by the Department of Parks and Recreation at Chase Palm Park on Thursday evenings. You can also book the Cabrillo Pavilion Arts Center for private special events.

CHANNING PEAKE GALLERY
County Administration Building
105 E. Anapamu St., Santa Barbara
(805) 568-3994
www.sbartscommission.org
Hidden away in the County Administration Building, the Channing Peake Gallery is a treasure trove of regional art. Walk over to the engineering building adjacent to the gallery and find all the county's recent art gifts and a large mural by one of SB's most famous landscape artists, Ray Strong. The exhibitions here seem to be an Insiders secret, but they are out in the open now! Walk out onto Anapamu Street, across from the library, to see the Jardin de las Granadas public sculpture exhibitions. And around the corner on the alley side of the Granada parking garage is the magnificent *Summer Solstice* murals by Benjamin Bottoms and Richard McLaughlin. Admission is free. Open Mon through Fri from 8 a.m. to 5 p.m.

SANTA BARBARA ARTS AND CRAFTS SHOW
Chase Palm Park, along Cabrillo Boulevard east from State Street, Santa Barbara
(805) 897-1982
You can shop for culture here—literally. Established in 1965 by local artists, the Santa Barbara Arts and Crafts Show is called the "Art Center of the West." Sponsored by Parks and Recreation since 1966, the show is now the only continuous, nonjuried arts festival of original drawings, paintings, sculpture, crafts, and photography in the world. Approximately 250 Santa Barbara County resident artists display their own works in an informal atmosphere under the palms of Chase Palm Park. All items are original art, created by the artists you meet. The show is held every Sun

and on designated holidays from 10 a.m. until dusk.

ℹ️ For a calendar of Santa Barbara performances, check out the Santa Barbara Performing Arts League website at www.sbstage.org.

SANTA BARBARA CONTEMPORARY ARTS FORUM (CAF)
653 Paseo Nuevo, 2nd floor, Santa Barbara
(805) 966-5373
www.sbcaf.org

Founded in 1976, CAF presents provocative, innovative contemporary art that explores aesthetic and social issues of our time. It has earned an international reputation as a leading alternative art space and is the primary contemporary arts center on California's Central Coast. CAF presents the work of local, regional, national, and international artists as well as a broad variety of performance and media art. In addition, it operates extensive education and outreach programs, including classes in contemporary art, lectures, poetry readings, panel discussions, workshops, catalogs, video programs, artists' gallery talks, and mentorship programs. The Santa Barbara Contemporary Arts Forum is located in a striking 2nd-story space in the Paseo Nuevo Mall and is open to the public Tues through Sat from 11 a.m. to 5 p.m. and Sun noon to 5 p.m. Admission is free.

UNIVERSITY OF CALIFORNIA AT SANTA BARBARA ARTS & LECTURES
UCSB Campus, Goleta
(805) 893-3535
www.artsandlectures.ucsb.edu

For nearly 50 years, the UCSB Arts & Lectures program has brought a unique and lively array of performing arts, films, lectures, and writers' readings to the university campus—and to the entire Santa Barbara community. Performances feature world-class touring artists: dance companies, chamber musicians, theater companies, and traditional musicians from all over the world. Examples of the diverse range of invitees include the Silk Road Ensemble and Yo-Yo Ma, Madeleine Peyroux, and the Lyon Opera Ballet.

Arts & Lectures also presents international cinema, rarely seen documentaries, independent films, and top Hollywood movies. Lectures and readings bring distinguished people from every area of public life to the stage, for example, Madeleine Albright, Gary Trudeau, the Dalai Lama, and Garrison Keillor.

Most events are presented in the 860-seat Campbell Hall on the UCSB campus, although recently productions and programs have been making more frequent appearances in downtown venues such as the Lobero Theatre, Granada Theatre, and Arlington Center (see the Performing Arts Venues section later in this chapter).

DANCE

Dance in all its forms is a favorite Santa Barbara activity. Although many talented local dancers have found it difficult to earn paychecks for their expertise, they have found numerous ways to practice dance and create high-caliber performance groups. The **Santa Barbara Dance Alliance** (805-966-6950; www.sbdancealliance.org) arranges for the country's best choreographers to visit the city and promotes local choreographers and dancers.

A number of local amateur dance companies—**Ballet Santa Barbara** (805-682-6872;

www.balletsantabarbara.org), **Santa Barbara Ballet Center** (805-966-0711; www.santabarbaraballetcenter.com), and **West Coast Ballet** (805-687-6086) give seasonal performances.

Are you "over" the plié and ready for something different? Then check out Irish step at **Claddagh School of Dance** (805-672-0167; www.claddaghdance.com) or Polynesian dance classes with **Hula Anyone?** (805-451-0589; www.hulaanyone.com).

i **Your foot is tapping, but you don't know the steps? Check out Santa Barbara Dance Alliance's website, www.sbdancealliance.org, for a complete listing of studios and schools offering dance lessons.**

STATE STREET BALLET
322 State St., Santa Barbara
(805) 965-6066
www.statestreetballet.com
This professional ballet company made its debut in 1994 and has succeeded in its goal of bringing the Santa Barbara community "high-quality ballet with a flair." The company strives to present energetic contemporary ballets mixed with the classics. It tours nationally but is in residence at the Lobero Theatre, with performances from Sept through Apr.

State Street Ballet manages to attract top-notch dancers thanks to the extensive dance-world contacts of its founder, Rodney Gustafson. Gustafson is a former American Ballet Theatre dancer who first came to Santa Barbara while on tour with the ABT in the 1970s. He noticed Santa Barbara was rich in all the arts except professional ballet. The beauty and potential of the area drew him back here in 1993 to start a professional company.

FILM

Since it's only 90 miles from Hollywood, Santa Barbara attracts not only celebrity residents from the motion picture industry but also visiting film crews. While you're here, you might even see a group filming a scene at the beach, the zoo, on the courthouse lawn, or on State Street.

At one time, Santa Barbara was the film capital of the world. In 1912 the Flying A Studio built the best-equipped and most innovative motion picture studio in the nation on the corner of Mission and State Streets. Flying A produced hundreds of films—from westerns to dramas set on tropical islands and the Arabian desert. At one point, nearly one film per day was being produced in Santa Barbara.

Hollywood eventually succeeded in drawing the motion picture industry farther south, and grand-scale film production in Santa Barbara ceased by 1921. Today you can satisfy your appetite for great film at a number of Santa Barbara movie theaters, film festivals, and other venues.

Movie Theaters

Metropolitan Theatres has a monopoly on just about all the movie theaters in this town. All theaters show the usual Hollywood releases as well as a few major foreign films. The Riviera Theatre tends to present popular artsy foreign films. The less popular or more offbeat films are often sent to Plaza de Oro.

Call the Metropolitan Theatres Movie Hotline, (877) 789-6684, for locations and showtime information for all the following cinemas or purchase tickets online at www.metrotheatres.com. **Santa Barbara Fiesta 5,** 916 State St.; **Metro 4,** 618 State St.; **Paseo**

Nuevo, 8 W. De la Guerra Place (in the Paseo Nuevo Mall); **Riviera Theatre,** 2044 Alameda Padre Serra; **Arlington Center for the Performing Arts,** 1317 State St. (805-963-4408); **Plaza de Oro,** 371 Hitchcock Way; **Camino Real Cinemas,** Camino Real Marketplace, 7040 Marketplace Dr., and **Fairview Theatre,** 251 N. Fairview.

Film Festivals & Other Movie Venues

SANTA BARBARA INTERNATIONAL FILM FESTIVAL
1528 Chapala St., Santa Barbara
(805) 963-0023
www.sbfilmfestival.org
Every January Santa Barbara turns into a mini Cannes, with film professionals, celebrities, press, and thousands of fans dashing from screen to screen for 11 straight days. Best known for its international films, panels of film professionals, and educational seminars, the Santa Barbara International Film Festival continues a tradition of diverse programming, showcasing independent films from around the world. It presents more than 200 international films to an audience of over 60,000.

UNIVERSITY OF CALIFORNIA AT SANTA BARBARA ARTS & LECTURES
UCSB, Goleta
(805) 893-3535
www.artsandlectures.ucsb.edu
The UCSB Arts & Lectures program sponsors a series of excellent films from around the world—internationals, documentaries, and independents—as well as top Hollywood movies.

ART GALLERIES

ARCHITECTURAL FOUNDATION GALLERY
229 E. Victoria St., Santa Barbara
(805) 965-6307
www.afsb.org
This tiny gem of a gallery is not to be forgotten when wandering around town with an eye toward viewing art. Located in the historic Acheson House, built in 1907, the Architectural Foundation Gallery has been presenting diverse exhibitions of paintings, drawings, watercolors, collage, and photography for over 20 years. Hours are Tues through Fri from 9 a.m. to 2 p.m.

ATKINSON ART GALLERY
Santa Barbara City College
721 College Dr., Santa Barbara
(805) 965-0581, ext. 3484
www.gallery.sbcc.edu
Located on the beautiful Santa Barbara City College campus in the Humanities Building, the Atkinson Gallery is the college's showcase for the visual arts. The gallery hosts 6 exhibits of contemporary art each academic year, featuring a wide range of styles and media, and culminating in the spring with the annual student exhibition. In the fall, artists may also submit work to the annual Small Images exhibition, which is juried by a different critic/arts professional each year. The Atkinson Gallery exhibits international and national artists as well as artists of the region. Gallery hours are Mon through Thurs 10 a.m. to 7 p.m., and Fri and Sat 10 a.m. to 4 p.m.

BROOKS INSTITUTE OF PHOTOGRAPHY GALLERIES

27 E. Cota St., Santa Barbara

(805) 585-8000

Call center: (805) 617-4503

www.brooks.edu

Brooks Institute of Photography is an internationally famous school for professional photographic education. Brooks hosts numerous cultural events for the Santa Barbara community, including exhibits by world-renowned photographers, international multimedia slide shows, student film festivals, undersea slide shows, and educational lectures. The public is invited to tour the campuses and view the numerous photographic images produced by students, faculty, and alumni. Admission is free.

First Thursdays

Art is alive and well in downtown Santa Barbara on the first Thursday of each month, when galleries, museums, and art-related venues showcase visual and performing arts in a lively social environment. From 5 to 8 p.m., locals and visitors mingle with neighbors and participate in the arts community revelry. Grab a *1st Thursday Passport,* the printed guide and map to all things First Thursday, available from participating galleries and venues, MTD shuttles, the visitor center, and hotel concierges. You can print a "passport" from the website www.santabarbaradowntown.com.

THE EASTON GALLERY

557 Hot Springs Rd., Montecito

(805) 969-5781

www.eastongallery.com

Ellen Easton's gallery focuses on contemporary landscapes by local artists. Easton represents the artists involved in the Oak Group, a local group of plein air artists. The gallery is open weekends from 1 to 5 p.m., and weekdays by appointment.

FAULKNER MAIN, EAST & WEST GALLERIES AND TOWNLEY ROOM GALLERY

Santa Barbara Central Public Library

40 E. Anapamu St., Santa Barbara

(805) 564-5608, (805) 962-7653

(no website)

Local sculptors, printmakers, and visual artists display their works at one of the 4 galleries located at the Santa Barbara Central Public Library. Walk through during library hours, or attend one of the special evening art openings. Check the library for a particular art showing schedule. Admission is free. Library hours are Tues through Thurs 10 a.m. to 8 p.m., Fri and Sat 10 a.m. to 5:30 p.m., Sun 1 to 5 p.m. Closed Mon.

GALLERY 113

La Arcada Court

1114 State St., Studio 8, Santa Barbara

(805) 965-6611

www.sbartassoc.org

Santa Barbara is not short on original artwork. Gallery 113 is a cooperative gallery where local sculptors, fine artists, ceramicists, jewelers, and other artists of the Santa Barbara Art Association display and sell their original works. Artists are often on hand to discuss their pieces. Be sure to pop upstairs.

The gallery is open Mon to Sat from 11 a.m. to 5 p.m. and Sun from 1 to 4 p.m.

JAMES R. MAIN FINE ARTS
27 E. De la Guerra St., Santa Barbara
(805) 962-8347
www.jamesmainfineart.com
Located in the Oreña Adobe, the heart of Santa Barbara's art scene, James R. Main Fine Arts features 19th- and early 20th-century fine art and antiques. With a collection of American, European, and Japanese art, this gallery offers an eclectic collection of oils, watercolors, and fine prints. The gallery is open Mon through Sat from noon to 5 p.m.

PEREGRINE GALLERIES
1133 Coast Village Rd., Montecito
(805) 969-9673
www.peregrinegalleries.com
Collectors of plein air art, Jim and Marlene Vitanza have been showcasing the finest in art to Santa Barbara residents for more than 27 years. In addition to paintings, Bakelite jewelry from the early 1930s and antique silverwork from masters William Spratling, Hector Aguilar, and Georg Jensen are represented, in addition to an array of vintage Miriam Haskell and Chanel costume jewelry and very fine Native American pieces. The galleries are open from noon to 5:30 p.m. Mon through Sat and 11 a.m. to 4 p.m. on Sun.

SULLIVAN GOSS GALLERY
11 E. Anapamu St., Santa Barbara
(805) 730-1460
www.sullivangoss.com
These galleries exhibit the works of America's great artists, focusing on Californian artists from the middle of the 19th century to the present. Visit the galleries to view important

sculptures and oil paintings as well as revolving exhibitions. The gallery at 7 E. Anapamu St. is home to the Arts & Letter Cafe and tends to show more vintage work; while the large contemporary space at 11 E. Anapamu St. showcases more contemporary and cutting-edge, as well as living artists.

UCSB'S WOMEN'S CENTER ART GALLERY
Women's Center
University of California at Santa Barbara
Santa Barbara
(805) 893-3778
This art gallery of ever-changing exhibits highlights art that specifically addresses women's issues. Mixed media art is presented throughout the gallery and usually carries very thought-provoking messages. Gallery hours are Mon through Thurs 10 a.m. to 9 p.m., and Fri 10 a.m. to 5 p.m. Admission is free, but a parking permit is required for parking on campus. The permit can cost $5 to $7 for 3 to 4 hours.

WALL-SPACE GALLERY
113 W. Ortega St., Santa Barbara
(805) 637-3898
www.wall-spacegallery.com
Housed in a delightful, restored cottage just 2 blocks off the beaten path of downtown State Street, this newcomer exhibits a combination of spectacular, serene, traditional, and modern photography. Providing the perfect breeding ground for interaction between curious art lovers and innovative, emerging, talented photographers, the original "mothership" gallery opened in 2004 in Seattle showcasing local and national artists' photographic works. If you like to see the world as viewed through the creative camera lens of some very exciting talent,

stop in or make an appointment. An online component called the Studio provides a juried gallery for purchasing prints from the Internet. Collectible is the third component in the Wall-Space Gallery, exhibiting four well-focused collections per year from new visionary artists like Jay Tyrrell, Mark Vercammen, and Grace Weston. Call for hours and days and openings, which are also tasty, indeed.

> **i** If you want to visit the studios of some of our talented local artists, call Santa Barbara Studio Artists at (805) 898-4471, or visit www.studio artists.org and arrange a guided tour.

WATERHOUSE GALLERY
1114 State St., Ste. 9, Santa Barbara
(805) 962-8885
www.waterhousegallery.com
Established in Santa Barbara in 1994, the Waterhouse Gallery carries art in the realist and impressionist styles and has developed quite a reputation for its showing of renowned painters whose work tends to be of the plein air, landscape, and floral still-life school of art. Conveniently located by the Santa Barbara Museum of Art. Open 11 a.m. to 5 p.m. daily.

WESTMONT MUSEUM OF ART
Westmont College
955 La Paz Rd., Santa Barbara
(805) 565-6162
www.westmontmuseum.org
A state-of-the-art venue located on Westmont's inspiring wooded campus, the Westmont Museum of Art is an educational resource for Montecito and the Santa Barbara community, offering family festivals, topical lectures, and exhibitions ranging from old master prints to contemporary installations. The museum is open weekdays 10 a.m. to 4 p.m. and Saturday 11 a.m. to 5 p.m. Closed on college holidays.

LITERATURE

Writers abound in Santa Barbara. The literary community sparkles with the extraordinary talents of novelists, poets, and screenwriters, including T. C. Boyle, Fannie Flagg, Sue Grafton, and Gayle Lynds. Famous authors of children's books associated with the area include Audrey and Don Wood and Lee Wardlaw. Santa Barbara also has more small publishers than almost any other US region of its size.

Nearly every day brings a reading, lecture, or book signing at bookstores, cafes, colleges, and libraries. The *Santa Barbara Independent* also includes book signings and other literary happenings in the weekly events listings.

If you're moving here and want to get involved in a writer's group, we suggest you attend a reading at one of the locales listed below and speak with other writers. They can point you in the right direction. You can also meet other budding scribes through Santa Barbara City College adult education classes. Each year, the continuing education division offers excellent writing courses in a number of different genres. After attending these courses, many students get together and form their own writers' groups. (See the Education & Child Care chapter for more information on this program, or visit www .sbcc.net/continuingeducation.)

Here are a few highlights of our literary scene.

SANTA BARBARA WRITERS CONFERENCE

Hyatt Santa Barbara
Santa Barbara
(805) 568-1516
www.sbwriters.com

This nationally renowned conference, founded in 1972, is now hosted at the Hyatt Santa Barbara Hotel located right across from the beach (see listing in Accommodations). The conference aims to sharpen the skills of aspiring writers and launch them on the path to publication. Registrants attend the full week of writing workshops, evening lectures by literary celebrities, and private writing sessions in June. Guest speakers have included Ray Bradbury (since the inception), Amy Tan, Sue Grafton, Gail Tsukiyama, and Carolyn See.

SMALL PUBLISHERS, ARTISTS & WRITERS NETWORK (SPAWN)

(805) 646-3045
www.spawn.org

SPAWN is a nonprofit organization providing information and networking opportunities for creative people interested in the publishing process. Dues are $65 annually, and include a free print or e-book, a subscription to their monthly Market Update, a listing in their member directory, the opportunity to post a book or service in their catalog, discussion group access, playbacks of audio recordings, and the opportunity to participate at various book festivals throughout the year.

SPEAKING OF STORIES

Center Stage Theater
751 Paseo Nuevo, Santa Barbara
Center Stage Theater Box Office: (805) 963-0408
www.speakingofstories.org

Pages come alive onstage during these magical evening performances, when professional actors read classics and short stories to a captivated audience. In the past, performers have included celebrities such as John Cleese, Jane Seymour, Jeff Bridges, and talented local actors. Readings are offered from January through May at the Center Stage. You can also attend special presentations at other times of the year. Tickets range form $13 to $35. Season subscriptions are also available for $69 to $134.

ART MUSEUMS

KARPELES MANUSCRIPT LIBRARY MUSEUM

21 W. Anapamu St., Santa Barbara
(805) 962-5322
www.rain.org/~karpeles

The Karpeles Library is the world's largest private holding of important original documents and manuscripts. David and Marsha Karpeles established the library because they wanted American children to gain a sense of destiny and hope for the future. They believe this can be achieved by helping people look closely at important accomplishments in various disciplines—particularly history, literature, science, government, art, and music. They opened the original Manuscript Library Museum in Montecito in 1983 but now operate out of the above location.

In addition to the Santa Barbara location, the library now operates museums throughout the United States.

The library features rotating exhibits that focus on about 25 documents at a time. Topics are drawn from the fields of history, music, science, literature, and art. Highlights of the museum's permanent collection include the original draft proposal for the US Bill of Rights and documents penned by such stellar scientists as Einstein, Galileo, Darwin, and Newton.

Past exhibits include "Anne Frank in the World 1929–1945," "Space," and "Great Women in History." Every 3 months the museum features different painting and photography exhibits showcasing the works of the community. The museum is open noon to 4 p.m. Wed through Sun. Closed on Mon and Tues, Thanksgiving Day, Christmas Day, and New Year's Day. Admission is free.

✳SANTA BARBARA HISTORICAL MUSEUM
136 E. De la Guerra St., Santa Barbara
(805) 966-1601

This fascinating museum will give you a sense of what it was like to live in the Santa Barbara of yesteryear. For more than four decades, the museum has celebrated Santa Barbara's artistic and cultural heritage through displays of unique artifacts, photographs, furnishings, and textiles dating as far back as the 15th century.

Artifacts from the Chumash, Spanish, Mexican, American, and Chinese cultures attest to Santa Barbara's multicultural heritage. The museum library holds rare literary and visual documents, including 30,000 historic photographs. Adjacent to the museum are two early-19th-century buildings, the 1817 Casa Covarrubias and the 1836 Historic Adobe. The Gledhill Library is brimming with even more rare literary and visual documents, including 70,000 historic photographs.

Museum hours are Tues through Sat 10 a.m. to 5 p.m., Sun noon to 5 p.m. You can also book a docent-led tour. Call for details. The museum is closed Mon. Admission is free, but a donation is appreciated. (See the listing in the Attractions chapter for more information).

✳SANTA BARBARA MUSEUM OF ART
1130 State St., Santa Barbara
(805) 963-4364
www.sbmuseart.org

Santa Barbara's Museum of Art ranks among the top 10 regional museums in the country. Its permanent collection includes Asian, American, and European treasures spanning more than 5,000 years, from ancient bronzes to vanguard contemporary art.

American art ranges from early portraits through 19th- and 20th-century landscapes, still lifes, and portraiture to Modernist painting and sculpture. The Asian collection encompasses the art of China, Japan, India, Tibet, and Southeast Asia.

While roaming the halls, you can view works by numerous well-known artists such as Eakins, Monet, Chagall, Picasso, and O'Keeffe. The museum also exhibits the acclaimed *Portrait of Mexico Today* (1932), the only intact mural in the United States by renowned Mexican artist David Alfaro Siqueiros. Touring exhibits are on display several times a year. Kids will love the Family Resource Center (open Tues through Sun 11 a.m. to 5 p.m.). You'll also find a cafe and gift shop on the premises. The Constance and George Fearing Library stocks a wide range of reference books, art periodicals, and art exhibition and auction catalogs. Library hours vary, so call before you visit.

Museum hours are Tues through Sun 11 a.m. to 5. It is closed on Mon. Admission (Tues through Sat) is $9 for adults, $6 for seniors/students with ID and children ages 6 to 17; children under 6 are admitted free. Suggested donation on Sun.

SUSAN QUINLAN'S DOLL & TEDDY BEAR MUSEUM

122 W. Canon Perdido St., Santa Barbara
(805) 730-1707
www.quinlanmuseum.com

Susan Quinlan grew up taking art classes at the Cleveland Museum of Art. Upon earning her degree in library science, she became a librarian for the Cal State University system for over 30 years. During those years, she must have focused an inordinate amount of time on collecting, because she amassed one of the largest displays of dolls and teddy bears in the United States, perhaps in the world. Three thousand of her historical and contemporary dolls and teddy bears are on display at the museum's three galleries. The gift shop has numerous one-of-a-kind and limited edition items and out-of-print books. The museum is open 11 a.m. to 5 p.m. Fri through Mon. It is closed Tues through Thurs and on holidays. Admission is $6.50 for adults, $3.50 for preteens, and children under 5 are free.

UNIVERSITY ART MUSEUM

UCSB, Goleta
(805) 893-2951
www.uam.ucsb.edu

Established in 1959, the University Art Museum is known for its creative programs focusing on vanguard contemporary art. The museum's 7,000-object fine art collection ranges from antiquity to the present. Of special note is the Sedgwick Collection of Old Master Paintings and the Morgenroth Collection of Renaissance Medals and Plaquettes. Modern holdings include sculpture by Henry Moore, Sam Francis, and George Rickey; paintings by Joan Mitchell and Robert Therrien; and works by Georgia O'Keeffe and Jean Tinguely.

One of the museum's particular strengths is works on paper, with drawings by Jonathan Borofsky and prints by Jean Arp, Richard Diebenkorn, and 1930s WPA artists. You'll also find more than 300 paintings and drawings by early 20th-century Santa Barbara artist Fernand Lungren and a substantial group of 19th- and 20th-century photographs here.

The museum's architecture and design collection, which focuses on the work of Southern California–based architects and designers, is considered one of the most comprehensive of its type in the country. It includes more than 750,000 historic drawings and related documents such as correspondence and writings, photographs, models, casts, and furniture.

A diverse educational outreach program of lectures, tours, films, performances, and symposia is scheduled throughout the year, and special educational programs are offered for schoolchildren. In addition, the Museum Store offers an array of unique art, design, and fashion items that reflect the museum's changing exhibitions.

For information about current exhibitions and programs, call the numbers above or visit the museum's website. The museum's hours are noon to 5 p.m. Wed through Sun. The museum is closed Mon and Tues. Admission is free. A parking permit is required for parking on the campus. It can cost from $5 to $7 for 3 to 4 hours.

WILDLING ART MUSEUM

2928 San Marco Ave., Los Olivos
(805) 688-1082
www.wildlingmuseum.org

Out of town but worth every minute of travel is the Wildling Art Museum, which is dedicated to the art of America's wilderness. Situated in quaint Los Olivos, the museum presents 3 to 4 exhibits a year focused on wilderness and nature, along with 10 to 12 smaller exhibitions, programs, and activities for children. The museum is open Wed through Sun from 11 a.m. to 5 p.m. The suggested donation is $2 per adult. Children and members are free.

MUSIC

CAMERATA PACIFICA SANTA BARBARA
(805) 884-8410
Info: (800) 557-BACH
www.cameratapacifica.org
Called "the best chamber music reason to get out of the house" by the *Los Angeles Times,* Camerata Pacifica is known for its intimate venues, inventive programming, and an inviting, often irreverent atmosphere full of discussion and banter. Offering monthly concerts from September to May, the ensemble's programs feature the exceptional artistry of Camerata Pacifica's musicians and a diverse repertoire, from Mozart to Musgrave, Beethoven to Berio. Camerata Pacifica has been part of Santa Barbara since 1989 and performs at Hahn Hall at Music Academy of the West, with monthly lunchtime and evening concert series. The group also performs monthly in San Marino, Los Angeles, and Ventura.

COMMUNITY ARTS MUSIC ASSOCIATION (CAMA)
2060 Alameda Padre Serra, Ste. 201, Santa Barbara
(805) 966-4324
Tickets for individual performances through the Granada Box Office, (805) 899-2222, or the Lobero Box Office, (805) 963-0761
www.camasb.org

Founded in 1919, CAMA is the grande dame of Santa Barbara arts groups. It's devoted to bringing the world's greatest symphony orchestras, maestros, and soloists to Santa Barbara's balmy shores.

The roster of artists and orchestras presented by CAMA over the past 85 years represents a who's who of music in this century: Horowitz, Rachmaninoff, Segovia, Mehta, the New York and Berlin Philharmonics, and the Concertgebouw Orchestra, to name just a few. The Los Angeles Philharmonic has performed in Santa Barbara every year since 1920.

CAMA's season runs October through May, and concerts tend to sell out quickly; in fact, it's sometimes hard to get tickets to certain performances at all unless you're a season subscriber. Call right away if you have any interest in attending a performance. All concerts are held at the Granada Theatre, at 1214 State St., or the Lobero Theatre at 33 E. Canon Perdido St.

✳MUSIC ACADEMY OF THE WEST
1070 Fairway Rd., Montecito
(805) 969-4726, box office: (805) 969-8787
www.musicacademy.org
The Music Academy of the West is internationally renowned and widely considered one of the finest summer music festivals and schools in the country. Every summer it offers 8 weeks of richly varied music performed by exceptional musicians—much to the delight and benefit of Santa Barbara residents and visitors.

The academy was established in 1947 by a group of dedicated arts patrons and celebrated musicians, including legendary German opera singer Lotte Lehmann and Dr. Otto Klemperer, music director of the Los Angeles Philharmonic from 1933 to 1939. The group wanted to create a summer music academy on a par with such East Coast institutions as Juilliard and Tanglewood.

The academy has provided gifted young musicians with the opportunity for advanced study and performance under the guidance of internationally known faculty artists (including Metropolitan Opera star Marilyn Horne, director of the Music Academy's voice program, and piano pedagogue Jerome Lowenthal).

In 1951 the academy took up permanent residence at Miraflores, an elegant, Mediterranean-style estate on a bluff overlooking the Pacific Ocean. Today the campus occupies 9 acres of wooded, beautifully landscaped grounds and gardens.

Events are open to the public during the academy's Summer Festival, which starts in mid-June and ends in mid-August. Picnic Concerts at the Miraflores campus are popular events. Concertgoers enjoy a picnic supper in the gardens followed by a concert showcasing brilliant young musicians in Hahn Hall.

Master classes—the academy's signature program, in which faculty artists give feedback to the performers—are held in piano, strings, brass, winds, percussion, and voice, and are open to the public. Call or visit the above website for more information. Also, free community-outreach concerts are presented at various locations around town, including the Santa Barbara Museum of Art and the Presidio. Some of the Summer Music Festival events are free of charge. Subscriptions are available, or you can purchase single tickets from the Music Academy Box Office (805-969-8787).

OPERA SANTA BARBARA
1330 State St., Ste. 209, Santa Barbara
(805) 898-3890
www.operasb.com

When this nonprofit organization opened its first official season in 1996, it was the first opera company in the region in nearly 35 years.

Opera Santa Barbara is the dream child of opera singers Marilyn Gilbert, a lawyer by profession, and her husband, Nathan Rundlett, a retired teacher. They wanted to bring opera on a grand scale back to town and started making the dream a reality in 1993. They staged five full operas and countless operatic excerpts at many locations to build an audience. A following emerged, and the company opened its first official season in fall 1996.

Opera Santa Barbara attracts first-rate singers, technical staff, conductors, and stage directors. Many of the stars sing with major opera companies, for example, the Metropolitan, San Francisco, and Munich operas. The orchestra is composed of professional players from Santa Barbara and Los Angeles.

Productions are fully staged, thanks to set designers from California and New York, choreographers, award-winning costume designers, and a large chorus. The season runs from September through March. For tickets to small productions, call the Lobero Theatre Box Office (805) 963-0761, or visit www.lobero.com; for large productions, call the Granada Theatre Box Office (805) 899-2222, or visit www.granadasb.org.

i If you like the blues, visit www .sbblues.org and sign up for the free Blues Lovers e-mail updates. You'll receive all the latest information on blues events in Santa Barbara.

SANTA BARBARA BLUES SOCIETY
(805) 897-0060
www.sbblues.org
Founded in 1977, Santa Barbara Blues Society is the oldest existing blues society in the United States. This not-for-profit organization sponsors and produces performances of well-known blues musicians, supports local blues artists, and has an active Blues for Youth program.

SANTA BARBARA CHAMBER ORCHESTRA
(805) 966-2441
www.sbco.org
Directed by renowned violist Heiichiro Ohyama, this acclaimed orchestra consistently presents classical chamber music of the highest standards and spotlights world-renowned guest soloists.

The orchestra's season runs fall through spring, with concerts taking place on Tuesday evenings. Seats are almost always sold out through season subscriptions, but when they are available, individual tickets can be ordered through the Lobero Theatre Box Office (805-963-0761). To order subscriptions, call the Santa Barbara Chamber Orchestra at the number above.

SANTA BARBARA CHORAL SOCIETY
1330 State St., Ste. 202, Santa Barbara
(805) 965-6577
www.sbchoral.org
The Santa Barbara Choral Society, founded in 1948, is the oldest performing arts organization in Santa Barbara. It's renowned for the high quality and discipline of its singers and its challenging, innovative repertoire. Composed of about 100 members, the society aims to open up avenues for study and performance to all qualified singers and to encourage public interest in choral music. The society has presented several world premieres and devotes a significant number of its programs to 20th-century music by American composers.

> **i** Feeling jazzy? The Santa Barbara Jazz Society (www.sbjazz.org) is a nonprofit organization whose mission is to promote and support jazz through a variety of activities. Concerts are usually held on the second Sunday of each month at SOhO Restaurant and Music Club 1221 State St., Santa Barbara, from 1 to 4 p.m., and there's a small admission fee.

SANTA BARBARA MASTER CHORALE
(805) 967-8287
www.sbmasterchorale.org
Created in 1984, Santa Barbara Master Chorale performs major choral works accompanied by a professional orchestra and soloists. Conducted by Dr. Steven Hodson, the group presents 3 concerts a year.

SANTA BARBARA SYMPHONY
1330 State St., Ste. 102, Santa Barbara
Office main line: (805) 898-9386
www.thesymphony.org
For more than a half century the Santa Barbara Symphony has been celebrated for its unique ability to deliver brilliant orchestral concerts. Led by internationally renowned music director Nir Kabaretti, the Santa Barbara Symphony performs traditional symphonic, choral, and popular music. They present a series of 7 concerts per season at the beautifully restored Granada Theatre in the heart of downtown Santa Barbara.

SINGS LIKE HELL
Lobero Theatre
33 E. Canon Perdido St., Santa Barbara
(805) 963-0761
www.singslikehell.org
Top singers/songwriters come to the Lobero Theatre to play a range of music, from folk, rock, jazz, reggae, and pop to hip-hop and country. Performers in this series are chosen for their talent, regardless of fame or fortune. In the past they have included Peter Case, Tom Russell, the Persuasions, David Crosby, Tracy Chapman, Charlie Musselwhite, Greg Brown, Laura Love, and Shawn Colvin. Season ticket holders receive a backstage pass for a meet-the-artist reception after each show. Tickets are available at the Lobero Theatre Box Office (see above) or online at www.lobero.com.

THEATER

It's not New York, but Santa Barbara comes pretty darn close to offering a similarly wide range of high-quality dramas, musicals, contemporary plays, and offbeat comedies.

CIRCLE BAR B DINNER THEATRE
Circle Bar B Guest Ranch
1800 Refugio Rd., Goleta
(805) 967-1962
www.circlebarbtheatre.com
The Circle Bar B Guest Ranch, just north of Santa Barbara, hosts a lively dinner theater on Friday and Saturday evenings, as well as a Sunday matinee. Theater runs from April through October, and tickets for dinner and the show are $45 per person, with senior and student rates available on Friday and Sunday. Dinner is a tri-tip and chicken BBQ, complete with mashed potatoes and gravy, green beans, chili, salad, garlic bread, and

dessert. A vegetarian option is available with advance notice, and there is a full bar in the main lodge for the purchase of alcohol, beer, and wine.

✳ENSEMBLE THEATRE COMPANY OF
SANTA BARBARA
Box office: (805) 965-5400
www.ensembletheatre.com
Founded in 1979, the award-winning Ensemble Theatre Company is Santa Barbara's longest-running professional theater company. ETC has built an excellent reputation for producing a range of classic and modern comedies, dramas, light musicals, and off-Broadway hits. It produces 5 fully staged productions each season from October through June. ETC's professional company members have performed on Broadway and appear regularly in films and on television. Guest directors come from major regional theaters, and set designers work in regional theater, film, and television.

It also offers a Storybook Theatre, which stages an original musical play for children every year. The company resides at the intimate 140-seat Alhecama Theatre in the Presidio State Park. Call the number above for tickets.

PACIFIC CONSERVATORY OF THE
PERFORMING ARTS THEATERFEST
(805) 928-7731, box office: (805)
922-8313
www.pcpa.org
This unique regional theater group is not technically within the geographic region we're focusing on in this book. However, many Santa Barbarans head up to Solvang and Santa Maria in the North County for the excellent performances of comedies, dramas, and musicals.

PCPA is based at Allan Hancock College in Santa Maria and appears at three different North County facilities, the closest being the 700-seat Solvang Festival Theatre, an outdoor amphitheater. PCPA is the only training program of its kind in the country offered by a community college. It supports a unique, fully accredited vocational training program for aspiring actors and theater technicians.

PCPA Theaterfest is home to a core company of resident and visiting professionals. Past productions include such classics as *Les Misérables, Macbeth, West Side Story,* and *Ragtime.* You can order season subscriptions or tickets to individual performances from the PCPA website or by calling the box office number above. Note that arrangements for patrons with special needs are subject to availability and must be made in advance.

PERFORMING ARTS VENUES

A number of area arts centers, auditoriums, theaters, and halls host a wide range of performances by local and traveling companies and troupes.

ARLINGTON CENTER FOR THE PERFORMING ARTS
1317 State St., Santa Barbara
(805) 963-4408
This exquisite city landmark is probably the most unusual theater you'll ever visit. It's also Santa Barbara's main performing arts venue, and it has held that title for more than 50 years. It's built on the site of the grand Arlington Hotel, which opened in 1875. Arlington House was the name of the Virginia mansion owned by Robert E. Lee and later occupied by the Union army, and the posh hotel was so named to appeal to post–Civil War sympathizers of both the

North and the South. The hotel burned to the ground in 1909, and a new Arlington rose from the ashes in 1911. Bad luck befell that building too, as it was heavily damaged in the 1925 earthquake and subsequently demolished. The site lay as a patch of weeds until Fox West Coast Theatres erected the third and present structure as a showcase movie house in 1930–31. The stunning tile-roofed building was designed to resemble the Moorish kings' Alcazar in Seville. The unique architectural style is actually a combination of numerous styles from Spanish architecture. The Andalusian exterior features a tall spire and an arched courtyard with fountains.

The interior is adorned with sweeping staircases of glazed Tunisian tiles, antique chandeliers, and iron lanterns that are copies of Catalonian street lamps from the 14th through the 16th centuries. The walls depict authentic Spanish villages, each building completely detailed with roof, chimney, lighted windows, balconies, stairways, and ironwork. The ceiling boasts a moonlit sky and twinkling stars. Actor Seth Rogen likened it to "a movie theater inside a Mexican restaurant" at a fete there during the Santa Barbara International Film Festival.

✵CAMPBELL HALL
UCSB, Goleta
(805) 893-3535
Opposite the University's Cheadle Hall administration building, Campbell Hall is the main venue for Arts & Lectures performances by comedians, musicians, dance troupes, and all types of touring artists. This 860-seat facility on the UCSB campus was originally designed as a recital hall, and the acoustics and sight lines are excellent.

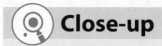 **Close-up**

Alhecama Theatre

The Alhecama, 914 Santa Barbara St., a cozy 140-seat theater next to the Old Presidio, was originally the centerpiece of the Santa Barbara School of the Arts. The school, which was a branch of the Community Arts Association, boasted a powerhouse teaching staff of nationally known artists, including Buckminster Fuller, Carl Oscar Borg, Ed Borein, and Colin Campbell Cooper. The school closed when its director died in 1932, and the association handed over the property to a bank during the Depression to pay off creditors.

Philanthropist and civic leader Alice Schott saved the arts complex from becoming a parking lot when she bought the property in 1939. She renamed the property and the theater Alhecama—a word coined from the first two letters of her four daughters' names: Alice, Helen, Catherine, and Mary Lou. Later she deeded the property to what's now called the Continuing Education Program, which held well-attended classes there from 1945 to 1981. The California Department of Parks and Recreation purchased the property in 1981, handing management over to the Santa Barbara Trust for Historic Preservation. Today the theater is home to the Ensemble Theatre Company. The facilities feature a climate-control system and free parking next to the theater.

CENTER STAGE THEATER
751 Paseo Nuevo, Santa Barbara
(805) 963-0408
www.centerstagetheater.org
Center Stage Theater opened in 1990 thanks to an unusually successful collaboration between Santa Barbara's business, civic, and art communities. The theater is located on the upper level of the Paseo Nuevo mall in downtown Santa Barbara. Center Stage is a 130-seat professional black-box theater featuring a full spectrum of events including dance, music, theater, lectures, meetings, and films. Each year 60–70 different producers rent the theater to present performances that range from young dancers and actors appearing onstage for the first time to seasoned professionals from Santa Barbara and beyond.

✳EL CAPITÁN CANYON
US 101 North to El Capitán State Beach
(805) 685-3887
www.elcapitan.com
Historic groves of oaks and sycamore trees surround you in this outdoor luxury campground site, where a summer concert series offers families a night of rocking-good fun. For a $10 admission, local bands play every Saturday night from April through October. Adults, kids, and young-at-hearts dance on the Creekside Greens near a blazing fire pit and under a canopy of twinkling stars. Barbecue dinners with humongous portions of chicken, salad, beans, and garlic bread are offered for $18, or you can bring your own picnic and drink.

*GRANADA THEATRE
1214 State St., Santa Barbara
(805) 899-2222
www.granadasb.org

After a $40 million-plus restoration, the Granada Theatre has become one of the premier entertainment venues on the South Coast. Seating for 1,550 patrons includes loge and balcony sections, plus 8 side boxes. From Santa Barbara's very own Santa Barbara Symphony to sold-out guest performances of Gustavo Dudamel conducting the Los Angeles Philharmonic Orchestra, the Granada has returned to her former glory.

The Granada Theatre is proud to be the home of the area's finest performing arts companies: Opera Santa Barbara, Santa Barbara Symphony, Community Arts Music Association, State Street Ballet, and Santa Barbara Choral Society. The venue is also a favorite stop for UCSB Arts & Lectures' events on tour as well as Music Academy of the West's Summer Festival Concert Series and the ever-popular Broadway Series. Additionally, 2011 saw the launch of the exciting Granada Theatre Concert Series. Every month the Granada Theatre showcases popular entertainers, such as the Moody Blues, Big Bad Voodoo Daddy, and world-famous comedians. A dynamic array of outside presenters also brings top-level touring productions to the Granada Theatre.

*LOBERO THEATRE
33 E. Canon Perdido St., Santa Barbara
Box office: (805) 963-0761
www.lobero.com

The beloved Lobero, which is the oldest continuously operating theater in the state, is a theater with a history. In the 1870s there were no opera houses in California south of San Francisco. A Santa Barbara opera aficionado named José Lobero changed all that by establishing the first opera house in Southern California. He raised money and built the original theater—supposedly the largest adobe structure in existence at the time—in 1873. It soon became a major cultural center, attracting traveling shows, vaudeville, and performances by community groups. The building fell into disrepair and was condemned in 1922. The Community Arts Association purchased the structure and tore it down. The group then contracted famous local architects George Washington Smith and Lutah Maria Riggs to design the "new" Lobero, a stately Spanish Revival structure with soaring columns, graceful arches, and a red-tile roof. The new theater opened in August 1924.

Today the Lobero Theatre is not only a major performing arts center for the community but also a city and state historic landmark that enjoys the aforementioned title of California's oldest continuously operating theater. The nonprofit Lobero Theatre Foundation has operated the 680-seat theater since 1938. It provides an intimate setting for many types of performances and events, from chamber music, modern dance, ballet, and opera to lectures, contemporary music, and children's theater. It was voted one of *DownBeat* magazine's "Best Places to See Jazz" in 2011, and the Jazz at the Lobero series is just one of many fine, popular performances you can catch here.

MARJORIE LUKE THEATRE
Santa Barbara Junior High School
721 E. Cota St., Santa Barbara
(805) 884-4087, ext. 1
www.luketheatre.org

This theater is named in honor of the late Marjorie Luke, the well-loved, former performing arts instructor at Santa Barbara Junior High School. The theater's Spanish Colonial Revival architecture, similar to the courthouse and Mission Santa Barbara, provided a perfect framework for the $4 million renovation (2003) that created this stunning 812-seat space. Features include vaulted wood ceilings, ornate relief work, handmade tiles, and hand-forged wrought iron. Santa Barbara Junior High students use this theater, as do community arts organizations. Mentoring and technical workshops are held here.

SANTA BARBARA BOWL
1122 N. Milpas St., Santa Barbara
(805) 962-7411
www.sbbowl.com

The renovated (and continuing to be improved) Santa Barbara Bowl is one of Santa Barbara's most evocative venues. Music lovers of all types (but primarily rock) flock to to see top performers and internationally acclaimed acts from April through October. Built in 1936 of local stone, the 4,562-seat outdoor amphitheater in the Riviera foothills provides an outrageously scenic setting for rock bands, a mariachi festival, and singers of all stripes. The sloped seating makes for fantastic views. On clear evenings, you can see the ocean shimmering in the distance, and with the stars glittering above and onstage, you can't beat the bowl for ambience. In recent years, the bowl has hosted a long list of popular stars, including Sting, Sheryl Crow, Alanis Morissette, Bob Dylan, the B-52s, the Gypsy Kings, Tom Petty and the Heartbreakers, and Jack Johnson.

PARKS

It's true that Santa Barbarans love their beaches, but eventually we all get a hankering for a change of scenery, a wide expanse of green grass, and a shady grove for picnicking. Luckily, maintaining a thriving system of parks has always been a high priority in Santa Barbara, and whether you're looking for a tranquil garden or a rugged spot to hike, you'll find enough wide-open spaces to fit your every mood (not to mention plenty of room for the kids to run around). The Channel Islands National Park and Marine Sanctuary are so spectacular, they get their own separate chapter in this book—don't miss it!

OVERVIEW

In this chapter, we show you the best of our beautiful parks, covering Santa Barbara first, and then heading west to east from Goleta to Carpinteria. Next, we'll go inland for a look at Cachuma Lake Recreation Area, one of the county's most popular parks. City, county, and state parks are listed according to the geographical area in which they are found, along with their major features and other useful information.

For information about parks within the city of Santa Barbara, contact **Santa Barbara Parks and Recreation** (805-564-5433; www .sbparksandrecreation.com), which administers the daily workings and programs at more than 55 parks citywide (a total of 1,764 acres). The Adapted Programs Office (805-564-5421) can answer questions about wheelchair accessibility to the parks; call between 8 a.m. and 5 p.m. weekdays. A free city park map which lists all the parks and their features is available at the main office at 620 Laguna St.

All city parks are open from sunrise until a half hour after sunset, except where posted otherwise. During summer daylight saving time, many parks remain open until 10 p.m., but be sure to check the posted hours when you arrive. All city park restrooms are closed at dark, and no overnight camping is allowed.

More than 20 county parks (900 acres) fall under the auspices of the **Santa Barbara County Parks Department** (805-568-2461; www.countyofsb.org/parks), headquartered at Rocky Nook Park in Mission Canyon. You can make reservations for facilities at any county park by calling (805) 568-2465. You can also read about park facilities or download printable maps at the department's excellent website (listed above). Park hours are from 8 a.m. to sunset year-round.

SANTA BARBARA

ALAMEDA PARK
1400 Santa Barbara St., Santa Barbara
(805) 564-5418
www.sbparksandrecreation.com
One of the city's oldest parks, Alameda is best known today as the site of Kids' World (see the Playgrounds section in the Kidstuff chapter), a very cool 8,000-square-foot fun zone for—who else?—kids. But while the kids are playing, Mom and Dad will appreciate the park's unique collection of more than 70 species of trees, the gazebo, and the acres of shady lawn. Since this park is close to downtown, it provides a good respite from the hustle and bustle, even though the street-only parking can sometimes present a problem. Many downtown workers grab lunch, hoof it over from their offices, and relax in the shade.

ALICE KECK PARK MEMORIAL GARDENS
1500 Santa Barbara St., Santa Barbara
(805) 564-5418
www.sbparksandrecreation.com
A relative newcomer on the city parks scene, Alice Keck Park Memorial Gardens is a gorgeous 4.6-acre sanctuary right in downtown Santa Barbara. With the focus on an impressive botanical collection complemented by a koi-filled lily pond and small streams, the park has an especially tranquil feel. It's the perfect spot to contemplate the meaning of life. A Sensory Garden for the visually impaired, with audio posts and interpretive Braille signs, is one of few such areas on the Central Coast. Within the garden, visitors can touch trees and bubbling water as well as smell the flowers and enjoy other nonvisual experiences. Alice Keck also boasts a low-water demonstration garden. Pick up a

pamphlet here and you'll find lists of all the plant species used in its creation. Parking is on the street.

ANDREE CLARK BIRD REFUGE
1400 E. Cabrillo Blvd., Santa Barbara
(805) 564-5418
www.sbparksandrecreation.com
Once a tidal marsh known as the Salt Pond, the bird refuge was donated to the city in 1909. Mary Clark, a local philanthropist, had the pond drained and converted to a freshwater lake, then named it after her deceased daughter, Andree. You can ride your bike to the refuge, which sits at the east end of Cabrillo Boulevard. Be sure to pack your binoculars. This is one of the best spots in town for observing waterfowl, migrating songbirds, and resident species that thrive in the water and surrounding foliage. Stroll around the pond and you'll find interpretive signs and observation platforms. It's an easy walk.

Although the city has done its best to remove domesticated fowl from the refuge, there are always a few hanging around, and you should be aware that feeding the birds here is against the law (not to mention unhealthy for the birds). If you choose not to walk or bike, you can park your car in the small lot on Los Patos Way.

ARROYO BURRO BEACH (HENDRY'S BEACH) PARK
2981 Cliff Dr., Santa Barbara
(805) 687-3714
www.sbparks.org
Better known as Hendry's Beach, Arroyo Burro is one of the most popular county parks in Santa Barbara. It was part of the original lands that the king of Spain granted to Santa Barbara in 1782. You can walk your dog off leash here in the area east of

the slough as long as you remain within voice control range. For more information on recreational facilities, see the Beaches & Watersports chapter.

CHASE PALM PARK
E. Cabrillo Boulevard, Santa Barbara
(805) 564-5418
www.sbparksandrecreation.com

Named in honor of the venerable Pearl Chase (1909–1979), Chase Palm Park stretches along the beachfront from Stearns Wharf to East Beach. The 35 acres include a bike path and walkway, large stretches of lawn, a soccer field, and restrooms.

Once consisting mainly of just palm trees and grass, the park seems to be ever evolving. Across the street, Chase Palm Park Expansion, completed in early 1998, includes a fantastic children's playground with a nautical theme (read more about it in the Playgrounds section of the Kidstuff chapter), a carousel, and a public pavilion. Arts and crafts booths line the park each Sunday and holiday, and the rest of the time you'll see people of all ages enjoying the lovely seaside setting. The only problem is—you guessed it—parking. Parking is found along the street or in city lots, but on weekends and holidays, it can be difficult to get a space.

> **i** For a taste of quintessential Santa Barbara, check out the free summer music concerts from July through August at Chase Palm Park (www.sbparksandrecreation.com) on Thursday evenings. Pack a picnic, round up the family, kick back, and enjoy some great tunes while the kids run wild.

DOUGLAS FAMILY PRESERVE
End of Linda Road on the Mesa, Santa Barbara
(805) 564-5418
www.sbparksandrecreation.com

Overlooking Arroyo Burro (Hendry's Beach), the Douglas Family Preserve is one of the last undeveloped pieces of oceanfront property in Santa Barbara. At one point developers wanted to change that, but in late 1996 the citizens of Santa Barbara had a chance to save the property from development when the owners, tired of trying to get financing, offered to sell it for $3.5 million.

The fate of what was formerly known as the Wilcox Property (it was once owned by nurseryman Roy Wilcox) had been a subject of public debate for years, and preservation-minded Santa Barbarans were not about to let this chance go by. So they started sending in money. Cash, checks, and even pennies from children's piggy banks flooded in from all parts of the city and county.

When the total didn't quite add up to enough, actor and local resident Michael Douglas chipped in $600,000 to put the fund-raising campaign over the top. On March 1, 1997, the 70-acre Douglas Family Preserve, named by the largest contributor in honor of his father, Kirk, became the property of the City of Santa Barbara.

Truly a "people's park," it's basically undeveloped, but it's a good place for a solitary stroll on bluffs overlooking the ocean, and it's one of the few parks in the city where dogs can run free. Park on the 300 block of Linda Road and enter through the metal gate, or park at Arroyo Burro and walk up the newly developed path access. There are no restrooms or recreational facilities.

i If you want to take a walk in the park and enjoy spectacular Santa Barbara views, Shoreline Park, Franceschi Park, and Douglas Family Preserve are the best picks. Don't forget your camera!

ELINGS PARK
1298 Las Positas Rd., Santa Barbara
(805) 569-5611
www.elingspark.org
Run by the Elings Park Foundation, which has donated untold amounts of money and time to make it one of the city's most beloved recreational areas, beautiful Elings Park comprises 230 acres and is the largest public green and recreational space in Santa Barbara City. Of these, 135 acres remain undeveloped. Facilities include 3 lighted fields, 2 soccer fields, a BMX track, a radio control car track, mountain bike trails, jogging and hiking trails, picnic and barbecue facilities, a playground, and restrooms. Stand on the hilltops here and you can breathe in panoramic views of the city and ocean.

The undeveloped south part of the park boasts the area's best hang-gliding and paragliding training hill and is the site of the annual New Year's Day Hang Gliding and Paragliding Festival (see the Annual Events chapter). Soaring gliders are a common sight in this area of the park, and you are welcome to watch.

If you're planning a get-together, you can reserve one of 3 picturesque special event areas. Godric Grove, especially for weddings, boasts a 300-seat amphitheater, a sprawling lawn, and a deck area shaded by oak trees. Singleton Pavilion, also for weddings, has a lovely gazebo in the middle of a meadow as well as picnic tables tucked in a grove of liquid amber trees. The South

Bluffs are also available for ceremonies, and they boast a 180-degree view of the ocean. Four picnic venues include Cappello Picnic Area, with a canopy top; Fenton Davison Picnic Area, with horseshoe pits and barbecue; Sunrise Rotary Picnic Area, with a large barbecue and beautiful view; and Pine Grove Picnic Area, with a large barbecue and small playground. These areas are often booked on weekends, so be sure to make a reservation well in advance (up to a year ahead if you want a group area on a weekend during the months of June, July, August, and September). Parking is usually ample, but when several events are going on at once, cars can spill out onto the adjoining streets.

The park is one of the few in Santa Barbara that allow off-leash dogs in certain areas. But you'll need to pay for a permit and tags. The yearly fee is $125. For information, e-mail the Elings Park Dog Owners Group (EPDOG) at info@elingspark.org.

Park hours vary depending on the time of year but are generally from sunrise to sunset. Office hours for reservations are from 9 a.m. to 5 p.m., Mon through Fri. Once you've enjoyed this wonderful place, you might be moved to make a donation to the Elings Park Foundation, which will gladly accept your contribution. Just walk into the office and write a check, or send your donation to the foundation at 1298 Las Positas Rd., Santa Barbara 93105. Overnight camping is not allowed.

i Try to find the likeness of Francesco Franceschi, an Italian botanist, carved into stone at Franceschi Park. His serene face gazes out toward the Pacific Ocean. (Hint: It's easier to see it from Mission Ridge Road.)

FRANCESCHI PARK
1510 Mission Ridge Rd., Santa Barbara
(805) 564-5418
www.sbparksandrecreation.com
Named for Francesco Franceschi, who made a name for himself in horticulture, the 18-acre park actually encompasses a portion of a nursery he owned until 1925. In addition to an impressive botanical collection, the park offers a panoramic view of the city and ocean from its lookouts and winding walkways. Of special interest is Franceschi's home, built in 1905 and still within the park's boundaries. Plans are currently in the works for house and park restoration. In the meantime, check out the 63 medallions (see if you can find them all!) placed around the house by a previous wealthy owner. The medallions pay tribute to places and people, although no one knows for sure what the meaning is behind them. You'll also find a small picnic site and restrooms within the park, and it has its own parking lot. This is not necessarily a good "kid" park, however, as there is no play area and no lawn for romping. It is an excellent place for romance, though, as it has one of the best views in town.

MACKENZIE PARK
State and De la Vina Streets,
Santa Barbara
(805) 564-5422
www.sbparksandrecreation.com
MacKenzie Park, the site of El Mercado del Norte (the Northern Marketplace) during the annual Old Spanish Days celebration (see the Annual Events chapter), is fairly busy the rest of the year, too. In addition to one of the city's few lawn-bowling greens, plus an adjacent clubhouse, the 9-acre park has a playground, baseball diamonds, picnic areas with barbecues, and restrooms.

A recreational building in the park has a kitchen, fireplace, barbecue pit, and large patio and is available for meetings or other functions. Parking is available in an on-site lot.

MISSION ROSE GARDEN
Los Olivos and Laguna Streets,
Santa Barbara
(805) 564-5418
www.sbparksandrecreation.com
Tended carefully by local volunteers, the Mission Rose Garden and surrounding grassy area provide a popular place to toss the Frisbee around, stretch out for a nap, or literally stop and smell the roses. Inhale the fragrance of more than 1,500 rose plants in the garden, which is across the street from Mission Santa Barbara (see the Attractions chapter). You can also walk along the paths to the ruins of old aqueducts, a reservoir, a grist mill, and even a jail. This is a must for rose lovers. Park on the street.

OAK PARK
300 W. Alamar Ave., Santa Barbara
(805) 564-5418
www.sbparksandrecreation.com
Oak- and sycamore-studded Oak Park, bisected by Mission Creek, plays host to all the city's ethnic festivals, and it's one of the most visited parks in the city. It also provides a few extras, such as a raised dance floor where dancers from the festival of the moment can entertain the crowds.

When the park is not full of festivalgoers, you'll find folks playing tennis on 2 public courts and kids splashing in the wading pool (open June through August) or romping on the playground. You can also play a serious game of horseshoes in the lighted horseshoe pit. The park has plenty of places

Dog Guidelines

Dogs must be on a leash at all times in county parks, and there are only four leash-free areas in the city of Santa Barbara: the Douglas Family Preserve, the area east of the slough at Arroyo Burro (Hendry's Beach) Park down to Shoreline Park steps, the eastern end of Tucker's Grove Park at Kiwanis Meadow, and a posted off-leash area of Elings Park (with a special permit). The dog's human companion must be at least 18 years of age, be able to leash the dog immediately if there are any signs of trouble, and keep the dog out of picnic sites, sports fields, and playgrounds. Any damage done to a park by an unleashed dog is the owner's responsibility, and doggie messes must be cleaned up immediately using "poop station" supplies, which are found in most city and county parks.

You can bring your dog with you to a California state park, but you must be able to show the dog's rabies vaccination certificate or license. During the day, dogs must be on a leash no more than 6 feet long, and they are not allowed on trails, on the beach, or in buildings unless they are service animals.

to picnic and barbecue. Restrooms and a parking lot are also available.

ORPET PARK
Alameda Padre Serra and Moreno Road, Santa Barbara
(805) 564-5418
www.sbparksandrecreation.com
This charming park on the Riviera is filled with exotic plants and trees and is a good place for birding in the fall and spring. Park on Alameda Padre Serra, then meander along the footpaths and enjoy the botanical wonders.

PERSHING PARK
100 Castillo St. at W. Cabrillo Boulevard, Santa Barbara
(805) 564-5422
www.sbparksandrecreation.com
Known for its lighted ball fields and 8 lighted tennis courts, Pershing Park doesn't have much more in the way of recreational

facilities, but you can spread a blanket out on the lawn and picnic. Restrooms are on-site, and there's a parking lot, but it fills up fast on weekends so you may have to park on the street.

ROCKY NOOK PARK
610 Mission Canyon Rd., Santa Barbara
(805) 568-2465
www.countyofsb.org/parks
Donated to Santa Barbara County in 1928, 19-acre Rocky Nook Park is a charming spot for a stroll along the banks of Mission Creek or a quiet lunchtime picnic. Studded with oaks and sycamores and dotted with boulders, the park is almost completely shaded, which makes it a cool respite from the heat during the summer. It's also a great place for birding, especially in spring, when migrating birds gather in the dense foliage.

You'll find 2 large group picnic and barbecue areas here as well as several smaller picnic sites, and a small playground for the kids. Permanent restrooms are on-site, and parking is plentiful. After a relaxing picnic lunch, you can pop across the street to the Santa Barbara Museum of Natural History or stroll to Mission Santa Barbara, which is also within walking distance. You won't find any expansive lawns here, but that's part of the charm of this little "rocky nook."

SHORELINE PARK
Shoreline Drive and La Marina, Santa Barbara
(805) 564-5418
www.sbparksandrecreation.com
One of the most popular parks in Santa Barbara, Shoreline Park encompasses 15 manicured acres that overlook the beach just west of the Santa Barbara City College campus. It's the perfect place to fly a kite, or you can gaze out toward the Channel Islands and maybe see a whale swimming by (a bronze whale's tail marks the best vantage point for whale-watching).

You can access the beach by going downstairs to the sand, or you can opt to relax in the park's grassy areas, which include facilities for picnics and barbecues. Kids will love the playground here, and you'll find restrooms on-site. The park has a fairly generous parking lot, so you usually don't have to go looking on the street.

SKOFIELD PARK
1819 Las Canoas Rd., Santa Barbara
(805) 564-5418
www.sbparksandrecreation.com
High in the Santa Barbara foothills, oak-studded Skofield Park is just below the trailhead for Rattlesnake Canyon Trail, the most popular hiking trail in Santa Barbara (and yes, you do need to watch out for rattlers in the spring and summer). You'll find lots of other trails here for mountain biking, walking, or hiking. Group picnic and barbecue facilities, restrooms, and on-site parking are available.

Skofield has a more rugged feel than some of our other parks, but there is a wide expanse of lawn for those who don't want to rough it. Reservable camp areas are available for nonprofit groups dedicated to youth. One caution: Because of its foothill location, temperatures in the park during the day are often much warmer than those down below in the city, so dress accordingly.

> **i** Some of Santa Barbara's parks are favorite weddings spots. Among the most popular are the ocean-view bluffs of Shoreline Park, the Rose Garden near the Mission, Alice Keck Memorial Garden with its koi-filled lily pond, Chase Palm Park by the beach, and the panoramic hilltop at Elings Park.

STEVENS PARK
258 Canon Dr., Santa Barbara
(805) 564-5418
www.sbparksandrecreation.com
Tucked into the foothills at the end of Canon Drive, Stevens Park is another great spot for hiking, birding (white-throated swifts can be found here almost all year long), and picnicking. A small playground sits along the banks of a creek, and the park has barbecues and restrooms. Parking is available in a small lot at the entrance. If you're going to hike, watch out for rattlesnakes, especially in spring and summer.

TUCKER'S GROVE PARK
805 San Antonio Creek Rd. at Cathedral Oaks, Santa Barbara
(805) 967-1112
www.countyofsb.org/parks

Tucker's Grove is hugely popular with large groups, partly because of its easy access and partly because it has group picnic areas that can accommodate up to 400 people. The lower portion of the park is almost completely level and covered with lawn, which means that it's easy to keep an eye on the kids, and they aren't likely to go climbing off someplace where you can't find them. On this level there's a large playground area, a volleyball court, horseshoe pits, and lots of picnic areas for large or small groups. There is also a fenced off-leash area for dogs. Kiwanis Meadow, the upper area of the park, has a very large group picnic area with a barbecue, play equipment, a ball field, and a volleyball court. From Kiwanis Meadow you can hike up San Antonio Creek Canyon on foot or ride up on horseback (although you're responsible for getting the horse) all the way to San Marcos Pass Road. Both areas have permanent restrooms and parking lots, although the lots may fill up during large group events or on holidays.

GOLETA

EVERGREEN OPEN SPACE
Evergreen Drive and Brandon Drive, Goleta
(805) 967-2500
www.goletavalley.com
A greenbelt area in west Goleta, Evergreen has tennis courts and playground equipment and is a great spot for a picnic. It's the home of the only official 18-hole Frisbee (or "disc") golf course between here and Los Angeles. If that's your game, this is your place! Parking is on the street, and there are no restrooms.

GOLETA BEACH COUNTY PARK
5986 Sandspit Rd., Goleta
(805) 967-1300
www.countyofsb.org/parks
Located just east of the University of California at Santa Barbara campus, Goleta Beach sits at the entrance to the Goleta Slough, which makes it a great birding spot as well as a first-rate day-use facility for sunbathing, swimming, or fishing off the pier. A playground, restrooms, and ample parking are on-site, and the excellent Beachside Bar-Cafe (805-964-7881) sits right on the sand. For more information about the park, see the Beaches & Watersports chapter.

LAKE LOS CARNEROS PARK
Los Carneros Road and Calle Real, Goleta
(805) 568-2461
www.countyofsb.org/parks
Lake Los Carneros, bounded by Los Carneros Road, Covington Way, Calle Real, and La Patera Lane, is a hidden jewel in the center of busy Goleta. The grounds include the lovely Stow House (see the Attractions chapter) and outbuildings, the restored Goleta Train Depot, which houses the South Coast Railroad Museum (also listed in the Attractions and Kidstuff chapters), and a 25-acre artificial lake that has been declared a natural preserve.

Pathways (of dirt, decomposed granite, or wood-chip-covered) circle the lake, making it easy to do the loop on foot or on a bike. At the north end of the lake, a wooden footbridge crosses the channel, offering the perfect vantage point for observing the birds, turtles, frogs, and other fauna that populate the area.

The garden around the Stow House, planted with a variety of exotic plants, is also a wonderful birding spot, especially in spring. Fish inhabit the lake, and local anglers swear that some of these are big, but we've never seen anything bigger than a large minnow. Still, you can take your chances by casting off the bank if you want. No swimming is allowed in the lake.

Near the railroad depot is a small picnic area, but people often eat lunch on the Stow House lawn, stretching out in the shade to enjoy the sights and sounds of nature. The park is a perfect place to exercise your dog, but please remember that pets need to be on a leash and should never be allowed to disturb the local wildlife by leaping into the lake. You can park on any of the streets that border the park, but most people opt to use the parking lot on Los Carneros Road, between Cathedral Oaks and Calle Real. Restrooms are on-site.

STOW GROVE PARK
580 La Patera Ln., Goleta
(805) 961-7500
www.cityofgoleta.org

Truly unique for the Santa Barbara area, this Goleta City park is dominated by a large grove of California coastal redwood trees that tower over wood-chip-covered walkways lined with low wooden fences. Also scattered throughout the park are mature sycamores, oaks, and eucalyptus, and a small grove of giant sequoias grows north of the children's play area.

The south section of the park is newer, with a large redwood play area, lots of picnic tables, and a wide lawn sheltered by oaks and pines. The north section includes group picnic areas, a smaller playground, 2 volleyball courts, horseshoe pits, and a softball diamond. Stow Grove has a permanent restroom, and parking is available in the on-site lot. If the lot fills up, park on La Patera

Lane or on the street north of Cathedral Oaks Road.

MONTECITO

MANNING PARK
449 San Ysidro Rd., Montecito
(805) 969-0201
www.countyofsb.org/parks

Divided into two distinct sections—upper and lower—Manning Park is a lovely shady spot in the middle of Montecito. It's a popular site for weddings and family celebrations. All the vegetation in the park has been introduced, and California live oaks as well as native plant species such as toyon, coffeeberry, and maple trees have been planted.

In addition to the charm of its terrain, the park offers many recreational facilities, including 3 group picnic areas with barbecues (the largest accommodating up to 250 people), a softball field, a tennis court, a volleyball court, 4 horseshoe pits, and a playground. The upper park has a permanent restroom, while the lower park offers only a chemical toilet. Small parking areas are scattered throughout the park, or you can park on School House Road, which borders the southwest side of the upper park. If you are going to a gathering here, be certain to check both sides of the park, or you may miss the party!

SUMMERLAND

LOOKOUT PARK
2297 Finney Rd., Summerland
(805) 568-2465
www.countyofsb.org/parks

Known for its spectacular view of the ocean and the Channel Islands, 4-acre Lookout Park is perched above the sea just north of Carpinteria. The beach below (you must descend a steep paved hill or a small footpath through a eucalyptus grove to reach the sand) has a secluded feel to it, and it's a great spot for swimming, surfing, or surf fishing. In the park area, you'll find 2 large picnic areas with barbecues, a playground on a sand surface, volleyball courts, and restrooms.

TORO CANYON PARK
576 Toro Canyon Rd., Summerland
(805) 969-3315
www.countyofsb.org/parks

You are miles from the beach at this county park, but the rugged oak woodland provides a pleasant change of scenery. The 74 acres remain in their natural state, with only a small, 1-acre grassy area breaking up the chaparral, oak, manzanita, sage, and other indigenous plants.

Toro Canyon has 2 main parking areas, 3 large group picnic areas (one accommodating more than 200 people), and a network of paths and hiking trails throughout, one of which will reward you with an overlook gazebo at the end. Recreational facilities include horseshoe pits and a playground.

A park ranger lives here year-round.

Note: Fire danger can be extremely high here during the summer and fall.

CARPINTERIA

CARPINTERIA BLUFFS NATURE PRESERVE
Bailard Avenue, Carpinteria
(805) 684-5405
www.carpinteriabluffs.org

Perched high above the sparkling Pacific, this stunning expanse of wilderness is one of the largest tracts of open space left along the county's south coast. In October 2000, after a passionate fund-raising campaign by a local group known as Citizens for the Carpinteria Bluffs, this 52-acre property was officially deeded to the City of Carpinteria to be protected as a natural open-space preserve. Stretching west from Bailard Avenue, the bluffs encompass a spectacular area of quiet meadows, thick eucalyptus groves, and rugged sea cliffs. As you stroll along the hiking trails, you'll be treated to gorgeous views of the Carpinteria Valley, the Santa Ynez Mountains, and the Santa Barbara Channel. It's also a fantastic place to hike and look for wildlife. In a rocky cove below the bluffs lies one of only two publicly accessible harbor seal colonies in Southern California. To access the bluffs, take the Bailard Avenue exit, turn right, and park in the lot at the end of the street.

CARPINTERIA SALT MARSH NATURE PARK
Ash Avenue and Sandyland Road
(805) 684-5405

A remnant of a wetland that once extended from the Santa Ynez Mountains to the Pacific, this 230-acre reserve is one of the largest remaining coastal estuaries in California. A few years ago, this vast wetland resembled little more than a wasteland, but it's made an incredible comeback. Native plants are flourishing, halibut and other marine and estuarine fish nurseries are thriving in the channel, and waterfowl flock to the fish-rich waters. Not surprisingly, birding is excellent. Visitors have spotted more than 200 species here, including ospreys, long-billed curlews, pelicans, egrets, and endangered species such as Belding's savannah sparrow and the light-footed clapper rail. To access the park, exit US 101 at Linden Avenue and drive south less than a mile. Just before the avenue hits Carpinteria Beach, turn right on Sandyland Road. Continue 3 blocks to the park entrance on Ash Avenue, and park along the street. Near the entrance, you'll find a small amphitheater, interpretative signs, and restrooms. For a relaxing mile-long stroll, follow the nature trails to the edge of the channel, where you can watch fish jumping and waterfowl stalking the banks. You can join a 90-minute docent-led tour at the park entrance on Sat at 10 a.m.

CARPINTERIA STATE BEACH
Linden Avenue and 6th Street, Carpinteria
(805) 968-1033
www.parks.ca.gov

In addition to camping spaces, this 48-acre park has a mile of beachfront perfect for swimming, fishing, tide pooling, surfing, beach volleyball, and soaking up the sun. If you'd rather not get sand in your shorts, there's a grassy play area that's relatively sand-free. Nearby, seals and sea lions are often visible, and occasionally you can even spot a whale swimming by. Stop by the visitor center to view natural history exhibits or take one of the scheduled nature walks.

EL CARRO PARK
El Carro Lane and Namouna Street, Carpinteria
(805) 684-5405
www.carpinteria.com/activities/parks/ElCarro

This small neighborhood park has a playground for the kids, a picnic area with a barbecue, a multiuse field, and restrooms. It's a great place to spread out a blanket, and there's plenty of room to run on the expansive lawn.

MONTE VISTA PARK
Bailard Avenue and Pandanus Street, Carpinteria
(805) 684-5405
www.carpinteria.com/activities/parks/montevista/

One of Carpinteria's most popular parks, its open spaces encourage soccer games. A jogging trail, multiuse field, and playground are also in the park. The park is set back behind some condominiums outside the city of Carpinteria, just above the Ventura County line.

California State Parks

Southern Santa Barbara County has 4 California state parks on the beach. There is a day-use fee of $8, or $10 for all state parks in Santa Barbara; it's payable at the entrance kiosk. (If you pay an entrance fee to one state park, you can use the permit to enter another park the same day.)

Annual passes ($125 a year) are also available and entitle you to a 9-person passenger vehicle or motorcycle entry and parking at most state parks for a 12-month period. Discount passes are available for the disabled and for seniors 62 and older. For complete information on all California state park passes, call (916) 653-6995, visit www.parks.ca.gov, or write to PO Box 942896, Sacramento, CA 94296.

WEST OF GOLETA

We mention El Capitán, Gaviota, and Refugio beaches briefly here. For detailed information (including camping information) see the Recreation and Beaches & Watersports chapters.

And while you may be heading "north" toward San Francisco to reach these beaches, it is important to remember that Santa Barbara actually faces south so you are heading west, as weird as it seems.

EL CAPITÁN STATE BEACH
**Off US 101, 17 miles west of
Santa Barbara
(805) 968-1033
www.parks.ca.gov**
One of our favorites, El Cap is open from dawn to dusk year-round and offers swimming (the beach is accessible via a stairway on the bluffs), fishing, picnicking, and camping as well as tide pooling and birding. The bike trail here connects with Refugio State Beach, 2.5 miles up the coast. Along the bike trail are some lesser known but very rewarding accesses to the beach.

GAVIOTA STATE PARK
**Off US 101, 33 miles west of
Santa Barbara
(805) 968-1033
www.parks.ca.gov**
Made up of 2,700 acres that rise from sea level to the top of Gaviota Peak, Gaviota is a popular park for swimming and camping. Anglers, divers, and surfers can use the pier at the west end of the beach. In addition to the normal beach activities, the park has great hiking trails, including one that takes you to Gaviota Hot Springs, and it's a beautiful spot for a picnic. High winds can sometimes be a problem so be prepared. Nearly

half the campsites can now be reserved ahead of time from the end of May through August.

REFUGIO STATE BEACH
**Off US 101, 23 miles west of
Santa Barbara
(805) 968-1033
www.parks.ca.gov**
Just 2.5 miles west of El Capitán State Beach, Refugio is an excellent spot for surf fishing, picnicking, camping, and hiking. The waters off Refugio also offer some great swimming and diving, with reefs and kelp beds to explore.

SANTA YNEZ VALLEY

CACHUMA LAKE RECREATION AREA
**CA 154, 20 miles northwest of
Santa Barbara
(805) 686-5054
www.sbparks.org**
Although the Santa Ynez Valley is technically out of Santa Barbara proper, we include this recreation area because it's a local favorite and less than an hour's drive from Santa Barbara. It's especially popular for fishing and camping (see the Fishing and Recreation chapters for details) as well as for boating and wildlife viewing.

You can rent boats (with or without motors) and kayaks at the lake on an hourly, or daily, basis, and private boat-launching facilities are also available. Kayaking and canoeing are now allowed on the lake. Boats less than 10 feet in length are not allowed.

Because Cachuma is a domestic water reservoir, swimming, wading, waterskiing, sailboarding, and any other bodily contact with the water are not allowed, but there are 2 swimming pools in the campground open during the summer months. You can also rent a bike or arrange for horseback riding in the vicinity.

The nonprofit Cachuma Lake Nature Center features hands-on displays of local flora and fauna as well as Chumash and settler history. For a fun family outing, join a Santa Barbara County park naturalist for the nature walks scheduled every Sat from 10 to 11:30 a.m. Some of the animals you might expect to see around the lake are deer, wild pigs, bears, and as many as 150 species of birds.

Cachuma is especially proud of its small, but permanent, American bald eagle population, and this is the only place in the county where, in the winter months, you can reliably spot this majestic symbol of America. To get a close-up look at the eagles and other wildlife, we recommend taking a 2-hour, county park naturalist–led Eagle Cruise aboard the *Osprey*.

The 30-passenger *Osprey* departs from the marina on Friday, Saturday, and Sunday. Check park schedules on the web and bulletin boards in the park for current departure times. The cost is $15 for adults; $7 for children 12 and younger (sorry, no children under 4 are allowed). Be sure to make a reservation (805-686-5050), and bring your binoculars and a warm jacket, as it can be quite chilly on the lake. Because you are riding on a relatively stable pontoon vessel, seasickness is rare.

Cachuma Lake is open for day use from 8 a.m. to sunset; admission is $10 a vehicle. Plenty of parking is scattered throughout, and restrooms (or chemical toilets) are available in each camping area, at the marina, and near the pool.

CHANNEL ISLANDS
NATIONAL PARK

The Channel Islands are 11 to 60 miles from the mainland, but they're an entire world apart. When you step ashore, you feel as if you've traveled a century back in time to the pristine California land and seascapes that once dominated the coast. You won't see hotels, restaurants, and museums lining the shores. Instead, you'll find spectacular white-sand beaches, sea caves and hidden coves, barren mountains, rocky reefs, and incredibly clear water.

Eight islands in the waters off Southern California make up the Channel Islands. Often referred to as "the Galapagos of California," these remote islands and the waters surrounding them are filled with unusual flora and fauna, dramatic geological formations, rare archaeological finds, and other oddities that occur nowhere else on earth.

One reason the channel is so unique is because it's an unusual transition zone called the Southern California Bight. At Point Conception, the islands and the mainland run east–west rather than north–south. The waters lying between the islands and the mainland form the Santa Barbara Channel—a melting pot of currents from different directions. The California current brings cold waters from the Arctic into the channel from the north. Warm currents from Mexico come in from the south, carrying more subtropical marine life along with them.

The result of this complex blend of currents is an exceptional variety of cold-water and warm-water plants and animals, including giant kelp forests, seabirds, whales, seals, and sea lions. In addition, the remoteness of the islands has allowed plants and wildlife to evolve in isolation. This is the only part of the world where you'll find the Santa Cruz Island scrub-jay, the Channel Island fox, the Anacapa deer mouse, and many other endemic species.

FROM ISOLATED ISLANDS TO PROTECTED SANCTUARIES

For approximately 11,000 years, the Chumash, or "island people," lived on these islands, regularly traversing the channel in swift canoes called *tomols* to trade with mainland Indians. They lived in peaceful isolation on the islands until 1542, when explorer Juan Rodriguez Cabrillo cruised through the channel while leading an expedition for Spain. He supposedly fell on San Miguel and died as a result, but his body has never been found.

The 1700s and 1800s brought more explorers and eventually fur traders, hunters, settlers, and ranchers—all of whom threatened the Channel Islands' resources and habitats. It wasn't until the late 20th century that the incredible biodiversity, important cultural artifacts, and stunning natural beauty of the islands triggered a succession of moves to protect the region. In 1980 Congress officially recognized the significance of the region's natural and cultural resources and declared five of the islands—San Miguel, Santa Rosa, Santa Cruz, Anacapa, and Santa Barbara—and their surrounding 1 nautical mile of ocean as the Channel Islands National Park. Later that year, 1,252 nautical miles of ocean extending from mean high tide to 6 nautical miles offshore around each of the islands in the park were designated a National Marine Sanctuary. The Channel Islands National Marine Sanctuary encompasses 1,110 square nautical miles (1,470 square miles).

The islands themselves fall under the jurisdiction of the National Park Service, while the National Oceanic and Atmospheric Administration (NOAA) administers the marine sanctuary program, and the National Park Service and the National Marine Sanctuary share jurisdiction of the nautical mile closest to the island shores.

CONTINUED CONSERVATION

In 1988 the Nature Conservancy, a nonprofit international environmental organization, acquired the western 90 percent of Santa Cruz Island from a private owner and formed the Santa Cruz Island Preserve. The National Park Service continued to own and manage the remaining eastern side of the island. Then in August 2000, the

Nature Conservancy transferred 8,500 acres of its holdings on Santa Cruz Island to the National Park Service, a donation designed to reinforce the partnership between the two organizations. Since the transfer, the Conservancy owns and manages the western 76 percent of the island, while the eastern 24 percent is owned and managed by the National Park Service.

The 8,500 acres of Santa Cruz Island donated by the Nature Conservancy to the National Park Service adjoin the park's western boundary and includes the 5-mile-long narrow section of the island called the isthmus. The land transfer was great news for visitors to Santa Cruz Island, who now have much more land to explore. The public can come ashore on the isthmus at Prisoners' Harbor, hike the trails, explore the beach, and camp in the designated areas. The Nature Conservancy limits public access to the Santa Cruz Island Preserve due to recovering ecosystems in this part of the island. See the Santa Cruz Island Project section below for more information.

BACK IN THE NEST

In the early 1960s, the bald eagle population disappeared in the Channel Islands. The pollution from DDT and other pesticides was to blame; the chemicals caused the birds to lay thin-shelled eggs. Thankfully, the subsequent banning of toxic pesticides allowed the islands to slowly recover to their natural state. With the islands in a healthier condition, bird restoration began.

In 2002 funding from the Montrose Settlements Restoration Program allowed for the reintroduction of 61 young bald eagles to the northern Channel Islands. With the assistance of the National Park Service and the Institute for Wildlife Studies, the bald eagle population is returning to its roost.

In spring 2006, efforts paid off when the first bald eagle chick hatched (unaided by humans for the first time in over 50 years) on the islands. This important conservation event made national headlines. It was so big that a webcam (http://chil.vcoe.org/eagle_cam.htm) to live feed the action to the entire country was installed. (In fact, the chick identified as A-49 was recently tracked flying over the mainland near Santa Barbara.) Spring 2007 brought yet another birth of a bald eagle chick on Santa Cruz Island, an extremely positive indicator that the islands are one chick closer to recovering their bald eagle population.

In 2011, there were 34 bald eagles establishing their old territory on the Channel Islands. Before 2006, the last known successful nesting of a bald eagle pair on the northern islands was on Santa Rosa in 1950. Four pairs were discovered nesting on Santa Cruz Island, while Anacapa Island hosted its first nest in more than 60 years.

Bald eagles aren't the islands' only comeback chicks. Another is the peregrine falcon. It, too, disappeared from the islands in the mid-20th century. Scientists recently discovered the first pair of peregrine falcon chicks in over 50 years, all signs of good things to come.

i In 2010, the bald eagle webcam connected more than 160,000 visitors from more than 145 countries worldwide who generated 1.5 million hits. These viewers keep a daily watch over the raptors and contribute to the biologists' monitoring efforts. For your own peek through the webcam, go to www.nps.gov/chis/photosmultimedia/bald-eagle-webcam.htm.

A WEALTH OF NATURAL RESOURCES

In the areas of the Channel Islands that are currently protected, scientists have been following a remarkable comeback by Mother Nature. Native flowers and plants are beginning to bloom anew after years of grazing by cows and sheep. Sea lions and seals are multiplying, and fish are restocking their schools.

People come from all over the world to see and experience the wonders of the Channel Islands. The national park is home to more than 2,000 terrestrial plants and animals, and 145 of these are found nowhere else on earth. Thousands of seabirds nest on the islands because of the absence of ground predators.

The marine life surrounding the Channel Islands is equally amazing. The giant kelp forest alone supports nearly 1,000 species of marine life. Key species in the park and sanctuary include the California sea lion, elephant and harbor seals, blue and gray whales, dolphins, and the blue shark, brown pelican, western gull, abalone, garibaldi, and rockfish.

Pinnipeds (seals and sea lions) were once hunted nearly to extinction for their meat, fur, oil, and ivory. But the Marine Mammal Protection Act passed in 1972 made it illegal to kill, harm, or capture any kind of marine mammal without a permit. Four species of pinnipeds live and breed on the Channel Islands and in the surrounding waters.

More than 27 species of cetaceans (whales and dolphins) inhabit the park and sanctuary during the year. From December through April, thousands of gray whales swim through the channel on their annual migration from Alaska to Mexico and back. (See the Whale-Watching section of our Beaches & Watersports chapter if you'd like to go on a whale-watching trip). In the last decade, increased numbers of whales have shown up in the channel, including blue, minke, and humpback whales.

The common dolphin practically owns the channel. They travel in large groups and love to play and surf in the wake of passing boats. Sometimes you can spot a Dall's porpoise or Risso's dolphins. Other dolphins here include the Pacific white-sided and bottlenose dolphins.

More than 25 species of sharks have been sighted in the channel, but some only vacation here from time to time. Resident sharks include the giant basking, leopard, thresher, blue, horn, and Pacific angel.

We humans are invited to experience this natural wonderland in all its splendor—as long as we respect and care for its precious resources.

THE NATIONAL PARK, MARINE SANCTUARY & NATURE PRESERVE

The National Park Service, the National Marine Sanctuary, the Nature Conservancy, and other partners all work to protect the fragile ecosystems of the islands and the sea, while educating the public about the plants, animals, marine life, and other natural phenomena. Following are descriptions of the special services each provides.

CHANNEL ISLANDS NATIONAL PARK
Robert J. Largomarsino Visitor Center
1901 Spinnaker Dr., Ventura
(805) 658-5730
www.nps.gov/chis
The Channel Islands National Park Headquarters and Visitor Center is in Ventura, 35 miles southeast of Santa Barbara. Although

it's not technically in the geographic area covered by this book, we do need to tell you about the visitor center, which is not only a one-stop resource for information about the islands but also a fun and fascinating place to visit. Wander inside and you'll find a museum, a bookstore, a living tide pool and interactive touch-screen exhibit, telescopes, and other interesting displays, including "Channel Islands Live." You can also see a 25-minute movie in the auditorium. The visitor center is open daily 8:30 a.m. to 5 p.m.; it's closed on Thanksgiving and Christmas. On weekends and holidays at 11 a.m. and 3 p.m., park rangers offer free public programs.

> **i** The most complete skeleton of a pygmy mammoth was discovered on Santa Rosa Island in 1994. The mammoths roamed the Channel Islands during the Pleistocene epoch.

CHANNEL ISLANDS NATIONAL MARINE SANCTUARY
113 Harbor Way, Ste. 150, Santa Barbara
(805) 966-7107
www.channelislands.noaa.gov
The Channel Islands National Marine Sanctuary is part of the National Marine Sanctuary System that consists of 14 protected marine areas that encompass more than 150,000 square miles of marine and Great Lakes waters from Washington State to the Florida Keys, and from Lake Huron to American Samoa. The system includes 13 national marine sanctuaries and the Northwestern Hawaiian Islands Marine National Monument. The mission of NOAA's National Marine Sanctuaries is to serve as the trustee for the nation's system of protected marine areas, to conserve, protect, and enhance

their biodiversity, ecological integrity, and cultural legacy.

SANTA CRUZ ISLAND PRESERVE PROJECT OF THE NATURE CONSERVANCY
3639 Harbor Blvd., Ste. 201, Ventura
(805) 642-0345
www.nature.org

The Nature Conservancy is a private, international, nonprofit membership organization. Its mission is "to preserve the plants, animals, and natural communities that represent the diversity of life on Earth by protecting the lands and waters they need to survive." The Nature Conservancy currently owns and manages the Santa Cruz Island Preserve, which comprises 76 percent of the island. The organization also offers a variety of daylong and occasional overnight educational trips to the preserve through local concessionaires and museums. Call for more information.

WHAT TO SEE & DO

If you're looking for direct interaction with nature, you'll love the Channel Islands. They offer a fantastic array of recreational opportunities amid gorgeous scenery. You can hike, fish, camp, dive, snorkel, and even surf within the park. You can go diving, birding, whale-watching, and sailing, explore tide pools, and lounge on the beaches, which locals think are among the most beautiful in the world.

From certain overlooks on some islands, you can observe hundreds of seals and sea lions hauling onto the beaches. You can kayak in coves, sea caves, and lagoons or go on a ranger-led hike and discover the island's human history. Many Santa Barbara companies offer scuba diving, kayaking, and

sailing trips—see our Beaches & Watersports chapter for details on specific sports. You'll also find complete information on angling in our Fishing chapter.

If you're interested in kayaking, contact the Channel Islands National Park and Robert J. Largomarsino Visitor Center at (805) 658-5730 and request its special sea-kayaking information brochure.

i For guided camping adventures and customized tours on the islands, contact Santa Barbara Adventure Company (805-898-0671, 888-773-3239; www.sbadventureco.com).

Camping

You can camp year-round in National Park Service–managed campgrounds on all five islands, but no camping is allowed in the Santa Cruz Island Preserve. Beach camping is allowed on Santa Rosa Island.

Camping reservations are required for all campgrounds and can be obtained by calling Recreation.gov at (800) 365-CAMP or visiting the National Park Service online Reservation Center at www.nps.gov. Before you can reserve a campsite, however, you are required to arrange your transportation. That's because the boats tend to fill up before the campgrounds.

The camping fee is $15 per campsite per night. Reservations can be made no more than five months in advance, and we recommend that you reserve well ahead of time, not only to ensure that you get a site but also to allow time for the permit to travel in the mail. When you call, you will need to have some information at hand: camping dates, transportation information, and number of campers.

Facilities are very primitive. You will need to bring all your own water and food. You also have to carry your gear from landing areas to the campgrounds, so don't go overboard when packing. All campgrounds have picnic tables and pit toilets. Fires are not permitted. Bring along an enclosed camp stove for cooking.

On Santa Rosa Island and Scorpion Ranch on Santa Cruz Island, you can enjoy the luxury of running water. Santa Rosa even has a shower. Fierce winds often blast the campgrounds on Santa Rosa and San Miguel Islands. The National Park Service has built windbreaks to shield campers from their full force. You won't blow away, but your maps and lightweight items might, so stow them tightly away.

The National Park Service can send you detailed camping information specific to each island, or refer to the website. Call the Visitors Information line at (805) 658-5730 or visit the camping website at www.recreation .gov and weave your way through to the page you need.

Diving

The Channel Islands have some of the most fascinating dive destinations on the planet. Divers from all around the nation and the world come to explore the magnificent kelp forests and the incredibly diverse marine life. Visibility here is usually much better than off the mainland beaches.

If you're a diver, contact the Channel Islands National Park or the Marine Sanctuary websites for information on diving and shipwrecks you can visit. Permits to dive are not required (fishing licenses are however). For information on diving excursions, refer to the Diving section of the Beaches & Watersports chapter. In the meantime, here are a few guidelines to keep you safe in the sometimes-treacherous channel waters.

- Use standard safe diving procedures.
- Know the area.
- Be aware that changing weather affects currents and surge.
- Never dive alone.
- Always fly the diver's flag when underwater.

The sea has claimed more than a few divers over the years, so take heed and do your homework before venturing underwater.

ISLAND BY ISLAND

Although the Channel Islands have a lot in common with each other, each has distinct features that set it apart. Here are brief descriptions of each island. You also can request a park newspaper for each island from the Channel Islands National Park Visitor Center in Ventura (805-658-5730).

Note that there are no food and drink concessions on the islands. When you visit, you must bring all your own supplies, including drinking water. You will also need to pack out all your trash.

Anacapa Island

Anacapa Island's name is derived from the Chumash word "Eneepah," which means island of deception or mirage. That's because the island gives the illusion of changing shape when the weather is foggy or very warm. Anacapa is actually a chain of three small islets (East, Middle, and West Anacapa) connected by shallow sandbars. It's not very big—5 miles long and 0.25 mile wide—and the land area totals just 1 square mile. Since this island is closest to the mainland (Ventura), it's also the most visited. It's only about 90 minutes by boat from the mainland and is a good choice if you're visiting the islands for the first time.

Anacapa has 130 sea caves, 29 Chumash archaeological sites, and towering cliffs. The islands attract large populations of seabirds, including California brown pelicans and the largest breeding colony of Western gulls in the world. Tide pooling is also excellent—the best area is said to be near Frenchy's Cove on the southeastern tip of West Anacapa.

> **i** The lighthouse on Anacapa Island was the last permanent lighthouse built on the West Coast.

Almost all trips to Anacapa are to East Anacapa Island, where you'll find ranger residences, a visitor center, a lighthouse, and a churchlike building containing two 50,000-gallon redwood water tanks, all built before 1932. Until 1990, the lighthouse had a handmade Freshnel lens. It now uses a modern lighting system, but you can see the original lead crystal lens in the visitor center.

You can hike on about 1.5 miles of trails on East Anacapa. During the summer, the park rangers offer daily, guided nature walks. A self-guided trail booklet is available at the visitor center trailhead. Picnic tables for day use are available in three areas on East Anacapa. You can snorkel and swim in the Landing Cove, but you might want to wear a wet suit—the water's cold, even in summer.

Santa Cruz Island

Santa Cruz is the largest and most topographically diverse of all the Channel Islands. It's about 24 miles long, with a total of 60,645 acres of mountains, valleys, grasslands, woodlands, beaches, and dunes. Most visitors hike, camp, picnic, and explore on the eastern end of the island, which is managed by the Channel Islands National Park. Be prepared for a skiff landing on the beach—there are no piers at any of the landings.

A number of rugged hiking trails and roads lead you to bluffs and mountaintops for spectacular views, and along the coastline are sea caves, rocky ledges, reefs, and tide pools. On land, the island supports an exceptional array of flora and fauna. More than 600 plant types flourish here, and eight types are found only on Santa Cruz Island. The most famous endemic plants include the Santa Cruz Island ironwood and the island oak.

More than 260 species of birds inhabit the island, including the endemic Santa Cruz Island scrub-jay—a bigger, bluer version of its mainland cousin. The Channel Island fox is the most famous mammal in these parts, next to the seals and sea lions that bask and play in the coves.

Painted Cave

Santa Cruz Island is home to the largest and deepest known sea cave in the world—Painted Cave. Named for the colorful rocks and lichens covering its surface, the cave is 160 feet high at its entrance and extends a quarter of a mile into the side of the island. In the spring a waterfall cascades down through its mouth. Depending on conditions, you might be able to visit the cave on a summer whale-watching cruise aboard the *Condor Express*. (See the Beaches & Watersports chapter.)

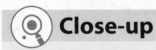

Close-up

Blue Whales—Repeat Visitors to the Channel Islands

At one time of year or another, 27 species of cetaceans (whales, dolphins, and porpoises) have been documented in the Channel Islands National Marine Sanctuary. Among these are the rare and magnificent blue whales—the largest animals to ever exist on Earth.

Blue whales (*Balaenoptera musculus*) have been on the endangered species list since 1966. Before the whaling industry severely depleted their numbers, about 300,000 blue whales cruised the world's oceans. Today, there are fewer than 10,000. About 2,000 are found off the coast of California—the greatest concentration of blue whales in the world.

In 1992, for reasons still not entirely understood by marine experts, blue whales began coming in increasing numbers to feed in the Channel Islands National Marine Sanctuary, usually from late May through October. Approximately 200 blue whales have been sighted at the peak of the feeding season, which is an incredibly large number considering that blue whales are usually very shy, very fast, and as a result, seldom seen. Also, they generally travel alone or in pairs, and their migratory patterns are not entirely predictable.

The whales that feed near the California coast typically go south in the winter (usually to Mexico) to breed and give birth. In the summer, they return to California to feed, traveling wherever they can find abundant krill, which are small, shrimplike crustaceans found mostly near continental shelf waters. It seems as though blue whales have discovered a sumptuous krill buffet in the Channel Islands National Marine Sanctuary, and they keep coming back for more.

Blue whales are truly amazing creatures. When a calf is born, it already weighs 2 to 3 tons and is 20 to 24 feet long. Adults weigh approximately 150 to 200 tons, which is equal to about 30 elephants, or 1,600 people. They reach about 80 to 100 feet in length. An adult blue whale's heart is about the size of a VW Beetle, and its tongue is heavier than an African elephant.

The island is a superb destination for swimming, snorkeling, diving, and kayaking. It lies right in the transition zone for warm currents from the south and colder currents from the north, so this is where you'll find a mingling of marine species.

If you're in any type of kayak or a private boat and want to land or hike in the Nature Conservancy–owned preserve, you must apply for a day-use landing permit in advance. See the Rules & Regulations section later in this chapter.

Santa Rosa Island

Santa Rosa is the second-largest island in the park (53,000 acres, or 84 square miles). It's also one of the most remote, which means you won't run into many people. Because of its size and seclusion, Santa Rosa is a great choice for multiday visits. Or you can take a day trip over to fish for surf perch and halibut off the windswept beaches or wander the rugged trails. The island's many landscapes—mountains, canyons, sand dunes, grasslands, woodlands, and freshwater

Despite their weight and girth, blues are incredibly fast swimmers, traveling at speeds of 8 to 25 knots. They can also dive up to 630 feet. When a blue whale blows, the spout rises up to 50 feet.

The jury's still out on why the blue whales have decided to become regular vacationers in the Santa Barbara Channel. One thing's for certain, though—they do like the gourmet krill the channel serves up. During the spring and summer months, there's something of a "krill machine" phenomenon in the channel, out near a deep canyon close to the Channel Islands. The winds cause an upwelling of dense, cold water that is rich in oxygen and nutrients. When the strong summer sunlight hits this nutrient-rich water, it triggers photosynthesis. The miniscule plants that result attract tiny, but slightly larger, animals such as krill, which feed on the plants. Two hundred krill weigh about one ounce, and it takes about 3,200 to top a pound. They float around in swarms measuring about 330 by 660 feet. Blue whales simply flap their flukes, open their jaws wide, and swim fast through the swarm, and in a short time they pick up literally tons of krill and other marine life that happens to be in the way. One adult blue whale can eat up to 4 tons of krill a day.

Blue whales are particularly sensitive to low-frequency sound. They can hear certain frequencies, including the ones produced by seismic testing, for thousands of miles. The government ceased the testing in 1989, and, lo and behold, in 1992 the blue whales in the vicinity increased in number.

Could it be the lack of disturbance or a larger volume of krill that lured the blue whales back? No one knows for certain, but in the meantime, wildlife enthusiasts are trying to see them while they can.

You can view a 67-foot skeleton of an adolescent blue whale outside the Santa Barbara Museum of Natural History. But if you'd like to see the real thing, make a point of taking a whale-watching cruise sometime during the blue whales' May through October feeding season. See the Whale-Watching section in the Beaches & Watersports chapter for details.

marsh—make hiking along the dirt roads and trails a real treat.

We've visited Santa Rosa in the summertime and enjoyed walking along the beautiful windswept beaches and up to the grove of Torrey pines—one of the rarest trees in the world. The only other Torrey pines on this half of the planet are found near San Diego, at the Torrey Pines State Reserve. Three native terrestrial mammals make their home on the island—the Channel Island fox, spotted skunk, and deer mouse, all of which are endemic to the Channel Islands.

Santa Rosa is also famous for its remains of the pygmy mammoth, a miniature mammoth that roamed the island during the Pleistocene era. A fossil skeleton of a pygmy mammoth discovered in 1994 on Santa Rosa is the most complete specimen ever found.

Santa Rosa Island was long home to a commercial cattle ranch, Vail & Vickers Company, which began ranching here in 1902. In 1986 the company sold the island to the National Park Service and negotiated a special-use permit allowing it to continue the business until 1998, when the last of the cattle were removed. Currently, the company holds a special-use permit allowing it to hunt introduced species such as deer and elk for a few months of the year.

i Archaeologists believe the 13,000-year-old bones from an ancient woman discovered on Santa Rosa Island in 1959 are the oldest known human remains in North America.

Other characteristics unique to Santa Rosa include six endemic plant species that occur nowhere else on Earth and extensive archaeological findings that divulge much about the Chumash, who thrived on this island for thousands of years. Santa Rosa is the only island that allows backcountry beach camping at certain times of the year. Call the visitor center for more information.

San Miguel Island

San Miguel lies closest to Point Conception, the westernmost end of the channel. Since it is more exposed to prevailing northwest winds and blasting Pacific storms, this island is more barren and weather-beaten than the others. It's often foggy and windy, but if you can put up with the less-than-perfect weather, you'll be rewarded with scenes of wildlife you won't find anywhere else.

Animals like their privacy, and they know that San Miguel is about as private as you can get among the northern Channel Islands. San Miguel's major draw is the Point Bennett rookery and haul-out spot for pinnipeds (sea lions and seals), including northern fur seals, California sea lions, elephant seals,

and harbor seals. At certain times of year, more than 30,000 of these pinnipeds crowd the beach, creating one of the largest congregations of wildlife in the world.

Another unique thing about San Miguel is its caliche forest. Sort of a petrified forest in sand, it was formed by caliche (calcium carbonate) casts around plant roots and trunks. The plants are gone, but you can still see the very strange stone forms that enveloped them.

Between 1948 and 1970 the US Navy used San Miguel as a bombing range, which didn't exactly do much for its natural environment. But Mother Nature has made a huge comeback on the island, and it's now a fertile and scenic preserve for many species of animals and plants. Whales (gray, killer, and blue), dolphins, and porpoises grace the surrounding waters, and zillions of birds, including western gulls, cormorants, pelicans, and auklets fill the skies during the spring and summer months.

Hiking is a fantastic way to experience San Miguel. However, if you leave the Cuyler Harbor and ranger station area, a park ranger must lead you.

Santa Barbara Island

Santa Barbara Island lies much farther offshore than the other islands in the park, so be prepared for a longer boat ride (4 or more hours). It's also the smallest of the group— only 1 square mile, or 640 acres. Most of the island is a giant mesa, surrounded by steep cliffs.

Although the island is small, it offers a surprisingly rich array of wildlife and scenery. We once asked a ranger which island she preferred in the park, and she named Santa Barbara as her perennial favorite.

Santa Barbara Island is most famous for its large sea lion rookery, and you can observe the seals and sea lions from a number of excellent overlook spots. More than 11 species of seabirds nest along the steep cliffs, making the island excellent for birding. The island is also an outstanding destination for snorkeling, swimming, diving, and kayaking.

PERMITS & REGULATIONS

To protect the delicate resources of the National Park and Marine Sanctuary, all visitors are required to follow specific regulations and obtain appropriate landing, day-use, and camping permits. Here's an overview.

Permits

Channel Islands National Park

Landing and hiking on the islands is limited, and in most cases (except day use on Anacapa and Santa Barbara Islands), you will need a permit to access an island beyond the beaches. All permits are issued free of charge and are available at the park's headquarters and visitor center in Ventura or by calling (805) 658-5730.

Santa Cruz Island Preserve

Access to the preserve is limited, and commercial vessels or commercial charter parties are not allowed to land or let passengers off here. However, if you go by private boat, you can apply for a permit that allows you to land and hike on this part of the island. Contact the Nature Conservancy at (949) 263-0933 to get an application and a list of the strict rules governing activity on the island. The Conservancy issues permits to owners or captains of private charter boats but not to commercial

vessels. Permits cost $60 for a calendar year or $20 for 30 consecutive days. You can also sign up for one of the naturalist-led day trips to the island scheduled throughout the year or, if you represent an educational, research, or nonprofit organization, you can organize a charter day trip. Contact Island Packers at (805) 642-1393 or www.islandpackers.com (see the listing under By Boat in this chapter).

Rules & Regulations

Going out to the National Park and National Marine Sanctuary is a fantastic way to view wildlife up close and personal. But you have to remember that all the island's natural resources are protected. The Channel Islands National Marine Sanctuary's brochure *Protecting Your Channel Islands* summarizes the rules all visitors must follow. It's available at the National Park Service Visitor Center in Ventura, the Marine Sanctuary office in Santa Barbara, or online at http://channelislands .noaa.gov/edu/pdf/pyci-09.pdf.

Following are a few of the major regulations you should know about:

- You may not feed, collect, harass, or otherwise harm the wildlife, plant life, or other natural and cultural resources of the Channel Islands National Park. That means you may not bring back any shells, plants, feathers, animals, Chumash artifacts, or other things you might be tempted to stash in your backpack. When you're tide pooling, don't collect anything. Take only pictures, and leave everything else where it is.
- The water, too, is protected, so don't dump any type of refuse in the ocean.
- Under federal law, it is illegal to disturb and/or harm marine mammals and seabirds in the National Park or the Marine Sanctuary at any time. They are

very sensitive to any type of human disturbances, especially during nesting and pupping seasons. Kayakers, hikers, and other visitors should stay at least 100 yards away from marine mammals, both in the water and on the beaches.

- Fishing in waters within the park and sanctuary requires a California fishing license, and fishing restrictions apply in Channel Islands Marine Protected Areas (MPAs), which are sections of the ocean set aside to protect and restore habitats and ecosystems, conserve biodiversity, provide a refuge for sea life, enhance recreational and educational opportunities, provide reference areas for scientists to measure changes elsewhere in the environment, and help rebuild depleted fisheries. There are a variety of types of MPAs, ranging from limited to full protection.

Channel Islands MPA classifications include:
- **Marine Reserves (MR),** which prohibit all take of living, geological, or cultural resources. Scientific take may be permitted.
- **Marine Conservation Areas (MCA),** which prohibit specific commercial and/ or recreational take of living, geological, or cultural resources on a case-by-case basis. Scientific take may be permitted.

Unless specifically prohibited, nonconsumptive activities, such as diving, surfing, swimming, and boating, are allowed within all of the above MPA designations, as long as "take" restrictions are followed. Anchoring within and transit through MPAs with catch onboard is allowed, so long as fishing gear is not deployed and stowed away.

The California State Fish and Game Commission and NOAA established 13 MPAs

in the Channel Islands. The 13 MPAs form a network that covers approximately 240 square nautical miles and 21 percent of sanctuary waters. Eleven of the MPAs are no-take marine reserves, where no extractive activities, such as fishing, are allowed. Two MPAs are marine conservation areas allowing recreational fishing for pelagic fish and lobster. One of these areas also allows commercial lobster trapping. The Channel Islands marine protected area network is currently the largest system of no-take marine reserves in the continental United States. Nearly 80 percent of the sanctuary remains open to fishing, in accordance with state and federal fishing regulations. For more specific information contact the **Department of Fish and Game** at (562) 342-7100 (www .dfg.ca.gov/marine/channel_islands), or the **Channel Islands National Marine Sanctuary** at (805) 966-7107 (http://channelislands .noaa.gov). You can get a license at any bait and tackle shop or onboard a Truth Aquatics vessel out of Santa Barbara (see subsequent listing under By Boat). Check out the Fishing chapter for more specifics on licenses.

Pets are not allowed onshore on any of the islands.

GETTING THERE

The easiest way to get to the Channel Islands is to hop aboard a commercial passenger boat operated by one of the official park concessionaires. You can also fly to Santa Rosa Island or catch a ride on a private charter boat.

By Boat

For years, Island Packers Company in Ventura was the sole concessionaire providing public boat transportation to the islands.

In recent years the National Park Service added another, Truth Aquatics, located right in Santa Barbara, making it easier for locals and visitors to get out to the islands.

ISLAND PACKERS COMPANY
1691 Spinnaker Dr., Ste. 105B, Ventura
Reservations: (805) 642-1393
www.islandpackers.com
Island Packers offers various trips to Anacapa and Santa Cruz Islands year-round, to Santa Barbara and Santa Rosa Islands from April through October, and to San Miguel in May through October. Trips include half-day cruises, all-day excursions, nature discovery tours, and transportation for campers and kayaking expeditions.

Weekend and holiday trips fill quickly during the spring and summer months, so you should make your reservations at least 2 weeks in advance. Fees range from $42 for a half-day trip to Anacapa Island to $102 for a 2-day visit to San Miguel Island.

TRUTH AQUATICS
SEA Landing, 301 W. Cabrillo Blvd.,
Santa Barbara
(805) 962-1127, (805) 963-3564
www.truthaquatics.com
Truth Aquatics has three fully equipped dive boats and has been taking divers on regular excursions to the Channel Islands for years. There are also island excursions geared more toward kayakers and hikers, but divers are also welcome. You can take a 3-day weekend trip, for example to Santa Rosa and San Miguel. The boat departs from Santa Barbara in the early morning. You reboard the boat for evening activities, slide shows, videos, or education workshops. After sleeping onboard, you wake up and spend the day exploring another island before returning to Santa Barbara. A 3-day trip to Santa Rosa and San Miguel, including meals, costs approximately $530. Private charters may be arranged for 1-day trips.

Other Commercial & Private Boats

A number of commercial and private boats offer island excursions—see our Beaches & Watersports chapter for an overview of your boating options. If you plan to take your own boat out to the islands, you can find navigational information in NOAA charts 18720, 18727, 18728, 18729, and 18756. If you need emergency assistance, call the Coast Guard on Channel 16 of your marine band radio. National Park Service patrol vessels regularly monitor the channel.

By Air

CHANNEL ISLANDS AVIATION
Camarillo Airport, 305 Durley Ave.,
Camarillo
(805) 987-1301
www.flycia.com
If you really can't face being on a boat or your time is limited, just cruise to the islands by air in only 25 minutes aboard a nine-passenger Britten Norman Islander aircraft. Channel Islands Aviation offers year-round departures from Camarillo Airport. In business since 1976, CIA provides camper transportation, day trips, and 1-day and weekend camping and surf fishing safaris to Santa Rosa Island. Camper transportation costs $330 per person. Scheduled day trip rates are $160 per person, plus tax. The company can also provide charter flights to the island from Santa Barbara Airport.

RECREATION

For a city its size, Santa Barbara has an incredible number of recreational opportunities. Part of this is due to the number of tourists who come to town looking for fun, but it's also a result of the Santa Barbara lifestyle, which places a heavy emphasis on being health-conscious, active, and fit. We think you'll find just about everything you'd ever want to do listed below, but if you wake up one morning and get the urge to do something else spur-of-the-moment, pick up the *Santa Barbara News-Press* and look in the "Public Square" section for a listing of the day's activities and events around town.

On Sunday look for the "What's Doing on the South Coast" calendar, which includes everything happening in the upcoming week. Also check "The Week" listings in the *Santa Barbara Independent* (distributed free each Thursday). Remember that facilities such as tennis, volleyball, and basketball courts, gyms, pools, and running tracks at local colleges may be available for limited public use. Call UCSB (805) 893-3738; the Santa Barbara City College Community Services Department (805) 965-0581, ext. 2726; or the Westmont College Athletic Department (805) 565-6010, for information.

This chapter begins with a list of local sports and recreation companies, facilities, and organizations, then covers area sports and activities alphabetically. It ends with a list of local athletic clubs and spectator sports.

ORGANIZATIONS & FACILITIES

The following companies, organizations, and facilities sponsor a variety of sports and recreational programs and events in Santa Barbara.

**LOUISE LOWRY DAVIS RECREATION
  CENTER**
1232 De la Vina St., Santa Barbara
(805) 897-2568
**www.santabarbaraca.gov/resident/
recreation_and_sports/seniors**
Headquarters for the Senior Citizens Information Service, the Louise Lowry Davis

Center offers weekday recreational activities for adults, with many programs specially designed for the older set. The center offers bridge, Scrabble, Italian and French classes, bingo, Stretch-and-Tone classes, porcelain painting, yoga, crochet, and knitting. The **Carrillo Recreation Center** (100 E. Carrillo St., Santa Barbara; 805-897-2519) also offers many classes for adults, including dance and fitness. Both centers are run by the Santa Barbara Parks and Recreation Department. You can pick up activity schedules for both centers at either location.

SANTA BARBARA ADVENTURE COMPANY
(877) 885-WAVE, (805) 884-WAVE
www.sbadventureco.com
Launched in 1998, Santa Barbara Adventure Company offers a range of guided outdoor adventures. Trips are tailored to your interests, with activities ranging from kayaking, biking, hiking, surfing, and rock climbing to camping adventures, Channel Island trips, and wine country tours. The emphasis is on escaping crowds and getting back to nature. One of the most popular trips is the coastal kayaking excursion. Experienced guides lead kayakers along the spectacular Gaviota coast while sharing their knowledge of the area's natural history and marine ecology. Multisport adventures are also available (biking and kayaking, for example). Prices range from $85 per person for a 2-hour kayaking tour to about $495 per person for a fully outfitted multisport 3-day adventure. All trips include qualified guides, equipment, transportation, and any necessary permits. Day trips require advance reservations. For overnight trips, book at least 2 weeks in advance. Call or visit the company's website for more information.

SANTA BARBARA CITY COLLEGE CONTINUING EDUCATION DIVISION
www.sbcc.edu/ce
Numerous locations

Alice F. Schott Center
310 W. Padre St., Santa Barbara
(805) 687-0812

Selmer O. Wake Center
300 N. Turnpike Rd., Santa Barbara
(805) 964-6853
This comprehensive program of inexpensive classes is a huge hit with Santa Barbarans, who anxiously look forward to the quarterly Continuing (or Adult) Ed schedule (it can be picked up at Continuing Ed offices or viewed on the website above). In addition to business classes, computer courses, lectures, foreign-language classes, and self-improvement courses, Adult Ed offers a plethora of recreational and arts classes, including dance, fitness, ceramics, drawing, painting, quilting, cooking, birding, nature walks, writing, cooking, film studies, music, and more. We can only scratch the surface of the possibilities here, so call for a copy of the schedule of classes and tempt yourself to try something new.

SANTA BARBARA OUTFITTERS
1200 State St., Santa Barbara
(805) 564-1007
www.sboutfitters.com

SANTA BARBARA PADDLE SPORTS
117B Harbor Way, Santa Barbara
(805) 899-4925
www.kayaksb.com
Hailed as a year-round indoor playground, Santa Barbara Outfitters retail store's claim to fame is its huge indoor wall for rock-climbing enthusiasts. It's open Sun through Thurs from 10 a.m. to 6 p.m., and Fri and Sat from 10 a.m. to 7 p.m. The Outfitters' sister location, Santa Barbara Paddle Sports, focuses on kayaking adventures to the Channel Islands and in and around the Santa Barbara waters. For full details, visit both Santa Barbara Outfitters' and Santa Barbara Paddle Sports' websites.

SANTA BARBARA PARKS AND RECREATION DEPARTMENT
620 Laguna St., Santa Barbara
(805) 564-5418
www.sbparksandrecreation.com

The Santa Barbara Parks and Recreation Department provides a wide range of recreational activities for the whole family. Among these are the city's youth and adult sports leagues, dance, gymnastics, art and music classes, dog-obedience training, teen programs, fitness classes, aquatics, tennis programs, and a wide range of camps and sports clinics over school breaks and the summer months.

Information on all of the programs can be found in the free *Parks & Recreation Activity Guide*, which is issued twice a year (spring/summer and fall/winter) and published on the department website. Fees vary according to the class or activity you choose but are generally very affordable. City residents receive a 10 percent discount on most programs. Special needs persons need not feel left out of the local recreation scene. In addition to hundreds of other events, Parks and Recreation provides both specialized and inclusive sports and recreation activites for children and adults of all ages and abilities. You can register online for most recreational classes. Visit the website listed above and click on "e-Recreation."

SANTA BARBARA SEMANA NAUTICA ASSOCIATION
PO Box 5001, Santa Barbara, CA 93150
www.semananautica.com
Back in the mid-1930s, five Navy battleships were moored outside the Santa Barbara Harbor, filled with bored crew members. The locals hit upon an idea: Why not challenge the sailors to a series of contests on our beach, just for the fun of it? Originally dubbed "Fleet Week," the celebration still happens every summer, but with a new name to honor Santa Barbara's Spanish heritage.

This festival draws crowds of spectators, but we list it here for those of you interested in participating. With contests as diverse as swimming, tennis, lawn bowling, cycling, softball, running, fishing, paddleboarding, volleyball, Krazy Kardboard Kayak Race, Ironman in-line hockey tournament and tug-of-war—to name a few—you're sure to find something you're good at. Designed for people of all ages and skill levels, the contests appeal to both serious athletes and weekend warriors, plus kids and older adults. Most events require entry fees, which vary widely depending on the event. For a brochure listing all events and relevant phone numbers, contact the Santa Barbara Semana Nautica Association at the address listed above or visit the website.

The East Beach Bathhouse, 1118 E. Cabrillo Blvd. (805-897-1944), and the City of Santa Barbara Parks and Recreation Department, 620 Laguna St., (805-564-5418), also have Semana Nautica brochures. This is Santa Barbara–style recreation par excellence, so start getting in shape now!

i If you live in the city of Santa Barbara, you are eligible to receive 20 percent off the regular fees for facility rental, and 10 percent off the regular fees for activities and programs. Proof of residency, such as a CA driver's license, must be shown. For details, call (805) 564-5418, or visit www.sbparksandrecreation.com.

SANTA BARBARA SPORTS LEAGUES
(805) 564-5422
www.sbparksandrecreation.com
The Santa Barbara Parks and Recreation Department organizes city leagues in a

variety of sports, including volleyball, basketball, soccer, softball, and tennis. Men's, women's, and coed leagues are available, so get your friends together and join the fun. Registration fees vary depending on the type of league you join.

UNIVERSITY OF CALIFORNIA AT SANTA BARBARA
Off CA 217, Goleta
(805) 893-3738
www.recreation.ucsb.edu

UCSB's Exercise and Sports Studies Recreation offers a packed schedule of recreational programs and classes held on the campus or nearby. Most are excellent, and all are open to the public, although you'll have to pay more if you're not a student (and you'll also have to pay for parking). Especially popular are the Leisure Arts classes (805-893-3738), which include everything from aquatics, dance, and group fitness to martial arts, sailing, and kayaking. Call for a current brochure or visit the department's website for information.

BIKING

As you might expect in a fitness-conscious city like Santa Barbara, there are miles of bike trails that will literally take you from the mountains to the sea (or from downtown Santa Barbara to Goleta). Nearly all county roads have bike paths marked by a solid white line on the right side of the road. These lanes must be kept clear of vehicular traffic, and by the same token, bikes are expected to stay out of the vehicle lanes.

A good investment is Map No. 7 of the Santa Barbara County Recreational Map Series, "Santa Barbara Road Bicycling Routes," available for about $3.50 from bookstores

and bike shops (we suggest **Bicycle Bob's,** 15 Hitchcock Way [805-682-4699]; **Open Air Bicycles,** 1303 State St. [805-962-7000]; or **Velo Pro Cyclery,** 633 State St. [805-963-7775] or 5887 Hollister Ave., Goleta [805-964-8355]). City maps are available at these locations for free. You can also receive a free map by calling Traffic Solutions at (805) 963-SAVE or by visiting its website at www.traffic solutions.info and sending an e-mail request.

i For free biking resources, including scenic South Coast bike tours, maps, and information on bike shops, bike safety, and cycling events, contact the Santa Barbara Bicycle Coalition (805-617-3255; www.sbbike.org), a county-wide biking advocacy group.

One of the favorite in-town spots to bike is the 2-lane Cabrillo Bike Path, which spans the entire waterfront from Leadbetter Beach to the east end of Cabrillo Boulevard. This path is open to bicycles, quadracycles, and in-line skaters, so it is often crowded, and you never know whom you might (literally) run into.

Caution is the byword here, especially on weekends or holidays, when massive numbers of bikers and skaters (as well as many pedestrians who walk across bike paths) make for a harrowing ride. Of course, in addition to casual biking, many Santa Barbarans love cycling the county's rugged hills and canyons. To get the buzz on what's hot for training or racing, ask at any of the bike shops.

Outfitters

The following companies organize biking trips:

SANTA BARBARA ADVENTURE COMPANY

(877) 885-WAVE, (805) 884-WAVE
www.sbadventureco.com

Bike through the back streets of town, cycle around the wine country across rolling hills and farmland, or bump your way along a rugged single-track forest trail. Santa Barbara Adventure Company offers a range of excursions for bikers of all levels, and they'll customize tours to suit your skills and interests. If you don't want to break a sweat climbing any hills, choose the Mountains to the Shore trip and zoom downhill with the wind in your hair. Prices range from $115 per person (four-person minimum) for the mountains to the shore trip to $155 per person for a wine country bike tour (two-person maximum).

SANTA BARBARA WINE COUNTRY CYCLING TOURS

3630 Segunto St., Santa Ynez
(888) 557-8687

Tim Gorham and Corey Evans are the quintessential hosts on biking tours around the breathtakingly beautiful Santa Ynez wine country. Half-day guided tours begin at $135 per person (four-person minimum). If you'd rather bike to the beach, you can try the "Bike to the Beach" tour from Santa Ynez to Refugio Beach. The tour includes a gourmet picnic and is $175 per person (two-person minimum). Still looking for more touring action? Multiday and customized trips are also available.

Rentals

Ever want to ride in a surrey with a fringe on top? Pedal your way along the waterfront in one of these, or even an electric car if you are feeling lazy.

FESS PARKER'S DOUBLETREE RESORT

633 E. Cabrillo Blvd., Santa Barbara
www.fessparkersantabarbarahotel.com
(click on "resort activities")

WHEEL FUN RENTALS

23 E. Cabrillo Blvd., Santa Barbara
22 State St., Santa Barbara
(805) 966-2282
www.wheelfunrentals.com

CAMPING

Camping is a fantastic way to experience Santa Barbara's famed natural beauty. Few things are more exhilarating than waking up in the morning to the call of the birds and wildlife, then going for an early morning hike or walk along the beach, with views of the ocean, islands, and mountains everywhere you look.

One thing we can't emphasize enough: Make reservations as early as possible. The state park campgrounds fill up very quickly, especially during the summer months and on holiday weekends. Many people make their summer reservations at least 6 months in advance.

Los Padres National Forest also has a number of campgrounds. Many of these sites are available on a first come, first served basis with varying fees depending on the facility. You will, however, need a permit to park or camp at most of these sites. For reservations, call (877) 444-6777 or visit www.reserveamerica.com. If you have any questions, you can call the Los Padres National Forest Service headquarters (805-968-6640) or the Santa Barbara Ranger District (805-967-3481). For a truly unique camping experience, try one of the Channel Islands. You'll find detailed information in the Channel Islands National Park chapter.

State Parks

Four state parks with year-round campgrounds are in the area covered in this book. Three of them—El Capitán, Refugio, and Gaviota—occupy prime beachfront along the scenic coastline that stretches northwest between Goleta and Gaviota. The fourth, Carpinteria State Beach, lies on the shores of Carpinteria, just 12 miles south of Santa Barbara. Each welcomes hundreds of thousands of day-use visitors and campers every year.

To reserve a site at El Capitán, Gaviota, Refugio, or Carpinteria, call Parknet (800-444-7275) or visit www.reserveamerica.com. We highly recommend reserving your campsite well ahead of time. You can make reservations up to 7 months in advance (but do so at least 2 days before your planned arrival). Sites are available on a first come, first served basis. Note that a $7.50 reservation fee will be added to the campsite cost.

You can camp in these parks for up to 7 days from March 1 through November. At other times of year you can stay longer—up to 14 days. During the off-season and on weekdays, you might be able to get a campsite without advance reservations, but don't count on it—these parks are amazingly popular, even during the winter months. Lifeguards are generally on duty at state beaches from mid-June through Labor Day weekend.

Keep in mind that all California state parks have strict regulations regarding noise, curfews, parking, trail access, and litter (you will be advised of these regulations when you arrive). Dogs are allowed on a 6-foot leash, but you may not take them on trails or beaches. Be prepared to pay a fine if you do. And don't forget to clean up after your pets!

CARPINTERIA STATE BEACH
5361 6th St., Carpinteria
(805) 684-2811
Info: www.parks.ca.gov
Reservations: (800) 444-7275
www.reserveusa.com

Because of its excellent facilities and programs, Carpinteria State Beach is almost always booked to capacity throughout the summer and on every major holiday. The park has a visitor center with natural history exhibits and nature programs as well as a convenience store. Birding, swimming, fishing, hiking, surfing—you name it—are popular activities here. You can also spot harbor seals nearby from December through May.

The 48-acre park has more campsites and facilities than any other state park in the region. Each of the 213 narrow family campsites has a parking space, picnic table, and fire ring. Restrooms in each campground feature hot showers (there's a charge). Drinking water is available nearby. You'll find sites here for tents as well as campers, trailers, and motor homes up to 30 feet. Water, sewer, and electrical hookups are available in one of the campgrounds ($65 per night).

Adults and kids alike can sign up for naturalist-led nature walks to the shore and tide pools. Check the schedule at the visitor center. The park is about 12 miles south of Santa Barbara off US 101. Take the Casitas Pass exit to Palm Avenue and follow it 3 blocks into the park.

> ℹ️ Many of the beaches have naturally occurring black tar. Keep some vegetable oil at hand to remove it from your feet, and wear old shoes when hiking.

RECREATION

EL CAPITÁN STATE BEACH
Off US 101, 17 miles northwest of Santa Barbara
(805) 968-1033
www.parks.ca.gov for information
(800) 444-7275
www.reserveamerica.com for reservations

"El Cap" ranks among the most beautiful state parks in Southern California. The 133-acre park was formerly the site of a large Chumash village. Today it features 130 developed campsites and 5 group sites, restrooms, a snack bar, showers, barbecue grills, and open fire pits. Trailers up to 27 feet in length and campers to 30 feet in length are allowed to park here.

Rates start at $35 per night for a standard site (beach sites with hookups are $50 and $65). There's a lot to see and explore at El Cap. Walk down a path from the bluffs and you'll arrive at the sandy beach, where you can sunbathe, fish, sailboard, and explore tide pools. You can hike along nature trails or along the bluffs—and if you take the blufftop trail just 2.5 miles west, you'll end up at Refugio State Beach. There is a nice bike trail between the two campgrounds. From June 19 through Labor Day, lifeguards patrol daily.

GAVIOTA STATE PARK
Off US 101, 33 miles west of Santa Barbara
(805) 968-1033
www.parks.ca.gov

Named after the Spanish word for "seagull," given to the area by soldiers of the Portola Expedition who supposedly killed a seagull while camping here in 1769, this sprawling, 2,700-acre park is smaller and a bit more primitive than El Capitán and Refugio, but it offers fantastic views from mountainside

trails. It lies near where the coastline turns north at Point Conception, 33 miles north of Santa Barbara. Thirty-nine developed sites are available on a first come, first served basis; 37 of these can now be reserved in advance between the Friday of Memorial Day weekend and the Sunday of Labor Day weekend each year. You'll need to bring your own drinking water.

Park facilities include pay showers, food service, restrooms, and picnic areas. You can swim, fish off the pier, and hike on numerous trails, including one that leads to Gaviota Hot Springs. US 101 cuts across the park. So does a railroad trestle (down by the day-use parking lot). Trailers up to 25 feet and campers as long as 27 feet may park here, but there are no hookups.

Camping fees start at $35 per site per night year-round.

REFUGIO STATE BEACH
Off US 101, 20 miles northwest of Santa Barbara
(805) 968-1033
www.parks.ca.gov for information
(800) 444-7275
www.reserveamerica.com for reservations

Palm trees line the beach and campgrounds at Refugio, so the place looks like a picture-postcard scene from Hawaii. The park offers 66 developed campsites and 3 group sites, many picnic areas, excellent coastal fishing and nature trails, and a seasonal kiosk. Trailers up to 27 feet and campers up to 30 feet in length may park here, but there aren't any hookups. Refugio is a great place for picnicking, diving, snorkeling, and exploring nature trails. A 2.5-mile (4.0-kilometer) bike trail connects Refugio with its neighboring state park, El Capitán. A fantastic, mostly uninhabited beach, just north of the cove, is accessible during low tide. Depending on the time of year, camping fees start at $35 per night; $50 for the row closest to the beach.

i When hiking in the county, it's possible to run into a rattlesnake, especially in the spring and summer. So watch your step!

Other Public Camping Areas

CACHUMA LAKE RECREATION AREA
CA 154, northwest of Santa Barbara
(805) 686-5054 (recorded information)
(805) 686-5050
www.cachuma.com

Cachuma Lake is a 3,200-acre county reservoir and recreation area in the Santa Ynez Mountains about 20 miles northwest of Santa Barbara. It's the pride and joy of the Santa Barbara County park system, and you can count on friendly staff, gorgeous scenery, and diverse wildlife in the area at any time of year.

Tent and RV campsites are available year-round, and a campsite reservation system was put in effect in fall 2011. More than 400 campsites are available, each with a picnic table and barbecue pit. One hundred sites have full electrical, water, and sewer hookups; 30 have electrical and water. All campsites are close to showers, restrooms, and water. The limit is 14 days, but from October 1 through March 31 there is no limit, so stay as long as you like. Group sites for 32 to 120 people can be reserved up to a year in advance; call (805) 686-5050 for information or go to www.cachuma.com.

Campers can now enjoy the outdoors and have comfortable accommodations at Cachuma Lake. Central Coast Cabins rents 1- and 2-bedroom cabins equipped with electricity, full bathrooms, fully equipped kitchenettes, a living room, private porches, picnic tables, and fire pits. You need to bring your own sleeping bags/bedding, pillows, towels/toiletries, and groceries. Cabins may be reserved year-round, and up to 1 year in advance. Rental rates range from $100 to $210 per night based on cabin selection and season. Visit www.centralcoastcabins.com, or www.cachuma.com for more details. To make reservations, phone (805) 934-1441.

For an unusual camping experience, you can reserve a yurt, which is basically a tent covering the frame of a round cabin, for $65 to $85 per night. Fees vary, depending on the yurt size and season. Each yurt is insulated and has bunk beds, a skylight, and a wooden deck. The yurts are very popular with families and can be reserved up to a year in advance. There is a 2-night minimum weekend stay and 3-night minimum stay for holidays.

There are also 3 six-sleeper cabins located near the marina and 1 four-sleeper cabin, ranging from $100 to $125 during peak season and $80 to $100 during nonpeak season. Call (805) 686-5050 for reservations.

Cachuma Lake provides numerous facilities, including a fully stocked general store, a gas station, a Laundromat, a snack bar and grill, a marina, a bait and tackle shop, bike rentals, boat and kayak rentals, and an RV dump station. You're allowed to bring a dog as long as it stays on a leash. You'll need to pay a $3 daily pet fee and show proof of rabies vaccination.

If you're looking for a place to pursue lots of different recreational activities while camping, you can't go wrong by choosing Cachuma. It's a recreational paradise, with boating, fishing, naturalist programs, wildlife and eagle cruises, and trails for horseback riding and hiking.

However, swimming, waterskiing, sailboarding, or any bodily contact with the lake is strictly forbidden because it's a reservoir, and much of the water ends up in someone's home down the mountain.

Rates range from $20 to $35 per night, depending on the type of site. A second vehicle at the same site costs an additional $10 (maximum two vehicles and eight people per site). If you're going to visit Cachuma more than once, you might consider buying a season pass at the entrance. The Parks chapter contains a complete description of the Cachuma Lake Recreation Area.

LOS PADRES NATIONAL FOREST
Various campsites off CA 154, about 20 miles northeast of Santa Barbara
Headquarters: (805) 968-6640
Santa Barbara Ranger
District Office: (805) 967-3481
(877) 444-6777
www.reserveusa.com for reservations
www.rockymountainrec.com

Los Padres National Forest is a huge region (nearly 2 million acres) stretching across the coastal mountain ranges from Los Angeles County in the south to Monterey County in the north. You'll find 16 developed family campgrounds in the Santa Barbara Ranger District of this national forest; the closest to the city of Santa Barbara lie near CA 154, near Paradise Road, the upper Santa Ynez River, and Cachuma Lake. Amenities at each site vary from rustic campgrounds with toilets (but no piped drinking water) to full-service sites with piped water, fire pits, toilets, paved roads, picnic tables, and stoves. You can also

camp by permit in designated backcountry areas. You can even tie up your horse at some spots (equestrian sites at Upper Oso are $24 a night and $116 at Sage Hill, for example).

Reservation sites are Upper Oso, Paradise, and the group area at Sage Hill. All the other sites are available on a first come, first served basis, and the fees are about $19 per night. It costs around $91 for a group and $5 for rustic campgrounds with an adventure pass. You will, however, need a permit to park and/or camp at most of these sites. For information, call the Forest Service office, 6755 Hollister Ave., Ste. 150, Goleta, at (805) 968-6640 or (805) 967-3481.

Reservations must be made 4 days in advance. Two-day minimum stay required on weekends.

Private Campgrounds

OCEAN MESA AT EL CAPITÁN
100 El Capitán Terrace Ln., Santa Barbara
(866) 410-5783
www.oceanmesa.com

Located 20 minutes north of Santa Barbara on the Gaviota coast, Ocean Mesa is right next door to sister site El Capitán Canyon, and guests of both properties can share the facilities, which include 2 fun convenience shops, 2 heated pools (1 with spa) and deli/cafe. Wired for Internet and TV, you can stay plugged in if you must, but with the wonderful tide pools and beach across the highway, amazing views up and down the coastline, we recommend you just relax and chill. Outdoor movies are shown on a big blow-up screen during the summer, and there's even a company (see Insider Tip) that will rent you an RV all set up and ready to go—no driving required!

SUNRISE RV PARK
516 S. Salinas St., Santa Barbara
(805) 966-9954, (800) 345-5018
Sunrise is the only private RV park in Santa Barbara, and it's only 13 blocks from East Beach, 1.5 miles from State Street, and 2 blocks from a bus stop. It has been in operation for more than 50 years and has 33 RV sites. Each site offers full hookups (water, 50-amp electricity, sewer, and even cable TV). The park has 4 restroom areas with free hot showers, free wireless Internet service, and laundry facilities.

Rates start at $50 per night per person in an RV up to 30 feet in length. Each additional person costs $5 per night. If your rig is longer than 30 feet, you pay extra for each additional 5 feet. You can stay for as long as 28 days. After that, you can request an extension, which is sometimes available during the off-season. The ultimate maximum length of stay is 6 months. Sunrise RV Park is booked year-round. Advance reservations are highly recommended. Pets are welcome as long as they remain leashed and owners clean up all pet messes.

i Want the thrill of RV camping—but without the hassle of driving and high cost of gas? Check out Vacation Trailers 2 U (877-EZ-CAMPING; www.vacationtrailers2u.com), which operates under contract with California State Parks, Santa Barbara County, and other campground organizations and will deliver your "home away from home" for $200 a night.

DANCING

The Santa Barbara Parks and Recreation Department offers an impressive lineup of dance lessons and dances, including swing, salsa, Argentine tango, folk dancing, ballet, tap, and hip-hop. After you practice, show off your steps at the Carrillo Recreation Center, at 100 E. Carrillo St. (805-965-3813). The center's ballroom is one of only two spring-loaded dance floors in the country. Swing dances, held on the first and third Friday of the month, often feature live dance bands. Two Saturday dances a month rotate between country and western, ballroom, and West Coast swing. Lessons begin at 7 p.m., followed by dancing from 8 to 11 p.m. Cost ranges from $10 to $15.

For a schedule of dance programs, pick up an activity guide from Santa Barbara Parks and Recreation (see the listing at the beginning of this chapter) or download one at the department's website (www.sbparksandrec reation.com). You can also contact the Santa Barbara Country Dance Society (www.sbcds .org) for contra and English country dance schedules and information.

LESLIE SACK DANCE STUDIO
20 W. Calle Laureles, Santa Barbara
(805) 965-0651
www.lesliesack.com
Many styles of dance are offered here, and practice parties twice a month (usually the second and fourth Friday, $5 admission) run from 9 to 11 p.m. in order for students to practice their new moves with other students in a "safe and fun environment."

THE SANTA BARBARA DANCE CENTER
127-A W. Canon Perdido, Santa Barbara
(805) 899-2901
www.santabarbaradancecenter.com
Here you can choose from a full array of classes in all styles of dance. Ballroom, Latin, and swing dance classes are offered every Saturday night for $7.

HANG GLIDING & PARAGLIDING

Hang gliding and paragliding are alive and well in Santa Barbara, and an active association in town promotes the sports. If you're new to gliding, you can take lessons (it costs about $200 for an introductory lesson) using the company's equipment. After that you'll have to decide whether to buy a glider, as they are usually not rented.

Local launch points include La Cumbre Peak, the Douglas Family Preserve, and the beloved 200-foot training hill—which is considered one of the best in the country—in an undeveloped area on the south side of Elings Park. Contact **Fly Away Hang Gliding** (805-957-9145) or **Fly Above All AirSports** (805-965-3733; www.flyaboveall.com) to talk to real enthusiasts of the sport who are anxious to tell you all about it. (Also see the listing for the New Year's Day Hang Gliding and Paragliding Festival in our Annual Events chapter.)

i For quick information on Santa Barbara hikes, log on to Santa Barbara Hikes at www.santabarbara hikes.com.

HIKING

Santa Barbara is a haven for hikers. In fact, hiking is one of our most popular weekend recreational activities. With miles of scenic trails accessible year-round, you'd be hard-pressed to find a better place to explore the wilderness.

Maps and information (as well as the permits needed for backcountry hiking) can be found at the Los Padres National Forest Headquarters, 6755 Hollister Ave., Ste. 150,

Goleta (805-968-6640). Or you can pick up a copy of the *Santa Barbara Trail Guide* at a local bookshop or outdoor equipment store; it lists 25 hiking trails in the Santa Barbara area, including trail ratings, access information, descriptions, maps, and trail logs.

Santa Barbara Day Hikes by Raymond Ford Jr. and *Day Hikes around Santa Barbara, 2nd edition: 82 Great Hikes* by Robert Stone are also good resources, as is Map No. 2 in the Santa Barbara County Recreational Map Series, titled "A Hiker's Guide to the Santa Barbara Front Country." Trail maps are also available at Pacific Travellers Supply, 12 W. Anapamu St., Santa Barbara (805-963-4438). If you'd rather not wander off by yourself, the Sierra Club (805-966-6622) sponsors a variety of day and evening hikes that range from easy to strenuous. These and other local club hikes are usually listed in the "Events Today" or "What's Doing" sections of the *Santa Barbara News-Press* or in the *Santa Barbara Independent* under "The Week."

One of our favorite easy hikes is Rattle Snake Canyon, a serpentine trail with waterfalls, pools, and plenty of shady picnic spots. The moderately easy Cold Springs Trail is also popular. Once a stagecoach route, this trail begins in the shade by a cool running creek and ends with a steep and rocky climb up the mountain.

i There's nothing like springtime at Figueroa Mountain in the Santa Ynez backcountry. Blue lupine, chocolate lilies, purple shooting stars, and orange poppies create a panorama of colorful wildflowers. Don't forget to bring a picnic lunch!

HORSEBACK RIDING

CIRCLE BAR B GUEST RANCH AND STABLES
1800 Refugio Rd., Goleta
Stables: (805) 968-3901
Guest ranch: (805) 968-1113
www.circlebarb.com

Well-known for its riotous dinner theater, the Circle Bar B, 20 miles north of Santa Barbara, offers public horseback riding for all levels with spectacular views of the ocean and local canyons. Half-day (4-hour) horseback rides are $75 per person, and depart daily at 9 a.m.; 1.5-hour-long rides are $45 per person and leave daily at 9:30 a.m., 11:30 a.m., 2 p.m., and 4 p.m. Private and group rides are available by appointment. Children must be 7 and up to ride. From US 101, take the Refugio State Beach exit and drive 3.5 miles toward the mountains until you see the large stone entrance.

LOS PADRES WILDERNESS OUTFITTERS
(805) 331-5252
www.lospadresoutfitters.com

Whether it's horseback riding in the mountains, along the beaches, or camping out for a few days, Los Padres Wilderness Outfitters creates unforgettable experiences. Half-day and 2-hour rides are available as well as full-day rides with lunch provided. The full-day ride is $275 per person with a two-person minimum. For a true taste of the backcountry, try a 3- or 4-day pack trip with guides. For real adventurers, there's the Spot Pack trip: Cowboys and cowgirls are dropped off at a chosen destination with food and supplies (apart from a sleeping bag and hiking gear) for your stay. Pack trip rates range from $250 to $300 a day per person (and $170 to $270 per person a day for hikers). Spot Pack trips cost $475 to $575 per person. Call for details.

RANCHO OSO STABLES AND GUEST RANCH
3750 Paradise Rd., Santa Barbara
(805) 683-5686
www.ranchooso.com

You'll be riding into history at this old ranch, once a Spanish land grant in the local mountains. Rancho Oso offers trail riding starting at $40 for a 1-hour ride. Little cowboys and cowgirls ages 3 to 8 and younger can practice their skills on hand-led pony rides for $20. On the weekends, the chuckwagon food service lets you refuel after your ride. Rancho Oso offers equestrian group camping as well as overnight accommodations in cabins and covered wagons. Reservations are required, so call ahead. Beginners and children are welcome. Take CA 154 to Paradise Road and look for the sign approximately 5.5 miles from the turnoff.

JOGGING

The beach is the most popular jogging site in Santa Barbara, either on the sand, along the Cabrillo bike path, or along Shoreline Drive. If you're looking for something away from the coast, head for one of these parks, which have jogging trails: **Monte Vista Park,** Bailard Avenue and Pandanus Street, Carpinteria; and **Elings Park,** Las Positas Road and Jerry Harwin Parkway, Santa Barbara.

LAWN BOWLING

Santa Barbara has 2 lawn bowling clubs, and free instruction is offered at both. Since they are open on alternate days, it's possible to play every day if you're so inclined.

MACKENZIE PARK LAWN BOWLS CLUB
State Street at Las Positas Road,
Santa Barbara
(805) 563-5494
www.mackenzieparklbc.org
This club has 2 greens, which are open to visitors as well as club members. Call the club to arrange a 1-hour free lesson. (After your lessons, you'll need to buy your own bowls.) Walk-ins are welcome. The club is open Mon, Wed, and Fri from 9 a.m. to 3 p.m., and Sat from 9 a.m. to noon. Join in at the noon game (sometimes there is a 2 p.m. game as well). From May to Oct, Twilight Bowl occurs Tues and Thurs from 5:30 to 7:30 p.m.

SANTA BARBARA LAWN BOWLS CLUB
1216 De la Vina St., Santa Barbara
(805) 965-1773
www.santabarbaralbc.org
The 2 greens here are open to club members and novices, who learn to bowl during a short training course. Out-of-town visitors need to be a member of a lawn bowls club to play and pay $2 per game. Walk-ins, either beginners or experienced lawn bowls club members, are welcome. Open bowling times are 9:45 a.m. and 12:15 p.m. on Tues, Thurs, and Sat, and noon on Sun.

MARTIAL ARTS

Whether it's karate, tae kwon do, kung fu, t'ai chi, or sambo, you can find a variety of local schools willing to teach you the skills you seek. We've included a few and suggest you

check the Yellow Pages of the local phone directory for others. Call for complete information on class schedules and prices, which vary widely.

THE CULTURAL SCHOOL: AIKIDO WITH KI
255 Magnolia Ave., Goleta
(805) 967-3103
www.goletaaikido.net
Learn aikido (mind and body coordination) and judo from a master at this small school, which has been in Goleta for more than 40 years. There's a free introductory lesson, and classes for men, women, and children are available.

Nite Moves

Need some exercise? Sign up for the popular **Nite Moves Summer Sunset Series,** and you can walk, run, jog, or swim with other fitness enthusiasts every Wednesday evening at beautiful Leadbetter Beach. After your workout, stick around for the sunset party and awards ceremony with a free dinner buffet, drinks, and live entertainment. Kids are welcome. For details, call (805) 564-8879 or visit www.runsantabarbara.com.

MACOMBER MARTIAL ARTS TRAINING CENTER
5950 Hollister Ave., Goleta
(805) 683-6617
www.macomberkarate.com
Macomber is a family martial arts center offering a range of classes for preschoolers,

children, and adults. The specialized curriculum combines techniques from Korean Tang Soo Do, American Kenpo, and Okinawan Kobudo (weapons) as well as ground fighting and grappling skills.

VAHILLA ELITE TRAINING CENTER
1722 State St., Santa Barbara
(805) 687-1514

Kickboxing, jujitsu, mixed martial arts (MMA), kung fu, and weapon training. On-site personal training and opportunities to progress onto martial arts competitions are offered here.

THE WU SHU STUDIO
23A W. Gutierrez St., Santa Barbara
(805) 965-5316

This is the oldest martial arts studio in Santa Barbara and is consistently voted the best martial arts studio in local newspaper polls. You'll find a good range of martial arts taught here, including kenpo, kickboxing, kung fu, and t'ai chi. There are classes for adults, children, seniors, and disabled persons.

ROCK CLIMBING

Set against the rugged backdrop of the Santa Ynez Mountains, Santa Barbara has some great crags for climbing. From huge boulders and steep sandstone cliff faces to dramatic overhangs and bluffs, avid climbers will find plenty to challenge them. If you're serious about the sport, we suggest you pick up a copy of *Rock Climbing: Santa Barbara and Ventura* by Steve Edwards. It lists more than 1,000 climbing routes in the area.

One of the most popular climbing spots in Santa Barbara is Gibraltar Rock. It's easily accessible and offers routes for climbers of all levels. To get there, wind up Mountain Drive past Sheffield Reservoir, veer left, and turn right on Gibraltar Road. Continue about 5 miles up Gibraltar Road and you'll see the rock on the left-hand side. Painted Cave has some of the best bouldering in Santa Barbara. The boulders hang over Painted Cave Road off CA 154. You'll find them about a mile before the Chumash Painted Cave Historical Park.

If you're just starting out in the sport or want to brush up on your skills, **UCSB Adventure Progams** (805-893-3737; www.recreation.ucsb.edu) offers instruction for climbers of all levels—from total beginners to more advanced climbers. Start out your climbing expedition at the indoor Adventure Climbing Center, with the reputed "largest imprint wall on the West Coast." The 30-foot main wall has a dedicated bouldering section, top rope climbing, lead bolts, 3 crack features, and more. It's the perfect place for beginning learners or for those attempting to bone up on their skills. The center is open daily starting at 11:30 a.m. Harness or rock shoes may be rented at the center. A day pass or membership is required. If you're ready for a bona fide course, take a class at the university. Beginning to advanced rock-climbing classes are taught for around $109. Belay and rescue classes are also available. An outdoor climbing rock can be found at **Trigo-Pasado Park** (6633 Pasado, Isla Vista; 805-968-2017).

Santa Barbara Outfitters at 1200 State St. also has an indoor wall with routes for all skill levels—from children to more experienced climbers. Rates are $5 per adult visit, $3 per child, or $30 for an unlimited monthly pass, and you can call the store to arrange climbing instruction (805-564-1007).

Goleta Valley Athletic Club, 170 Los Carneros Way, has an outdoor wall that nonmembers can use for $12 a day. Certified belayers are on duty Mon through Thurs from 6 to 8 p.m. and Sun from 2 to 5 p.m. Call (805) 968-1023 or visit www.gvac.com for details. If you're interested in guided outdoor climbs, Santa Barbara Adventure Company (877-885-WAVE, 805-884-WAVE; www.sbadventureco .com) offers guided climbs and instruction for all skill levels.

SKATING

Although Santa Barbara has no skating rinks, in-line skating is one of the most popular activities along the Cabrillo Boulevard waterfront. If you don't have your own, you can rent them from the places listed below. (Just remember to stay out of the way of bikes and quadracycles as you zip along the bike path.) All rentals include protective gear.

WHEEL FUN RENTALS
Multiple locations (see website)
(805) 966-2282
www.wheelfunrentalssb.com

FESS PARKER'S DOUBLETREE RESORT
633 E. Cabrillo Blvd., Santa Barbara
(805) 966-2282

SOCCER

Soccer is one of the fastest-growing sports in Santa Barbara. There are countless leagues (both adult and children's—see the Youth Sports section in our Kidstuff chapter for information on children's leagues), and hard-fought matches take place all over town on just about any weekend. Soccer fields (called "multiuse" fields because they also accommodate a good old American football game as well as Ultimate Frisbee) are found in Santa Barbara at **Chase Palm Park,** East Cabrillo

and Santa Barbara Street; **Dwight Murphy Field,** Por la Mar Drive at Niños Drive; **Elings Park,** Las Positas Road and Jerry Harwin Parkway; **MacKenzie Park,** State Street and Las Positas Road; **Pershing Park,** Castillo Street and West Yannonali Street; **Shoreline Park,** Shoreline Drive; **Girsh Park,** Phelps Road, Goleta; **Children's Park,** Picasso Road, Isla Vista; **Estero Park,** Camino del Sur and Estero Road, Isla Vista. In Carpinteria, a field is located at **Monte Vista Park,** Bailard Avenue and Pandanus Street.

> **i** Looking for a spot to kick a soccer ball, flick a Frisbee, or hit a few tennis balls? Visit www.totalsanta barbara.com. The site lists neighborhood parks, complete with colorful keys to all their facilities. Once you've found your destination, you can click on the link for maps and directions.

SOFTBALL

Softball is actually more popular than baseball around here, and a number of city leagues (see the earlier Santa Barbara Parks and Recreation listing) take to the fields during the spring and summer season.

Even if you don't join a league, if the ball fields are not occupied by league play, you're welcome to round the bases at these locations in Santa Barbara (all fields are lighted): **Cabrillo Ball Park,** Cabrillo Boulevard; **Dwight Murphy Field,** Por la Mar Drive at Niños Drive (one field); **Girsh Park,** Phelps Road; **Elings Park,** Las Positas Road and Jerry Harwin Parkway (three fields); **Ortega Park,** E. Ortega Street and Calle Cesar Chavez (one field); and **Pershing Park,** Castillo Street and West Cabrillo Boulevard (two fields).

Other area venues include **El Carro Park,** El Carro Lane and Namouna Street, Carpinteria (one field); **Toro Canyon Park,** Toro Canyon Park Road, Summerland (one field); **Manning Park,** San Ysidro and E. Valley Roads, Montecito (one field); **Stow Grove Park,** La Patera Lane and Cathedral Oaks Road, Goleta (one field).

SWIMMING

With all our sunshine and warm weather, swimming is a popular form of aerobic exercise in these parts, and there are a couple of public pools to choose from. For information on children's wading pools, see the Swimming Pools section of the Kidstuff chapter.

CARPINTERIA VALLEY COMMUNITY SWIMMING POOL
5305 Carpinteria Ave., Carpinteria
(805) 566-2417
www.carpinteria.ca.us
Aqua aerobics, master classes, Aquacamp, and children's swim lessons are just some of the activities and classes held at this community pool. Walk-ins are welcome for most classes, and lap swimming usually goes on all day (hours vary and are subject to change). Winter and summer hours vary for recreational swimming. Admission is $6 for an adult, $4 for youth, $4.50 for seniors, and $8.50 for the master's day pass. Annual memberships are $525 for individuals and $675 for families. A punch card is available for $55 and allows 30 swims.

LOS BAÑOS DEL MAR POOL
401 Shoreline Dr., Santa Barbara
(805) 966-6110
This 50-meter, 7-lane outdoor pool, opened in 1914 and formerly called "the Plunge," accommodates up to 300 swimmers every day. Especially popular with lap swimmers, the pool is used for Parks and Recreation programs such as year-round noon lap swims, adult swim lessons, aquamotion sessions, and coached morning and evening workouts. It is heated to 79 to 80 degrees Fahrenheit (26 to 27 degrees Celsius). Fees are $4 for adults and teens and $1 for ages 18 and younger. Los Baños is open to the public only during limited summer afternoon hours.

TENNIS

In addition to its swanky private tennis clubs, the Santa Barbara area has 28 public courts that are available on a first come, first served basis. Seventeen of the courts are lighted until 9 p.m. Contact (805) 564-5573 or www.santabarbaraca.gov/resident/recreation_and_sports/tennis for more info.

Santa Barbara

In the city of Santa Barbara, permits are required for most public courts. They may be purchased on-site or from the Parks and Recreation Department at 620 Laguna St. Daily permits are $5 per person; $4 with Resident Discount Card; students 18 and older with a student ID are $4. Annual permits are $125 ($105 with Resident Discount Card) for adults and $105 ($95 with Resident Discount Card) for seniors 60 and older. Teens and children 17 and younger play free and do not need a permit. For information on any courts in the city of Santa Barbara, as well as on lessons, leagues, or local tournaments sponsored by the city, call (805) 564–5517.

The largest tennis facility in Santa Barbara is the **Municipal Tennis Courts complex,** at 1414 Park Place. You'll find 12 courts here, and the 1,000-seat center court stadium is the main venue for local tournaments. Open from dawn to dusk, the center has lockers, showers, restrooms, and equipment rentals. Three courts are lit until 9 p.m. Mon through Fri.

> **i** Tennis anyone? The Santa Barbara Parks and Recreation Department offers classes and lessons and organizes singles, doubles, and team tennis leagues. For details, call (805) 564-5573 or visit www.sbparksandrecreation.com.

The **Las Positas facility,** at 1002 Las Positas Rd., includes 6 lighted courts, backboards, showers, and restrooms, and is open until 9 p.m. nightly. The only other lighted courts in the city are at **Pershing Park,** 100 Castillo St. The 8 courts here (4 lighted) are used by the Santa Barbara City College tennis team and are open to the public only on weekends and on weekdays after 5 p.m. Play is available until 9 p.m. Mon through Fri. **Oak Park,** at 300 W. Alamar Avenue, has 2 unlighted courts open for public use daily from dawn to dusk. You can also play on 6 hard courts at **Santa Barbara High School** (1031 Nopal St.) after 5 p.m. weekdays and all day on weekends and during school holidays.

Montecito

Montecito has one public court in **Manning Park,** at San Ysidro and E. Valley Roads. You can play for free here.

Goleta

In Goleta you'll find two courts at the **Evergreen Open Space,** in the 7500 block of Evergreen Drive; two at the **Emerald Terrace**

Open Space, at Berkeley Road and Arundel Road; four at the **Kellogg Tennis Courts,** in the 600 block of Kellogg Avenue; and two in the **Stow Open Space,** located in the 6200 block of Stow Canyon Road.

ULTIMATE FRISBEE

Santa Barbara has been described as a hotbed of Ultimate Frisbee. In fact, UCSB's team, the Black Tides, has captured the National Championship six times. Check out www.santabarbaraultimate.com for more information. There's also a Frisbee Golf course in Goleta at the Evergreen Open Space, in the 7500 block of Evergreen Drive.

VOLLEYBALL

Volleyball is big in Santa Barbara, especially on the beach, where you can show off your tan (and your body) while getting a good workout. The **East Beach volleyball courts** on E. Cabrillo Boulevard (there are 14 of them) are the most popular venues for beach volleyball, and they are generally available on a first come, first served basis. Most major tournaments are held here, and tournament or league play sometimes takes up most of the courts, but you're welcome to snag one if it's free. Several other local beaches and parks have volleyball courts, including **Manning Park** in Montecito (1 court); **Leadbetter Beach** in Santa Barbara (2 courts); and **Goleta Beach Park** (one court), **Stow Grove County Park** (2 courts), and **Tucker's Grove Park** (2 courts) in Goleta. Other locations include **Lookout Park** in Summerland and **Toro Canyon Park** in Carpinteria.

Men's, women's, and coed indoor volleyball leagues are organized by Santa Barbara Parks and Recreation, with games at

Santa Barbara City College and the Goleta Valley Youth Center. Call (805) 564-5418 for information.

YOGA

BIKRAM YOGA SANTA BARBARA
3891 State St., 2nd Floor
(805) 687-6900
www.bikramyogasb.com
Bikram Yoga of Santa Barbara is one of a kind in central California. This particular type of yoga, named after Bikram Choudhury, the founder of the worldwide Yoga College of India, follows a specific regimen of 26 asana poses and two breathing exercises that are conducted in a room heated to 105 degrees! This practice has been scientifically designed to warm and stretch muscles, ligaments, and tendons in the order in which they should be stretched to achieve maximum effectiveness. There are 5 classes each day during the week, 3 on Saturday and Sunday, and each class is 90 minutes long (first timers are expected to arrive 15 minutes prior to class for a brief overview given by an instructor). Whether you are a seasoned "yoga-er" or you simply want to try something unique, Bikram Yoga is the place to go. Just make sure to bring a towel and water, because you're going to sweat! On a side note, frequent Bikram-goers advise not to eat a large meal 2 hours prior to a class.

SANTA BARBARA YOGA CENTER
32 E. Micheltorena St., Santa Barbara
(805) 965-6045
www.santabarbarayogacenter.com
You'll find more than 100 yoga classes a week at this busy center, including gentle yoga, Ashtanga, pre- and postnatal yoga, and Restorative Yoga, just to name a few.

Introduction to Yoga workshops are scheduled twice a month. Prices range from about $10 for a community class to $275 for a 90-day, 24-class pass.

SOURCE YOGA STUDIO
1911 De la Vina St., #G, Santa Barbara
(805) 569-2505
www.sourceyogastudio.com
Say "om" to peace and restoration. Vinyasa, restorative, and core strength are just a few of the styles of yoga taught at the Source. Class costs are $13 per adult, $10 for seniors and students. A $125 pass entitles you to an unlimited number of classes in a month's period.

YOGA SOUP
28 Parker Way, Santa Barbara
(805) 965-8811
www.yogasoup.com
Eddie Ellner is quite locally renowned for offering mind, body, and spirit-bending yoga classes. His classes are usually packed with yoga-loving individuals who are trying to detox from the stresses of the every day. Because of Ellner's own inability once-upon-a-time to pay for yoga classes, he and fellow teachers at his studio offer classes on a donation basis, with a suggested donation of $14 a class. This studio is in a pleasingly rejuvenated part of downtown. You can even book a facial or a massage afterwards at Crimson Day Spa & Boutique right across the street. For easy parking, use the public lot on the corner of Gutierrez and State Streets.

ATHLETIC CLUBS

The greater Santa Barbara area has a large number of health and fitness clubs with varied programs and facilities. Most will not quote membership prices over the phone but require you to come in, take a tour, and then choose from several membership options.

Generally, individual and family memberships are offered at each club, and special packages and discounts are often available, so be sure to ask if you are considering joining. Many clubs also allow a complimentary session to familiarize you with the facilities. If you're in town for a few days, ask about day-use fees, which are also commonly available.

Santa Barbara

EAST BEACH BATHHOUSE
1118 E. Cabrillo Blvd., Santa Barbara
(805) 897-2680
Open 8 a.m. to 5 p.m. Mon through Fri and 11 a.m. to 4 p.m. on weekends, the bathhouse is situated right on the beach and offers weight rooms, beach volleyball courts, lockers, showers, and beach supplies and rentals. Daily fee is $4 per day. A 10-visit punch pass is $31 to $34. Call for other options and resident discount information.

SANTA BARBARA ATHLETIC CLUB
520 Castillo St., Santa Barbara
(805) 966-6147
www.sbathleticclub.com
Aerobics, yoga, and self-defense classes are available here as well as an outdoor lap pool, a weight room, squash and racquetball courts, an outdoor workout center, and spinning and Pilates studios. You'll also find saunas, steam rooms, cafe, and spas, plus a child-care facility. A free towel and a locker are provided on each visit. The SBAC is open 5 a.m. to 10:30 p.m. Mon through Fri, 6 a.m. to 8 p.m. on Sat, and 7 a.m. to 8 p.m. Sun.

SANTA BARBARA FAMILY YMCA
36 Hitchcock Way, Santa Barbara
(805) 687-7727
www.ciymca.org
The usual family-oriented YMCA atmosphere prevails here, with classes and activities for the young and old. Serious fitness buffs will appreciate the circuit, free-weight, and cardio-training equipment, racquetball and tennis courts, and aerobics classes as well as the large pool, which is open for lap swimming, water aerobics classes, and recreational swimming.

The kids can take swim lessons, romp in the fantastic Kids' Gym, or join in group recreational programs. Child care is available. The Y is open weekdays 5:30 a.m. to 9:30 p.m., Sat 6:30 a.m. to 6:30 p.m., and Sun 10:30 a.m. to 6:30 p.m. Membership fee is $100 for adults and seniors, and $150 for families, with monthly fees of $57 for adults, $47 for seniors, and $98 for families.

SPECTRUM ATHLETIC CLUB
21 W. Carrillo St., Santa Barbara
(805) 965-0999

3908 State St., Santa Barbara
(805) 563-8700, (888) 867-5860
www.spectrumclubs.com
Voted the top club in Santa Barbara, Spectrum has state-of-the-art weight-training equipment, nationally certified trainers, cardio machines with personal televisions, and a host of exercise classes. The club is open Mon through Thurs from 5 a.m. to 11 p.m., Fri from 5 a.m. to 9 p.m., and Sat and Sun from 7 a.m. to 8 p.m. (Club hours may vary according to location. Call first.)

WOMEN'S ATHLETIC CLUB
4141 State St., Suite D 1.2, Santa Barbara
(805) 845-4545
www.womensathleticclub.net

A "non-threatening" workout haven "for women, by women" that offers classes ranging from spinning and cardio & strength circuit training to boot camp. Top-level equipment includes free weights and machines. WAC follows current trends in the fitness world, such as TRX suspension training. There is an emphasis on high-quality personal training. All fitness levels are welcome. Facility is accessible 24 hours a day.

Goleta

CATHEDRAL OAKS ATHLETIC CLUB
5800 Cathedral Oaks Rd., Goleta
(805) 964-7762
www.wcaclubs.com

This popular family swim, tennis, and athletic club features a full fitness area with Stairmasters, treadmills, stationary bikes, and free weights; 2 outdoor heated pools; a Jacuzzi; and 12 tennis courts, 8 of which are lighted. Also available are aerobics, step aerobics, aqua aerobics, and yoga classes, plus a variety of programs for children and teens, including child care at the Kids' Club. There's a definite family feel here. It's open 5:30 a.m. to 9:30 p.m. Mon through Fri and 7 a.m. to 8 p.m. weekends.

GOLETA VALLEY ATHLETIC CLUB
170 Los Carneros Way, Goleta
(805) 968-1023
www.gvac.com

One of the largest fitness clubs in town, the Goleta Valley Athletic Club offers aerobics classes, fitness and cardiovascular equipment, free weights, handball, racquetball, yoga, kickboxing aerobics, self-defense

classes, and senior fitness classes. In addition, it has an outdoor lap pool, indoor and outdoor whirlpools, a sauna, and facilities for massage and yoga. Rock climbing and volleyball are also available. Hours are 5 a.m. to 11 p.m. Mon through Thurs, 5 a.m. to 9 p.m. Fri, and 8 a.m. to 8 p.m. weekends.

SPECTRUM ATHLETIC CLUB
6144 Calle Real, Goleta
(805) 964-0556
www.spectrumclub.com

This 15,000-square-foot space offers everything a fitness buff is looking for. Weight-training equipment, yoga and Pilates classes, nationally certified trainers, and cardio machines with personal televisions are just a few of its amenities. Club hours are Mon through Thurs from 5 a.m. to 11 p.m., Fri from 5 a.m. to 9 p.m., and Sat and Sun from 7 a.m. to 8 p.m.

Montecito

MONTECITO ATHLETIC CLUB
40 Los Patos Way, Montecito
(805) 969-4379

This 3,500-square-foot facility opened in February 1998 to rave reviews. Facilities include state-of-the-art Life Fitness equipment, free weights, a Pilates studio, custom-designed men's and women's locker rooms, and a second-floor mezzanine with the latest cardiovascular equipment. Hours are 4 a.m. to 8 p.m. Mon through Fri, 7 a.m. to 5 p.m. on weekends.

MONTECITO FAMILY YMCA
591 Santa Rosa Ln., Montecito
(805) 969-3288
www.ciymca.org

The family-friendly atmosphere of the Y appeals to many, and you'll find a full lineup of youth lessons, classes, and sports, as well as facilities for adults who are serious about keeping fit. Facilities include a large pool, free weights, and cardio training equipment, as well as tennis and handball courts. Pilates, yoga, aerobics, and aqua aerobics are offered, and child care is available. The Y is open 6 a.m. to 9 p.m. Mon through Fri, 7 a.m. to 6 p.m. Sat, and noon to 6 p.m. on Sun.

Summerland

PLATINUM FITNESS
2488 Lillie Ave., Summerland
(805) 969-1570
www.sbplatinumfitness.com
Platinum Fitness provides goal-oriented plans to suit everyone's needs and specializes in event-specific, sports training, general fitness, and post-physical therapy training for everyone from the weekend warrior to the professional. Their serious, focused, no-frills training programs are designed to put people in the best shape of their lives.

SPECTATOR SPORTS

Baseball

SANTA BARBARA FORESTERS
Caesar Uyesaka Stadium
UCSB, Santa Barbara
(805) 684-0657
www.sbforesters.org
The Foresters are Santa Barbara's next best thing to professional baseball. Part of the Coastal Collegiate League, the Foresters play at UCSB's Caesar Uyesaka Stadium in a June-through-August season. Players come from college teams all over the country, including UCSB, USC, UCLA, Stanford, Florida State, and Wichita State. The Foresters are good, too.

The team is a 12-time California Coastal Collegiate League winner and 7-time California State Champion. The team also is a two-time national champion, having won in 2003 and 2006.

There's an old-time family atmosphere at Foresters games, with promotions, contests, and races between innings, so bring the kids and enjoy. Tickets are available at the gate. Season and family passes are available online, making this a great deal for summertime family fun.

Basketball

SANTA BARBARA BREAKERS
City College Sports Pavilion
Santa Barbara City College
721 Cliff Dr., Santa Barbara
(805) 965-4667
www.sbprohoops.com
Santa Barbara welcomed its first professional minor-league team in a very long time with the West Coast Professional Basketball League franchise—the Santa Barbara Breakers. Curt Pickering, known locally as the former director of basketball of the Santa Barbara Islanders during their yearlong stint with the Continental Basketball Association, is owner/head coach. The WCBL rules are slightly different than the NBA, in that there are fewer timeouts and a 23-second shot clock. The average WCBL league points scored is 116 points per team per game, which promises action-packed seasons for Santa Barbara. In addition to WCBL play, the Breakers are annually invited to China to play international professional games. The Breakers have been touring there since 2008, and 11 players have secured professional playing opportunities in China since that time. Tickets are sold through Ticketmaster or by calling (805) 963-4408.

College Athletics

Although nationally ranked teams and over-flowing stadiums are not the rule in Santa Barbara, we're proud of our local schools and love to cheer them on. If there's a hot contest going, Santa Barbarans turn out in droves to support the home team, and everyone gets into the spirit. The cost for watching college athletic events varies—some events are free and others require an admission fee. Only UCSB offers tickets in advance, with Santa Barbara City College and Westmont selling tickets at the door or gate.

SANTA BARBARA CITY COLLEGE
721 Cliff Dr., Santa Barbara
www.sbcc.edu/athletics
SBCC has fielded some fine football, vol-leyball, and basketball teams, and the public is always welcome to attend any sports event on campus. The Vaqueros' football team plays in La Playa Stadium across from the beach.

SBCC also fields baseball and softball teams and has men's and women's golf, soccer, tennis, and volleyball teams. Tickets to all SBCC athletic events can be bought at the door or gate and are not available in advance.

UNIVERSITY OF CALIFORNIA AT SANTA BARBARA
Athletics Ticket Office
(805) 893-8272
www.ucsbgauchos.com
UCSB's Gauchos, who play in the Big West Conference, host a variety of sports events that are open to the public. The Lady Gau-chos basketball team won the Big West Con-ference regular season title for eight straight seasons and received the conference's

automatic NCAA Tournament bid for seven straight years.

The men's basketball team is blazing a trail to victory under coach Bob Williams as the 2002, 2010, and 2011 Big West Tourna-ment Champions and 1991, 2003, and 2008 Big West regular season champions. Join the Gauchos in the "Thunderdome," so named because the thousands of stomping feet during a tight game rumble like thunder.

UCSB almost always has great men's and women's volleyball teams. In the past, the men's team has ranked among the top five teams in the nation, and in 2011, it played for the NCAA Championship. Other spectator sports on campus include baseball, softball, swimming, soccer, tennis, track, and water polo. You can buy tickets to Gaucho games on the website or by calling the number above.

i For a chance to see some future major league baseball stars, check out a UCSB Gaucho game. More than a few players have been plucked from the team's ranks in major league drafts.

WESTMONT COLLEGE
955 La Paz Rd., Santa Barbara
(805) 565-6010 (athletics)
www.westmont.edu/sports
The Westmont Warriors invite the public to basketball, soccer, volleyball, tennis, and other spectator sports events played by its six men's and six women's teams. Part of the Golden State Athletic Conference, the War-riors have won 48 conference titles in the past 18 years. Westmont has also claimed seven NAIA national championships, includ-ing titles in women's soccer in 2001, 2002, and 2003. Westmont Field & Track won the women's marathon and NAIA Outdoor Track

and Field Championships in 2007. In addition, the men's basketball and soccer teams, plus the women's volleyball squad, have been highly ranked in recent years. When athletic events have an admission fee, tickets are sold at the gate or the door.

Polo

*SANTA BARBARA POLO AND
  RACQUET CLUB
3375 Foothill Rd., Carpinteria
(805) 684-6683
www.sbpolo.com

The public is invited to watch Sunday afternoon matches during the polo season, which runs from April through October. Matches are played at 1 and 3 p.m., and admission is $10 at the gate for adults (children under 12 are free). Food and beverage service is available, or you can bring your own picnic. Not only is the "sport of kings" exciting to watch, but the venue provides great people-watching, especially during special events such as the "Best Hat Day." You can pack a picnic and tailgate, purchase food at the Centennial Cafe, or if you know a member, partake in Sunday brunches or parties during the season. Be certain to wear comfortable shoes, as "divot stomping," a long-standing tradition of stomping the torn up turf at half time at this historic, century-old hallowed polo grounds, is all part of the fun.

GOLF

In a survey conducted by *Golf Digest,* golfers rated where they played as more important than how they played, which makes it clear why Santa Barbara is one the world's top destinations for golf. Over 6 public 18-hole courses, three 9-hole courses, and a variety of private courses in Santa Barbara provide for excellent golf accentuated by a backdrop of pristine natural beauty.

Tee off on one of Sandpiper Golf Course's six holes perched above the Pacific Ocean (now, there's a water trap!). This championship course was rated as one of the top 25 public courses in the country by *Golf Digest.* Or play on the Rivers Course in Solvang amid the caramel landscape dotted with dark green oaks.

Ty Warner has snapped up several of the courses in the last few years, which means only one thing: He'll continue his quest to take great things and make them even greater. His holdings now include the public Sandpiper Golf Course, Rancho San Marcos Golf Course, and Montecito Country Club.

Driving ranges abound in Santa Barbara. You'll discover them at Glen Annie, La Purisima, Rancho San Marcos, Alisal River Course, Sandpiper, Santa Barbara Golf Club, Tee Time Driving Range, and Twin Lakes.

Greens fees can be pricey, but discounts are offered during the week, later in the afternoon, or at one of the more affordable public courses. Note that all fees listed here include the use of a cart so you can save money if you walk the course. Most courses offer discounts to Santa Barbara residents and seasonal specials. Be sure to inquire when you call.

Now, pick up your bag and get ready to enjoy a day of golf. We'll provide the views and the excellent greens. The rest is up to you!

SANTA BARBARA

HIDDEN OAKS GOLF COURSE
4760 Calle Camarada, Santa Barbara
(805) 967-3493

This picturesque little 9-hole, 1,027-yard course is almost literally hidden in the oaks south of Hollister Avenue. Once a lemon orchard, Hidden Oaks is a rather hilly par 27, and you play the whole course with irons. This is a great little practice course, especially for chipping and putting. The longest hole is 173 yards. Fees are $12 on weekdays, $14 on weekends for adults. Students ages 18 to 24 and seniors are $9 on weekdays and $11 on weekends. Juniors ages 17 and under are $6 on weekdays and $7 on weekends. Monthly passes and 10-play discount cards are available. No electric carts are available, but you can rent a pull-cart if you wish. Hidden Oaks operates on a first come, first served basis. Note that credit cards are not accepted.

SANTA BARBARA GOLF CLUB
Las Positas
3500 McCaw Ave., Santa Barbara
(805) 687-7087
www.sbgolf.com

One of the most popular courses in town, the par-70, 18-hole Santa Barbara Golf Club is owned by the City of Santa Barbara. In addition to public golf, the 6,037-yard course offers many activities including leagues for men, women, and couples. The club also sponsors a junior golf program in conjunction with the city's Parks and Recreation Department. This course has been called the most affordable course of its quality in town, so it's definitely worth checking out. Also on-site are Mulligan's Cafe (with a banquet room), a putting green, and a 19-stall driving range with ocean views. Fees are posted online and there are discounted fees for county residents. Internet tee times are available from their website or call (805) 687-7087 to reserve a tee time. Soft spikes are required on the course. Reservations are recommended.

Nine-hole rounds are also an option. Golf carts are available.

GOLETA

GLEN ANNIE GOLF CLUB
405 Glen Annie Rd., Goleta
(805) 968-6400
www.glenanniegolf.com

An environmentally friendly course supporting habitats for endangered wildlife, the 6,420-yard, par-71 championship Glen Annie Golf Course was expertly designed by Damian Pascuzzo and Robert Muir Graves and is a local favorite. Snuggled into the foothills in west Goleta, it offers panoramic ocean and mountain views and exceptional personal service.

Your clubs are picked up when you arrive in the parking lot and are loaded into a cart, which will be ready to go when you reach the clubhouse. After you finish play, staff will whisk the clubs away and clean them for you.

Among the more challenging holes are the par-5 10th, which is the longest at 577 yards (uphill). A lake and 10-foot waterfall are visible on holes 4, 7, 8, and 18.

In addition to a pro shop, a grass driving range, and other amenities, the club boasts an excellent restaurant, the Frog Bar & Grill (see the Restaurants chapter).

Fees are $59 Monday through Friday ($41 for tri-county residents), $74 on weekends ($51 for tri-county residents). Proof of residency is required. Twilight rates represent a significant savings over regular greens fees. An annual pass is available with unlimited golf and preferred tee times for as little as $103 per month. Check out the discounted "Stay and Play," which lets you check into a hotel, play golf, and have the golf outing conveniently billed back to your hotel. The packages range from economy to higher-end hotels, such as the Fess Parker Doubletree Resort. Call for details.

OCEAN MEADOWS GOLF CLUB
6925 Whittier Dr., Goleta
(805) 968-6814

A 9-hole, par-36, 3,250-yard course that has been operating in Goleta for more than 30 years, Ocean Meadows offers one of the most affordable games in town, and you'll rarely have to wait for a tee time. There are 2 par-5 holes and 2 long par 3s, with water at the sides of most holes. Since the course borders Devereux Slough, you might even see some wildlife. Ocean Meadows has putting and chipping greens, and sand bunkers for practicing, and you can arrange a lesson if you want to improve your game. Fees are $20 on weekdays and $22 on weekends for 9 holes. Student, junior, and senior discounts are available, as are twilight rates of $24 for an entire day of play.

Duffers who live in Santa Barbara County receive resident discount rates by merely showing proof of address with their California driver's license or other form of ID at the golf course. Course discounts vary depending on time of day and day of the week. For current rates, go to www.sbgolf.com, where you can also access a fun, free YouTube golf lesson courtesy of Chris Talerico of the Santa Barbara Golf Club.

✳SANDPIPER GOLF CLUB
7925 Hollister Ave., Goleta
(805) 968-1541
www.sandpipergolf.com
Sandpiper provides an inspiring combination of challenge and beauty for championship golf situated at the edge of the Pacific Ocean with breathtaking ocean and mountain views from every hole. The championship golf course at Sandpiper has been rated by *Golf Digest* in the top 25 public golf courses in the country. It was designed by William F. Bell and opened in 1972 featuring beautiful rolling fairways and challenging greens in a seaside links-style layout.

Sandpiper's dynamic design attracts players of all skill levels including those of the highest caliber. Measuring over 7,000 yards with a championship rating of 74.5, Sandpiper has challenged the abilities of PGA and LPGA players alike, playing host to several professional tournaments including the PGA Tour Tournament Players Series, the LPGA Tour Santa Barbara Women's Open, and the prestigious final stage of the PGA Tour Qualifying School.

Sandpiper offers a full range of golf services that include an experienced and courteous staff, golf carts, driving range, practice putting greens, Titleist rental clubs, PGA instruction, and a well-stocked golf shop. Sandpiper combines a tradition of championship golf and spectacular surroundings to provide its visitors with something much more than a round of golf.

TWIN LAKES GOLF COURSE AND LEARNING CENTER
6034 Hollister Ave., Goleta
(805) 964-1414
www.twinlakesgolf.com
Twin Lakes, which sits near the bank of a Goleta creek, is a 9-hole, 1,501-yard executive course. It has several challenging holes with water and tight dogleg turns, and a mere slip of the wrist may put you out of bounds.

Twin Lakes boasts one of the best driving ranges in the greater Santa Barbara area, with 30 high-tech driving stations that are lighted at night. In fact, it is estimated that almost 50 percent of the golfers who come to Twin Lakes do so for instruction and practice.

Greens fees are very affordable—$12 on weekdays and $13.50 on weekends. Cart rental is an additional $6 per person. This is an Insiders' favorite for hitting a bucket of balls.

CARPINTERIA

Carpinteria doesn't have a golf course, but its **Tee Time Driving Range,** at 5885 Carpinteria Ave. (805-566-9948), is open for practice from 8 a.m. to dusk daily. The lighted range includes sand traps and putting greens, so you can practice all your skills. Golf lessons are also available. Fees are $12 per hour, $18 for an hour and a half, and $24 for all day. There are discounts for seniors (60 and older) and juniors (11 to 18 years old) of $20 for all day and $10 an hour. Kids accompanied by an adult get free admission, and even Fido is welcome here!

OVER THE PASS

LA PURISIMA GOLF COURSE
3455 CA 246, Lompoc
(805) 735-8395
www.lapurisimagolf.com
Dubbed by *Golf Digest* as the 33rd-toughest course in America, this 18-hole, championship 7,105-yard course is one to be reckoned with. Not only is it difficult, but it was also rated at 4.5 stars by *Golf Digest* and voted "Best Value" and "Best Conditioned" course by Southern California golfers.

A picturesque 45-minute drive from downtown Santa Barbara, La Purisima was designed by renowned architects Robert Muir Graves and Kenneth Hume Hunter Jr. What began as 300 acres became an architecturally landscaped course that continues to draw rave reviews and attention.

Beginners needn't sweat. Even though the course is challenging, it's also accessible and rewarding for novices. Call for fees and details about the Golf Getaway packages, with golf and hotel stays given at a discounted price.

RANCHO SAN MARCOS GOLF COURSE
4600 CA 154, Santa Barbara
(805) 683-6334, (877) 776-1804
www.rsm1804.com
Previously rated as one of the top 10 courses in California by *Golf* magazine, the original 18-hole, 6,817-yard championship course was designed by renowned golf architect

Robert Trent Jones Jr. More than 1,700 valley oaks dot the course, many of them two centuries old.

An already excellent course has been renovated into an outstanding one. Changes include: the reestablishment of greens and bunkers on Hole #1, new green and bunkers at Hole #3, refurbishment of all bunkers, new bunkers at fairways #17 and #11, new target greens on the practice range, opened up sight line on fairway #18 and hole #15, and a new cart path and bridge from green #3 to tee #4. Perhaps best of all, Rancho now serves cold beer and wine at Davy's Stable Cafe.

RIVER COURSE AT THE ALISAL
150 Alisal Rd., Solvang
(805) 688-6042
www.rivercourse.com
The soft caramel yellows and the deep oak greens of the valley and the Santa Ynez Mountains create a stunning vista for the River Course, which features four lakes and, for the most part, follows the path of the Santa Ynez River. The 6,830-yard championship 18-hole course (rated 73.1) is a local favorite.

Although the course is challenging, it isn't unforgiving, except maybe at the 7th hole, known for its multiple challenges. You can easily sink your ball into a vineyard, bounce it off a tree, or land it in the lake.

The Monday through Friday rates are $60, and $72 for Saturday and Sunday; seniors and students are afforded generous discounts, and twilight play after 2:30 p.m. offers discounts, too.

The River Course is part of the striking Alisal Guest Ranch, known as a destination resort getaway. Horseback riding, tennis, and fly fishing can be added to your menu of weekend activities.

FISHING

Santa Barbara has some great spots to cast a line. While it may not compare with some of the more famous sportfishing areas of the world, such as Cabo San Lucas or the Florida Keys, there are still plenty of fish in the sea as well as in freshwater streams and artificial lakes.

Santa Barbara has always been blessed with an abundance of fish, mollusks, crustaceans, and other forms of marine life. The Chumash Indians found fish aplenty in the channel, rivers, and creeks, and for more than a century, successful commercial fishing enterprises have supplied residents and restaurants with a wide range of tasty bounty. In fact, there's a fresh seafood market down at our harbor and a Saturday morning fresh market as well.

Given this bounty, angling is a cherished local pastime. You can cast your line from a party boat near the islands, off the Breakwater, into the surf, or beneath the calm waters of Cachuma Lake. Even if you don't catch "the big one," you can at least enjoy a few relaxing hours surrounded by incredibly beautiful scenery.

A CHANNEL FULL OF SURPRISES

Santa Barbara County is the northern part of what's called the Southern California Bight. From Point Conception about 50 miles to Ventura, the coastline stretches east–west rather than following the north–south orientation that dominates the rest of the California coast.

About 25 miles off the coast lie the Santa Barbara Channel Islands, which also stretch from east to west. This unusual orientation has created the Santa Barbara Channel, an area often protected from the larger ocean swells of the open Pacific.

The channel is a crossroads where cold water masses from the north converge with warmer masses from the south. North of Point Conception, the water is cold most of the year because the prevailing northwest

winds cause an upwelling of water. South of the point, ocean waters gradually warm, although Santa Barbara waters are cool most of the year.

As the channel waters warm and cool with the seasons, game fish from the north and south migrate in and out of the area, resulting in an incredible diversity of species. At certain times of year, for example, you might catch warm-water barracuda and cold-water king salmon on the same day. This is one of the only places in California where you'll find such a mix.

USEFUL GUIDES

Pick up a free copy of the California Department of Fish and Game's *Guide to Ocean*

Sportfishing in Santa Barbara and Ventura Counties. This clear, easy-to-read booklet is useful for any angler, but it especially targets novices and people who are unfamiliar with channel resources. It gives a general description of popular fishing sites, catch species, and fishing techniques. You can also pick up the *Guide to California Marine Fish Identification.* These guides are available at the Department of Fish and Game's office at 1933 Cliff Dr., Ste. 9, Santa Barbara (805-568-1231), and you can access a PDF version of them at www.dfg.ca.gov.

FISHING LICENSES & REGULATIONS

Anyone 16 or older needs a sportfishing license to take any fish, including mollusks and crustaceans, from California waters. However, you do not need a license to take fish from a public pier. Everyone must adhere to catch and season restrictions and size limits. Ask for a current list of regulations when you buy your license.

FISHING LICENSES

- **Annual:** $43.46 for residents, $116.90 for nonresidents
- **10-day nonresident sportfishing:** $43.46 (valid for 10 consecutive days from purchase date)
- **1-day sportfishing:** $14.04 for residents and nonresidents (valid for fishing in both inland and ocean waters)
- **2-day sportfishing:** $21.86 for residents and nonresidents (valid for fishing in both inland and ocean waters)

By state law, you must display your valid sportfishing license by attaching it to your outer clothing at or above the waistline so that it is plainly visible. If you're diving from a boat or shore, you may leave your license on the boat or within 500 yards of shore. Don't be caught fishing without a license. The fine is expensive. Many hundreds of dollars, we hear. Licenses can be obtained at authorized bait and tackle stores, most sporting goods stores, SEA Landing and Harbor Tackle at the harbor, and most county and state campgrounds.

The *California Sport Fishing Regulations* book provides details on the seasons, limits, and sizes allowed for each fish species. You should also ask about any supplements to this manual, as the state often issues periodic updates to be used in combination with the larger publication. Both books and supplements are available at bait and tackle shops and sportfishing enterprises.

For more information regarding regulations and licenses, call or write the California Department of Fish and Game, 1933 Cliff Dr., Ste. 9, Santa Barbara (805-568-1231). Better still, visit the website at www.dfg.ca.gov.

WHERE TO FISH

To help you become more familiar with the different places you can fish around Santa Barbara, we've divided this section into five areas: the Coast, the Islands, Pier Fishing, Surf Fishing, and Freshwater Fishing.

The Coast

The three main habitats along the Santa Barbara coast are the kelp beds, sandy bays and beaches, and open waters up to several miles from shore.

The main characteristic of our coastal waters is the presence of giant kelp (actually an algae) that grows in waters from 20 to 80 feet deep. Although rooted mainly to rocky bottoms, kelp can take root in soft bottoms in the more protected regions of the coastline.

Giant kelp can create dense underwater forests that provide shelter for a variety of marine life. The tops of the kelp canopies look like glassy brown patches spread along the surface of the water. While a source of many catches for anglers, kelp beds can also be a huge source of frustration. Lines often get tangled and break in the rubbery strands.

Stretches of sandy beaches break up the kelp beds along the coastline, giving you a chance to troll freely for bottom species. Open waters generally encompass areas up to several miles offshore and provide an ideal home for pelagic species.

i The weather in the channel often turns nasty in the afternoon, when the winds pick up. Be sure to tune in to your weather radio or the Weather Channel (46 on the local Santa Barbara cable system) to get the latest forecast, especially if you're going out in a private boat.

In the kelp beds, the kelp (or calico) bass reigns as king of the coast. They are generally found in dense kelp beds but also make their home in rocky reefs. You can catch calicos many ways; the most common is casting with scampi lures or live anchovies. Calicos are present just about any time of year but seem to be most active during summer and fall months.

Other edible species you can catch in the kelp bed areas include cabezon, sheepshead, a variety of rock fish, sculpin, and lingcod. The prime season to catch each species varies, but most are generally available year-round.

The California halibut is probably the most sought-after prize in Santa Barbara coastal waters. This flat fish tends to dwell on wide expanses of sandy bottoms, but you can also find it on sand patches in kelp forests. Although fish in excess of 40 pounds (18 kilograms) have been taken, large halibuts these days average about 25 pounds (11 kilograms). The sweet, flaky flesh of this hard-fighting fish makes for excellent dining.

To maximize your chance of catching halibut, you should troll on the bottom with a salmon-type rig—a large flasher baited with an anchovy and weighted with a 1- to 2-pound sinker. Drifting and casting with a small flasher and anchovy or live anchovy can also produce a good catch. The best time of year to catch halibut is during the spring and summer, when the water warms and the fish begin to spawn.

Other fish inhabiting the sandy coastlines include barred sand bass, corbina, and barred surf perch.

In the open waters offshore, you can catch pelagic species. One of the most popular is the Pacific bonito, but its numbers have seriously declined in recent years. You can catch it on live anchovy or by trolling a variety of lures, including green gobblers or "Cojo" flies.

Although smaller than its Atlantic cousin, the California barracuda still puts up a good fight and can weigh up to 15 pounds. You'll have the best luck catching this fish with live anchovies, but you can also achieve success by trolling with a bright lure. The peak season for most pelagic species is during the summer and early fall.

Every few years during the spring, migrating salmon can be found in the waters off the Santa Barbara area. King and silver salmon are the two most common species.

These elusive fish usually appear when the local water is coldest. When a salmon run arrives, Santa Barbaran anglers hit the water en masse.

About the only way to catch these fish locally is to use a salmon rig with a flasher and a 1- to 2-pound weight with a quick release and baited with an anchovy. The slow troll required for salmon fishing can be extremely boring, but the rewards are more than worth the effort.

Occasionally during summers with very warm water temperatures, such as those produced by El Niño, tropical species can visit the coast of Santa Barbara. The most consistent visitor of this group is the yellowtail, a member of the jack family. It's the sign of a landmark season when anglers can catch these prized fish within several miles of the coastline. Yellowtail range from 10 to 30 pounds, but the larger ones can reach a weight of 45 pounds (20 kilograms) or more.

The preferred areas for yellowtail fishing include the offshore oil rigs near Naples reef (west of Santa Barbara) and Carpinteria. Use live bait, such as squid, mackerel, or anchovy, for the best shot at catching these fish. However, you can also catch them by trolling white feathers and larger lures that look like mackerels.

The Islands

Before you head out to the islands, you need to know about the marine reserves. A new ruling establishes 110.5 square nautical miles as marine reserves and 1.7 nautical miles of marine conservation. If you're caught fishing in one of these reserves, you can be fined a hefty sum, so we recommend you contact the Department of Fish and Game (805-568-1231; www.dfg.ca.gov) or visit the Channel Island Marine Sanctuary Website at www .cinms.nos.noaa.gov/marinere/mail.html for a map of restricted areas before you venture out on your own. That said, you'll still find plenty of fruitful fishing areas around the islands. Best of all, the "spillover" effect from the new reserves should help boost fish populations in other areas of the channel.

Four islands in the Santa Barbara Channel Island group run in an east–west chain about 25 miles offshore from the Santa Barbara coast: Anacapa, Santa Cruz, Santa Rosa, and San Miguel. In general, these islands offer better fishing than along the mainland due largely to the diversity of habitats and lower fishing impact. This windswept region of rock and water is famous for bottom fishing, and anglers routinely come home with a gunnysack full of fish.

Species include several types of rockfish. The most popular species include the vermilion rockfish or red snapper (the meat and potatoes of island fishing), lingcod, ocean whitefish, cabezon, sheepshead, and sculpin. It's not uncommon to see anglers reel up a rock cod rig of six hooks from the depths with a fish on each hook.

The peak season for bottom fishing is usually during the winter months, but any time of the year can be fruitful. Halibut fishing along some of the sandy stretches of the islands during the warmer months can produce trophy-size fish.

i **Thresher shark is a popular game fish. Tinker's in Summerland has shark burgers on the menu if you want to try this tasty treat from our waters.**

If you don't have your own boat, the only regular, full-time private charter to access the islands from Santa Barbara Harbor is aboard Captain David Bacon's custom sport fisher

WaveWalker (805-964-2046; 805-895-3273; www.wavewalker.com). There are a few part-timers that can be found via the Internet. Costs range from $1,020 (full day) to $840 (three-quarters of a day; includes 20 percent gratuity to the crew) and $660 per half day. All rods and tackle provided.

However, be prepared for cold temperatures and rough seas, as the exposed outer channel is typically much windier than the coastal waters.

Pier Fishing

The traditional roots of most local anglers are in pier fishing. You can cast a line off Stearns Wharf or the Breakwater at the Santa Barbara Harbor. Licenses are not required unless you step out onto the sand and/or use live bait. You can also pier fish at Goleta and Gaviota Beaches, about 10 and 30 miles west of Santa Barbara, respectively. Both piers lie on sandy bottoms.

Off the pier, you're most likely to reel in barred surf perch, with a sprinkling of halibut, mackerel, jack smelt, white croaker, yellowfin, and spotfin croaker.

Surf Fishing

Casting from shore is a popular form of fishing, both at sandy beaches and rocky coastlines. Some of the best sandy beaches for surf fishing include Goleta, Jalama, and Gaviota Beaches, and Carpinteria.

The main catches at these beaches are barred surf perch and an occasional halibut. You can also catch cabezon in the rough waters of Jalama and the scrumptious corbina (whose northern range is Santa Barbara) in Carpinteria. The best bait for these fish varies, but sand crabs, which can be dug from these beaches, usually bring the most

success. Fly fishermen are an increasingly common site along the beaches in Santa Barbara and Carpinteria. If you want to try your luck with a fly line, you'll find that surf perch, halibut, yellowfin croaker, and corbina are especially partial to clouser minnow flies, sand crab imitations, and surf rat flies.

The rocky coastlines in the region can offer some profitable fishing for rockfish, calico bass, and cabezon. The reefy areas near Gaviota and Goleta, about 10 miles west of Santa Barbara, are prime spots. Many of the fishing techniques used for kelp beds apply here.

> **i** For local saltwater fly-fishing information, surf-fishing clinics, and monthly fishing reports, check out the website of fly-fishing guide Gary Bulla at www.garybulla.com. You can also purchase flies specially designed to lure local species on the site.

California grunion ranks as one of the wonders of the Southern California marine world. This member of the silversides family has the unique habit of coming ashore through the surf onto sandy beaches to mate and bury its eggs. Between March and September, these fish spawn 3 or 4 nights following each full or new moon and then for a 1- to 3-hour period immediately after high tide.

Females swim onto the beach and dig themselves into the sand to lay their eggs, while males flop next to them and fertilize the eggs. They achieve all this in a matter of seconds, then ride back into the ocean in a passing wave.

Grunion fishing (or hunting, as many locals call it) has been equated to snipe hunting, as a person can search for a lifetime and never experience this amazing phenomenon. Many people claim that the whole thing is really a hoax. In reality, grunion running does occur, but mainly on the darkest nights and on the darkest beaches away from human development.

In the Santa Barbara region, the best places to see grunion runs are Goleta Beach and beaches in the Carpinteria area. It is legal to take grunion by hand. However, just seeing a grunion run is reward enough for most people, as very few can truthfully say that they've seen this remarkable quirk of nature.

Freshwater Fishing

Drive 35 miles northwest of Santa Barbara and you'll come across **Cachuma Lake** (805-686-5054; www.countyofsb.org/parks)—the best freshwater fishing area in the county and one of the best bass-fishing lakes in Southern California. Cachuma was created when the Bradbury Dam was built in the 1950s on the Santa Ynez River.

Surrounded by the Santa Ynez Mountains, the lake offers spectacular scenery as well as great fishing. On the shores you can spot many types of wildlife, from mountain lions, mule deer, and endangered pond turtles to osprey, kingfishers, and golden eagles. At certain times of year, you can also view a pair of resident as well as migratory American bald eagles and their offspring.

The lake water provides plenty of action for serious and not-so-serious anglers. Here you can find trout, small- and largemouth bass, catfish, bluegill, crappie, and redear perch. The lake is stocked with trout from October through April. Approximately 70,000 rainbow trout are planted annually. Licenses, bait, and tackle are available at the marina along with fish-cleaning stations. You

can also rent a boat or kayak by the hour or day (see the Charter & Party Boats section).

If you're into stream trout fishing, you'll find a few opportunities at the Los Padres National Forest north of Santa Barbara. The main fishery is in the Santa Ynez River above Cachuma Lake, where trout are stocked occasionally during the cooler months of the year. Other smaller streams in the backcountry offer small trout, but expect to hike a long distance to reach many of the more productive areas.

All forms of fishing appear to result in some success, for example, using flies, spinners, and natural baits. A small steelhead trout fishery once existed below Bradbury Dam on the Santa Ynez River, which created Cachuma Lake. Due to dwindling numbers, however, no fishing is permitted on any rivers from Bradbury Dam to the ocean. That means no casting for any species, and steelhead are listed as an endangered species—so hands off!

Although Lake Casitas in Ventura County lies outside the geographic region covered in this book (it's about 20 miles east of Santa Barbara), it merits mention because it's one of the best spots in California for catching trophy-size largemouth bass. It's also a great place for trout, catfish, bluegill, crappie, and redear perch. Call the Lake Casitas Marine Bait & Tackle Shop at the lake for more information, (805) 649-2043.

CHARTER & PARTY BOATS

If you want to fish the coastal waters and don't have access to a private boat—or you just want the luxury of having someone else do the driving—Santa Barbara offers the party/charter boat *Stardust* (805) 963-3564 and the charter sport fisher *WaveWalker*.

If money is no object, the *Channel Cat,* a luxury catamaran owned by Charlie Munger, can be chartered for private occasions. For info, go to www.channelcatcharters.com or phone (805) 455-4228.

Santa Barbara

STARDUST
SEA Landing
301 W. Cabrillo Blvd., Santa Barbara
(805) 963-3564
www.stardustsportfishing.com
Depending on the time of year, the 65-foot *Stardust* offers half-day, three-quarter day, and twilight deep-sea fishing trips. From Mon through Thurs half-day trips are from 9 a.m. to 3 p.m., Fri and Sun three-quarter day trips are from 7 a.m. to 4 p.m. Two Sat half-day trips happen from 7 a.m. to noon and 12:30 p.m. to 5:30 p.m. Twilight trips occur early June to late Aug from 6 to 9:30 p.m. On board, you'll find a custom sundeck and a galley serving breakfast, lunch, and beverages—including beer. Prices vary from $50 for adults and $41 for children under 12 on a half-day trip to $72 for adults and $60 for children on a three-quarter day trip. Twilight trips are $40 for adults and $30 for children. Senior and children rates are available on weekdays only. Rod and tackle rental is available, and you can also charter the *Stardust* for group fishing trips.

WAVEWALKER CHARTERS
Marina 3 Gate at the harbor,
Santa Barbara
(805) 964-2046 home
(805) 895-3273 cellular phone
www.wavewalker.com
Seasoned skipper and writer Captain David Bacon and his custom Grady-White sport fisher *WaveWalker* are available for charter

for small groups of four to six passengers. The cost ranges from $1,020 (full day) and $840 (three-quarter day; includes 20 percent gratuity to the crew) to $660 for half day.

i Tide books are available free at all local tackle shops and many other stores in Santa Barbara.

Cachuma Lake

CACHUMA BOAT RENTALS
Cachuma Lake Marina
(805) 688-4040
If you're planning to fish at Cachuma Lake, you can rent boats and kayaks right at the marina. Motorboat rates range from $45 an hour for a four-passenger, 6-horsepower boat to $120 for a full-day rental of a six-passenger, 9.9-horsepower boat. Boats without motors are $30 an hour. Patio deck boats start at $110 an hour for a 10-passenger, 25-horsepower boat to $288 for a full day on a 14-passenger boat.

BAIT & TACKLE SHOPS

You can find bait and tackle shops near any of the piers, at the harbor, at charter boat landings, and at Cachuma Lake and Lake Casitas—here are three of the more popular ones in town.

ANGEL'S BAIT & TACKLE
230B Stearns Wharf, Santa Barbara
(805) 965-1333
Conveniently located right on Stearns Wharf, Angel's sells salt- and freshwater tackle, live bait, and cold drinks and snacks. You can also rent fishing rods here. Once you've caught the "big one," you can bring your fish to Angel's for filleting and vacuum sealing.

FISHING

HOOK, LINE AND SINKER
4010 Calle Real, #5, Santa Barbara
(805) 687-5689
Hook, Line and Sinker is regularly named "Best Bait and Tackle Shop in Santa Barbara" in local media polls. It's conveniently situated near the intersection of State Street and CA 154, which is right on the way to Cachuma Lake.

SEA LANDING
301 W. Cabrillo Blvd., Santa Barbara
(805) 963-3564
www.sealanding.net
Heading out for some saltwater fishing? The SEA Landing has everything you need and is open Mon through Thurs 7:30 a.m. to 6:30 p.m., and Fri through Sun from 6 a.m. to 6:30 p.m.

BEACHES & WATERSPORTS

When you think of Santa Barbara, the first thing that probably comes to mind is "beach." For most residents, the beaches, bluffs, and the blue channel waters provide both recreational and spiritual rejuvenation. We take long walks, sunbathe, frolic, relax, and pursue our favorite watersports, which run the gamut from boating to surfing to paddle surfing.

However, there is a slightly less-than-perfect side to our waters you should probably know about before you plunge into the ocean. The water temperatures are not like those off the shores of the Hawaiian Islands or Mexico, where they average in the upper 70s (20s Celsius). During the summer months, water temperatures here tend to be in the mid-to-high 60s (teens Celsius). During the winter months, they drop about 10 degrees to the mid-50s (teens Celsius). In fact September is about the best month to test the waters around here. You won't see your feet here, like other vacation waters in the Caribbean or Kauai either. Many people wear wet suits or surf shirts so they can stay in the water for hours. Some hardy souls, however, dive and dip without any extra coverage every month of the year.

Only the bravest take part in the annual Polar Beach swim in the winter, and they are no spring chickens. If you find the water a bit cold for your taste, just remember that these very temperatures are what allow for the incredible diversity of marine life in the channel.

OVERVIEW

Here's an overview of where you can go and what you can do in, on, under, over, and next to the water. From our most popular beaches and places to rent or buy beach equipment to the area's major watersports, listed alphabetically, we have covered boating (including sailing), boat excursions/sightseeing, diving and snorkeling, kayaking, Jet-Skiing, kiteboarding, parasailing, whale-watching, surfing, and the popular paddle surfing.

If you're visiting between February and the end of April, you might want to check out the Whale-Watching section of this chapter right away. Don't miss the chance to view one of nature's most amazing events—the annual gray whale migration. Blue whales, humpback whales, and other types of marine mammals traverse our channel year-round.

Whatever time of year you're here, our beaches and waters beckon you to enjoy and explore. Even a solitary walk, on a chilly, windy winter day, can soothe the soul.

PARKING

Before you set out on your waterfront adventures, you have to actually get to the beaches and watersports within the Santa Barbara city limits. Which means you must find parking. Looking for a vacant, affordable spot can be a real frustration during the summer and on busy holiday weekends. Here are a few pointers. The city operates a number of parking lots along the beach side of Cabrillo Boulevard: near East Beach, Chase Palm Park, Garden Street, at the harbor, and at Leadbetter Beach. Although these lots are extremely convenient (who wants to cross Cabrillo Boulevard with beach equipment and children in tow?), they can also be expensive if you park there for more than a few hours.

i   **If you're headed out for a whale-watching or fishing trip from SEA Landing, ask for a parking validation when checking in for the trip, and you'll score free parking in the harbor lot.**

On off-season weekdays (November through April) you can park for free in the lots at Leadbetter, Garden Street, and Chase Palm Park. But from May through September, during holiday seasons, and on weekends you will have to pay an hourly or day rate. In the Cabrillo East, Cabrillo West, and Harbor West lots, the honor system applies year-round and parking fees are slightly cheaper. Look for the signs directing you to the collection boxes and drop your fee in the one that corresponds with your parking stall. The harbor lot is open 24 hours, so if you need to leave your car overnight while you're out on a boat, you don't have to worry. The Harbor Patrol cruises the lot regularly.

If you're going to be here for a while, we recommend buying an annual parking permit, which allows you to park free at any of the beachfront city lots except on Stearns Wharf. The permit (a sticker that goes on your windshield) costs $80 a year and is valid from January through December. Buy your permit on December 1 when they go on sale, and it will be valid for 13 months of parking. Buy it midway through the year and the fee will be prorated. They're available from the kiosks at the parking lot entrances or at the Harbor Patrol Office above the Chandlery on the harbor front. For waterfront parking information, call (805) 564-5523 or (805) 897-1965.

BEACHES

The Santa Barbara coastline stretches more than 50 miles between Gaviota and Carpinteria, with many excellent beaches all along the way. Some are ideal for a family day at the beach—they have full facilities, including restrooms, playgrounds, restaurants, snack bars, and showers. Others have no facilities but boast great tide pools, perfect surfing waves, and wide stretches of sand for sunbathing.

Even if the weather isn't conducive to sunbathing, our beaches can be fantastic places to enjoy the natural surroundings. Here we describe most of our favorite beaches. A few others are not listed because they have very limited parking in residential areas and/or difficult-to-explain access by trails or paths through private property. Besides, you can reach most of these "secret" beaches by walking from the beaches described here at low tide.

Lifeguards are on duty at East, West, and Leadbetter Beaches daily from Memorial Day weekend (or mid-June) through Labor Day weekend and on weekends during spring and fall. They are also on duty other weekends in May and September and sometimes in October if warm weather prevails. If lifeguards are not available at a beach, we've noted it in the description.

Please keep a few rules in mind during your day at the beach. Bottles are not allowed on Santa Barbara city beaches (cans are fine). The same goes for open fires and burying coals. Smoking is also a no-no. Use the designated barbecue pits if the beach has them. Dogs are not allowed at all on most city beaches, which includes East Beach, West Beach, and Leadbetter Beach. Nor are they allowed on the beaches in the state parks including El Capitán, Gaviota, and Refugio Beaches. However, you can walk your dog on a county beach, as long as it's on a leash. Dogs are also allowed off leash east of the slough at Arroyo Burro Beach Park.

With that said, we wish you many happy hours in the surf, sand, and sun!

Santa Barbara

**ARROYO BURRO BEACH PARK
(HENDRY'S BEACH)
2981 Cliff Dr., Santa Barbara
(805) 687-3714
www.countyofsb.org/parks**
Most Insiders call this popular beach "Hendry's Beach." It stretches beneath the bluffs of Hope Ranch and continues for nearly 2 miles west toward Goleta and a short way east toward the Mesa. It's a great place to surf, sailboard, fish from the shore, watch dolphins swim by, and look at tide pools. From February through May you might also spot some gray whales passing by (bring your binoculars).

At low tide you can walk or run as far as Goleta Beach Park to the west and Shoreline Park to the east. At high tide, especially during the winter, you might not be able to walk as far, but the views are still wonderful. You're allowed to walk dogs here off leash east of the slough as long as you keep your pet within voice control range. At all other areas, dogs must be leashed. Lifeguards are on duty every day from mid-June through Labor Day.

Arroyo Burro has restrooms, outdoor showers, public telephones, and a grassy area with picnic tables. The Boathouse offers beachside seating, ocean views, good food, and a lively bar with a great happy hour. It serves breakfast, lunch, and dinner and a popular Sunday brunch inside or on the patio. The beach parking lot lies about a half-block west of the Cliff Drive/Las Positas Road intersection.

**EAST BEACH
E. Cabrillo Boulevard, Santa Barbara
(805) 897-1983
www.sbparksandrecreation.com**
East Beach, with a wide swath of glorious sand that stretches from Chase Palm Park toward the Bird Refuge and numerous facilities, is another popular beach that has been cited as one of the best beaches in the nation, probably due to the volleyball players and "volley belles" in their bikinis. Unfortunately, East Beach often scores high for bacteria counts, so make sure you check the beach status report before you go swimming. Call the Beach Hotline at (805) 681-4949, or visit www.sbcphd.org.

Volleyball courts dominate the east end of the beach. This is where world-renowned beach volleyball champ Karch Kiraly (a native son) practiced and played for years. Big-time beach volleyball tournaments often take place here, although less so now than in the past.

At the East Beach Bathhouse (beneath the Cabrillo Arts Pavilion) you'll find public restrooms, cold-water outdoor showers, lockers, a weight room, equipment rentals (chairs, umbrellas, volleyballs, beach-friendly wheelchairs, etc.), and East Beach Grill, a casual restaurant/snack bar (see the Best Breakfasts Close-up in the Restaurants chapter). The beach also has a large picnic ground and playground. There's virtually no surfing here, but sometimes you can enjoy decent boogie-boarding.

i For beach status reports, call the Santa Barbara County Environmental Health Services Beach Hotline at (805) 681-4949 or check the website at www.countyofsb.org/phd. To be safe, try to avoid contact with ocean and creek water for at least 3 days after a storm, when runoff pollutes the water.

LEADBETTER BEACH
Shoreline Drive at Loma Alta Drive, Santa Barbara
(805) 897-2680
www.sbparksandrecreation.com
"Leds" is a fantastic family beach tucked between the harbor and Shoreline Park. The waves are usually small except at the point near Shoreline Park, where beginner and intermediate surfers and boogie boarders can usually count on catching some rides. When the breeze picks up, it's great fun watching the colorful sailboards, catamarans, and sailboats whiz by.

Volleyball courts, restrooms, outdoor showers, and a grassy expanse with family picnic areas and barbecues are all available

here. You can enjoy breakfast, lunch, dinner, and drinks at the Shoreline Beach Cafe with your toes in the sand. Park in the city lot right at the beach.

WEST BEACH
W. Cabrillo Boulevard, Santa Barbara
(805) 897-2680
www.sbparksandrecreation.com
If you walk directly west on the sand from Stearns Wharf toward the marina, you'll be treading across West Beach. This small, quiet expanse has hardly any waves (it's at the entrance to the harbor) and is ideal for swimming and watching the boats cruise in and out of the harbor. Several kayak rental outfits park themselves on West Beach during the summer (see the Kayaking section of this chapter for information).

If the kids get tired of the beach, they can head over to the nearby playground and wading pool (open in the summer only) next to the Los Baños del Mar Pool. Park in the harbor parking lot and walk toward Stearns Wharf to reach the beach.

West of Goleta

The following three state beaches are just off US 101 near Gaviota. They all have camping facilities and are very popular. Day-use parking fee is $8. See the Camping section of the Recreation chapter for camping information.

EL CAPITÁN STATE BEACH
Off US 101, 17 miles west of Santa Barbara
(805) 968-1033
www.parks.ca.gov
El Capitán was once the site of an extensive Chumash village, and it's easy to see why the Chumash chose to live in this area for so long. This is one of our all-time favorite

beaches. At "El Cap" you can spend many hours exploring rocky tide pools, spotting sea lions and seals, and relaxing on the beach. The stands of sycamore and oak trees form a beautiful backdrop for swimming, fishing, surfing, and walking. From February through May you might even spot the gray whales swimming close to shore.

You can hike the nature trails in the adjacent park, and if you walk or ride a bike just 2.5 miles west, you'll arrive at Refugio State Beach. If you wander off the trail at designated places, you'll find public accesses to the beach that are relatively unused.

GAVIOTA STATE PARK
Off US 101, 33 miles north of Santa Barbara
(805) 968-1033
www.parks.ca.gov
This huge, 2,700-acre park lies close to where the coastline turns north at Point Conception. It has a cove at the mouth of a creek where you can fish, swim, and picnic. You can also fish off the pier or hike up to Gaviota Hot Springs. Facilities include food service, restrooms, and picnic areas. (See the Parks chapter for more details.)

REFUGIO STATE BEACH
Off US 101, 23 miles west of Santa Barbara
(805) 968-1033
www.parks.ca.gov
If you saw a picture of Refugio, you might think it was a tropical beach on a Hawaiian island because of the many palm trees planted along the beach and camping area. The beach stretches for 1.5 miles along the coast, next to a 39-acre park. It's a great place for picnicking, diving, swimming, snorkeling, and exploring nature trails. Refugio lies just 2

miles west of El Capitán State Beach—a bike trail along the bluff connects the two.

Goleta

GOLETA BEACH COUNTY PARK
5986 Sandspit Rd., Goleta
(805) 967-1300
www.countyofsb.org/parks
This 29-acre county park has long been a favorite destination for families and UCSB students. A palm-lined grassy expanse fronts the mile-long sandy beach. Waves tend to be small here, which makes the beach ideal for children and beginning surfers. You can fish off the pier (no license necessary), play volleyball on a court in the sand, and toss horseshoes in a designated area. Children can romp in the playground.

The park also has picnic facilities, barbecue areas, pay phones, dressing rooms, restrooms, and a snack bar. The Beachside Bar-Cafe serves lunch and dinner and drinks daily.

To reach the park, take the Ward Memorial Freeway from US 101 toward UCSB. You'll see the Goleta Beach exit just before you get to campus. Park in the free parking lot at the beach.

i Keep our beaches and ocean healthy. The beaches that allow dogs have biodegradable doggy-poop bags free from kiosk dispensers, thanks to Heal the Ocean, a local nonprofit dedicated to safe ocean waters.

Montecito

BUTTERFLY BEACH
End of Butterfly Lane, Montecito
(805) 568-2460

Butterfly Beach is one of the few west-facing beaches, and it lies across the street from the posh Four Seasons Resort The Biltmore Santa Barbara. If you're hoping to run into celebrities, you have a fairly good chance here. This is where many Montecito residents take beach walks because it's one of the only places along the shore where you're allowed to walk your dog.

Lots of celebrities also stay at the Four Seasons and head to the beach for a few moments of R&R. It's a great beach for swimming and sunbathing, and when the tide is low, you can walk to East Beach. You won't find any facilities here, but the Coast Village Road shopping area is just a few blocks away. If you do spot a celebrity, we recommend you do what Insiders do—leave him or her alone.

Summerland

SUMMERLAND BEACH
Lookout Park
2297 Finney Rd., Summerland
(805) 568-2460
www.sbparks.org
Summerland Beach is quiet and clean and a great place for families to spend the day. Lookout Park sits on the bluffs above the beach. There you'll find picnic tables, barbecue areas, restrooms, telephones, a volleyball court, and a playground. Walk down the steep, asphalt path from the parking lot to reach the sand, where you can swim, sunbathe, and stroll along the shore. However, be forewarned: There is natural tar on the beach here, and you will need baby or vegetable oil to remove it, and in recent years, efforts have been underway to deal with what appears to be oil leaking from capped wells that have become compromised over time. Take the Evans Avenue exit from US 101

and head toward the ocean. You'll dead-end into the free parking lot, which closes at dusk.

> **i** Remember, all "private" beaches are public below the mean tide line. You're free to be there, as long as you don't trespass on residents' property. Use the legal access trails to get there.

Carpinteria

CARPINTERIA CITY BEACH
End of Linden Avenue, Carpinteria
(805) 684-5405
www.carpinteria.ca.us
The City of Carpinteria's beach is very popular with families, since it was once billed as the "world's safest beach." Protected by a natural reef breakwater, the beachfront waters are ideal for swimming, bodysurfing, and boogie-boarding. One word of caution: Stingrays also love this area—especially where Franklin Creek meets the beach—so be sure to shuffle your feet when wading along the shore toward Sandy Point; this scares them away. You can rent bikes, kayaks, and other equipment, buy snacks and lunch at the snack bar, and play volleyball on one of the beach courts.

CARPINTERIA STATE BEACH
Linden Avenue and 6th Street,
Carpinteria
(805) 968-1033
www.parks.ca.gov
Nearly 800,000 visitors trek to this 48-acre beach park every year to enjoy the glistening sands, tide pools, and campgrounds. You'll find day-use and camping facilities here (restrooms, picnic areas, and telephones) and a visitor center with natural history exhibits and nature programs.

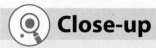

Close-up

The Gaviota Coast & Naples

Most people who visit Santa Barbara do the "downtown thing" or luxuriate in Montecito or maybe even visit Santa Barbara wine country. By not slowing down along one artery that links Santa Barbara to the Santa Ynez Valley, they may be missing one of the great natural treasures of our area: the magnificent unspoiled stretches of the Gaviota coastline. The area runs "north" (actually west) from Goleta before the 101 turns inland through the Gaviota Pass and winds it's windy way toward the Santa Ynez Valley. En route, there are state beaches (outlined in this book) and a wonderful canyon with a rustic, special retreat nestled within called El Capitán Canyon where you can stop off for a bite to eat, slumber in tents or in style, and even listen to live music outdoors during summer concerts.

Efforts are underway to save a 1,000-plus acre section of this coastline at Naples, an area once slated to be a railroad town, that developers have been trying to get their hands on since the late 1800s. It remains one of the last unspoiled stretches of coastline, both on the Pacific ocean side and the mountain side of the 101. Over the past decade, ongoing efforts have been underway to save Naples. The entire region stretches to the west of Goleta to Point Conception and, some would argue, 20 miles north to Point Sal. Members from the Sierra Club, Surfrider, Citizens Planning Association, SBCAN (Santa Barbara County Action Network), Audubon Society, League of Women Voters, and the Gaviota Coast Conservancy, as well as individuals, formed the Naples Coalition to preserve the view sheds, restore the biodiverse habitat, maintain wildlife corridors, protect the sensitive coastal bluff, and provide appropriate public access. Their goal is to not only be stewards of the landscape, but preserve it for future generations. Take a look, learn more about Save Naples, and check out www .savenaples.org. You may just be inclined to join the effort.

This is a fantastic place to watch birds—in fact, it's one of the best birding spots in the area. You can also swim and fish at the shore, hike on the beach and nature trails, and picnic in the grassy play area. There's an excellent swimming beach and a designated area for surfing. For camping information, see the Camping section of the Recreation chapter.

RINCON BEACH PARK
US 101 at Bates Road,
Carpinteria
(805) 568-2460
www.countyofsb.org/parks

The point at the east end of this beach is world famous for its excellent surf waves (see the Surfing section of this chapter). But during the warmer months, when the waves are smaller, Rincon is a great beach for sunbathing and cooling off in the water, as long as you steer clear of the rocky point.

Rincon has public telephones, restrooms, and picnic tables. But bring your own picnic—there's no snack bar here.

To find Rincon, drive 3 miles east of Carpinteria and turn toward the ocean at the Bates Road exit, right at the Santa Barbara/Ventura County line. Park for free in the upper or lower Rincon Beach lots.

BOAT EXCURSIONS & SIGHTSEEING TRIPS

Most of these boats also offer special whale-watching excursions. (See the Whale-Watching section later in this chapter.) Schedules and excursions vary, depending on the season, so it's always best to call ahead for current departure times. The schedules in this section reflect summer options and rates, unless otherwise indicated. We recommend you wear rubber-soled shoes and try to dress in layers so you're prepared for sudden changes in weather. Remember to bring a sweater, hat, sunglasses, sunscreen, and your camera. If you have binoculars, bring those, too, for a close-up glimpse of the wildlife.

*AKA *SUNSET KIDD* SAILING
125 Harbor Way, Santa Barbara
(805) 962-8222
www.sunsetkidd.com

The *Sunset Kidd* is a 41-foot Morgan Out Island Ketch, Coast Guard–certified for 18 passengers who seek a truly tranquil sailing experience. Narration is kept to a minimum. *Sunset Kidd* takes people out on romantic sundowner cocktail cruises, 2-hour coastal excursions, and overnight Channel Island trips. Morning and afternoon 2-hour trips along the coast cost $40 per person. The romantic sunset-twilight sail also costs $40 per person. You can quench your thirst at the full-service bar on board, then relax and enjoy a quiet glide along the coast. The *Sunset Kidd* is also available for private charters. *Sunset Kidd* is located at Cabrillo Landing in front of the Santa Barbara Maritime Museum at the harbor.

*CONDOR EXPRESS
SEA Landing
Cabrillo Boulevard at Bath Street, Santa Barbara
(805) 882-0088, (888) 77-WHALE
www.condorcruises.com

Watch the sunset and dine, dance, and drink cocktails on the new 149-passenger high-speed catamaran *Condor Express*. It's the perfect party boat. You can charter the *Condor Express* for group sunset cocktail and dinner cruises or for a pelagic bird trip. The boat has a large galley that will provide anything from light hors d'oeuvres to three-course meals, and the full bar keeps guests well imbibed. Bands and DJs can also be arranged. Rates for summer party cruises are about $30 per person including hors d'oeuvres (but not including drinks), and prices for private charters start at $950 per hour on weekends and $850 per hour during the week with a 2-hour minimum.

> **i** *Lil' Toot* ferries passengers, young and old, back and forth from Stearns Wharf to the harbor. Kids fare is only $1, and they get to take the helm. Bubbles and the "little toot" of the horn make this a fun way to get on the water for a nominal fee, and it's a short ride for those who suffer from mal de mer.

DOUBLE DOLPHIN/SAILING CENTER OF SANTA BARBARA
Next to the boat launch ramp at the harbor, Santa Barbara
(805) 962-2826, (800) 350-9090
www.sbsail.com

Sail in style on the 49-passenger *Double Dolphin*, a 50-foot catamaran. The *Double Dolphin* offers coastal trips, sunset champagne cruises, cigar cruises, jazz cruises, weekend dinner cruises, and Channel Island safaris. During the summer, coastal cruises are scheduled between 1 and 4 p.m., and the sunset champagne cruises are at 6 p.m. The cost is $25 for adults and children. The 2-hour trips include a narrated tour of the harbor, then a cruise past Stearns Wharf along the coastline toward Montecito. Jazz cruises are scheduled on Friday evenings from April to September and cost $40 for adults and $22 for children 12 and under. Dinner cruises are available on Sat from 6 to 8 p.m. during the summer months. Fares are $65 for adults, $35 for children 12 and younger. Whale-watching and trips to the Channel Islands are also offered.

TRUTH AQUATICS
301 W. Cabrillo Blvd., Santa Barbara
(805) 962-1127
www.truthaquatics.com
Truth Aquatics offers 1-, 2-, and 3-day summer excursions to Channel Islands National Park, the four-island chain that many refer to as the "Galapagos Islands of California." The trips aboard Truth Aquatics' fleet of custom-designed liveaboard dive boats *Truth, Conception,* and *Vision,* allow visitors opportunities to discover the endangered ecosystems of Santa Cruz Island as well as see the lesser-visited Santa Rosa and San Miguel Islands. Overnight excursions include all meals, bunkhouse lodging with hot showers, instructive guides, and good company. Day-trip prices are $90 for adults and $50 for children ages 12 and under; overnight excursions begin at $200 per person.

BOATING & SAILING

Santa Barbara Harbor

If you're moving to Santa Barbara and want a permanent slip for your boat, we have bad news for you. There's a very long waiting list for permanent slips in the 1,133-slip harbor. Most people sell their boat and their permit together, so the list rarely shrinks. Call the Waterfront Department (805-564-5531) to find out the latest developments.

If you're just visiting the area with your boat, you'll have better luck. Guest slips are available on a first come, first served basis. Call Visitor Slip Information, (805) 564-5530, regarding visitor slip assignments. Availability depends on the type of vessel.

If you arrive in Santa Barbara by boat and the marina is full, you can be added to a waiting list and then drop anchor in the open anchorage area to the east of Stearns Wharf. The list is updated daily.

Slip fees are payable in advance. The base rate for the first 14 days is 90 cents per linear foot per 24-hour day; the rate doubles after 14 days. The permit is valid until noon of the last day paid for. You can renew it by contacting the Harbormaster's Office (805-564-5530) before 11 a.m. of your checkout day.

You'll pay a $35 fine if your visiting vessel is tied up without permission and $5 per day for not paying for your visitor slip permit in advance. If you leave the harbor owing visitor fees, you pay $10 plus double the amount you owe.

Alcoholic beverages are permitted in marinas but not on public sidewalks. Pets must be confined aboard your boat. Dogs must be leashed when walking to and from your boat. Parking (maximum vehicle length 20 feet) costs $2 an hour ($12 maximum per day). No in-and-out privileges. Boat trailers in the launch ramp cost $2 an hour ($8 maximum per day). Three-night maximum stay.

Public Boat Ramps

If you have a boat and want to put it in the water, you have only a few choices. The Santa Barbara Harbor maintains a boat launch ramp that can handle most types of boats. It's at the east end of the harbor parking lot, near the intersection of Cabrillo Boulevard and Bath Street.

There's a small-vessel launch in Carpinteria off Ash Avenue. You'll need to go to the Santa Barbara Harbor if you have a real boat.

The piers at Goleta and Gaviota have winches from which you can launch boats up to 2 tons.

Powerboat Rentals

SAILING CENTER OF SANTA BARBARA
Next to the boat launch ramp in the harbor, Santa Barbara
(805) 962-2826, (800) 350-9090
www.sbsail.com
The Sailing Center rents three 13-foot Boston whalers, one 18.5-foot Blue Water ski/fishing boat, as well as 36- to 50-foot yachts with skippers by the hour and day. Prices start at $30 an hour for the smaller boats and range up to more than $1,000 a day for the large yachts with skippers.

i If you notice a lovely array of white sailboat masts on a Wednesday afternoon out at sea, that's "Wet Wednesday" sailing races put on by the historic Santa Barbara Yacht Club. The SBYC is open to members only, but anyone can enjoy the views.

Useful Numbers

These numbers might come in handy if you're boating or sailing in the Santa Barbara area:

Santa Barbara Marine Emergencies: 911

Coast Guard/Search and Rescue: (800) 221-8724, (310) 732-2044

Waterfront Department: (805) 564-5531

Harbor Patrol: (805) 564-5530 24-hours a day/7 days a week

Marine Weather: (805) 897-1942

Sailing

Sailing the Santa Barbara Channel can be an incredible experience. As you cruise along the coastline, you'll see the Santa Ynez Mountains looming beyond the bluffs and the Channel Islands shimmering on the horizon. Although infrequently windy, the area has a wide range of challenging conditions.

Breezes along the coastline average 10 to 15 knots, and swells average 2 to 4 feet during most of the year. Out in the channel, especially close to the islands, it's very common to experience light winds in the morning and winds of 20 to 30 knots in the afternoon.

If you have any questions regarding sailing in the Santa Barbara region, you can call the Sailing Center of Santa Barbara (see next listing). They have expert sailors on staff that can help you navigate a safe course through our waters.

SAILING CENTER OF SANTA BARBARA
Next to the boat launch ramp in the harbor, Santa Barbara
(805) 962-2826, (800) 350-9090
www.sbsail.com

The Sailing Center of Santa Barbara is one of the largest sailing schools on the West Coast.

The center offers one-stop shopping for sailboat rentals, group charters, cruises, and more. Its many other services include sailing lessons, from basic learn-to-sail classes to bareboat chartering certification; skippered and bareboat charters; and single- and multiple-day trips to the Channel Islands. Call for information and rates.

To rent a smaller boat, you'll need to pass a short checkout to show that you won't hurt yourself or others and that you know how to get back to the dock. If you plan to rent a larger boat to sail to the islands, you'll need to complete a 4-hour checkout. To access the Sailing Center, park in the harbor lot and walk to the center's docks by the boat launch ramps.

Marine Supply Stores

WEST MARINE
132C Harbor Way, Santa Barbara
(805) 564-1334
www.westmarine.com

West Marine offers all types of boating, nautical, fishing, and navigation equipment, and marine-oriented clothing. Hours vary slightly by location but are generally from 8 a.m. to 6 p.m. Mon to Sat, and 9 a.m. to 5 p.m. Sun. A second Santa Barbara location is at 26A S. Calle Cesar Chavez (805-564-1005).

DIVING

The Santa Barbara Channel is one of the world's top spots for scuba diving. There's an incredible diversity of marine life, and many species are found nowhere else on earth. Along the coastline you can explore the kelp forests and shallow reefs. Many divers from all over the world head out to the Channel Islands Marine Sanctuary, which surrounds the Channel Islands (see the Channel Islands National Park chapter). The experts at the following are your best bet for getting the scoop on where to dive.

SANTA BARBARA AQUATICS
5822 Hollister Ave., Goleta
(805) 967-4456
www.sbaquatics.com

Santa Barbara Aquatics has been around for more than 20 years. It offers a full range of classes, plus equipment sales and rentals for scuba diving, kayaking, surfing, and swimming. You can take SSI, NAUI, or PADI courses in just about every type of diving: night, deep, dry suit, kayak and boat diving, navigation, search and recovery, rescue, assistant instructor, dive master, and instructor.

The shop also sells wet suits and dry suits; rents skin-diving gear and assorted watersport accessories (but no masks, snorkels, or fins); and operates a repair station.

Dive Boats

TRUTH AQUATICS
301 W. Cabrillo Blvd., Santa Barbara
(805) 962-1127
www.truthaquatics.com

Truth Aquatics operates three excellent dive boats from SEA Landing at the Santa Barbara Harbor: *Truth, Conception,* and *Vision.* All were designed and custom-built for divers. Truth Aquatics runs 1- to 5-day excursions to the Channel Islands year-round. A great thing about this company is that you can show up in just a bathing suit, and the staff will outfit you with everything you need.

Single-, 2-, and multiday dives are scheduled throughout the year. Trips may be customized for your diving pleasure. Kayaking, hiking, and Channel Island trips are also provided by Truth Aquatics—their 3 boats may be chartered for groups for up to 5 days. (See earlier listing on trips to the Channel Islands National Park).

JET SKIING

SANTA BARBARA JET BOATS
SEA Landing
301 W. Cabrillo Blvd., Santa Barbara
(805) 570-2351
www.sbjetboats.com
Santa Barbara Jet Boats operates during the summer out of the harbor, next to the boat-launch ramp near SEA Landing. You can rent a Sea-Doo jet boat (seats up to 4, $225 per hour), a WaveRunner III (seats 1 to 3 people, $135 per hour), or the *Challenger* (seats up to 7 people, $235 per hour). All prices include fuel, life vests, wet suits, and safety orientation. You must be at least 18 years old to rent any watercraft, and a $500 security deposit with a credit card is required. Reservations are essential.

KAYAKING

The following firms offer kayak rentals and/or guided tours along the coast or out to the Channel Islands. Ocean kayaks are much more stable than the narrow, tippy river kayaks, so you don't need much experience to use one effectively. They're a fantastic way to explore the Santa Barbara coastline and marine world.

AQUASPORTS
111 Verona Ave., Goleta
(805) 968-7231, (800) 773-2309
www.islandkayaking.com
In business since 1988, Aquasports rents sea kayaks for groups and will deliver them to beaches from Goleta to Leadbetter Beach in Santa Barbara. Rental fees include an introductory lesson—no experience is required.

Aquasports also offers guided kayak trips along the Santa Barbara coast. Launch the kayak near Stearns Wharf and paddle out into the open ocean along the coastal bluffs for a 2- to 3-hour round-trip. Prices are about $79 per person for a group of four. Another trip takes you along the spectacular Gaviota coastline, a succession of small, secluded coves about 15 minutes west of Santa Barbara. This is a more remote experience—some of the beaches along here can only be accessed by kayak, so you'll really feel like you're getting back to nature. This trip costs about $89 per person for a group of four paddlers.

Guided kayak trips to the Channel Islands are one of the most popular excursions (you cross the channel by powerboat, then kayak off the islands). No special athletic ability or prior sea-kayaking experience is required. You can arrange custom trips with advance notice.

i In the spring of 2011, Cachuma Lake allowed kayaking on the man-made reservoir in the Santa Ynez Valley. However within the first few weeks, due to heavy winds, a stranded kayaker had to be rescued by helicopter, so don't assume that lake kayaking is a safer alternative!

CAPTAIN JACK'S SANTA BARBARA TOURS, LLC
(888) 810-8687
www.captainjackstours.com
Captain Jack's boasts that it provides more tours than anyone else and, you know what? We think they're right. Their plentiful menu of adventurous tours leaves you wanting to book not one, but at least two or more. Here's a sample of what they have to offer: A 2-hour harbor introductory kayak tour for $35 with a two-person minimum or $60 with an individual lesson beforehand; an Evening Champagne/Harbor Tour for $50 per person with a two-person minimum; the popular Gaviota Kayak/Hot Spring Hike Tour, a 6-hour trip that costs $175 per person or $260 for two people; and the glider/kayak tour and horseback/kayak/wine-tasting tour. Phew. The choices just keep going on and on. Check out the website for more information.

PADDLE SPORTS
117-B Harbor Way, Santa Barbara
(805) 899-4925, (888) 254-2094
www.paddlesportsofsantabarbara.com
Owned by a local kayak enthusiast, Paddle Sports is the oldest and largest kayak shop on the central coast of California. The convenient Santa Barbara Harbor store rents all types of kayaks, both singles and tandems, as well as kayak-related gear (helmets, wet suits, paddles, etc.). You can launch your kayak on flat water a short stroll from the store. The store also sells kayaks and accessories, and when the weather's fine, it rents kayaks on the beach between the Harbor and Stearns Wharf. Prices for single-person kayak begin at $25 for the first 2 hours. Rates for tandem kayaks begin at $40 for the first 2 hours. Paddle Sports also rents stand-up paddleboards (SUP). A standard SUP starts at $40 for the first 2 hours, and a demo SUP starts at $50 for the first 2 hours. Day, week, and group rates are available.

Their additional location in Carpinteria, at 3825 Santa Claus Ln., has 3,000 square feet of kayaks and gear, as well as a consignment shop. The staff are experts in the sport and will outfit you with everything you need to get on the water.

Paddle Sports has years of experience guiding kayakers in local waters. During the summer, the store offers guided trips to the Channel Islands National Park and along the coast (call the harbor store).

SANTA BARBARA ADVENTURE COMPANY
(805) 452-1942, (888) 773-3239
www.sbadventureco.com
Launched in 1998, Santa Barbara Adventure Company offers a wide range of kayaking excursions led by experienced and knowledgeable guides. Choose from coastal paddling adventures along the spectacular Santa Barbara and Gaviota coasts, evening stargazing trips, and full- or multiday paddles around the sea caves and secluded coves of the Channel Islands. As you paddle, the guides share their knowledge of the area's natural history and marine ecology, so you'll enrich your mind as well as your spirit. The company will also customize trips to suit your skills and interests. Prices range from about $85 per person for a 4-hour paddle to $175 per person for a 1-day paddle around Santa Cruz Island. If you're not completely confident on a kayak, sign up for a lesson. Santa Barbara Adventure Company offers kayak instruction for beginners as well as kayak surfing classes for more advanced paddlers. All trips include qualified guides, equipment, transportation, and any necessary permits.

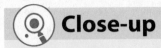

Close-up

What's SUP?

Don't let the chilly Santa Barbara water scare you off: try one of the hottest water-sports around. **Stand-up paddleboarding,** or **SUP,** is a watersport that has gained immense popularity in recent years in Hawaii and other places. Stand-up paddleboarding is a fast calorie burner, doesn't take much practice to master, and has quickly become a favorite pastime with Santa Barbarans. Modern paddleboards derive from the huge "olo" surfboards previously ridden by Hawaiian royalty. Even though they are much smaller, paddleboards still range from 9 to 14 feet in length, and can be made from a variety of materials depending on the board's purpose (surfing, racing, etc.).

As the name implies, stand-up paddleboarding, at its most basic level, simply involves getting past the wave break, standing up (which can at first be harder than it sounds) and paddling (with an outrigger-type paddle). When paddling, form is very important, so be sure to listen closely to your instructor when you take your first lesson. Once you've perfected your proper form and gained your "sea legs," paddleboarding is a cinch.

There are three basic levels—beginner, aerobic (which includes racing), and surf-ing—to this ocean sport, but if you've mastered this fun recreational activity, you might want to try stand up paddleboarding aerobic or yoga classes.

For all ages and all fitness levels, as long as you know how to swim, SUP is an excellent core workout, but it also benefits the rest of the body, as well as the mind (a quiet morning out above the kelp beds can be very meditative). Also, when care-fully supervised by an instructor, stand-up paddleboarding can serve as physical therapy for back, shoulder, and even knee problems.

The harbor location of Paddle Sports of Santa Barbara is one of two places where you can simply rent your board and walk it down to the beach (the other is A Frame Surf on Padaro Lane in Carpinteria); everywhere else, you'll have to transport your rented equipment.

Don't be surprised if you spot seals, dolphins, and possibly even a whale while out on your SUP!

The company operates on an open calendar, so day trips require advance reservation. For overnight trips, book at least 2 weeks in advance. Call or visit the company's website for more information.

SANTA BARBARA AQUATICS
5822 Hollister Ave., Goleta
(805) 967-4456
www.sbaquatics.com
Santa Barbara Aquatics sells and rents kayaks and accessories. Rentals average $40 a day

for a single kayak and $55 a day for a tandem, including life vests and paddles.

SANTA BARBARA SAILING CENTER
Next to the boat launch ramp in the harbor, Santa Barbara
(805) 962-2826, (800) 350-9090
www.sbsail.com
The Sailing Center rents kayaks and all the accessories starting at $10 per hour for a single kayak and $15 for a tandem with a 2-hour minimum (add tax and insurance).

Full-day rentals are $40 and $60, respectively. The center also offers an Olympic-style rowing scull for $20 an hour or $80 per day.

KITEBOARDING

Gaze out at the water from East Beach when the wind picks up and you might see brightly colored kites flying through the air with bodies attached. Kiteboarding made a huge splash in Santa Barbara when it first hit watersports lover's radar. Prevailing light, steady breezes make ideal conditions, and our wide-open beaches provide safe landing sites. In the right wind conditions, pilots can launch themselves from flat water and reach speeds of up to 20 to 30 miles per hour. East Beach is the most popular venue due to its wide landing area, but you can also kiteboard at Leadbetter Beach, and in the winter Arroyo Burro (Hendry's Beach) and Isla Vista offer challenging conditions for more experienced pilots.

SALT AIR KITEBOARDING
(805) 698-0432
www.saltairkiteboarding.com

From May to mid-September, check out kiteboarding with PASA-certified kiteboarders like Amy Naff. Amy and her crew teach you all about this unique sport that combines kite flying, wakeboarding, windsurfing, and surfing all into one. At least four 3-hour lessons are recommended for beginners. Learning is best done in pairs, and partnerships will be created for solos. Salt Air also has a supply of kites, kiteboards, and other gear available online for purchase. Call for more details and pricing.

SURFING

The Santa Barbara coast is one of California's premier surfing areas. The best waves hit the coast in the winter and fall, but good wave conditions for beginner to advanced surfers roll in regularly just about every month of the year.

The Channel Islands help protect the Santa Barbara coast from storm winds and create manicured conditions during strong winter swells. Unfortunately, these islands also block the coastline from almost all southerly swells, which tend to dominate during the warmer months. So from about May through September, the surf along the Santa Barbara coastline is typically quite small—perfect for beginners or intermediate surfers, but less than thrilling for experts.

Now for the surf scoop. Here's a brief overview of the main surf spots along the Santa Barbara coast, from east to west. We've tried to give you a good idea of their locations and basic information about access. For surf instruction and for more details on the local surfing scene, call one of the surf shops listed after the surf spots—they can arrange lessons and point you toward the best wave conditions for the day. Santa Barbara Adventure Company also offers surfing instruction. Call (888) 773-3239, or visit www.sbadventureco.com for the sample schedule of the 1-day lessons that cost $110 per person, with a two-person minimum.

Rincon Point

The Rincon is internationally renowned in the surfing world. It's located a few minutes' drive to the east of Carpinteria, right at the Santa Barbara/Ventura county line. Sometimes called the "Queen of the Coast," this wide, cobblestone point offers long, classic

California point-break waves. It's mainly a winter break, and waves during the cooler months are often excellent.

Since Rincon has a rocky bottom along most of the break, and conditions are often very crowded, this break is most appropriate for intermediate to advanced surfers.

You can easily access the spot from the US 101 Bates Road off-ramp. Park in the county or state parking lot.

Leadbetter Point

You'll find this small point at the west end of Leadbetter Beach, just below Shoreline Park. It typically has small waves that break on a rocky bottom into a sandy beach. It's an excellent spot for beginner and intermediate surfers. You can access the break from the Leadbetter Beach parking lot on Shoreline Drive.

Arroyo Burro Beach Park (Hendry's Beach)

This beach-and-reef break sometimes creates some decent surf waves during small- to medium-size swells. It's also a good wind-swell spot (typically in the afternoons) and a fun spot for kids to catch some waves. Park in the Arroyo Burro parking lot off Cliff Drive. The break is directly in front of the parking lot and Boathouse restaurant.

i You will need a full-length wet suit most of the year, although you can usually get away with a spring suit during the warmer months.

Campus Point

Campus Point is a large point break named after the UCSB campus, which sits along its shore. It's one of the best breaks in Santa Barbara, with three or four sections that are good in nearly all conditions. Consequently, it offers great surfing for beginners to advanced surfers. However, it does have a rocky bottom, so it's not the safest place for beginners. It can also be packed with UCSB students.

To access Campus Point, take the Ward Memorial Freeway from US 101 to the UCSB campus gate, where you will need to pay a parking fee on weekdays. Once you're inside the gate, turn left. On weekends you can park in the first parking lot to the left. On weekdays, you're only allowed to use visitor parking spots, which are quite a distance from the beach.

Another approach is to take the Goleta Beach off-ramp, just before the entrance to UCSB. Park in the beach lot and walk west along the coast about 0.5 mile (1 kilometer).

Sands Beach

You'll find this sandy reef break just west of Isla Vista, the densely populated student community adjacent to UCSB. Sands offers very nice surfing experiences in a beautiful location. You can expect to find small to medium surf; the best conditions occur during wind swells. The only negative here is that you often have to put up with tar globs in the water and on the beach, thanks to offshore oil seeps.

To reach Sands Beach, take Del Playa Road to its west end, then walk about 0.5 mile (1 kilometer) to the trail, just past Devereaux Point (also a decent surf spot on occasion).

El Capitán State Beach

The point at El Capitán ranks among the most beautiful surf spots along the Santa Barbara coastline. A small rocky point that ends in a sandy bay, this spot can have excellent and hollow surf. Follow US 101 north from Santa Barbara about 17 miles and take the El Capitán State Beach off-ramp. Go through the park gate (the day-use fee is $10), then take the beach trail east of the parking lot.

Hollister Ranch

Known by name to most surfers on the planet, "the Ranch" has some of the best surf in California. It's located about 30 miles west of the city of Santa Barbara and stretches from Gaviota State Beach to Point Conception. Unfortunately (or fortunately for those lucky enough to get to live and surf there), access to this stretch of coastline is very limited. There are only two ways to get there: by boat or by driving through private, gated Hollister Ranch property.

Boaters usually launch their crafts from the winch at the end of the Gaviota Beach pier, just east of the ranch property. As you motor westward, you'll run into several breaks with varying surf conditions. Recent subdivision of ranch property has substantially increased the number of property owners (many of whom buy pieces of land just to have surf access) and the number of people who are allowed to drive to the pristine beaches by vehicle. Local surfers frequently try to cajole, entice, and bribe their fortunate friends who own ranch property to drive them into the ranch for a session.

Jalama State Beach

Although not in the geographic area covered in this book, Jalama State Beach is often frequented by Santa Barbara surfers. This coastal area is well exposed to the open Pacific waters, and unlike Santa Barbara, it catches swells from southerly to northerly directions. With often windier, colder, and rougher surf, Jalama challenges even the most experienced surfer. Beach and reef breaks occur all along this stretch of wild and scenic coastline.

To access the area, take US 101 to just north of Gaviota, then take the CA 1 turnoff. From there, go about 8 miles to the Jalama Road turnoff on the left, then follow this winding road 12 miles to the beach. The state campground offers day-use facilities as well as dozens of overnight camping spots.

Surfing Equipment & Lessons

A-FRAME SURF SHOP
3785 Santa Claus Ln., Carpinteria
(805) 684-8803
www.aframesurf.com
Run by two local brothers, this surf shop opened in 2000 right by Santa Claus Beach. The store sells short boards from local designers such as Progressive and Wayne Rich as well as some hard-to-find smaller lines of surf- and beachwear for men, women, and children. You can also rent surfboards, body boards, wet suits, fins, and skim boards here, and surf lessons are available year-round, but you should book at least a week in advance and 2 weeks in advance during the summer. Surf lessons are $75 per person for 90 minutes and $65 per person for two or more people. Stand-up paddleboarding lessons are $90 per person.

CHANNEL ISLANDS SURFBOARDS
36 Anacapa St., Santa Barbara
(805) 966-7213
www.cisurfboards.com
Tourists and surf experts alike shop at Channel Islands Surfboards. This is where you can find surfboards by Al Merrick, one of the best board designers and shapers in the surfing industry. You can also purchase a range of other surfing equipment and apparel.

SURF COUNTRY
Calle Real Center
109B S. Fairview Ave., Goleta
(805) 683-4450
www.surfcountry.net
This complete surf and beach shop is a good place to pick up Insider information on the best surf and beach spots. It rents soft or hard surfboards, body boards, and wet suits. Rates for surfboard rentals are $30 a day and $15 for each additional day. Surfing lessons are also available.

SURF HAPPENS SURF SCHOOL
(805) 966-3613
www.surfhappens.com
Founded in 2003, this local surfing organization offers personal instruction for surfers of all ages, including year-round surf camps for kids, family surf camps, international surfing safaris, and free surfing competitions around the world. The school takes a martial arts approach to instruction, teaching discipline and focusing on both mental and physical fitness. Lessons start at $80 an hour for a personal lesson, and go down depending on the number of people who join the group. Surf Happens provides all the equipment, including wet suits and sunblock—all you have to do is show up in your swimsuit.

WHALE-WATCHING

Every year in late September, about 28,000 Pacific gray whales begin migrating south from Alaska to the warm lagoons and bays in Baja California, where they mate and give birth. In early February, the adult males, pregnant females, and a few juveniles start heading back north to their summer Arctic feeding grounds. The new mothers and their calves hang around the lagoons a bit longer before following along. This migration— among the longest of any mammal's—is one of nature's most incredible spectacles, and you can get a ringside seat to watch it right here in the channel.

The following is a list of boats that will take you out to watch the whales and give you a bit of whale education in the process. It's a good idea to call to verify the current schedule, as departure days are often added or dropped, depending on how many whales are in the channel that week. All these boats work as a team. If one boat is enjoying a spectacular appearance by a whale or pod of whales, the captain will radio other whale-watching boats in the vicinity and share the sighting.

i If you're heading out for a whale-watching trip, dress in layers with flat-soled shoes and take a windbreaker. It's cold on the water even in summer. Also, bring binoculars, if you have them, for a close-up view of the wildlife.

*AKA *SUNSET KIDD* SAILING
125 Harbor Way, Santa Barbara
(805) 962–8222
www.sunsetkidd.com
Sunset Kidd is probably the least touristy of the whale-watching trips. This excursion is

for those who love sailing and prefer the tranquility of gliding up to the whales on a wind-powered vessel (the motor is used as little as possible). Narration is kept to a minimum. The *Sunset Kidd*, a 41-foot Morgan Out Island Ketch, takes up to 18 passengers on 2-hour whale-watching cruises twice daily from mid-February through May. The fare is $40 (no discounts for kids or seniors).

CAPTAIN DON'S WHALE WATCHING
219 Stearns Wharf #G, Santa Barbara
(805) 969-5217
www.activitiessantabarbara.com

Captain Don's power yacht, the 149-passenger *Rachel G*, has a full galley and bar, an upper deck with great views and seating, and a lower deck with indoor seating, air-conditioning, and heating. Trips go out along the coast to see gray whales at 9 a.m., 12 p.m., and 3 p.m. daily. Trips last about 2.5 hours. May through September, blue and humpback whales can be seen by the Channel Islands; October through December, the Channel Islands also host gray whales. Trips to the Channel Islands leave daily at 10 a.m. and 2:30 p.m., and generally last 4.5 hours. Call for prices and reservations.

✳ *CONDOR EXPRESS*
SEA Landing
301 W. Cabrillo Blvd. at Bath Street,
Santa Barbara
(805) 882-0088, (888) 77-WHALE
www.condorcruises.com

The 75-foot, 149-passenger high-speed catamaran *Condor Express* is the only whale-watching vessel offering a whale-watch guarantee. If you don't see whales or exceptional sightings of other marine animals on your trip, the captain will issue a free trip on another excursion during the same season. All cruises include informative narration about the whales and other wildlife you might encounter on the trip. Check out the southern gray whale migration from December through early February, the gray whales northerly migration from mid-February through early May, and the humpbacks and blue whales from May to September (nearly 100 percent guaranteed whale sighting on these cruises). Call for prices and reservations.

i A giant sperm whale washed ashore in Isla Vista, near the University of California at Santa Barbara, in April 2007. Uncommon to Santa Barbara waters, this whale was believed to have been snacking on giant squid, cephalopods that were once minimal in our waters but are now abundant along the Central Coast.

DOUBLE DOLPHIN/SAILING CENTER OF SANTA BARBARA
Santa Barbara Harbor near the boat launch ramp
133 Harbor Way, Santa Barbara
(805) 962-2826, (800) 350-9090
www.sbsail.com

The *Double Dolphin*, a 50-foot catamaran, takes up to 49 passengers out for 2.5-hour, narrated whale-watching cruises, leaving in the morning and afternoon daily from mid-February through mid-May during the gray whale migration. Rates are $30 for adults, $10 for children 12 and younger and college students under 25 with ID. On Sunday during the summer, the *Double Dolphin* runs full-day island safaris to Santa Cruz Island, and the boat often encounters whales during the Channel crossing. See the Boating & Sailing section in this chapter for details.

Appendix

LIVING HERE

In this section we feature specific information for residents or those planning to relocate here. Topics include real estate, education, health care, and much more.

RELOCATION

Santa Barbara isn't just a popular vacation destination; it's also one of the most desirable residential areas in the country. If you've ever visited, you'll know why. Where else can you bask in sunshine more than 300 days a year, spend one day strolling the beach and the next hiking in the mountains or sailing to unspoiled islands? In Santa Barbara we have access to top-notch educational institutions and high-quality health care. We enjoy a year-round calendar of theater, art, music, and dance, and if we want to, we can dine at a wide range of quality restaurants 7 days a week. Remember, Santa Barbara isn't a big, bustling city with high crime and high pollution. It's a small, fairly safe Southern California beach town. It's also friendly, relaxed, and ravishingly beautiful. Let's face it, Santa Barbara has it all.

No wonder so many people are scrambling to buy a house or condo here. But there is a downside to this incredible desirability. Consider the age-old formula of supply and demand, or the adage you get what you pay for, which in this case translates to one of the most desirable places to live in the country. As more and more people want to move here, real estate prices skyrocket, leaving the average home buyer standing on the pavement with a serious case of sticker shock. Even college students do a double-take when they realize they have to pay $700 dollars to share a room in Isla Vista, adjacent to UCSB. There's just no way to sugarcoat Santa Barbara's housing situation. Sure, you'll find the home, or apartment, of your dreams. But the question is, can you afford it?

OVERVIEW

Since the economic crisis, pricing has been on a bit of a roller-coaster ride, and prices did drop considerably. What once cost $1 million is now closer to $600,000. Foreclosures and short sales have entered the picture, making real estate investment and prices uncertain. Even seasoned real estate agents have difficulty pricing properties for sale these days.

Despite tremendous philanthropy, community organizations and the general civic-mindedness of Santa Barbarans, homelessness and panhandling continue to be an issue. There is also the threat of living in an area that experiences more drought than rain as well as gusting Santa Ana winds: Devastating wildfires have been a regular occurrence, especially in the foothill neighborhoods.

Once you have a good feel for the different neighborhoods, continue on to the Real Estate section for the inside scoop on the local market, how to choose an agent, and a list of local real estate companies that can help you find your dream home.

If you absolutely can't afford a permanent real estate commitment in Santa Barbara, check out the Vacation Rentals section of the Accommodations chapter and line up a condo, mansion, or beach cottage for the summer. It's the next best thing to living here.

NEIGHBORHOODS

Santa Barbara

If all you've ever seen of Santa Barbara is the touristy beachfront area, you've missed the flavor of the charming neighborhoods that make up our beautiful city. In fact, as you cruise the jacaranda-lined streets of Santa Barbara, you'll discover many highly desirable residential areas—probably more than you'd expect for such a small town. Scenic enclaves such as the Mesa, downtown Santa Barbara, Mission Canyon, and the Riviera all evoke contrasting images for Insiders, and each is worth exploring. We begin with an overview of the popular, downtown beachfront.

The Beachfront

The Santa Barbara beachfront area along Cabrillo Boulevard is the most tourist-oriented section of the city. State Street and Stearns Wharf divide this strip into East Beach and West Beach, our classic palm-fringed stretches of sand. Not surprisingly, hotels and motels line the street opposite the beach on the north side of Cabrillo. If you're not walking to the beach from one of these nearby accommodations, you will find parking a nightmare along here, especially on weekends when the Sunday Santa Barbara Arts and Crafts show is set up along E. Cabrillo Boulevard from 10 a.m. to dusk (www.santabarbaraartsandcraftsshow.com).

A few public parking lots are available if you're willing to pay; otherwise, arrive early or park on a side street and walk.

East Beach has volleyball courts on the sand and is the site of many local tournaments. Across the street from these you'll notice some upscale condos, known as the first stop for many a divorcé! West Beach includes the area west of Stearns Wharf to the Santa Barbara Harbor. This wide expanse of sand is home to beach-rental and kayaking concessions as well as a calm area for swimming. Across the street, motels and restaurants are jammed in from one end of West Beach to the other, drawing hordes of tourists during the summer. If you continue to the far west end, you'll hit SEA Landing, the boarding point for whale-watching trips, and just beyond that, Santa Barbara's picturesque harbor.

The Mesa

Heading west up the hill from the harbor lies the Mesa, a large family-oriented residential neighborhood bisected by Cliff Drive. Properties here range from Mediterranean and ranch-style homes to contemporary dwellings and shingled cottages with prices starting at about $600,000 for small single-family homes and reaching up to more than $4 million for larger homes on prime property with ocean views. You'll also find many apartments here rented by Santa Barbara City College students.

A thriving shopping district sits at the intersection of Meigs Road and Cliff Drive, and Mesa residents head to Shoreline Park for recreation. This 15-acre stretch of rolling lawns, on a bluff overlooking the ocean, is a favorite venue for family outings and picnics. It's also one of the best places in Santa Barbara to watch the sunset and fly a kite. Perched on a Mesa bluff top to the east of Shoreline, you'll find Santa Barbara City College, which arguably has the best panoramic view of any educational institution in the country and was deemed one of the top community colleges in the country by *Forbes* magazine in 2011. SBCC's La Playa Stadium sits majestically across the street from beautiful Leadbetter Beach and the Santa Barbara Harbor. The stadium steps and track are a popular exercise spot—when a game or track and field event is not taking place.

i The Santa Barbara Chamber of Commerce (805-965-3023; www .sbchamber.org) offers a relocation packet. For $20 ($30 mailed) you can order a personal packet with a map and real estate and demographic information as well as an economic profile, contacts for commercial real estate, a calendar of events, and information on arts and cultural activities.

Downtown

The retail center of downtown Santa Barbara lies on "lower" State Street, between Stearns Wharf and Carrillo Street. Its busy shops, restaurants, sidewalk cafes, theaters, and the Paseo Nuevo outdoor mall are a natural draw for visitors, as well as panhandlers.

On the outskirts of this downtown area is a mix of gorgeous historic homes, smaller single-family dwellings, apartment and condo complexes, and small California cottages that are prevalent in the tree-lined Craftsman-style "bungalow district" near Santa Barbara High School. Also lovely are the old Victorian homes and gardens interspersed throughout the city. To give you an idea of prices, small bungalows on the more affordable west side of the city start at $600,000, while many grand old Victorian homes closer to the city center may soar into the millions.

Downtown Santa Barbara contains a large number of tourist attractions, including the Santa Barbara County Courthouse, the Presidio, and the Santa Barbara Museum of Art, so it's easy for a visitor to shop, dine, and see the sights and movies or theater productions within a fairly compact area. If you want to explore this historic district, we recommend the Red Tile Walking Tour (see the Close-up in the Attractions chapter for more details). Downtown always seems to be decked out with banners or decorations of some sort, adding to the neighborhood's festive feel. Your best bet is to nab a spot in a public parking lot and explore on foot. Better still, you can take the electric shuttle, which will whisk you around the downtown area for less than you'd spend to park in one of the pay lots. (See the Getting Here, Getting Around chapter for more information on local parking and transportation.)

Upper State Street

If you continue your drive up State Street, you'll reach Mission Street, the beginning of the "upper" State Street district, a mix of commercial and residential properties extending to La Cumbre Road. Unlike the downtown area, upper State lacks the Spanish ambience and has a much more modern feel. La Cumbre Plaza mall, which was revamped in an upscale Mediterranean style, anchors the furthermost end of State Street shopping.

San Roque

San Roque, between upper State Street and the foothills, is another charming residential neighborhood populated by a mix of families with young children and older retirees. Despite its close proximity to a busy shopping and commercial district, it manages to retain a quiet and secluded feel. Meticulously maintained homes with well-manicured lawns line the sunny streets, and you'll notice a variety of architectural styles, from imitation Tudor cottages and Spanish haciendas to classic ranch-style homes. Real estate (you're probably getting used to this by now) is expensive, with prices beginning at $800,000 and rising to over $1 million. A small three-bedroom house can sell for more than $1 million. Smaller two-bedrooms may go for just around $1 million.

Mission Canyon

Mission Canyon is the quiet, thickly wooded neighborhood around Mission Canyon Road and the adjacent foothills. It's a beautiful area of old oaks and sycamores, rocky streams, and hiking trails. Lured by the area's natural beauty, many artists, writers, and musicians make their home here. It's only a 10-minute drive to downtown, but the rugged wilderness makes it feel more remote. In lower Mission Canyon you'll find the Santa Barbara Museum of Natural History, Rocky Nook Park, and Mission Santa Barbara, while upper Mission Canyon is home to the Santa Barbara Botanic Garden and many popular hiking trails. Architecture in the area tends to be more contemporary in style. Real estate prices in Mission Canyon Heights range from $700,000 to $2.5 million—even well over $4 million for more exclusive homes secluded in the woodlands or homes offering remarkable views.

The Riviera

Driving up from Mission Canyon on meandering Alameda Padre Serra (Insiders call it "APS") puts you on the sunny Santa Barbara Riviera, with its magnificent views of the ocean, the Channel Islands (on a clear day), and the city of Santa Barbara. Not all the homes on the Riviera are large, but their location makes them expensive, with prices ranging from $700,000 to well over $3 million. The Santa Barbara Middle School resides on prime property here, and just above Alameda Padre Serra you'll (hopefully) find the newly renovated El Encanto Hotel and Garden Villas, with its Mediterranean-style restaurant and spectacular views of the city and sea reopened at long last (be sure to call ahead and find out).

Goleta Valley

The Goleta Valley ("Go-LEE-ta," from the Spanish word for "schooner"—and yes, we know that's not the correct Spanish pronunciation) is the fastest growing area on the South Coast. In 2001, after years of struggling to control the area's future, voters created a new City of Goleta stretching roughly from Patterson Road in the east to the western Urban Rural Boundary Line at the Bacara Resort. Many of the 29,000 residents of this new city are committed to curbing the huge boom in development that has changed the face of the Goleta Valley in the last 40 years. Once home to lemon groves and wide-open spaces, the area is now sprouting major high-density housing developments and apartment complexes. The Goleta Valley also has more high-tech firms than any other area in the county. Development aside, the new City of Goleta has one of the lowest crime rates in the state and nation for its size and attracts many families looking for a safe and relatively affordable place (by Santa Barbara standards) to raise their children.

The unincorporated area of the Goleta Valley includes Isla Vista (pronounced "EYE-la VIS-ta"—and yes, we've tweaked the Spanish pronunciation again), where thousands of UCSB students cram into several square blocks of rental complexes. You'll also find the recently renovated Santa Barbara Airport here, although it technically sits on a patch of the City of Santa Barbara (just to complicate things).

The Goleta Valley has its own county beach, and you'll find several excellent golf courses here, including the celebrated Sandpiper Golf Course. Camino Real Marketplace, a massive new retail center at Hollister Avenue and Storke Road, draws throngs of bargain shoppers for Costco, Home Depot, Best Buy, and other nearby big box stores, including Kmart across the way.

Other attractions in the area include the historic Stow House, a 2-story Victorian home built in 1872; the California Lemon Festival held each October on the Stow House grounds; and, of course, the cultural and educational offerings of UCSB. (See the Arts and Education & Child Care chapters for more information.)

The Goleta Valley's popularity with home buyers is pushing prices up here, too, but it has always been a more affordable option to Santa Barbara living. At the low end, you might find a small, older home for around $300,000. But you can still pay over $1 million for a home with a view.

Hope Ranch

Isolated between the area west of Modoc Road and the ocean, Hope Ranch, an affluent Santa Barbara County neighborhood, is a community unto itself. Sprawling ranch-style homes and secluded mansions line the main thoroughfare of Las Palmas Drive, and

the scores of winding, maze-like roads make it easy to get lost if you don't know where you're going. This is probably just fine with Hope Ranch residents, who value their privacy and employ their own security police.

Homes here sell for very big bucks, with low-end properties in the $1.5 million range and the most extravagant estates zooming upward of $10 million.

You won't find any commercial businesses or tourist attractions in Hope Ranch, but we recommend taking at least one sightseeing tour on Las Palmas Drive just to get a feel for the place. As you enter Las Palmas from Modoc Road (under the famous Hope Ranch gateway), to the left you'll see Laguna Blanca, a small lagoon that's part of the private La Cumbre Country Club. Originally the lagoon was surrounded by a horse-racing track designed by Thomas Hope, an Irishman who was granted the land in 1870.

You'll also notice a lot of bridle trails. Riding, as well as raising and showing horses, is a popular Hope Ranch pastime. Residents have access to bridle paths and a horse show ring as well as a private beach and tennis courts.

Montecito

Lying between Carpinteria and the city of Santa Barbara, Montecito has a well-deserved reputation as an enclave of the rich and famous. Unfortunately for the curious, most of the wealth is hidden behind massive gates or at the end of long, winding drives lined with trees or other lush vegetation. Movie stars do live here, including Rob Lowe, Oprah and Stedman (part-time), Carol Burnett, Drew Barrymore (she paid around $7 million for her manse), Jonathan Winters, and Billy Baldwin, among others, but you'll be lucky to catch a glimpse of them unless you see them out shopping or browsing the local market.

Montecito's sense of elegance and seclusion is carried over into its luxurious lodging places, including the exclusive San Ysidro Ranch, built in the 1930s and a vacation retreat for the likes of John and Jacqueline Kennedy, Jean Harlow, and Katharine Hepburn, and the posh Four Seasons Resort The Biltmore Santa Barbara, a beautifully landscaped complex of elegant rooms and cottages constructed in 1927 and perched just above Butterfly Beach (for more details, see the Accommodations chapter).

Shopping tends to be upscale and exclusive, with two main shopping areas, the "lower village," along Coast Village Road, and the "upper village," at San Ysidro and E. Valley Roads, which contain boutiques, antiques shops, high-end real estate offices, and restaurants. In our opinion, the most rewarding attraction in Montecito is Lotusland, a stunning collection of wildly imaginative gardens and exotic plants created by the eccentric Polish opera singer Madame Ganna Walska. (See the Attractions chapter for more details.) But we also love Tecolote Bookstore, one of the few remaining independent bookstores in Santa Barbara and the only bookstore in Montecito where locals, including T. C. Boyle, get their literary fix.

The highly respected Westmont College and Music Academy of the West are located within the boundaries of Montecito. Many families with young children also hope to buy homes in Montecito because of the two excellent public elementary schools—Cold Springs and Montecito Union—but unless you have big bucks, there's probably not much of a chance you'll be living here. Home prices range from about $2 million and soar to the mega-millions. In fact, Montecito has always vied with Hope Ranch for the most stratospheric estate sales. In 2001 Oprah Winfrey snapped up a 42-acre estate here for a reported $50 million, giving Montecitans cause to gloat over their lattes again. Not only is this a record real estate sale for the county, it's also one of the biggest real estate transactions for a private home in US history.

Summerland

Rambling up the hillsides on the north side of US 101, between the exclusive enclave of Montecito and laid-back Carpinteria, sits a community of funky houses, Victorian-style jewels, apartments, and Cape Cod–style abodes on the hillside above the "downtown" known for its antiques stores, hamburger joints, and local post office. Blink and you might miss it. But in recent years, this cute little coastal enclave has become quite a hot spot. Home buyers are scrambling for a prime piece of ocean-view property here, and its diminutive nature is a big part of its charm.

Tinged with a faintly bohemian air, Summerland (or "Spookville," as it was once called) used to be a stomping ground for Spiritualists, who gathered here for séances in the late 1800s. Today it's a popular hangout for antiques shoppers, surfers, and a steady gush of tourists who flock here on weekends to enjoy its quaint atmosphere and friendly cafes, and even a wine-tasting room, Summerland Winery, part of the Urban Wine Trail.

i Find out about Summerland's "ghostly" past by purchasing local author Rod Lathim's book, *The Spirit of the Big Yellow House: A History of Summerland's Founding Family.*

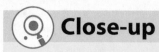

Close-up

Affordable Housing: Santa Barbara Style

Home ownership in Santa Barbara is expensive and out of reach for many. However, there is an option for prospective home buyers dreaming of living in paradise without paying through the nose. One alternative lifestyle is mobile-home parks (some are 55-over only). Manufactured homes aren't just a cheap, last resort; many offer more square footage at half the price of traditional houses and can be custom designed with up-to-date, stylish details. Many mobile-home park communities offer amenities that include gyms, pools, spas, clubhouses, and even views—if you don't mind living cheek-to-jowl with others. As far as your investment is concerned, mobile home values tend to stay fairly steady. Prices can begin as low as $50,000 and soar to close to half a million dollars. Expect to pay over $200,000 for a nice two-bedroom, two-bath pad. Remember association dues can vary from park to park, and there have been lawsuits over park fees in recent years. We like **Vista de Santa Barbara Mobile Home Park** (805-684-2313; www.vistadesantabarbara.com) in Carpinteria near the beach and salt marsh. **Rancho Goleta Mobile Home Park** (805-964-5515; www.ranchogoleta.org) in Goleta has a tranquil man-made lake that attracts local birdlife. One resident says she's spotted swans, great blue herons, cormorants, snowy egrets and great egrets, Canada geese, Ross geese, mallard ducks, and a variety of other waterfowl on the Pacific flyway, and the freshwater is a draw to seabirds. Even swans have traveled from the park to Devereux Slough and Lake Los Carneros.

A few sell the ground (many are on leased land), including Rancho Goleta and Summerland by the Sea mobile-home park, where the views of the Pacific Ocean are as stellar as the roar of the 101 freeway. Grab a free copy of *Casa Magazine* or do a search on www.realtor.com for current listings.

Carpinteria

An incorporated city located about 12 miles south of Santa Barbara, Carpinteria has a friendly, small-town Mayberry sort of feel. Named for the Chumash carpenters that Gaspár de Portol encountered here on a 1769 expedition, "Carp" (as the locals call it) contains acres of flower fields, greenhouses, and avocado groves. The annual California Avocado Festival is held here each October (see the Annual Events chapter), and a weekly farmers' market on Thursday afternoons also shows off the local bounty.

Carp's main attraction is its natural beauty, but it does maintain a small historical museum and boasts the area's only polo fields, just north of the city at the Santa Barbara Polo & Racquet Club. The downtown area, situated around the intersection of Linden and Carpinteria Avenues, has small shops and restaurants. A strip mall with more modern businesses occupies both sides of Casitas Pass Road. The area is especially good for antiques hunting, and the city has an excellent beach, once dubbed "the World's Safest Beach," with a wide sandy stretch and relatively riptide-free waters. Carpinteria State Beach is visited by about a million people annually. It boasts 4,000 feet of ocean frontage for swimming and tide pooling as well as facilities for picnicking, hiking, and surf fishing (see the Parks chapter).

Because everything is cheaper in Carpinteria, many families choose it over Santa Barbara for vacations, especially because it offers easy beach access, numerous motels, and better odds of finding a vacation rental. Historically, housing prices tend to be lower here than in Santa Barbara; you can find a home for $400,000 and lavish homes on exclusive Padaro Lane on the beach or in the foothills running as high as $5 million or more.

But there are several mobile-home parks in Carpinteria that make home ownership more affordable.

REAL ESTATE

In 1974 a struggling young couple with a down payment provided by their parents bought a three-bedroom, 20-year-old Santa Barbara tract home for $36,500. Making the payments was a stretch, but they managed, even while the mother stayed home to raise the kids.

More than 30 years later, the same home, with only a new coat of paint and some new carpet, sells for more than 25 times that amount. Mom and Dad, still living in the house, could not afford to buy it today, nor could they afford the mortgage payments, even though they're both working now. As for their grown-up children, they have to pack up and move out of town to be able to afford a home of their own.

And so it goes in Santa Barbara. Residents joke that they could sell their houses and buy mansions elsewhere, but the same scenario almost never happens the other way around. Facing a job transfer or other reason for relocation, many Santa Barbarans

rent out their homes rather than sell and risk cutting off any chance of being local homeowners again if they ever come back. And then there are all those ripe-aged, wealthy baby boomers looking for a quiet place to retire. For them, Santa Barbara has it all: sun, sea, surf, and fabulous golfing.

Median home prices are all over the map due to a number of factors including a fluctuating market, foreclosures, and the mega-billionaire who comes in and buys a house in Montecito for tens of millions of dollars and skews the results. In March of 2011 the median was $787,500; the condominium median price was $399,000. (The median price marks the point at which half the homes on the market sell for more and half sell for less). As we said, the multimillion-dollar estates in Hope Ranch and Montecito skew the figures a bit, too, but even at the lower end, homes in Santa Barbara are out of reach for many buyers.

To qualify for a loan of $800,000 for a $1,000,000 house in Santa Barbara (with 20 percent down payment), your household income needs to be at least $150,000 a year. Considering Santa Barbara's median income hovers in the mid-$50,000 range, it's not surprising home buyers are frustrated. At this rate, most renters can only dream of owning a home in the area.

That being said, prices have dropped considerably in recent years due to foreclosures and other market influences. Cash is king, and there are deals to be found—if you have the money and don't have to borrow from a bank or mortgage lender. Despite historically low interest rates, money continues to be tight from lenders and harder to come by, frustrating not only home sellers and buyers, but all the ancillary services including realtors and mortage brokers.

Some government officials say the solution to high-cost housing is simple: Build more houses. This scenario makes conservation-minded Santa Barbarans (and there are a lot of them) cringe. Historically, the market moves in cycles. But even during the dips here, demand remains relatively strong and prices are still high. After all, there's only one Santa Barbara in the world, and so many people want to live here. Just remember this general rule of thumb: You may have to work twice as hard to pay twice as much in order to afford to live here.

i New to Santa Barbara? Become one of the over 450-members of the Newcomer's Club. This dynamic group plans social functions so you can get to know the area and the people. Hospitality coffees for prospective members are held the first Monday of the month at Fess Parker's Doubletree Resort. Visit the website at www.sbnewcomers.org, or call (805) 564-2555 for more information.

Real Estate Firms

The companies below represent a partial list of real estate firms located in the greater Santa Barbara area. They are generally considered to have experienced agents who have good track records in assisting both buyers and sellers.

CENTURY 21
Gold Star Realty
3412 State St., Santa Barbara
(805) 687-7591, (800) 350-2733
www.century21ahart.com
This well-respected office of more than 30 agents has won the coveted Centurion Award for outstanding customer service

every year since 1983. The office specializes in residential real estate, but it also handles commercial and investment properties in all areas of greater Santa Barbara. This office is independently owned but offers the benefits of affiliation with a large chain, such as Century 21's national relocation program.

CENTURY 21
Butler Realty
1635 State St., Santa Barbara
(805) 563-2121, (800) 421-4452
www.c21butler.net
In addition to being the top-producing Century 21 office in Santa Barbara, Century 21 Butler Realty offers a property management and vacation rental division. This division, founded and run by Eric Penner for over 10 years, is an excellent resource for vacation rentals. Insiders know that it is the first place to turn to for their vacation rental needs.

COASTAL PROPERTIES
1086 Coast Village Rd., Montecito
(805) 969-1258
www.coastalrealty.com
In business since 1995, Coastal Properties has turned its extensive knowledge of the upscale vacation rental market into a successful "boutique" real estate venture. Specializing in Montecito, Hope Ranch, Santa Barbara, Carpinteria, and beach properties, the company's agents deal in everything from low-end condos to multimillion-dollar estates.

i Santa Barbara's strict building design guidelines arose from a stroke of Mother Nature's wrath. After a devastating earthquake in 1925, planners rebuilt the city in Spanish-Mediterranean style.

COLDWELL BANKER
3938 State St., Santa Barbara
(805) 682-2477
www.coldwellbanker.com
www.cbsocal.com
www.previewsestates.com
Frequently voted Santa Barbara's best real estate company in local newspaper polls, Coldwell Banker is a distinguished firm that sells multimillion-dollar estates as well as lower-priced family homes. The company has been in Santa Barbara for more than 30 years and has over 150 experienced agents. Coldwell Banker also has a national and international relocation department, a commercial division, an REO department, and a concierge service to help smooth your transition. Additional locations are in Montecito at 1290 Coast Village Rd. (805-969-4755) and 1498 E. Valley Rd. (805-969-0900).

MAIZLISH REALTORS, INC.
1514 Anacapa St., Ste. B, Santa Barbara
(805) 963-9555, (888) 963-9556
www.maizlishrealtors.com
Co-owners Morton and Alicia Maizlish are both brokers and the sole employees of this independent firm established in 1980. They believe in the single-agency approach, which means the company will only represent one party in a transaction. Recently they have been specializing in downtown, upper east, and Riviera properties. The Maizlishes deal with a full range of real estate, from condos to estates, and limit transactions to between 20 and 25 a year in order to provide personalized service.

PRUDENTIAL CALIFORNIA REALTY—
SANTA BARBARA
3868 State St., Santa Barbara
(805) 687-2666, (800) 326-3483
www.prusb.com
Doing business in Santa Barbara since 1950 (and voted the best local real estate company 5 years in a row in past *Santa Barbara News-Press* polls), Prudential California Realty–Santa Barbara has more than 105 agents working out of two local offices—a second location is at 1170 Coast Village Rd., Montecito (805-969-5026, 800-201-4364). The company deals in all types of properties including residential, commercial, and investment properties and specializes in helping first-time home buyers break into the market. Prudential's worldwide network of offices provides relocation assistance.

RE/MAX SANTA BARBARA
1715 State St., Santa Barbara
(805) 687-2600
www.remax-santabarbara.com
Part of a large national chain, this firm is a full-service agency handling a range of properties throughout the greater Santa Barbara area. Special divisions include estates, restaurants, residential, commercial, and investment properties. The company's broker has held many prestigious positions in the industry, including president of the California Association of Realtors. About 85 agents work out of two offices.

SOTHEBY'S INTERNATIONAL REALTY
1436 State St., Santa Barbara
(805) 963-1391
www.sothebyshomes.com/socal
Sotheby's displayed its brilliance when it moved into town by snapping up the local real estate giant Pitts and Bachmann. Adding Pitts and Bachmann real estate locations and agents to the firm really created a Santa Barbara presence. It doesn't matter whether the estate or house is large or small, Sotheby's realtors handle the transactions

with professional aplomb. Additional offices are located in Montecito at 1106 Coast Village Rd. (805-969-9993) and 1482 E. Valley Rd. (805-969-5005).

> **i** Yammering loudly on your cell phone in public is considered big-city behavior in this laid-back town. If you want to look like a local, you might want to tone it down a notch.

VILLAGE PROPERTIES
1250 Coast Village Rd., Montecito
(805) 969-8900
www.villagesite.com

Established in 1996, Village Properties is a locally owned and operated independent agency. Founded by Ed Edick and Renee Grubb, the company specializes in residential properties, including beachfront homes, estates, and new homes, but it also has experts in relocation, commercial properties, senior housing, affordable housing, and creative financing. More than 40 experienced agents with an average of 20 years experience serve Santa Barbara, Montecito, Goleta, Carpinteria, and the Santa Ynez Valley. Village Properties hosts a Teachers' Fund, which allocates dollars to teachers in the community. A second location is in Goleta at 4050 Calle Real, Ste. 120 (805-681-8800).

Other Resources for Finding a Home

The real estate pullout section in the Sunday *Santa Barbara News-Press* is a great resource; it's published in cooperation with the Santa Barbara Association of Realtors. *Casa,* a free tabloid, features real estate ads and photographs of homes for sale as well as a schedule of open houses for the week and a few classified ads for rentals. (They also cover the Santa Barbara arts scene quite extensively.) It's available in real estate offices and at more than 250 street stands in Santa Barbara.

Homes & Land runs photos of listed properties along with ads for the real estate companies that are listing them. Ads for fancy estates on the market in Montecito and Hope Ranch can be found in the slick quarterly *Santa Barbara Magazine,* which often shows both interior and exterior shots. Price tags on these homes are seldom below $1 million and are occasionally as high as $20 million.

> **i** Housing prices in the North County (including Santa Maria and Lompoc), as well as in Ventura and Ojai, are lower than those in the South County (greater Santa Barbara), but consider the cost of gasoline and the extra driving time before you buy.

THE RENTAL SCENE

If you can't afford to buy, you may have to rent, but don't expect to get off without paying a lot of money. (Hey, this is Santa Barbara!) Home rentals start at about $1,500 a month, and there is literally no ceiling, with large mansions and beachfront properties renting for $20,000 a month or more. Craigslist is a good place to start—and hopefully end your search. But word of mouth is often the best way to find a place. Tell everyone you know that you're looking, and follow up on every lead. If you are a college student looking for an apartment or room to rent, your best bet is the student housing office at the college or university you will be attending.

HEALTH CARE & WELLNESS

Illness and injury are never on anyone's agenda, but if the unexpected happens while you're in Santa Barbara, it's reassuring to know you have quick access to first-rate health care. The city offers the best concentration of health care facilities on the California coast between Los Angeles and the San Francisco Bay area. Every day, people from all parts of the state—and other areas of the country and the world, for that matter—come to Santa Barbara seeking quality health care services. Many of our hospitals and clinics date back a century or more, and our physicians and other health care practitioners rank among the best in the nation.

About the only medical services you won't have access to here are treatment for serious burns and organ transplants, and even those types of care can be found at highly rated institutions just an hour or two south of the county line.

Our community emphasizes preventive health care and offers many classes and services designed to promote good health. Most hospitals and clinics accept major insurance plans. However, health maintenance organizations (HMOs) are growing rapidly in the area, and along with the growth have come many changes, especially regarding physician choice. It's best to call and check beforehand with the individual hospital, clinic, or physician and your insurer to discuss coverage.

OVERVIEW

We begin this chapter with an overview of our main hospitals and affiliates, followed by descriptions of major clinics and alternative health care resources. We've also included handy lists of walk-in clinics, emergency numbers, and support services.

HOSPITALS

Cottage Health System

The nonprofit **Cottage Health System** (www.cottagehealthsystem.org) consists of Santa Barbara Cottage Hospital (with its associated Cottage Children's Hospital and Cottage Rehabilitation Hospital), Goleta Valley Cottage Hospital, and Santa Ynez Valley Cottage Hospital. Together they are the largest health care provider on the California coast between Los Angeles and the San Francisco Bay area.

Until the mid-1990s, the system's hospitals were all separate institutions. Santa Barbara Cottage Hospital merged with the smaller, community-based facilities so they could share services, save money, and expand their lists of health insurance providers. So far the merger has proved very successful, and you can count on excellent care at all affiliated centers. In 2007, Rehabilitation Institute at Santa Barbara also joined forces with Cottage, preserving its important inpatient and outpatient rehabilitation programs for the greater community. It is now known as Cottage Rehabilitation Hospital.

In 2003, Cottage purchased the beloved but fiscally beleaguered St. Francis Medical Center when it was closed by Catholic Healthcare West. Construction is now under way on the site to build workforce-affordable townhomes for Cottage employees.

The Cottage Health System presents a year-round wellness program (as do many of the facilities described below). The program's many offerings include Stop Smoking courses; annual heart, cancer, mental health and baby/family fitness fairs; flu shots; community CPR classes; healthy balance weight management clinics; and a series of maternity and childbirth-related courses.

SANTA BARBARA COTTAGE HOSPITAL
Pueblo at Bath Street, Santa Barbara
(805) 682-7111, (805) 569-7210
emergency department
www.cottagehealthsystem.org

Cottage Hospital is Santa Barbara's oldest and largest hospital. In the 1880s a group of civic-minded women led the vision to build a hospital for the growing community, then about 5,000 people. The goal was to provide medical care in a cozy, homelike "cottage" atmosphere that would help patients recover faster. Their vision, Santa Barbara Cottage Hospital, opened in 1891 in a 3-story wooden structure on the outskirts of town.

Since then Cottage has grown from a 25-bed facility to a comprehensive 345-bed, nonprofit acute-care medical center and teaching hospital that admits 20,000 patients a year and treats 42,000 emergency department visitors. Cottage has been nationally recognized for superior service, and it has

one of the only graduate medical education programs between the San Francisco Bay area and Los Angeles, with sought-after residencies in internal medicine, general surgery, and radiology.

Cottage Hospital's services run the gamut. The hospital has a Level II Trauma Center and provides 24-hour in-hospital coverage for illness and accidents as well as complete outpatient services for psychiatric and chemical-dependency services. About 600 specialists in all major clinical areas make up the hospital's medical staff. Cottage is particularly renowned for its interventional cardiology and cardiovascular surgery, its neuroscience and stroke program, its cancer services, and its inpatient and outpatient rehabilitation programs (Cottage Rehabilitation Hospital) as well as for its maternal/child services and pediatric program (Cottage Children's Hospital). Some 2,600 newborns are delivered each year, and the pediatric programs include neonatal and pediatric intensive-care units, a perinatal center for high-risk pregnancies, a perinatal/ pediatric ambulance, pediatric surgery, a pediatrics unit, and pediatric gastrointestinal and pediatric hematology/oncology departments. Outpatient services include cardiac electrophysiology, heart catheterization labs, and cardiac rehabilitation, comprehensive diagnostic imaging services, an eye center, and an outpatient surgery center.

Ground was broken in 2005 to rebuild Santa Barbara Cottage Hospital to meet new state earthquake safety standards, and the major portion of the new facility is scheduled to open in 2012—with 2 patient pavilions, a diagnostic and treatment pavilion, and new main entrance, all in the Spanish Colonial Revival architecture that is part of Santa Barbara's heritage. An added bonus—art and sculpture by Santa Barbara County artists—decorates the walls, hallways, and patios to help in the healing process.

GOLETA VALLEY COTTAGE HOSPITAL
351 S. Patterson Ave., Goleta
(805) 967-3411
www.cottagehealthsystem.org

Many residents love this small, neighborhood hospital for the friendly, personalized care it has offered since 1966. Formerly called Goleta Valley Community Hospital, the 122-bed institution joined forces with Santa Barbara Cottage Hospital in 1996 but maintains its intimate, community-based character and services. About 1,500 patients check into the hospital every year, and 18,000 people visit the emergency department for care.

Goleta Valley Cottage Hospital offers a full range of services, including its 24-hour emergency department, a comprehensive critical care unit, a subacute unit, specialized medical/surgical services for both inpatients and outpatients, a breast care center with specialized diagnostic and treatment programs, and a busy wound care center. The hospital is also being completely rebuilt, just south of the current facility, again to meet seismic safety standards. Completion is expected in late 2013.

CLINICS

CANCER CENTER OF SANTA BARBARA
300 W. Pueblo St., Santa Barbara
(805) 682-7300
www.ccsb.org

This nonprofit cancer treatment center, founded in 1949, offers radiation therapy, chemotherapy, and nuclear medicine for cancer patients. It also provides extensive support services for cancer patients and their families and friends. All support services are free and include counseling, home visits, a patient library, relaxation and stress management, support groups, and visitors programs.

> **i** Preferential hotel and transportation rates in Santa Barbara are available to Sansum–Santa Barbara Medical Clinic patients and guests. Visit www.sansum.clinic.org for a list of participating providers

SANSUM–SANTA BARBARA MEDICAL FOUNDATION CLINIC
Corporate Office: 470 S. Patterson Ave.
Santa Barbara
(805) 681-7500
www.sansumclinic.org

In October 1998, Santa Barbara witnessed the merger of two of the oldest medical groups in the region: Sansum Medical Clinic and Santa Barbara Medical Clinic. The parent organization is now called Sansum–Santa Barbara Medical Foundation Clinic and serves in an administrative capacity for the newly formed medical group of more than 140 physicians.

Sansum Medical Clinic was established in 1924 by William David Sansum, MD, who is widely credited as the first American to successfully isolate, produce, and administer insulin to treat diabetes. For decades, Sansum Medical Clinic has enjoyed a local, regional, national, and international reputation as a leading health care provider for medical evaluation, diagnosis, and treatment.

Santa Barbara Medical Clinic was founded in 1921 by three physicians. They succeeded in forming a carefully designed group practice to make comprehensive specialty care available to all segments of

Santa Barbara at a time when solo practitioners provided most of the care. In 1973 the physician-owners entrusted the clinic's assets, buildings, administrative operations, and contractual agreements to the nonprofit Santa Barbara Medical Foundation Clinic. The physician group kept the name Santa Barbara Clinic, Inc., and was retained by the foundation as a multispecialty physician group to administer health services.

In a nutshell, the merger of these two groups means that you are likely to find excellent health care that matches your needs, no matter what ails you or what type of health plan you have.

Sansum–Santa Barbara Medical Foundation Clinic operates the following facilities in Santa Barbara's South Coast region:

Sansum Multispecialty Clinics
51 Hitchcock Way, Santa Barbara
(805) 563-6100, main number
(805) 563-1994, pediatrics, community medicine
(805) 563-6100, urgent care
(805) 563-6190, Center for Wellness

215 Pesetas Ln., Santa Barbara
(805) 681-7500

317 W. Pueblo St., Santa Barbara
(805) 682-2621, (805) 898-3479,
(800) 472-6786

Sansum Specialty Clinics
FAMILY MEDICINE
1919 State St., Santa Barbara
(805) 563-6120

OBSTETRICS/GYNECOLOGY
515 W. Pueblo St., Santa Barbara
(805) 681-8911

OPHTHALMOLOGY/OPTOMETRY
29 W. Anapamu St., Santa Barbara
(805) 681-8950, main number
(805) 681-8969, Laser Eye Care Center

PHYSICAL THERAPY
27 E. Canon Perdido St., Santa Barbara
(805) 681-1711

41 Hitchcock Way, Santa Barbara
(805) 681-7781

PULMONARY/CRITICAL CARE MEDICINE
301 W. Pueblo St., Santa Barbara
(805) 898-3400

PSYCHIATRY/PSYCHOLOGY
1525 State St., Ste. 103, Santa Barbara
(805) 681-7517

Goleta Specialty Clinics
FAMILY MEDICINE
122 S. Patterson Ave., Goleta
(805) 681-7500

OCCUPATIONAL MEDICINE
101 S. Patterson Ave., Goleta
(805) 898-3311

PHYSICAL THERAPY
334 S. Patterson Ave., Goleta
(805) 681-1860

Carpinteria
FAMILY MEDICINE, INTERNAL, PEDIATRICS, URGENT CARE
4806 Carpinteria Ave., Carpinteria
(805) 566-5080

Community Resources

Refer to this list if you are experiencing an emergency situation or need information and assistance regarding community resources. Crisis lines are answered 24 hours a day.

Emergencies, 911

Fire Stations
   Santa Barbara, (805) 965-5254
   Gaviota, Goleta, and Isla Vista, (805) 681-5500
   Carpinteria, (805) 684-4591
   Montecito, (805) 969-7762
   Summerland, (805) 684-4591

Police or Sheriff Departments
   Santa Barbara, (805) 897-2300
   Gaviota and Goleta, (805) 681-4100
   Montecito, Summerland, and Carpinteria, (805) 681-4100

American Cancer Society, (805) 963-1576

California HIV, AIDS, and Sexually Transmitted Disease Hot Line, (800) 367-AIDS

California Poison Control, (800) 222-1222

Cottage Hospital 24-Hour Psychiatric/Substance Abuse Hotline, 211

Crisis/Suicide Intervention 24-Hour Helpline, 211

Coalition to End Family Violence 24-Hour Hotline, 211

Hospice of Santa Barbara, (805) 563-8820

Pollen and Mold Spore Hot Line, (805) 961-3951

Santa Barbara Rape Crisis Center 24-Hour Hotline, (805) 564-3696

Santa Barbara Council on Alcoholism and Drug Abuse, (805) 963-1433

Child Abuse Reporting Hot Line, (800) 367-0166

24-Hour Anger Management Hotline, (805) 656-4861

PLANNED PARENTHOOD OF SANTA BARBARA
518 Garden St., Santa Barbara
(805) 963-5801
www.ppsbvslo.org
The local Planned Parenthood center offers complete and confidential family-planning services at affordable rates. Services include pregnancy testing, counseling, birth control, testing and treatment for sexually transmitted infections and HIV, gynecological services, and education programs.

i Sansum–Santa Barbara Medical Foundation Clinic offers free flu shots in October and November. A $5 donation is requested. For more details, call the Influenza Hotline at (805) 681-7500.

WALK-IN CLINICS

Urgent care centers are located throughout Santa Barbara County. These smaller medical facilities provide services for a range of health and wellness needs. They are usually open every day and often have extended hours, typically 8 a.m. to 8 p.m. weekdays and shorter hours on weekends.

In most cases, you can just walk in—no appointment necessary. If you need quick treatment for minor accidents and emergencies or general family medical care, these are convenient facilities.

SANSUM–SANTA BARBARA MEDICAL FOUNDATION CLINIC URGENT CARE CENTERS
51 Hitchcock Way, Santa Barbara
(805) 563-6100

4806 Carpinteria Ave., Carpinteria
(805) 566-5000

MEDCENTER
2954 State St., Santa Barbara
(805) 682-7411

319 N. Milpas St., Santa Barbara
(805) 965-3011

271 N. Fairview Ave., #101, Goleta
(805) 681-7411

ALTERNATIVE MEDICINE

Many Santa Barbarans regularly turn to alternative medical treatments, and they don't have to go far to find them. You can find skilled practitioners in nearly every area of alternative health care, including naturopathy, homeopathy, clinical nutrition, acupuncture, and herbology. There are also numerous therapists with years of experience in massage, rolfing, shiatsu, and all types of bodywork therapy.

The weekly *Santa Barbara Independent* is a great resource for alternative medical services. You can also consult the Yellow Pages for listings.

PHYSICIAN REFERRAL SERVICES

Call these numbers to find out which physicians or dentists meet your particular medical and insurance needs.

DENTAL SOCIETY OF SANTA BARBARA–VENTURA COUNTY
(805) 656-3166
www.sbrcds.org

SANTA BARBARA COUNTY MEDICAL SOCIETY
Physician Referral: (805) 683-5333

EDUCATION & CHILD CARE

Given the intellectual atmosphere of the town, it should come as no surprise that Santa Barbarans have always placed great emphasis on high-quality education. For a relatively small community, Santa Barbara offers incredible educational breadth and diversity. If you're moving here, you'll have access to excellent schools, educational facilities, and programs for all ages, from preschool through retirement years.

At the preschool, elementary, and high school levels, parents have many choices for their children within the public and private sectors. At the higher education level, Santa Barbara is home to a University of California campus; Brooks Institute of Photography; Westmont College (a highly rated Christian college); and the prestigious Music Academy of the West summer full-scholarship program. Santa Barbara also has one of the nation's leading community colleges, Santa Barbara City College, as well as a number of continuing education and professional schools.

This chapter provides an overview of the many educational options available in Santa Barbara, as well as a brief overview of resources for finding appropriate child care and preschools for infants, toddlers, and prekindergartners.

PUBLIC SCHOOLS

About 25,000 students are currently enrolled in public schools in South Santa Barbara County, the area of focus in this book. Despite the funding cuts that have affected virtually every public school in California over the last 20 years, Santa Barbara's public schools have managed not only to stay afloat but also, in many cases, to thrive. At schools where "extra" programs have been eliminated, parents and local school districts have rallied to find innovative ways to raise funds to support them. Hardly a week goes by without a car wash, a jog-a-thon, an auction, or some other form of fund-raising event for local schools.

Many of our schools have earned California Distinguished School status over the years—a designation awarded to only 4 percent of all public schools in the state of California. It's a sure sign of excellent and innovative programs. A high proportion of our schools have also earned the prestigious National Blue Ribbon Award in the last 5 years (see the individual school districts below). Only about 200 schools in the United States achieve this prestigious designation following a rigorous application and screening process.

Most schools and/or districts in the area also offer GATE (Gifted and Talented Education), and all schools have special education programs. Santa Barbara also has four charter schools—public schools that operate free of many state statutes and regulations—and an Open Alternative School with an alternative curriculum and structure.

Legislation passed in July 1996 provides California public schools with incentive funding to reduce class size in the primary grades to improve instruction and student performance. The law made funds available to elementary schools so that they can reduce class size to 20 students or fewer in first and second grades and then in either kindergarten or third grade, at the school's discretion. Most elementary schools in the county, seizing the opportunity to create smaller classes, quickly arranged for extra classrooms and teachers. At nearly all schools, you can count on classes of 20 or fewer in kindergarten through third grade. Class sizes for grades four to six are typically 26 to 28 students.

If you're researching public schools in the area, be sure to call individual schools and request their School Accountability Report Card. School boards issue the Report Card annually across the state. It provides information about each school's resources, operations, successes, and areas of growth and improvement. Contents include a school profile, student achievement statistics, class sizes, budgets, expenditures, and other useful information. Most of the school districts in Santa Barbara County also post their report cards on the web. Go to www .sbceo.org/ schools and click on the "School Accountability Report Card" link.

Current Issues in the Public School System

The biggest issue Santa Barbara public schools face today is declining enrollment—especially in our elementary schools. Combine this with statewide budget cuts, and our schools are grappling with serious fiscal challenges. Both Santa Barbara and Goleta elementary schools are experiencing a decline in student enrollment that began almost a decade ago, and the districts expect this trend to continue. Recently, the Carpinteria Unified District also reported declines in student populations to the point where they may close one of the elementary schools.

It's not the quality of education that's affecting enrollment. So why are students leaving? Apart from lower birth rates, many blame the high cost of living on the South Coast. With the median home price hovering around $1 million, lower income families are forced to settle in more affordable satellite suburbs. At the same time, those who can afford to live here often choose to enroll their children in private schools or the more affluent public school districts. Goleta Union receives funds from the surrounding property tax base, but both the Santa Barbara and Carpinteria Union districts operate on a per-student funding allocation. When enrollment declines, these districts have less money to meet fixed expenses, and deficits can and do result.

i Researching Santa Barbara schools? Check out the Santa Barbara County Education website at www .sbceo.org. You'll find links to public and private schools, as well as API reports, School Accountability Report Cards, STAR test results, and other resources for parents, teachers, and students.

Faced with tough budgetary decisions, Santa Barbara school boards have so far managed to find creative ways to cut costs without sacrificing the quality of education. Parents rally to raise funds, and local businesses donate generous amounts of money and materials to schools in need. Of course, everyone has the best interests of the students at heart, and as long as this continues to drive future budgetary decisions, Santa Barbara public schools should continue to enjoy their excellent academic track record.

Public School District Overview

In this section we focus on the major school districts on the South Coast: Santa Barbara and Hope in Santa Barbara; Carpinteria; Cold Spring and Montecito Union in Montecito; and Goleta Union.

Santa Barbara

The Santa Barbara Elementary School/High School districts operated as separate districts until they officially became the Santa Barbara Unified School District on July 1, 2011. Facing a $10 million shortfall for 2012, district officials proposed the unification to generate $6 million. The increase in funding resulted from having the district size increase, which raised the funding limit per student. Without the increased revenue, the school district was going to be forced to make significant cuts, including layoffs and even a shortened school year. The district is governed by a single Board of Education, and under the California Education Code, the board operates independently from city or county governments. It has adopted an open-enrollment policy, meaning parents may enroll students at the school of their choice for as long as space permits.

SANTA BARBARA ELEMENTARY SCHOOL DISTRICT
720 Santa Barbara St., Santa Barbara
(805) 963-4338
www.sbsdk12.org
Kindergarten through grade 6

The Santa Barbara Elementary School District covers about 22 square miles in the City of Santa Barbara—and provides instruction for children in kindergarten through 6th grade.

It serves more than 5,900 students in 13 schools, including three charter schools (public schools that operate free of many state statutes and regulations) and an Open Alternative School (kindergarten through 8th grade), which has an open structure and curriculum. Some of the schools in this district have earned California Distinguished School status, an award that honors only the most exemplary of schools. In the past few years, Adams, Monroe, Roosevelt, and Washington Elementary and Peabody Charter School have received this prestigious award. In 2002 Adams was also the first school in Santa Barbara County to be recognized as a Title Achieving School for its success in meeting the needs of a diverse student population.

Seventy percent of the district's student enrollment is Hispanic, 25 percent is white, and the remaining enrollment comes from a variety of ethnicities.

In 1999 the district opened Santa Barbara Community Academy, a year-round elementary school requiring uniforms, which now enrolls about 300 students in kindergarten through 6th grade. The academy emphasizes a challenging academic curriculum, including foreign-language instruction starting in the early grades. If the number of applicants exceeds available space, students are selected via a lottery system.

In the fall of 2000, the Cesar Estrada Chavez Dual Language Immersion Charter School opened its doors. The school uses a 50-50 balance of both English and Spanish to teach a curriculum that meets state standards in all subjects. Most schools in the district offer a number of special programs, including GATE, Mentor Teacher programs, and Afterschool Enrichment Classes. On average, the district's student-to-teacher ratio is 20 to 1 in kindergarten through grade 3, and 27 to 1 in grades 4 through 6. Since about 45 percent of students do not speak, read, or write English proficiently, the district provides specialized programs such as English as a Second Language to help these students improve their English language skills.

SANTA BARBARA HIGH SCHOOL DISTRICT

720 Santa Barbara St., Santa Barbara
(805) 963-4331
www.sbsdk12.org
Grades 7 through 12

The Santa Barbara High School District serves approximately 10,600 students in grades 7 through 12. This district covers a much wider region than the elementary district—about 136 square miles—and draws students from all neighborhoods stretching from Goleta to Montecito. The district schools include five junior or middle schools (La Cumbre, La Colina, Santa Barbara, Santa Barbara Charter, and Goleta Valley), three high schools (Dos Pueblos, San Marcos, and Santa Barbara), and one continuation high school. About 18 percent are English Language Learners. Forty percent of the student enrollment is Hispanic, 47 percent is white, and the remaining enrollment comes from a variety of ethnicities.

Each school offers a comprehensive curriculum that meets all state and district standards. GATE, Advanced Placement, and ESL classes are available, and many of the schools have earned distinguished awards. In the past few years, La Colina Junior High, Goleta Valley Junior High, Santa Barbara Junior High, and San Marcos High School attained California Distinguished School status. Dos Pueblos High and Goleta Valley Junior High also received the illustrious National Blue Ribbon Award.

Consistently a standout in this impressive lineup of schools is Dos Pueblos High. For the past several years, students from the school earned the highest average SAT scores in the county: 119 points higher than the state average and 113 points higher than the national average. The Academic Performance Index places Dos Pueblos in the top 10 percent of all high schools in the state. Average scores at the other local high schools are slightly lower but also well above the national average.

Over the last few years, the district has launched some innovative on-campus academies or "school-within-a-school" programs. These academies are designed to prepare students for various careers. Santa Barbara High School has two on-campus academies for the visual arts and multimedia arts. In the fall of 2001, San Marcos High School introduced a Health Careers Academy, and Dos Pueblos High School launched an Engineering Academy in 2002 and the prestigious International Baccalaureate academic program in 2003. This pre-university course provides students ages 16 through 19 with a liberal arts curriculum to help them gain admission to top colleges and universities. Students wishing to enroll in these programs must submit an application for review.

All schools in this district offer a full range of athletic and extracurricular activities and are fully wired for the computer and Internet age. The student-teacher ratio is about 30 to 1 in grades 7 and 8 and 32 to 1 in grades 9 through 12. In grade 9, the student-to-teacher ratio for reading and mathematics is 20 to 1; in high school Advanced Placement, academies, and Reading for Success classes have a student-to-teacher ratio of 25 to 1.

Dos Pueblos Engineering Academy

Dos Pueblos High School students interested in science or engineering enroll in Dos Pueblos Engineering Academy, a hands-on college-preparatory program with a rigorous science curriculum. In 2010, the Engineering Academy (DPEA) Team 1717 took second place (out of 50 contending teams) at the San Diego Regional FIRST Robotics Competition, led by their physics professor, Amir Abo-Shaeer, a 2011 MacArthur Genuis Grant winner (which comes with a $500,000 no-strings-attached award).

HOPE SCHOOL DISTRICT
3970 La Colina Rd., Santa Barbara
(805) 682-2564
www.sbceo.k12.ca.us/~hopesd/
With approximately 1,350 students enrolled in kindergarten through grade 6, this small district consists of three excellent elementary schools in the Hope Ranch/San Roque/La Cumbre area: Monte Vista, Hope, and Vieja

Valley. Hope Elementary School reopened in September 1997 after being closed for more than 20 years. Monte Vista and Vieja Valley have both been named California Distinguished Schools in the last decade, and Monte Vista was recognized as a National Blue Ribbon School in 1997.

The Hope District provides a number of special programs, including GATE, Esperanza, and assistance for students with learning differences. Each school has computer labs with networked computers, and every classroom has a Macintosh computer with CD-ROM capabilities. The average number of students per teacher is 20 for kindergarten through grade 3 and 27 for grades 4 through 6.

Goleta
GOLETA UNION SCHOOL DISTRICT
401 N. Fairview Ave., Goleta
(805) 681-1200
www.goleta.k12.ca.us
Kindergarten through grade 6
The Goleta Union School District has nine schools with more than 3,500 students enrolled in kindergarten through grade 6. Class size is under 20 in grades K to 3 and 24 in grades 5 to 6. Approximately 35 percent of students are English Language Learners. The district has nationally recognized programs in bilingual education, composition, computer literacy, and mathematics. All the district's schools offer technology programs as well as music, art, and physical education. GATE is offered in grades 4, 5, and 6, and special education programs are available throughout the district. All schools have a computer center, and all classrooms are wired for high-speed communications.

Goleta Union parents and community members are very supportive and active participants in the schools, and the students' academic performance reflects this involvement. The district ranks consistently above the national average and state average in academic tests. In 2001 Mountain View was designated a Blue Ribbon School, the highest national honor bestowed upon a public or private school, and El Camino School and Kellogg School attained California Distinguished School status. El Camino also has a state preschool program known as the Children's Center for income eligible 4-year-olds. All the schools in this district have undergone extensive refurbishments in recent years.

Montecito
COLD SPRING SCHOOL DISTRICT
2243 Sycamore Canyon Rd., Montecito
(805) 969-2678
www.coldspringschool.net
Kindergarten through grade 6
Tucked in the lush foothills of Montecito, Cold Spring School is a one-school district serving approximately 200 students in kindergarten through 6th grade. Student academic performance at this excellent school consistently ranks in the top 5 to 10 percent of all elementary schools in California. Cold Spring School earned the California Distinguished School title in 1986 and 2010, and it was deemed a coveted Blue Ribbon School in 1997. In addition to its core teaching staff, the school employs a technology specialist; resource specialists for reading, special education, and language; and professional musicians and artists who provide instruction in visual arts, ceramic sculpture, drama, and music. The school integrates technology to support instruction and student learning with a 1-to-1 laptop program in grades 3 through 6,and if they wish, students can participate in an after-school enrichment program. The average number of students per teacher is 20 or fewer for kindergarten through grade 3 and 25 in grades 4 through 6.

MONTECITO UNION SCHOOL DISTRICT
385 San Ysidro Rd., Montecito
(805) 969-3249
www.sbceo.k12.ca.us/~montecit/
Kindergarten through grade 6
Set on a beautiful 8-acre site in an exclusive neighborhood, Montecito Union is a highly regarded one-school district with grades kindergarten through 6. Approximately 420 students are currently enrolled in the district, which has an outstanding academic record. Montecito Union remains one of the top 100 high-performing schools in California. In 1998 the school was awarded California Distinguished School status. It was one of only two schools in California to receive a perfect score on all 11 areas of evaluation. Montecito Union offers a GATE program and hires specialists to teach computer sciences, music, art, Spanish, physical education, and library sciences. In 2000 the district upgraded the campus, adding seven new classrooms and replacing six portable ones. Parents can expect an average of fewer than 20 students per teacher in kindergarten through grade 3, and 22 students per teacher in grades 4 through 6.

Carpinteria
CARPINTERIA UNIFIED SCHOOL DISTRICT
1400 Linden Ave., Carpinteria
(805) 684-4511
www.cusd.net/home
Carpinteria Unified serves the communities of Carpinteria and Summerland from Rincon

to Ortega Ridge Road and the Pacific Ocean to the Los Padres National Forest. The district's nine schools include five elementary schools one middle school, one high school and two alternative schools. About 3,000 students are enrolled in grades kindergarten through 12, and more than a third are classified as English Language Learners. In 2001, Carpinteria Middle School received the prestigious California Distinguished School award for the 2000–2001 school year, and Main Elementary and tiny 60-student Summerland Elementary received the award in 2002. Carpinteria High School has six academies—the Academy of the Media Arts, Culinary Arts Institute, Agriculture Science Technology Academy, Construction Technology, AVID, and Virtual Enterprise.

The district places a strong emphasis on integrating the tools of technology into its academic programs. Special education programs include GATE and assistance for those challenged in areas of learning, communication, and physical abilities. In addition, all English Language Learners receive primary language support through their core academic classes. The average number of students per teacher for the district is 20 for kindergarten through grade 3, 30 for grades 4 and 5, and 28 for grades 6 through 12.

PRIVATE SCHOOLS

Santa Barbara's private schools range from small, affordable, nonsecular schools to very expensive high schools that prepare students for entry into the best universities in the country. If you're looking into private schools, you'll have no trouble finding one that suits your children's academic interests and personalities. It might be difficult, however, to find one that pleases your pocketbook.

Typical annual tuition at private elementary schools can reach as high as $18,000 a year. Parochial schools are sponsored by parishes and usually cost considerably less. Many private schools offer some form of financial aid for qualified students—be sure to ask for information if your funds are limited.

Before you begin your search, be forewarned that applying to one of Santa Barbara's private schools does not guarantee admission. The most sought-after schools typically have only one or two classes per grade and are flooded with applicants. Some schools can have as many as 100 applications for a single, 20-student kindergarten class, which is often already filled with siblings of older students.

We recommend you apply to several schools to widen your options. At most independent schools, a child must be at least 5 and sometimes 5.5 years by September 1 in the year he or she enters kindergarten.

Santa Barbara also has a number of parish-supported elementary schools (Catholic, Episcopalian, and other denominations). Tuition at these schools is generally more affordable than at other independent schools. Keep in mind, however, that admission preference is given to registered active members of the parish. If you're interested in enrolling your children in a particular parochial school, we suggest you contact the parish directly.

Following is a roundup of many of the finest private schools in the area. All are coeducational. You can also check the Yellow Pages under "Schools" for a comprehensive list of local educational institutions.

EDUCATION & CHILD CARE

Santa Barbara

THE ANACAPA SCHOOL
814 Santa Barbara St., Santa Barbara
(805) 965-0228
www.anacapaschool.org
Grades 7 through 12
The Anacapa School is a college-prep day school. The student-to-teacher ratio is 6 to 1, and class sizes average 12 students. The curriculum emphasizes critical thinking, writing skills, creativity, and personal integrity and offers a wide range of classes from core academics to electives such as animation and organic gardening. Students go on regular field trips, day excursions, and two camping trips a year. Almost 100 percent of Anacapa graduates continue on to college, and many have gained admission to some of the nation's top tertiary institutions.

BISHOP GARCIA DIEGO HIGH SCHOOL
4000 La Colina Rd., Santa Barbara
(805) 967-1266
www.bishopdiego.org
Grades 9 through 12
Bishop Garcia Diego is a Catholic high school with an enrollment of approximately 300 students. It was founded in 1940 as Santa Barbara Catholic High and was later renamed to honor California's first bishop, Francisco Garcia Diego y Moreno. It operates in the Catholic tradition, teaching moral virtues and stressing a philosophy of scholarship and Christian service. The academic program offers a traditional, challenging, and comprehensive college preparatory curriculum. Advanced Placement classes are available to qualified students in English, American history, calculus, and Spanish. In recent years, 100 percent of Bishop graduates were accepted at colleges and universities throughout the country. The school

also offers a state-of-the-art technology program as well as courses in the creative arts. Average class size is 16 students, and the student-to-teacher ratio is 10 to 1. Bishop Garcia Diego is Santa Barbara's only Christian high school and admits students of all races, religions, and ethnic origins.

LAGUNA BLANCA SCHOOL
4125 Paloma Dr., Santa Barbara
(805) 687-2461
www.lagunablanca.org
Kindergarten through grade 12
Founded in 1933, Laguna Blanca School is a top-notch college-preparatory day school in Hope Ranch. The school offers advanced placement courses, an outstanding visual and performing arts program, a community-service component, interscholastic athletic competitions, student exchange opportunities, and a host of extracurricular activities. Not surprisingly, admission to Laguna is highly competitive. There is a maximum class size of just 13 students. Each year 100 percent of Laguna graduates are accepted to college.

MARYMOUNT OF SANTA BARBARA
2130 Mission Ridge Rd., Santa Barbara
(805) 569-1811
www.marymountsb.org
Kindergarten through grade 8
A member of the National and California Association of Independent Schools, Marymount is set on 10 acres of wooded grounds that were formerly an estate. The school enrolls about 243 students and welcomes qualified applicants of good character from all religious traditions, races, and ethnic origins for grades kindergarten through 8.

Marymount was founded in 1938 by the Religious of the Sacred Heart of Mary. Today it's a nonprofit corporation governed by a board of trustees and is one of the oldest and most respected private schools in Santa Barbara. Its two-track religion program (Catholic studies and religious studies) grows from the Judeo-Christian tradition and emphasizes moral development and community service. Students may choose an appropriate track, depending on their religious backgrounds.

The strong academic curriculum and small classes are designed to promote self-esteem and the love of learning in each student. Academic performance consistently ranks in the 50th percentile and above among the nation's independent schools. Marymount encourages creative expression and emphasizes physical fitness and good sportsmanship.

SANTA BARBARA CHRISTIAN SCHOOL
3723 Modoc Rd., Santa Barbara
(805) 563-4770
www.santabarbarachristian.com
Kindergarten through grade 8
Established in 1960, the Santa Barbara Christian School provides a program of high-quality, nondenominational Christian education. The curriculum focuses on helping students attain a balance of rigorous intellectual competence, healthy character development, and a personal commitment to Jesus Christ. Children from both Christian homes and those with no church affiliation are welcome. Total enrollment is around 100 students, and classes average about 18 students per teacher.

SANTA BARBARA MIDDLE SCHOOL
1321 Alameda Padre Serra,
Santa Barbara
(805) 682-2989
www.sbms.org
Grades 6 through 9
Founded in 1976, Santa Barbara Middle School spans grades 6 through 9 and seeks to develop well-rounded and self-confident teenagers through an innovative curriculum incorporating academics, creative arts and sports, community service, and outdoor education trips such as the Rite of the Wheel, where students bicycle more than 1,500 miles in seven states during the course of their enrollment. They hike and backpack, travel, eat, and camp with their headmaster and teachers. The annual trips teach students about the history, culture, and geography of a particular region, and they even learn to repair their own bikes! The school also boasts an excellent drama department and supplements its challenging academic curriculum with technology courses in computers, digital animation, and digital filming. The 120 students enrolled at the school are organized into age-appropriate academic villages with an average class size of about 16. Students also participate in a Career Study Week, during which students are exposed to career opportunities and are involved in community service.

THE WALDORF SCHOOL OF SANTA BARBARA
Main Campus: 401 N. Fairview, Goleta
(805) 967-6656
Early Childhood Campus: 5679 Hollister Ave., Goleta
Pre-kindergarten through grade 8
The Waldorf School of Santa Barbara is one of at least 1,000 Waldorf Schools. The 6-acre campus lies on a beautiful historical site between Mission Santa Barbara and the Natural History Museum. The school's approach to education is based on the principles of Waldorf Education, as initiated by Rudolf Steiner (1861–1925), an Austrian

philosopher/teacher. The role of teachers is to inspire imagination and intuition in the students so that they may develop their intellectual, creative, and social capacities. The curriculum integrates traditional academic subjects with the arts in a structured program tailored to the developmental age of each child. Subjects include math, science, music, art, foreign languages, humanities, handwork, dramatic arts, biodynamic gardening, and physical education. Grade classes average about 12 to 15 students.

Goleta
MONTESSORI CENTER SCHOOL
401 N. Fairview Ave., #1, Goleta
(805) 683-9383
www.mcssb.org
18 months old through grade 6
Founded in 1965, the Montessori Center School is a nonprofit organization offering preprimary, primary, and elementary education for approximately 300 students. Set amid beautiful gardens, the school adheres to the Montessori curriculum, which emphasizes hands-on, progressive, self-paced learning. Students work with specially designed learning materials at an early age to experience concrete principles and then move to greater complexity and abstraction. Most classes incorporate three different age or grade levels, which allows children to learn from one another and creates a "family" atmosphere. Spanish, art, music, and fitness are taught to children at a very young age, as well as theater and library studies for elementary students. Extracurricular classes range from sign language to t'ai chi. The school also serves children with special needs and offers before- and after-school care. Adult-to-child ratios are 1 to 6 in preprimary classes and 1 to 12 thereafter. In annual standardized tests,

MCS elementary students consistently average results between 2 and 3 years above their grade level, and graduates generally enroll in GATE or honors programs at middle and high school.

Montecito
CRANE SCHOOL
1795 San Leandro Ln.
Montecito
(805) 969-7732
www.craneschool.org
Kindergarten through grade 8
Set on 11 beautiful acres in affluent Montecito, Crane School offers a challenging academic curriculum. The school was established in 1928 and has an excellent reputation. Crane's teachers encourage independence and creativity while helping students use their education to become kind and responsible human beings. Art, drama, music, and athletics are critical facets of the syllabus, and the school offers a selection of special programs in areas such as technology, library media, visual arts, and physical education. The 8th-grade class trip to Bahia de los Angeles to work on a sea turtle preservation farm is something Crane alumni remember forever. Total enrollment is 230 students. Grades kindergarten through 5 have a maximum of 20 students per class, and grades 6 through 8 are divided into sections of 12 to 16 students. Admission is extremely competitive.

Carpinteria
CATE SCHOOL
1960 Cate Mesa Rd., Carpinteria
(805) 684-4127
www.cate.org
Grades 9 through 12
Cate School is regularly ranked among the top college-preparatory boarding schools

in the nation. The 4-year high school was established in 1910 and boasts a gorgeous, 150-acre campus set on a mesa overlooking the ocean and the Carpinteria Valley.

About 270 students from all over the world are enrolled at Cate, and approximately 220 of them live on campus. Average class size is 10 to 12 students, and the school offers Advanced Placement courses in more than 19 subjects.

Admission is competitive, and nearly 30 percent of the student body receives financial aid. In recent years Cate students have won National Merit Scholarships, National Science Scholarships, and numerous other awards. One hundred percent of Cate graduates go on to some of the nation's most selective 4-year colleges and universities.

THE HOWARD SCHOOL
5315 Foothill Rd., Carpinteria
(805) 745-8448
www.thehowardschool.org
Prekindergarten through grade 8
Known as Santa Barbara's oldest private school, this school was once located in Montecito but now is situated on the property of Girls Inc. in Carpinteria. The Howard School teaches the tools necessary for a comprehensive classical education. Its curriculum is based on the Carden method, established by Mae Carden in 1934. The approximately 80 students are taught in classes of no more than 15 students.

HIGHER EDUCATION

UNIVERSITY OF CALIFORNIA AT
**   SANTA BARBARA (UCSB)**
(805) 893-8000
www.ucsb.edu

UCSB is one of the 10 campuses that form the University of California system—widely regarded as the nation's leading public system of higher education. UCSB is unquestionably the academic jewel of the Santa Barbara area. Its presence extends well beyond the campus, influencing community arts, athletics, the intellectual scene, politics, and more.

Recently ranked one of the "hottest" colleges in the nation by *Newsweek*, UCSB offers 200 majors, degrees, and credentials. The campus includes three colleges: Letters and Science, Engineering, and Creative Studies. It's also home to two professional schools: the Gevirtz Graduate School of Education and the Bren School of Environmental Science and Management.

The university "family" includes about 18,000 undergraduates, 2,900 graduate students, and more than 1,050 faculty members. About 6,200 students live in campus housing, and most of the others live in adjacent Isla Vista, a high-density student

i No fewer than five Nobel Prize winners teach at UCSB. Nobel Prize laureates Finn E. Kydland (economics 2004), David J. Gross (physics 2004), Alan J. Heeger (chemistry 2000), Herbert Kroemer (physics 2000), and Walter Kohn (physics 1998) dazzled the community by winning Nobel Prizes in chemistry, economics, and physics.

community with shops, restaurants, and a zillion bicycles.

Since the campus consists of nearly 1,000 acres of prime coastal property on the edge of the Pacific, overlooking palm-lined beaches, lagoons, and some fantastic surf breaks on its doorstep, one might wrongly assume that academics are a low priority. On the contrary—since UCSB was founded in 1944, it has firmly established itself as a world-class research center and teaching institution.

A recent national study of America's top research universities ranks UCSB as one of the top public universities nationwide based on criteria such as research dollars, prestigious fellowships, and number of publications.

The university is best known for interdisciplinary research. In addition to its five Nobel Prize winners, the faculty also includes fellows of the National Endowment for the Humanities, recipients of the National Medal of Science, and members of the National Academy of Arts and Sciences, the National Academy of Sciences, the American Association for the Advancement of Science, and the National Academy of Engineering.

UCSB has 12 national research centers and institutes, including the Kavli Institute for Theoretical Physics, the Materials Research Laboratory, and the Southern California Earthquake Center. Eight of the centers are sponsored by the National Science Foundation.

UCSB is home to the California Nanosystems Institute, one of the first California Institutes of Science and Innovation. This research partnership between UCLA and UCSB is providing scientific advances that are critical to the California economy.

COMMUNITY COLLEGES & CONTINUING EDUCATION

SANTA BARBARA CITY COLLEGE (SBCC)
721 Cliff Dr., Santa Barbara
(805) 965-0581, ext. 7222
www.sbcc.net

Santa Barbara City College is renowned as a premier 2-year community college in California and the nation, ranked in the top 10 percent among community colleges nationwide. Founded in 1909, SBCC is among the oldest of the state's 112 community colleges. SBCC currently enrolls almost 20,000 credit students each semester along with more than 12,000 Continuing Education students each term.

As a public higher education institution, SBCC offers an extensive program of postsecondary education that is responsive to the needs of the state of California and adults in the local community. A wide range of associate degree and certificate programs is available, as are transfer programs that provide the first 2 years of study toward a baccalaureate degree. Through partnerships, qualified SBCC students are guaranteed transfer to a number of 4-year universities including campuses in the University of California System and the California State University System.

Responding to state and community needs, the college's programs address economic development, workforce and job training, skills enhancement, and lifelong learning opportunities.

Through SBCC's Continuing Education Division's Adult High School, the college also offers programs in basic skills, including Citizenship and English as a Second Language, and a variety of courses geared to a wide range of interests for the lifelong learner.

Students range in age from under 18 to over 80 years and represent the diversity of the state and the South Coast region.

SANTA BARBARA CITY COLLEGE
CONTINUING EDUCATION DIVISION
www.sbcc.edu/ce/

Alice F. Schott Center
310 W. Padre St., Santa Barbara
(805) 687-0812

Selmer O. Wake Center
300 N. Turnpike Rd., Santa Barbara
(805) 964-6853

SBCC Continuing Education is the noncredit division of Santa Barbara City College, dedicated to maintaining a strong program of lifelong learning that is affordable and accessible to the entire community.

Continuing Education's state-supported offerings include an adult high school program; short-term vocational programs; English as a second language classes; parenting, health, and safety courses; family and consumer sciences; and education programs for older adults.

Also offered are a number of community education courses (for a tuition fee) in disciplines including arts and crafts, cooking, literature, music, fitness, and personal development.

Please visit the website for more information about SBCC Continuing Education.

UNIVERSITY OF CALIFORNIA AT
SANTA BARBARA EXTENSION
6950 Hollister Ave., Goleta
(805) 893-4200
www.unex.ucsb.edu

UCSB Extension offers university-level certificate programs, seminars, and online courses designed for professional training and career advancement. The wide range of courses includes art and design, business and management, computers and technology, education, legal studies, and mediation.

Through the UCSB Extension, you can earn university credits and certificates and fulfill professional continuing education and relicensure requirements. Courses are offered every quarter, year-round.

Private Colleges, Universities & Specialty Schools

Santa Barbara

ANTIOCH UNIVERSITY SANTA BARBARA
801 Garden St., Santa Barbara
(805) 962-8179
www.antiochsb.edu

Antioch University Santa Barbara is an extension of Antioch University, which was founded in Yellow Springs, Ohio, in 1852. The Santa Barbara campus opened in 1977. Most of the students enrolled at Antioch are working adults who wish to earn an undergraduate or graduate degree. Antioch offers a BA program in liberal arts and MA programs in organizational management, education and teaching, clinical ·psychology, and social justice and educational leadership. You can also sign up for the weekend college courses in management offered once a month.

BROOKS INSTITUTE OF PHOTOGRAPHY
27 E. Cota Street, Santa Barbara
(805) 585-8000, (888) 276-4999
www.brooks.edu

Brooks specializes in professional photographic and motion picture education, with state-of-the-art resources, an outstanding faculty, and two campuses: one in downtown Santa Barbara; the other in Ventura for motion picture studies.

Ernest H. Brooks Sr., a professional photographer, founded the school in 1945 after his return from military service. Today the school has a faculty of more than 32 experts who pass on their knowledge to men and women from around the world. In the photography world, the institute is reputed to have the finest professors and facility in the nation.

Brooks prepares students for careers in the diverse disciplines of professional, commercial, and still photography and filmmaking. It also has programs geared toward the working photographer seeking new skills to advance within the industry.

Great emphasis is placed on a well-rounded general education; courses in communications, marketing, and business teach skills essential for success in the competitive marketplace. Students have access to the latest technology and practices in the field.

The institute offers AA, BA, and MS degrees and a diploma program, short-term courses, and weekend workshops in a variety of photographic disciplines. It also recently added a visual journalism program, which cross-trains students in still cameras, computers, and digital video cameras. Once every 2 years, Brooks students travel abroad on an international documentary project (for example, to China, Africa, India, Mexico, or Cuba) and present an exhibit when they return.

FIELDING GRADUATE UNIVERSITY
2112 Santa Barbara St., Santa Barbara
(805) 687-1099, (800) 340-1099
www.fielding.edu
Founded in 1974, Fielding Graduate University is a regionally accredited graduate school offering doctoral and master's degree programs and continuing professional education in the fields of psychology, human and organizational development, and educational leadership and change. Fielding's

postgraduate certificates include neuropsychology and respecialization in psychology and clinical psychology.

Also home to the Alonso Center for Psychodynamic Studies, this educational facility is perhaps best known for its innovative and flexible curriculum designed to serve mid-career professionals juggling work, family, and community commitments. The university's supportive competency-based approach to learning and assessment combines both theory and practice. Students build on their existing knowledge and professional experience and self-direct their learning through a mix of independent study, structured course work, and face-to-face and online collaboration with an extensive network of scholars, faculty members, and practitioners.

MUSIC ACADEMY OF THE WEST
1070 Fairway Rd., Santa Barbara
(805) 969-4726
www.musicacademy.org
The Music Academy of the West is one of the finest summer music schools in the country. It was established in 1947 by a group of dedicated art patrons and celebrated musicians, including legendary German opera singer Lotte Lehmann.

The academy's 8-week Summer School and Festival provides gifted young musicians with the opportunity for advanced study and performance under the guidance of internationally known faculty and visiting artists.

For more than 50 years, the school has attracted a stellar lineup of performing and teaching talent (for example, Metropolitan Opera star Marilyn Horne, director of the academy's voice program, and piano pedagogue Jerome Lowenthal) and thousands of gifted Fellows, many of whom later established critically acclaimed careers. More than 5,000 graduates have passed through the academy's gates, and they fill the ranks of major symphony orchestras and opera houses throughout the world. All those accepted to the academy through its rigorous audition process are awarded full scholarships, covering tuition, lodging, and meals for the entire 8 weeks.

The academy's permanent campus is located at Miraflores, a Mediterranean-style estate on a bluff overlooking the Pacific Ocean. It occupies 9 acres of wooded, beautifully landscaped grounds and gardens.

SANTA BARBARA COLLEGE OF LAW
20 E. Victoria St., Santa Barbara
(805) 966-0010
www.santabarbaralaw.edu
Conveniently located in the heart of downtown, the Santa Barbara College of Law opened in 1975. The school provides high-quality legal education through an affordable part-time evening program, leading to a juris doctor degree and eligibility to sit for the California State Bar Examination. Experienced attorneys and judges comprise the faculty, and the campus includes an extensive library and computer facilities. Students usually complete the program in 3.5 to 4 years.

WESTMONT COLLEGE
955 La Paz Rd., Santa Barbara
(805) 565-6000
www.westmont.edu
Founded in 1937, Westmont College is a residential 4-year college committed to the Christian faith. It provides a high-quality undergraduate liberal arts program in a residential campus community. About 1,330

students coming from within the nation and worldwide are currently enrolled at the school. The student/faculty ratio is 13 to 1, with 136 full-time faculty.

Westmont offers Bachelor of Arts and Bachelor of Science degrees in 26 liberal arts majors; 10 preprofessional programs; a 5th-year credential program; and numerous internships and practica. The extensive list of majors includes art, psychology, theater arts, religious studies, kinesiology, biology, and chemistry, just to name a few. Forty-three percent of students go on to graduate school. The average class size is 23. The gorgeous campus occupies 111 wooded acres—a collection of grounds from two former estates and a school for boys—in the Montecito foothills off Cold Spring Road. Westmont organizes numerous creative and performing arts programs, lectures, and sports events.

Carpinteria
PACIFICA GRADUATE INSTITUTE
249 Lambert Rd., Carpinteria
801 Ladera Ln., Montecito
(805) 969-3626
www.pacifica.edu
Accredited by the Western Association of Schools and Colleges (WASC), Pacifica Graduate Institute provides graduate degree programs in depth psychology (MA, PhD), depth psychology with an emphasis in psychotherapy (PhD), clinical psychology (PhD), counseling psychology (MA), mythological studies (MA, PhD), and humanities with an emphasis in mythology and depth psychology (MA). The school occupies a tree-studded, 13-acre campus in the Carpinteria foothills replete with wildlife-friendly plants, organic orchards, and vegetable gardens.

Reflecting the belief that human experience is diverse and multifaceted, Pacifica offers degree programs that are interdisciplinary in nature. Literature, religion, art, and mythology supplement the study of psychology. During the fall, winter, and spring quarters, students attend classes on campus during a 3-day learning retreat once a month. Most programs also include a 1-week summer session. Between sessions, students continue their course work through reading, research, and practicum experiences in their homes. This unique educational format is particularly suited to people who wish to pursue graduate education while continuing their current professional and personal commitments.

CHILD CARE

If you're working or just need time to get some "adult" things done, you'll be happy to know that Santa Barbara has many excellent facilities where your children can learn, play, and socialize with their pals under the careful supervision of qualified child care providers. Your options range from licensed homes to large, church-affiliated centers, to on-site child care programs at businesses or institutions.

We must advise you, however, that most child care facilities have long waiting lists, especially those with affordable fees and/or excellent reputations. It's not uncommon for parents to sign up their kids as soon as they're born—or even earlier. Many parents find it necessary to arrange for alternative care in their own homes (nannies, babysitters) until a child reaches preschool age.

Santa Barbara has many outstanding preschools, which typically accept children from ages 2 through 5. If you have a baby or toddler, we recommend that you visit the schools and get on the waiting lists as early as possible.

i Montecito über-mom Lisa Blades of the consulting service Nesting . . . 123 helps new parents with green nursery design for their babies, coaching new parents, creating organic environments, and childproofing the house. For info, go to www.nesting123.com or call Lisa at (805) 455-0687.

When choosing a preschool, don't immediately write off a school that isn't accredited. Preschool accreditation is a fairly new program. The National Academy of Early Childhood Programs (part of the National Association for the Education of Young Children) administers this voluntary accreditation system, which evaluates whether a program meets nationally recognized criteria for high quality. Accreditation is available to all types of preschools, kindergartens, child care centers, and school-age child care programs. But only a few local centers are currently accredited—it costs money to apply and the process is lengthy.

The best resources for finding out about child care are described below. You can also pick up *Santa Barbara Family Life*, a free monthly magazine that includes listings and ads on child care, preschools, and after-school day care; call (805) 965-4545 or check out www.sbparent.com.

**CHILDREN'S RESOURCE AND
  REFERRAL PROGRAM**
1124 Castillo St., Santa Barbara
(805) 962-8988
www.fsacares.org

The Children's Resource and Referral Program is administered through the Santa Barbara Family Care Center. It's one of more than 60 Resource and Referral Programs funded by the California Department of Education. The program provides information about all types of licensed child care centers and private providers and distributes information on choosing quality child care. It also has a lending library with videos, toys, and resources for caregivers, parents, and community members. Telephone and walk-in referrals are available Mon through Fri from 8 a.m. to noon and 1 to 3 p.m.

CHILDTIME PROFESSIONAL NANNY
Placement Service
536 Brinkerhoff Ave., Santa Barbara
(805) 962-4433
www.childtimenanny.com
ChildTime is a licensed and bonded nanny placement agency that specializes in matching nannies with families. Established in 1985, ChildTime sets high standards for its nannies. Selection is based on a careful screening and interview process. References, DMV records, and backgrounds are checked. Nannies are required to have CPR certification and to take a Nannies Skills Class.

Nannies are available for full-time or part-time positions on a live-in or live-out basis. ChildTime also has on-call temporary nannies who will come to your hotel or residence.

i *Want to meet other moms and dads whose babies are the same age as yours? Call PEP—Postpartum Education for Parents—at (805) 564-3888 or visit www.sbpep.org. This nonprofit volunteer organization will put you in touch with a group of local parents.*

After-School Care

All public and most private schools in the area offer after-school care, either on-site or at convenient locations in the vicinity of schools. When you enroll your child at a school, be sure to ask about your options. Some after-school care programs fill quickly, so be sure to do your research well in advance.

LOU GRANT PARENT CHILD WORKSHOP
Director: Ellen Stoddard
(805) 684-5310
www.lgpcw.org/learn.htm
Preschool
The Lou Grant Parent Child Workshop is officially one of four Santa Barbara City College Continuing Education programs in parenting. It allows parents to supervise their preschool-age children in various activities, letting them interact with other children of the same age. The family-oriented atmosphere allows parents to share new ideas and opinions on parenting with each other to cultivate original solutions to everyday issues. The funding for this program comes entirely from tuition and fund-raising activities. All of the money raised—100 percent—is put toward equipment, salaries, scholarships, and other items necessary for operation. There is a waiting list for the program, so plan accordingly.

School-Age Child Care

The Santa Barbara Elementary School District offers after-school child care at all elementary schools. Many of these programs are funded by the state Department of Education, Child Development Division. Several programs are funded through parent fees. One site (Peabody) is funded by a unique three-way partnership between the city, county, and school district. These programs run year-round. A staff member picks up kindergarten students from their classrooms during the school year. Children in 1st through 3rd grade walk to the center classrooms. Most centers close at 6 p.m. During the summer, and some other times when the elementary schools are closed, the centers are open 7:30 a.m. to 6 p.m.

The children are served a nutritious snack each day during the school year and breakfast, lunch, and snack are served when the centers are open full days. The major focus of the program is to provide a safe, enriching, and educationally sound environment that supplements and supports the regular school program. Homework, enrichment activities, outdoor organized and free-choice activities, and indoor small- and large-group activities are offered. During the summer, an academic program is offered and special enrichment themes are used. Field trips and specialists in music, drama, art, and physical education are also added to enhance the curriculum.

For information call the enrollment clerk, (805) 965-4633, or head teacher (805) 965-4633, extension 251.

RETIREMENT

When people dream of retirement, they often envision a comfortable home in a warm, dry climate, a region with plenty of social, recreational, and cultural opportunities, excellent health care, friendly people, and inspirational scenery. Santa Barbara, by all accounts, matches this dream. For more than a century, countless seniors and younger retirees from around the United States and the world have packed their belongings and moved to Santa Barbara. In this chapter, we focus on seniors, since they comprise the majority of retired folk in Santa Barbara.

The over-60 crowd makes its presence known everywhere. They play a major role in politics, the arts and culture scene, and adult education classes. Senior volunteers serve as docents at the museums, the zoo, the botanic garden, and other attractions; as helpers at our numerous service agencies; as tutors, teachers, guides, and mentors to younger Santa Barbarans. Our seniors also tend to stay active as long as possible. Folks from age 60 to 100 regularly attend fitness classes—it's not unusual to see a grandmother "crunching abs" right next to a 20-year-old. They walk, jog, play tennis and golf, attend concerts, travel, study, and read.

When seniors are no longer able to venture out as much as they'd like, Santa Barbara makes great efforts to bring services and activities to senior residences throughout the community.

OVERVIEW

Sound perfect? Well, there's one catch. As we've mentioned elsewhere in this book, the cost of living here is exorbitant. In fact, it's virtually impossible to live here on Social Security alone, and seniors with limited incomes find it extremely difficult to meet the costs of daily life. Housing and services for lower-income seniors have limited availability and long waiting lists.

Affordability aside, Santa Barbara offers many advantages for retired residents. In this

chapter we give you a sampling of our services and programs for seniors—with a special focus on those that can help stretch limited dollars.

We start with any general information resources; then move on to senior centers; ways to nourish the body and mind; recreation; employment and volunteer opportunities; retirement communities; and housing. For information on Santa Barbara's extensive health care system, see the Health Care & Wellness chapter.

TAPPING INTO THE SENIOR NETWORK

Your best resource for finding out about senior services and programs is the *Santa Barbara County Senior Resource Directory.* It includes listings of nearly all nonprofit and government agencies that provide services to senior citizens. Its contents are the foundation of this chapter, and you won't find a more comprehensive compendium of information for seniors anywhere else in the county. To receive a copy, call the nonprofit Central Coast Commission for Senior Citizens at (800) 510-2020 in California (which connects you to the area code you are dialing from) or the local branch number, (805) 925-9554, or visit the website at http://centralcoastseniors.org.

Senior Resources

The following organizations provide information on a variety of topics of interest to seniors.

AMERICAN ASSOCIATION OF RETIRED PERSONS (AARP)

Santa Barbara Chapter #72
333 Old Mill Rd., #263, Santa Barbara
(805) 967-9289
(916) 448-3614, regional headquarters
www.aarp.org

AARP is the nation's leading organization for people age 50 and older. AARP's motto, "The power to make it better," reflects its commitment to preserving the independence and autonomy of all older persons. It serves the needs of seniors through advocacy, research, and consumer information. An extensive network of local chapters and volunteers provides educational programs and community services for our nation's older population.

Local Santa Barbara Chapter #72 holds meetings the first Mon of each month at 1:15 p.m. at 1232 De la Vina St., Santa Barbara.

AREA AGENCY ON AGING/CENTRAL COAST COMMISSION FOR SENIOR CITIZENS

528 S. Broadway, Santa Maria (headquarters)
(800) 510-2020 (regional toll-free number), (805) 925-9554
www.centralcoastseniors.org

The Older Americans Act (1965) and its subsequent amendments in 1973 gave birth to Area Agencies on Aging, a network of federal, state, and local agencies, all working together to help seniors maintain independence and dignity in the environments they choose. At the local level, the Area Agency on Aging works in tandem with other public and private agencies to provide senior citizens with a wide range of services.

The Area Agency on Aging for the Santa Barbara region is the Central Coast Commission for Senior Citizens. The organization, which is based in Santa Maria, provides information over the phone and through its website and publishes the *Senior Resource Directory.* Its programs include home-delivered meals, senior lunches, in-home support services, respite for caregivers, information and referral, transportation services, legal assistance, senior day care services, senior citizen centers, home repair, and peer counseling.

Senior Connection is a special service of the Area Agency on Aging. The staff can give you information, refer you to appropriate programs and services, and help you with just about any question you have relating to senior citizens.

FAMILY SERVICE AGENCY SENIOR OUTREACH PROGRAM

123 W. Gutierrez St., Santa Barbara
(805) 965-1001
www.fsacares.org

FSA is Santa Barbara County's oldest non-profit human service agency. If you're older than 60 and live in Santa Barbara, Carpinteria, or Goleta, FSA will send a professional counselor to your home to assess your needs. Then it will connect you with the appropriate community resources. FSA will also provide individual, group, and family counseling if you so desire.

> **i** Need assistance with a critical but nonemergency issue? Call 211, the help line established by the Family Service Agency to help unburden the 911 lines.

SENIOR CENTERS

All the area community senior centers provide a vast range of information and resources, and each center offers different types of services. Typical examples are lunch programs, community education, recreational activities, music, health screenings, arts and crafts classes, computer training, and health insurance counseling. Senior centers are excellent places to meet with other seniors and stay active.

CARRILLO RECREATION CENTER

100 E. Carrillo St., Santa Barbara
(805) 897-2519

Active seniors love the Carrillo Recreation Center, with its Active Adult classes of stretch-and-tone and Jazzercise. Known for its spring-loaded dance floors, this center bursts with all kinds of dance classes for adults, including tap, salsa, folk, and tango. The Carrillo Street Gym next door offers table tennis and weight conditioning.

LOUISE LOWRY DAVIS RECREATION CENTER

1232 De la Vina St., Santa Barbara
(805) 897-2568

The Louise Lowry Davis Recreation Center is one of the most popular senior centers in the city. Located downtown on the corner of De la Vina and Sola Streets, the center serves as headquarters for the Senior Citizens Information Service. On fair-weather days, you can always see groups of smiling, laughing seniors bowling on the adjacent lawns. You can walk in and join various activities (e.g., chess and bridge) or sign up for weekday recreation programs. The center has a kitchen area, serving area, meeting rooms, restrooms, and on-site parking.

Frequently Called Numbers

Santa Barbara's senior citizens have access to a wealth of resources. Here's a list of telephone numbers that you'll probably want to have on hand for quick and easy reference.

The Eldercare Locator, (800) 677-1116

Family Service Agency, (805) 965-1001

Senior Connection, (800) 510-2020

Other Senior Centers

Other area senior centers also provide social, educational, and recreational services and facilities.

GOLETA SENIOR CENTER
5679 Hollister Ave., Goleta
(805) 683-1124

COMMUNITY ACTION SENIOR CENTER
941 Walnut Ave., Carpinteria
(805) 684-6090

NUTRITION

Grocery Resources

Call the Senior Connection at (800) 510-2020 for a list of stores in your area that deliver or for the names and phone numbers of services that will do your shopping for you.

Meals Delivered to Your Home

COMMUNITY ACTION COMMISSION MOBILE MEALS
5681 Hollister Ave., Goleta
(805) 692-4979
www.cacsb.com
For $3, Mobile Meals delivers a hot meal Mon through Fri from 10:30 a.m. to 2 p.m. to homebound seniors ages 60 and older. Frozen meals for weekends and holidays are also available. The delivery area includes Santa Barbara, Goleta, and Carpinteria.

MEALS-ON-WHEELS
(805) 683-1565
Meals-on-Wheels delivers hot midday meals to homebound seniors every day year-round, including holidays. They charge a modest fee for each meal—call between 9 a.m. and noon for more information.

i Need help picking up your groceries? Call the Market Van at (805) 965-1531. If you're 60 or older, of limited income, and have impairments that make it difficult for you to shop alone, the van will pick you up at your home every Friday for a $10 monthly donation. Call for details on eligible areas.

SENIOR BROWN BAG PROGRAM
4554 Hollister Ave., Santa Barbara
(805) 967-5741
A project of the Santa Barbara County Food Bank, Brown Bag distributes market-size bags of groceries twice a month to six different sites in Santa Barbara, Goleta, and Carpinteria. The bags are meant to supplement seniors' grocery shopping and include a variety of food items, including produce and bread. To be eligible for this free program, you must be 60 or older, have a limited income, and be in an independent-living situation. Singles or couples may apply.

Dining with Friends

CLIFF DRIVE SENIOR LUNCHEON
418 Santa Fe Place, Santa Barbara
(805) 965-4286
Join other seniors for lunch the first and third Thurs of the month (from 11 a.m. to 1 p.m.) in the recreation room across the road from the Free Methodist Church. A $3 donation is suggested. The program doesn't operate in August.

Community Action Commission Senior Nutrition Sites

If you're 60 or older, you're eligible for hot lunches at a nutrition site. You need to make reservations 24 hours in advance. Meals are free, but donations are suggested. If you need a ride to the site, transportation may be available. Call the commission headquarters for information and to make reservations at any of the following sites. It's located at 5681 Hollister Ave. in Goleta (805-692-4979; www .cacsb.com).

PRESIDIO SPRINGS
721 Laguna St., Santa Barbara

WESTSIDE COMMUNITY CENTER
423 W. Victoria St., Santa Barbara

GOLETA SENIOR CENTER
5679 Hollister Ave., Goleta

CARPINTERIA SENIOR CENTER
941 Walnut St., Carpinteria

RECREATION

Santa Barbara's recreational opportunities are available to active people of every age. See our Recreation chapter for a detailed overview of your many options. Many facilities offer senior discounts—be sure to ask whenever you inquire about information or pay fees.

SENIOR RECREATION SERVICES CLUB/ ACTIVE ADULTS PROGRAM
Santa Barbara Parks and Recreation
100 E. Carrillo St., Santa Barbara
(805) 897-2519, (805) 965-3813
www.sbparksandrecreation.com
If you're 50 years of age or older, you can join the Active Adults Program for only $41 a year ($45 nonresident). Club members are eligible for free or low-cost fees to a range of fitness and personal-enrichment classes.

Fitness activities include yoga, badminton, table tennis, various exercise classes, t'ai chi, Dancercise, slow-pitch softball, lawn bowling, and horseshoes. The stretch-and-tone class is particularly popular. Personal enrichment

classes and social events include dances, bingo, movie days, social luncheons, language classes, ceramics and painting classes, support groups, chess, and bridge games. Most fitness activities take place at the Carrillo Recreation Center, 100 E. Carrillo St., and Louise Lowry Davis Center, 1232 De la Vina St.

EDUCATION

There's no age limit for expanding the mind, and Santa Barbara offers an extraordinary array of educational opportunities. You'll find a variety of lectures, classes, forums, field trips, and poetry readings. Here we'd like to highlight one of Santa Barbara's shining stars—the Adult Continuing Education Program under the guidance of Santa Barbara City College—which actually targets seniors and provides special educational programs just for the over-50 set.

SANTA BARBARA CITY COLLEGE CONTINUING EDUCATION DIVISION
www.sbcc.edu/ce

Alice F. Schott Center
310 W. Padre St., Santa Barbara
(805) 687-0812

Selmer O. Wake Center
300 N. Turnpike Rd., Santa Barbara
(805) 964-6853
The Continuing Education Division of Santa Barbara City College, aka Adult Ed, offers an incredible range of noncredit and community service classes. During fall, winter, spring, and summer sessions, classes meet weekday mornings, afternoons, and evenings as well as Saturday. More than 12,000 people enroll in adult ed classes every year.

Most classes take place at the Alice F. Schott Center, others at the Selmer O. Wake Center, in addition to more than 100 locations in the greater Santa Barbara area. Many classes are free, with minimal fees for materials. This could change with the state budget cuts, however, and the notion of charging put the town in an uproar that unseated the longtime SBCC board of trustees and replaced them with a new board in 2011.

Many of the classes are specially designed for seniors. Subjects include the arts, business, finance, real estate, job training, computers, cooking and wine, crafts, current events and world affairs, literature, writing, home and garden, humanities, languages, music, and photography. The Omega Program (www.sbcc.edu/omega .htm), developed especially for seniors, offers classes and workshops related to the subject of aging. The Omega Program fosters self-esteem and dignity and helps seniors develop an appreciation of their past roles.

VOLUNTEER OPPORTUNITIES

Give the gift of your talent, skills, and time to the community. Many human service agencies such as hospitals, museums, homeless shelters, children's programs, wildlife agencies, and libraries depend on volunteers to keep things running smoothly. Contact specific organizations that interest you directly, or if you need help, check out the organization below.

**RETIRED SENIOR VOLUNTEER
PROGRAM (RSVP) SANTA BARBARA**
35 W. Victoria St., Santa Barbara
(805) 963-0474
www.rsvpsb.net
RSVP places seniors in volunteer positions at schools, hospitals, service agencies, senior centers, and other senior programs.

RETIREMENT COMMUNITIES & ASSISTED LIVING

It's very difficult for anyone to find affordable housing in Santa Barbara County. Low-cost rentals for seniors are available, but they are in extremely high demand and have long waiting lists. If you have a large nest egg put aside, you may be able to buy or rent a home in your choice of neighborhoods (see the Relocation chapter).

If you're like many seniors, you may be seeking the security and comfort of a retirement community where you can socialize with peers and take advantage of services that ease the challenges of daily life. All the retirement communities below offer, at the minimum, 24-hour security and housekeeping services. We've focused on communities with independent-living residences, although many of these also offer facilities for assisted living as well as skilled nursing.

People who opt for assisted living don't need full-time nursing care, but do need some help with dressing, bathing, eating, taking medications, and mobility. Assisted living facilities provide these services while allowing residents to retain privacy and independence.

We do not cover skilled nursing homes here. We recommend that you call Central Coast Seniors at (800) 510-2020 if you need information about this level of care in the community. If you're not sure what type of residence is best for you, just ask for guidance. The experienced staff will be more than happy to help.

Continuing Care Retirement Communities

These facilities offer a continuum of care: independent residential apartments or homes and separate facilities for assisted-living and skilled-nursing care. Costs vary significantly. Some require hefty entry fees plus monthly payments for services. At others, you pay month to month without a significant entry fee or endowment. Be sure to inquire about all the financial requirements when you request information.

Santa Barbara
THE SAMARKAND
2550 Treasure Dr., Santa Barbara
(805) 687-0701, (800) 370-5357
www.covenantretirement.com
This Christian continuing care retirement community is situated on a 16-acre, centrally located campus in a residential neighborhood bordered by Oak Park, Las Positas Road, and State Street. The Samarkand property was originally a boys' school, which closed in 1920. The land was then subdivided, and the complex became a resort hotel, which was named after the capital city of the Mongol conqueror Tamerlane. A group of local businessmen converted the property to a retirement community in 1955 and sold it to the Evangelical Covenant Church in 1966.

Today the Samarkand is one of 14 Covenant Retirement Communities run by a nonprofit corporation of the Evangelical Covenant Church. The Samarkand campus has between 400 and 500 residents in independent-living apartments ranging from residential independent living studios to 2-bedroom units, assisted living units, and beds in skilled nursing facilities. Amenities include a 24-hour emergency call system, housekeeping, linen service, 3 meals a day, comprehensive health services, and much more.

Residents of Samarkand have access to many recreational amenities. The grounds encompass a lovely swimming pool and Jacuzzi, exercise room, library, billiard room,

woodworking workshop, and hobby room, and residents can participate in organized activities and adult education programs. Community areas include a 220-seat fellowship hall, a private lounge for small groups, a dining room, and a chapel.

The Samarkand also has scheduled transportation for church, shopping, and appointments, as well as a gift shop, chaplain services, and a barber/beauty shop.

VALLE VERDE RETIREMENT COMMUNITY
900 Calle de Los Amigos, Santa Barbara
(805) 687-1571
www.valleverdesb.com
Valle Verde's 65-acre campus rests in the hills of the serene Hidden Valley neighborhood near Hope Ranch and Arroyo Burro (Hendry's Beach). It's owned and operated by American Baptist Homes of the West, a nonprofit corporation that has provided retirement housing and health care services since 1949. Valle Verde opened in 1966 and today offers several levels of care.

Many residents ride bikes, golf carts, or enjoy strolling around the flat, sprawling campus, which seems like a country club on a golf course. Amenities include a solar-heated pool and Jacuzzi, library, theater, private dining room, beauty/barber shop, and a convenience store. It also has a putting green, fitness center, hiking trails to the surrounding foothills, and city bus service. Activities include adult education and exercise classes.

All the apartments are ground-floor units with private patios and feature an emergency call system that connects directly with Valle Verde's Health Center, where registered gerontology professionals are always available. The wellness department offers a daily nursing clinic, and the dietary department can design a special diet if required.

If your needs change, you can move to assisted living accommodations in Quail Lodge or to the Health Care Center, a skilled nursing facility. Each spacious suite in Quail Lodge has a living area and private bath, along with a call bell system that connects you with staff 24 hours a day. The lodge serves 3 meals a day in a private dining room, and meals are tailored to the individual dietary requirements of each resident. It also provides housekeeping and maintenance services as well as activities. At the Health Center, licensed nurses and certified nursing assistants are on duty around the clock, providing postoperative and rehabilitative care and other support services.

Valle Verde also provides enhanced care for residents with Alzheimer's and other mild dementia in private apartments with specially trained staff available 24 hours a day.

Valle Verde welcomes pets.

VILLA SANTA BARBARA
227 E. Anapamu St., Santa Barbara
(805) 963-4428

Villa Santa Barbara is located just a few blocks from the heart of downtown Santa Barbara's arts and culture district. Residents can walk to the Arlington Theatre, cafes, restaurants, the central library, bookstores, movie theaters, shopping, churches, and the Museum of Art.

Villa Santa Barbara's spacious apartments are available for rent on a monthly basis, with no initial investment other than a nonrefundable service fee. The monthly fee covers 24-hour staffing, tableside dining service (3 meals a day, plus a 24-hour snack and beverage bar), housekeeping and linen services, transportation, and a full recreation program. Activities such as t'ai chi and craft classes, international dinners, and beach walks are available on-site or within walking distance.

Choose from studio alcove or 1-bedroom apartments, some with a kitchenette and a terrace overlooking the garden. On-site facilities include a hair salon for both men and women, a library, a TV room, billiards, a theater/music room, and a roof-garden terrace. Villa Santa Barbara is located near doctors' offices, Cottage Hospital, and Sansum–Santa Barbara Medical Foundation Clinic; the staff provides transportation to appointments. It also provides Alzheimer's care.

VISTA DEL MONTE
3775 Modoc Rd., Santa Barbara
(805) 687-0793, (800) 736-1333
www.frontporch.net

Vista del Monte is owned and operated by Front Porch, a not-for-profit organization that grew from a California teacher's service program established in 1928. Opened in 1964, this serene complex features beautiful landscaping, expansive lawns, and stately pines, and the entire complex has been vigorously refurbished to keep the buildings looking fresh and new. It's open to anyone 62 and older. The complex is located next to affluent Hope Ranch, near the Santa Barbara community golf course, hiking trails, and popular Arroyo Burro (Hendry's Beach).

Vista del Monte offers spacious independent-living and assisted-living apartments, a skilled-nursing facility, and specialized care for Alzheimer's patients. Residents also have access to a fitness and aquatic center with an excellent therapy pool, an adult education program, and an active residents' association. If you need limited assistance with daily activities, you can arrange for a home attendant to come to your residence. In assisted-living apartments, staff is available to help around the clock.

Montecito
CASA DORINDA
300 Hot Springs Rd., Montecito
(805) 969-8011
www.casadorinda.com

This lush retirement community on 48 beautifully landscaped acres is the ultimate place to spend your golden years. It originally operated as a for-profit institution, but since 1988 it's been owned and operated by the Montecito Retirement Association, a community-sponsored, not-for-profit corporation serving seniors through estate retirement living.

Casa Dorinda was originally designed by Carleton Winslow for Anna Dorinda Bliss and her husband, William, wealthy New Yorkers who relocated to Montecito in the early 1900s. The grand mansion had more than 80 rooms surrounding a central patio and was once a focal point of Montecito social life. It opened as a retirement community in 1970. Today, more than 300 residents enjoy one of three levels of retirement care, from independent living to hospital care.

Casa Dorinda offers an on-site swimming pool and Jacuzzi, croquet, lawn bowling, a fitness center, transportation services, food service, maintenance, housing care, health care, and walking trails through 24 acres of sycamore and oak groves. A full-time activity director plans trips to the theater, symphony, and other cultural events, including excursions to the Los Angeles area. Beaches, bikeways, and mountain trails are all nearby.

The wide selection of apartments ranges from studios to 2-bedrooms, all professionally updated and prepared for each resident. You can use the reception rooms for your own parties and to entertain guests. Other facilities include a nursing center, a separate clinic for everyday matters, a Personal Care Unit, and a state-of-the-art medical center. You must be at least 62 years old at the time of entry and meet the entry requirements.

Senior Apartments

These comfortable apartments appeal to active seniors who want to maintain total independence in a community with their peers.

RANCHO FRANCISCAN APARTMENTS
221 Hitchcock Way, #107, Santa Barbara
(805) 563-0343
www.towbes.com/residential/franciscan

Rancho Franciscan apartments are open to seniors only (minimum age 62). Built in 1988, the Spanish/Mediterranean-style complex is located in the upper State Street area. It's right next door to the Santa Barbara YMCA, which offers discounts to all seniors age 65 and older, and it's a few short blocks to grocery stores, La Cumbre Plaza Mall, movie theaters, and restaurants. The Metropolitan Transit District bus stops in front.

Rancho Franciscan's 111 units are divided among 4 stucco buildings with red-tile roofs. You can choose from 1- and 2-bedroom apartments in 2- and 3-story buildings (3 of the buildings have elevators). Each apartment has a private veranda and modern kitchen facilities. Shared amenities include a Jacuzzi, a recreation center, and outdoor barbecue grills. A social director organizes a monthly calendar of events and activities on the property.

RETIREMENT

SHEPARD PLACE APARTMENTS
1069 Casitas Pass Rd., Carpinteria
(805) 684-5589
www.towbes.com/residential/
shepardplace

This senior apartment complex for residents 55 and older is owned by the same people who own Rancho Franciscan. It features 169 garden-style apartments (1- and 2-bedroom), a swimming pool, a spa, and activities. Shepard Place is within walking distance of downtown Carpinteria and the beach. Residents sign a 12-month lease, then rent on a month-to-month basis after the lease expires. Monthly fees range from $1,215 to $1,305 for 1-bedroom apartments and $1,580 to $1,650 for 2-bedroom units.

DOOR-TO-DOOR TRANSPORTATION

EASY LIFT TRANSPORTATION
53 Cass Place, Ste. D, Santa Barbara
(805) 681-1181
www.easylift.org

Easy Lift is a nonprofit organization providing curb-to-curb, wheelchair-accessible van transportation service for frail elderly and handicapped people who cannot ride the bus. Service is available Mon through Fri from 5:25 a.m. to midnight, Sat from 6 a.m. to 11:20 p.m., and Sun from 6:20 a.m. to 10:45 p.m. The cost is $3.50 per one-way trip (exact change is required).

MEDIA

I t's rare that a news source becomes the news itself, but that is precisely what's happened with Santa Barbara's only daily newspaper, the *Santa Barbara News-Press* (steadily dropping circulation now at 25,563 compared to 41,000 a few years ago). In 2000, Santa Barbarans were thrilled when local billionaire and environmentalist Wendy McCaw purchased the paper from the New York Times Co., which had been running it since 1985. Changing ownership from a large conglomerate to an independent bucked the trends in media. But the change in ownership came at a cost, one that made national news (*Vanity Fair* wrote an exposé on it), and the story behind the squabble has been made into a documentary film.

The newspaper hit a snag, shall we say, when editors accused McCaw of meddling in editorial decisions. In less than a year's time, over 35 editors and reporters quit or were fired, leaving a newspaper that is strangely devoid of journalists and news.

For years, Santa Barbarans have been proud of their hometown newspaper. Now locals are hoping the fracas will be resolved soon so they may enjoy their hometown paper once again.

Where this will end, no one seems to know, as the feud between the journalists and their union officials and Wendy McCaw and her company, Ampersand Publishing LLC, and her copublisher/fiancé, Arthur von Wiesenberger, is being dueled out in the courts.

NEWSPAPERS

The much tamer historical origins of the newspaper in Santa Barbara began with the *Santa Barbara Gazette* in 1855. After struggling to survive with a small reader base, the paper eventually sold out to new owners, who moved to San Francisco and thereafter delivered the paper by steamship. This wasn't acceptable to subscribers, who sometimes got the "news" when it was weeks old, and the *Gazette* soon went out of business.

In 1868 the weekly *Santa Barbara Post* began publishing locally, but just over a year later, it was bought out, and the name was changed to the *Santa Barbara Press*. In 1871 it became Santa Barbara's first daily newspaper.

Other newspapers that packed some clout in their day included the *Morning Press, the Daily News,* and the *Daily Independent*. Thomas M. Storke, a local boy and Stanford graduate with deep Santa Barbara roots, owned all of these publications at one time or another and in 1938 merged the papers into one, the *Santa Barbara News-Press*.

Santa Barbara

Dailies

SANTA BARBARA NEWS-PRESS
De la Guerra Plaza, Santa Barbara
(805) 564-5200
www.newspress.com

The *Santa Barbara News-Press* is the city's main daily paper, with a daily circulation of under 30,000. It's a morning paper covering international, national, state, and local news. The Friday pull-out "Scene" section covers the local music, theater, and arts scenes and runs reviews of movies and local restaurants. Special sections such as the "Life" section of the paper give news about the thriving local nonprofit scene, and the Fiesta edition fills you in on all the events and parties happening in conjunction with the annual August celebration. Newsstand costs are 50 cents Monday to Saturday and $1.50 on Sunday.

SANTA BARBARA DAILY SOUND
411 E. Canon Perdido, Ste. 2,
Santa Barbara
(805) 564-6001
www.santabarbarafree.com

When the big presses start having difficulty, the little presses have an opportunity to jump in. That's exactly what Jeramy Gordon, president and CEO of NORDROG Publications and editor and publisher of the *Santa Barbara Daily Sound*, did. He launched the first edition of his tiny but mighty newspaper on March 23, 2006, and has successfully printed a free paper ever since. Delivered throughout town, this newspaper offers a quick snapshot of the daily news and includes favorite Santa Barbara journalists, including humor columnist Leslie Dinaberg and man-about-town Michael Bowker. The paper is published Tuesday through Saturday and can be found at local cafes and newsstands.

Weekly

THE SANTA BARBARA INDEPENDENT
122 W. Figueroa St., Santa Barbara
(805) 965-5205
www.independent.com

The *Independent,* published every Thursday, is a major source of news for the Santa Barbara community. This tabloid-style paper is packed with oodles of information on the theater, nightlife, sports, and dining scenes. The paper has taken on much of the "other paper's" story (*Santa Barbara News-Press*) and even some of its journalists. (The *Independent* has grown heftier since the *Santa Barbara News-Press*'s upheaval, perhaps the result of advertisers moving their ad dollars?) With a circulation of over 40,000, it's a common sight to see folks sitting at a juice bar or deli reading the *Independent*. The paper is distributed free of charge and may be found all over town, including at bookstores, cafes, and in front of markets and liquor stores.

Montecito

MONTECITO JOURNAL
1122 Coast Village Circle, Montecito
(805) 565-1860
www.montecitojournal.net

Calling itself "the Voice of the Village," the *Montecito Journal* is a weekly tabloid featuring social events, local news from Summerland (a column by yours truly) to downtown as well as Montecito, gossip, humor columns, political issues, real estate, and restaurant listings. This free publication is distributed throughout the local area and is available online as well.

MONTECITO MESSENGER
411 E. Canon Perdido, Ste. 2,
Santa Barbara
(805) 564-6001
www.montecitomessenger.com
The Santa Barbara Daily Sound decided in 2011 to shake up the town of Montecito a bit by introducing a new weekly paper delivered to homes in the 93108 zip code. A roster of regular columnists and news reporting brings more news to this tony neighborhood.

Carpinteria

COASTAL VIEW NEWS
4856 Carpinteria Ave., Carpinteria
(805) 684-4428
www.coastalview.com
Coastal View News is a small tabloid-type weekly that serves the Carpinteria Valley with news of local business, education, and community events. Its circulation is about 6,000, with free copies available at newsstands and other locations in Carpinteria, Summerland, Montecito, and Santa Barbara. Carpinteria events (except for major happenings like the annual California Avocado Festival) don't always get good coverage in the Santa Barbara press, so this is a great place to get the scoop on what's going on in Santa Barbara's neighbor to the south.

MAGAZINES

DINING & DESTINATIONS
www.dininganddestinations.com
This attractive, free glossy highlights Santa Barbara restaurants, home stores, fashion boutiques, art galleries, things to do, wineries and wine clubs, and local people. For in-depth home & garden features visit their sister site www.SBDigs.com. Distributed

to local coffeehouses, upscale boutiques, and stores.

805 LIVING
3717 E. Thousand Oaks Blvd.,
Westlake Village
(805) 413-1141
www.805living.com
Although published out of Westlake, some miles down the road but also within the 805 area code, this attractive informative free glossy covers the best of the region, including Santa Barbara, Ojai, and Ventura, and their motto, "living the good life in the 805," includes profiles in fashion, shopping, people, events, restaurants, home design, and more. Distributed free to shops and available at all Vons grocery stores.

MONTECITO MAGAZINE
1144 Edgemound Dr., Santa Barbara
(805) 682-8335
www.montecitomag.com
This handy palm-sized magazine highlights Montecito's scene with its well-written text and beautiful, full-color pictures. A quick thumbing through gives you a glimpse of Montecito's history, real estate, shops, galleries, restaurants, and entertainment. It's distributed free and is available by subscription.

SANTA BARBARA MAGAZINE
2064 Alameda Padre Serra, Ste. 120,
Santa Barbara
(805) 965-5999
www.sbmag.com
Santa Barbara Magazine is a slick, five-issues-a-year glossy showcasing the well-to-do. In addition to several feature stories and columns about local people, celebrities, and events, you'll find a large section of ads for Santa Barbara estates, private schools, art

galleries, expensive automobiles, fine jewelry, and upscale shops.

Its regular features, "SB Buzz," "SB People," "Art Scene," "Bits + Bites," and "Getaways" highlight people, fashion, places, and events the "average Joe" can only dream about. With its outstanding photography, it's an excellent depiction of Santa Barbara's elite.

SPECIAL INTEREST PUBLICATIONS

All of the publications listed below are free and generally distributed at local bookstores (Chaucer's is always a good bet) or newsstands. Visitor information publications are usually available at hotels and tourist stops.

FOOD & HOME
1525 Veronica Place, Santa Barbara
(805) 563-6780
www.food-home.com
This well-written quarterly glossy Santa Barbara lifestyle magazine is always a welcome read. In addition to the buzz on the local dining and bar scene, the magazine presents entertaining articles on food and wine trends, family issues, and home improvement. It also profiles local artists and recipes from restaurants around town. Free deliveries to selected homes, bookstores, premium hotels, and bed-and-breakfasts in the greater Santa Barbara area and beyond. A new publication, *Breathe In,* debuted in 2011 covering fitness, beauty, health, and travel.

SANTA BARBARA SEASONS
829 De la Vina St., Ste. 210, Santa Barbara
(805) 564-8804
www.sbseasons.com

The informative articles in this sophisticated quarterly spotlight Santa Barbara's history, architecture, culture, and natural beauty. A multiple award winner, *Santa Barbara Seasons* has a circulation of 36,000 with an estimated readership of over five times that. You'll see why when you pick up a copy for yourself.

INTERNET NEWS SOURCES

Let's face it, we are in a new millennium, and many people, especially the younger ones, are no longer turning to print publications for their news. Instead, they are searching for news and information online. The online edition of the *Santa Barbara News-Press* (www.newspress.com) is only available to subscribers, but the *Santa Barbara Independent* and *Santa Barbara Daily Sound* provide access to up-to-the-minute news online.

Here are local favorites—some serious, some quirky.

CRAIG SMITH'S BLOG
www.west.net/~smith/blog/index.shtml
"Covering Santa Barbara Law and Media like a Wet Blanket" is Craig Smith's tagline. His repartee and keen political conclusions are what has earned Smith, an attorney and professor, accolades in the community. He loves to give his perspective on events around town, with an emphasis on covering local media, but does go quirkily astray at times.

EDHAT
www.edhat.com
Log on and you'll get a very local glimpse of what's happening in Santa Barbara, from the citizen's point of view (ofttimes irreverent and wacky).

NOOZHAWK
www.noozhawk.com

Keep informed on what's going on politically and culturally on this online news source. Good reporting from on-the-beat writers and photographers under the watchful gaze of longtime publisher/editor Bill Macfayden.

RADIO

The oldest continuously broadcasting station in Santa Barbara is KDB (93.7 FM), which began operations in the Daily News building in 1926 under the call letters KFCR. (When George Barnes purchased the station in 1929, he changed the call letters to KDB, his wife Dorothy's initials.)

After several changes in physical location and formats, KDB began broadcasting classical music exclusively in 1980 and has been doing it 24 hours a day ever since. KDB is one of the only self-supporting classical music stations in the nation and is now owned and operated by the Santa Barbara Foundation and run under the watchful gaze of Tim Owens, a Peabody Award–winning former jazz producer at NPR in Washington, DC.

Radio listening in Santa Barbara is enhanced by many Ventura, Oxnard, and Los Angeles stations that have enough power to be heard in town, although several may fade in and out, depending on the weather or your reception. Nonetheless, for your listening pleasure, some of these are included on the list.

Adult Contemporary

KBBY 95.1 FM, www.b951.com
KRUZ 97.5 FM, www.kruz.com
KLITE 101.7 FM, www.klite.com
KFYV 105.5 FM, www.live1055.fm

Christian

KDAR 98.3 FM, www.kdar.com

Classical

KUSC 91.5 FM, www.kusc.org
KDB 93.7 FM, www.kdb.com

Classic Rock

KMGQ 106.3 FM, www.kmgq1063.com

College

KCSB 91.9 FM, www.kcsb.org (University of California Santa Barbara)

Country

KHAY 100.7 FM, www.khay.com
KRAZ 105.9 FM, www.krazfm.com

Hip-Hop

KCAQ 104.7 FM, www.q1047.com

Modern Rock

KJEE 92.9 FM, www.kjee.com

News

KFI 640 AM, www.kfiam640.com
KABC 790 AM, www.kabc.com
KTMS 990 AM, local news, www.990am.com
KNX 1070 AM, www.knx1070.com
KIST 1340 AM, www.talkradio1340am.com
KVTA 1520 AM, www.kvta.com

Oldies

KRTH 101.1 FM, www.kearth101.com

MEDIA

Public

KCLU 102.3 FM, www.kclu.org
KCBX 89.5 FM, www.kcbx.org

Rock

KOCP 95.9 FM, www.theoctopus959.com
KTYD 99.9 FM, www.ktyd.com

Spanish

KXLM, 102.9 FM, www.radiolazer.com
KVYB 103.3 FM, www.1033thevibe.com
KBKO 1490 AM, www.radiobronco.com

TELEVISION

Thomas M. Storke, who was on hand during the infancy of both the newspaper and radio businesses in Santa Barbara, seemed destined to be involved in the development of local television as well. It was not to be, however. Harry Butcher, owner of a local radio station, along with several members of a new media corporation, beat Storke to the punch by going on the air first in the early 1950s.

The new station was KEYT, Channel 3, which is still Santa Barbara's only homegrown commercial television station, and is considered to be an excellent one.

There are two nonprofit public access television stations in Santa Barbara, Channel 17 and Channel 21. Channel 17 offers free airtime to local community members who wish to create a program. Channel 21 is evolving into airtime for nonprofits by providing educational, arts, and cultural programming.

i Tune in to the Unity Telethon at the beginning of every December for a sample of celebrities who are donating their talents to raise money for the Unity Shoppe, a local nonprofit. Started by Kenny Loggins, this telethon has showcased Santa Barbara's celebrities and elite for over two decades.

Cable TV

Cox Communications (805-683-6651) provides cable and digital cable service to all of Santa Barbara County. If you like to watch TV, you'll need to do business with Cox, which will charge you from about $56.99 for limited basic cable (over 86 channels) to digital cable where the price depends on the package you choose.

Satellite Companies

If you want to beam programs from hundreds of stations down to your TV set, you can choose from a variety of full-service satellite companies. DirecTV has several affiliates. Call (800) 531-5000 or visit www.directtv.com. There's also Dish Network (800-823-4929; www.dishnetwork.com) and Direct Satellite TV (888-427-7125; www.directsattv.com).

INDEX

INDEX